Real Estate Principles

FIFTH EDITION

Charles F. Floyd
Marcus T. Allen

Dearborn
Financial Publishing, Inc.®

This publication is designed to provide accurate and authoritative information in regard to the subject matter covered. It is sold with the understanding that the publisher is not engaged in rendering legal, accounting or other professional service. If legal advice or other expert assistance is required, the services of a competent professional person should be sought.

Publisher: Carol L. Luitjens
Senior Acquisitions Editor: Tim Vertovec
Associate Development Editor: Nikki Loosemore
Managing Editor: Ronald J. Liszkowski
Art and Design Manager: Lucy Jenkins
Cover Designer: Elizandro Carrington
Interior Designer: Dale Beda

97 98 99   10   9   8   7   6   5   4   3   2   1

Library of Congress Cataloging-in-Publication Data

Floyd, Charles F.
    Real estate principles / Charles F. Floyd, Marcus T. Allen.–5th ed.
        p.   cm.
    Includes bibliographical references and index.
    ISBN 0-7931-1680-5
    1. Real estate business–United States.   I. Allen, Marcus T.
II. Title.
HD255.F57 1997   96-38392
333.33'0973–dc20   CIP

DEDICATION

This book is dedicated to
R. W. Barber
a man of the land
and
C. O. Floyd
a man of business

—Charles F. Floyd

This book is dedicated to
my family, friends and students.
Thanks for your support.

—Marcus T. Allen

Contents

Part Three   *Real Estate Services   145*

Preface

The study of real estate is inherently interesting because it is so relevant and practical. All students, regardless of their major, will face decisions regarding real property. This book is designed to help students prepare to make informed decisions about real estate transactions and investments.

NEW FOR THE 5TH EDITION

Real Estate Principles has long been recognized as one of the leading textbooks for the introductory real estate course. In response to the dynamic nature of the real estate discipline, the new *Fifth Edition* is our most extensive revision ever. It employs many of the teaching techniques we have used successfully for the more than 40 combined years that we have been in the classroom. There are four primary features of this revision:

Focus on Decision Making

There is a marked increase in the emphasis on decision making for users of real estate resources in this edition. This is evidenced by the following:

- Chapter 1: Introduction to Real Estate Decision Making
- Revised finance chapters which focus on decision-oriented topics such as how lenders decide to approve a loan

Reorganized Table of Contents

The content has been reorganized to follow the events of a real estate transaction, with an overall focus on improving the teachability of the material. The prose has been streamlined, and the total number of chapters has been reduced from 23 to 19. Deeds and legal description methods now appear in the same chapter, as do title examinations and the closing process. Appraisal has been condensed and is now covered in one chapter rather than two.

Latest Information Regarding Current Practice

The discussion of the brokerage process has been improved to include the latest information on buyer brokerage, dual agency and cooperating and transaction brokers. Residential mortgage financing has been emphasized and updated, with information on the structure of the housing finance system and the federal regulations that affect it, underwriting guidelines used by lenders as well as the loan application procedure.

Revised End-of-Chapter Problem Material

The end-of-chapter materials have been vastly improved to more closely focus on the material from the chapter and serve as a study guide for students.

TRADITIONAL STRENGTHS:

Readability

The first step in making the material interesting is to make the book readable. The language of the book is simple and straightforward. Terms are clearly defined in the text discussion as well as both in the End-of-Chapter and End-of-Book Glossaries. Adding to the text's readability are many special "Real Estate Today" feature boxes, which comment on the text discussion by describing and analyzing specific legal cases, real estate development and controversial issues involving the real estate industry. A listing of these features appears on pages xiii–xiv.

Relevance

We tried to present material that will adequately prepare the real estate student for his or her future dealings in real estate, either as a member of one of the real estate professions or as an investor and user of real estate resources. The text covers all traditional topics, including property law, real estate brokerage, finance and appraisal. In addition, topics that are often given only cursory attention in competing texts — real estate markets, real estate development, land-use controls, real property insurance and taxes affecting real estate — are covered in depth.

Special Features

As in prior editions of this book, we have included many new special features to enhance the students' learning experience. Close-Ups, Legal Highlights, Profiles and Case Studies are liberally sprinkled throughout the book to provide "real world" application of the concepts descried in the text. These features help round out the student's instruction in real estate by demonstrating the principles and concepts, both in action and in combination, as they occur in real estate as it is practiced today.

PEDAGOGICAL DEVICES

Teaching tools that facilitate learning about real estate are incorporated into the text. These tools include the following:

- Key Terms are boldfaced in the text and defined both in the End-of-Chapter and End-of-Book Glossaries.
- Many tables, graphs and photographs are included to aid today's visually-oriented student.
- Detailed chapter reviews are provided to highlight and emphasize the key concepts addressed in each chapter.
- Study exercises (designed to be used as "homework" should the instructor choose) are provided to give students an opportunity to reinforce their understanding of the topics developed in each chapter.
- Suggested reading lists for each chapter are included to direct students who wish to learn more about specific concepts to additional sources of information.

INSTRUCTOR'S SUPPORT

A comprehensive instructor's resource manual is available. Included in it are chapter outlines, overhead transparency masters, answers to end-of-chapter study exercises and a newly revised test bank of more than 800 questions. In addition, a computerized test bank is available for instructors to enable the creation of customized quizzes and exams.

ACKNOWLEDGMENTS

We wish to sincerely thank all of the people who provided comments and suggestions that have greatly improved this edition of the text. Our reviewers included Thomas E. Battle III, Center for Real Estate Education and Research; Douglas S. Bible, Louisiana State University—Shreveport; Donald E. Bodley, Eastern Kentucky University; Jay Q. Butler, Arizona State University; Lary B. Cowart, University of Alabama—Birmingham; Arthur Cox, University of Northern Iowa; Austin J. Jaffe, Penn State University; Don T. Johnson, Western Illinois University; Phillip T. Kolbe, The University of Memphis; Ivan J. Miestchovich, Jr., University of New Orleans; Edward L. Prill, Colorado State University; Ronald C. Rutherford, University of Texas—San Antonio; James L. Short, San Diego State University; Ronald Throupe, Washington State University.

We also wish to thank Tim Vertovec, Nikki Loosemore, Shirley Webster and the members of the production staff at Dearborn Financial Publishing, Inc., without whom this edition would not have been possible. In addition, special thanks are due to the students in our classes who served as guinea pigs for the new material and to Ronald Throupe, Washington State University, for revising and updating the instructor's resource manual and testbank.

Finally, we wish we could blame all of those mentioned above for the book's shortcomings, but we have to reserve that dubious honor for ourselves.

Charles F. Floyd
The University of Georgia

Marcus T. Allen
Florida Atlantic University

Real Estate Today Features

Profile

Legal Highlight

Close-Up

Case Study

CHAPTER 1
Introduction to Real Estate Decision Making

The decision to acquire real property requires the consideration of a variety of factors, including location, demographics, financing and the environment.

Chapter Preview

WHY SHOULD WE study real estate? Fundamentally, people must have places to live and businesses must have locations for their activities. As a result, real estate is a vital resource that touches the economic lives of all people and firms. A thorough understanding of the complexities of real estate resources and the markets in which they are traded enables us to make informed choices regarding real estate for either personal or business use. The objective of this text is to present the general principles necessary for effective real estate decision making. The text serves as a starting point for more advanced study of the concepts and issues facing real estate market participants.

To begin our discussion of the principles of real estate, we look to the objectives of this introductory chapter:

- Discuss the role of real estate studies in business education.
- Introduce the topics to be considered in the remainder of the book.
- Examine the characteristics of real estate that distinguish it from other economic resources.
- Consider the importance of real estate in the national economy.
- Describe various careers in the real estate industry.

1

THE ROLE OF REAL ESTATE STUDIES IN BUSINESS EDUCATION

When you first learned that your college or university offers a real estate principles course as part of its business school curriculum, you may have thought that the focus of the course would be to prepare you for a career as a real estate broker. While real estate brokerage is an excellent career choice for many people, this book does not assume that a career in brokerage is your sole motivation for taking this course. Instead, we present the principles of real estate from the perspective of the user of real estate resources. These principles provide a foundation for effective real estate decision making, whether you intend to manage a sizable real estate portfolio or simply to become more knowledgeable about your personal real estate transactions.

In most universities and colleges, real estate is regarded as a specialty area under the general umbrella of business studies. As such, a real estate principles course covers issues and topics unique to the real estate discipline and much too specific for adequate coverage in other areas of academic study. Because of the specialized knowledge required for effective real estate decision making, real estate issues deserve independent attention in a business curriculum. The intricacies of real estate resources and markets can baffle the ill-prepared decision maker, but a solid foundation in real estate principles will help you make effective business and personal real estate decisions throughout your career. In addition, the topics covered in this text will serve as a springboard for more detailed studies of real estate issues in subsequent courses for those students with specific interests in a career in the real estate industry.

Personal and Business-Related Real Estate Decisions

A thorough understanding of real estate principles is extremely important for real estate decision making for both personal and business-related real estate decisions. As individuals, all of us will probably face the following questions several times over the years: Should I buy a house or a condo or should I lease an apartment for my personal residence? What neighborhood do I want to live in or invest in? What type of financing should I use, and how do I arrange it? Should I use a broker to sell my property or sell it myself? How should I structure the sales contract to get the best deal? What type of deed should I use? How do I decide which property I should invest in?

The same issues that face us as individuals also apply in the business environment. Consider a company that requires additional office space to expand its operations and compete effectively in its product market. Such a company faces many questions that can be addressed only with knowledge of real estate principles. For example, should the company buy or lease additional space? If it leases space, how should it structure the details of the lease agreement to best serve its objectives? If the company decides to buy more real estate, should it build a new property or purchase an existing property? How should it finance the purchase or development? Should the company acquire a larger building than it currently requires and lease the additional space to tenants until the company needs it? Should the company consider relocating the corporate headquarters to a more central location, either in its current city or in another city altogether?

Appropriate answers to these and other important questions require familiarity with the overall operation of real estate markets, as well as specific knowledge of legal issues, transaction details and the financial framework of real estate resources. For this reason, real estate principles are a fundamental component of undergraduate business education, regardless of your chosen field of study.

Organization of This Book

Our goal is to present some of the basic principles of real estate in such a manner that you will be well prepared to anticipate and evaluate changing market conditions and make real estate decisions that best serve your personal and business objectives. We have divided the topics considered in the text into six categories: Real Estate Market Analysis, Real Estate's Legal Framework, Real Estate Services, Real Estate Transactions, Real Estate Investment Analysis and Real Estate Development. Understanding the issues in each topic area is essential for all participants in the real estate market, including homebuyers and homesellers, tenants, investors, developers, real estate professionals and business managers in non–real estate firms.

In Part One, Real Estate Market Analysis (Chapters 2 and 3), we consider the dynamics of real estate markets as a result of national, regional and local influences on property values and uses. In addition, we review the classic models of urban growth and discuss various aspects of the land development process. Part Two, Real Estate's Legal Framework (Chapters 4, 5, 6 and 7), considers issues related to the legal concept of real estate ownership. We define various ownership interests one can obtain in real estate, deeds and legal description methods, and private and public limitations on ownership. Part Three, Real Estate Services (Chapters 8, 9 and 10), discusses the real estate services industry, including brokerage, property management and appraisal. In Part Four, Real Estate Transactions (Chapters 11, 12, 13, 14 and 15), we examine the details of the transaction process by considering real estate contracts, property insurance, residential financing and the title verification and closing process. In Part Five, Real Estate Investment Analysis (Chapters 16 and 17), we consider the home purchase decision and the investment analysis process for income-producing properties. The final section is Part Six, Real Estate Development (Chapters 18 and 19), in which we examine the different types of residential, commercial and industrial development.

The remainder of this chapter sets the stage for the topics to be addressed throughout this text by describing the special economic characteristics of real estate, the economic importance of real estate and various career opportunities in the real estate industry.

SPECIAL CHARACTERISTICS OF REAL ESTATE

What is real estate? Simply defined, **real estate** is property in land and buildings. Technically, real estate consists of the physical land and structures, while **real property** consists of the legal interests associated with ownership of the physical real estate. In practice, however, the two terms are virtually synonymous. All other property—property that is movable—such as automobiles, furniture, boats and clothing, is known as **personal property.** (We will examine the legal concepts of "property" in Chapter 4.) As an economic resource, real estate has some very special characteristics that distinguish it from other types of resources and that give it distinct economic attributes. These characteristics are

- fixed location;
- uniqueness, or heterogeneity;
- interdependence of land uses;
- long life;
- long-term commitments;
- large transactions; and
- long gestation period.

Fixed Location

The characteristic of real estate that distinguishes it from all other types of economic resources is its fixed location. If there is an oversupply of wheat in Kansas, of automobiles in Michigan, of lawyers in Louisiana or of welders in Washington, they can move or be transported to areas of relative scarcity. This is not true of real estate resources. If there is an oversupply of condominiums in Palm Beach, of office space in Manhattan or of shopping centers in Minneapolis, they cannot be transported to other communities where the demand is stronger. A tract of land, of course, cannot be moved even a few feet up the street to help meet demand for space at that site. Thus, the success of real estate acquisition, development and investment decisions is directly affected by the forces of supply and demand in a local area.

Uniqueness

Because real estate is fixed in location, every parcel is unique, or to use a fancy term, is *heterogeneous.* Even subdivision lots located side by side are not perfect substitutes for each other because of differences in such factors as topography, tree cover and view. These factors often create large differences in property values. For example, lots fronting on a lake will probably sell for much more than lots just across the street; lots with a spectacular mountain view will sell for many times more than nearby ones without the view.

Interdependence of Land Uses

Real estate's fixed location leads to another economic characteristic—interdependence of land uses. The use of real property depends greatly on the provision of public services, the uses made of nearby land and the general economic vitality of the neighborhood and community.

It is extremely difficult to use land to its full economic potential, particularly in an urban setting, unless adequate public services are provided and neighboring land is used appropriately. Even agricultural lands need to be served by roads, and such basic utilities as electricity and telephone service are necessary for practical homestead use. As we move to denser residential development, public water and sewerage systems are essential, as are such governmental services as education, police and fire protection, and various social services. Land must be converted to public use for parks, schools and other governmental services, particularly transportation facilities. If adequate governmental services and public land uses are not available, it will be difficult or even impossible to develop land for residential, commercial or industrial use.

The use of land is also affected greatly by nearby land use. If a large tract of vacant land is located near areas of expanding residential and commercial development, this location should increase both the land's potential use and its value in the marketplace. Conversely, the value of land may be affected adversely by its proximity to "undesirable" uses. It would probably be difficult, for example, to develop a single-family housing development next to a chemical plant or slaughterhouse. Such uses, however, particularly if served by transportation facilities and other public services, may make nearby land valuable for industrial purposes.

The use of land depends heavily on public investments and the economic vitality of the surrounding neighborhood and community. Transportation improvements often increase the value of land by making it more accessible. Perhaps the opening of a new freeway or rapid transit line, for example, will make lands previously difficult to reach suitable for residential or commercial development. Conversely, increased congestion on existing streets resulting from population and economic growth may make houses located on those streets much less desirable for residential purposes.

The economic vitality of a neighborhood, community or region greatly affects the demand for real property and its value. If the economy of the area is expanding, the population also will increase, bringing about a corresponding increase in the demand for residential, commercial and industrial land. Conversely, if the economy of the area is in temporary or long-term decline, the demand for real estate and real estate values also will tend to decline.

It is the interdependence of land uses that leads to the necessity of both private and public land-use controls, topics we will study in Chapters 5 and 6. The use of land—more than the use of almost any other type of private property—affects the owners of other land and may create costs to the public at large. For example, the filling of floodplain lands (the low-lying land near streams) to make them suitable for high-density residential use may cause other owners of land on the floodplain to be affected adversely in periods of heavy rainfall. If other landowners also fill in their portions of the floodplain, a flood hazard that will require large public expenditures to alleviate may be created.

Long Life

Although its ability to generate income may change over time, land is virtually indestructible. Real estate improvements—that is, buildings on the land—also generally have very long lives. For example, a family would expect a new home to last as long as they wanted to live there, and many houses last for a century or more when maintained properly. Apartment houses, shopping centers and other types of income-producing property also have very long lives.

Long-Term Commitments

The long lives of real estate improvements mean that investment decisions are, by their very nature, long-term commitments. Although the immediate prospects for the production of income are very important in real estate investment analysis, the factors that influence income generation over the long term are equally critical. For example, the proximity of a motel to a heavily traveled highway is a predominant factor in the financial success of the motel. If the motel is built in a location that soon will be bypassed by a new freeway, it probably will not be a successful investment during much of its life. Conversely, shopping centers are often built somewhat ahead of the market to gain advantageous locations in advance of expected population growth.

The characteristics of long life and long-term commitments force the real estate investor and developer to take realistic, long-term outlooks if they want to make successful investment decisions. The real estate investor who merely assumes that favorable economic trends will continue will probably be unsuccessful. For example, most of the real estate failures during the real estate depression of the early 1990s occurred because investors and financial institutions regarded the future with unbridled optimism. Instead, investors should analyze carefully the factors that have caused economic trends to be favorable in the past and try to ascertain what will happen to these factors for some years into the future.

Large Transactions

Another important economic characteristic is the relatively large size of real estate transactions. Real estate purchases by their very nature involve large expenditures and are not entered into either lightly or frequently. A home is by far the average family's largest single purchase. Investment in income-producing real estate requires even larger outlays, beyond the financial means of most investors.

The large size and long-term nature of real estate transactions mean that buyers usually have to rely at least partially on some type of outside financing. This economic characteristic has led to the creation of the real estate finance industry, where long-term loans (25 to 30 years) are the norm.

The large size of real estate transactions and their resulting importance and complexity have also led to the rise of the real estate brokerage industry. Both buyers and sellers generally need assistance to analyze the marketplace, evaluate long-term investment decisions, arrange financing and, in general, deal with the complexities of these transactions.

Long Gestation Period

A final economic characteristic of real estate is the long **gestation periods** of real property improvements. The time between the conception of a real estate project and its actual completion and subsequent entry into the available supply may be several years. Suppose a group of investors decides to build an apartment complex. To complete this project, they first must acquire the land, then have engineering and architectural plans drawn for the site and buildings, secure zoning and other regulatory approval and arrange for financing before they can begin to build the project.

Long delays may occur at any of these steps: it may be difficult to secure approval from the zoning board; it may be necessary to wait several months for the completion of a new sewer line; bad weather may delay construction.

The long gestation period makes the supply of real estate slow to respond to increases or decreases in demand. Because the supply cannot be increased quickly, increases in demand often result in rapid upward price movements unless an excess supply exists. Conversely, demand may decline during a project's gestation period, leaving it to face a much reduced market when completed. This is yet another reason the real estate developer must analyze factors affecting future demand and supply. There may be a strong market for, say, office space in a certain area at present. This does not necessarily mean that the strong demand will continue. Many investors and financial institutions have discovered to their immense sorrow that by the time projects were completed, demand for the products had declined. Or they may not have fully considered the impact of other projects that were being built at the same time. Successful real estate investment requires a thorough, long-term economic analysis.

THE ECONOMIC IMPORTANCE OF REAL ESTATE

Real estate is a vital component of the national economy. Real estate constitutes a large portion of national wealth. Land and structures make up approximately two-thirds of the wealth of the United States, and the remainder consists of equipment and inventories. As individuals and businesses borrow against real estate assets, their borrowing activities give rise to the real estate finance industry. In 1995, mortgage debt in the United States totaled more than $4.6 trillion.

Real estate also is vital to the economy as a resource for current production. Expenditures for housing, housing operation, and furniture and household equipment totaled $1.3 trillion in 1995, or 26 percent of all personal consumption expenditures, and investment in structures and related equipment accounted for 49 percent of gross private domestic investment. The real estate and construction industries, which employ slightly more than 5 percent of all workers, account for more than 15 percent of the gross domestic product.

Although these figures give some indication of the impressive contributions of real estate to the national economy, they still underrepresent its total impact. Portions of the "real estate industry," notably real estate finance, are not included as part of "real estate" in the national income and product accounts. In addition, the industry generates a significant portion of the business of many other industries by creating a demand for products such as furniture and electrical appliances.

THE REAL ESTATE INDUSTRY: THE PRIVATE SECTOR

The real estate industry is diverse, offering many career opportunities. To many students, a career in real estate means selling homes — and, indeed, this is a significant part of the real estate brokerage industry. But many other fascinating careers in real estate exist, and one of the purposes of this book is to introduce these career opportunities, as well as to provide the basic knowledge needed to become a part of the real estate industry.

Real Estate Brokerage

In 1996, the National Association of REALTORS® (NAR), the largest trade group in the real estate industry, had more than 700,000 members, including brokers and salespersons. The compensation earned by participants in the brokerage industry fluctuates with the ups and downs of the real estate market, but the U.S. Department of Commerce estimated that compensation for real estate workers totaled $41.7 billion in 1995.

Real Estate Brokerage Specialties　Five principal classifications of real estate exist in the private marketplace: owner-occupied residential, renter-occupied residential, commercial, industrial, and farm and other open land. Because it is difficult to be an expert in all aspects of the real estate market, most brokers specialize in certain types of property. The extent of specialization depends on a number of factors, particularly the size of the local market. The real estate broker in a small city may deal in several or all types of properties. In larger cities, brokers may sell only one type of real estate or properties located in only one part of a city. Quite commonly, some brokers and salespersons sell only owner-occupied houses, while others deal only in the sale or leasing of income-producing properties. (See, for example, the profile of Arthur Rosenbloom on page 9.)

Property Management

Many people who invest in such income-producing real estate as apartments and shopping centers have neither the inclination nor the expertise to take care of the properties' day-to-day operating activities, such as leasing, rent collection, building repairs and building services. These tasks—and, indeed, the general objective of maximizing the income from a property—are delegated to the property manager. Some small brokers manage real estate as a supplementary activity, while many larger firms have separate property management departments. Still other property managers may be hired directly by the firms that own the properties. If the property manager does a good job, this function can add considerable value to a property.

Real Estate Finance

Several economic characteristics of real property, principally the long-term nature of real estate investment and the consequent need for large amounts of money over a long period of time, make mortgage credit both necessary for most purchasers and attractive to many lenders. This has given rise to the real estate finance industry.

Real estate loans are made by many types of institutions and even by individuals, and major employment opportunities are found in savings and loan associations, savings banks, commercial banks, mortgage banking firms and life insurance companies. Savings and loan associations and savings banks

Real Estate Today
Profile

Arthur Rosenbloom, Real Estate Broker

Real estate brokerage is one of the most demanding—but potentially rewarding—fields within real estate. Because it is a commission-only business, those who don't sell don't eat. But for those who possess the qualifications that make great salespersons, the financial rewards can be large. Arthur Rosenbloom is an example of a real estate brokerage superstar, one of a few who earn commissions of more than $1 million each year.

Rosenbloom entered the brokerage business about 30 years ago and spent nearly 10 years learning his trade—the leasing of office space in the highly competitive New York City market. At first, the business wasn't too glamorous as he tramped from building to building trying to find firms that needed more space. However, as he learned the market and gained the trust of both those who had space to rent and those who leased space, he began to do quite well indeed. Now he is responsible for leasing more than 600,000 square feet of office space each year at lease rates averaging around $40 per square foot. Commissions in this megabuck market often exceed $1 million for a single long-term lease, and Arthur obviously gets his share. When asked about the most essential factor for success in office leasing, Rosenbloom quickly answers: "Integrity. Unless people can count on your word, in this business, you are dead." ∎

specialize in residential loans and do most of their lending locally. Commercial banks also lend money on real estate, particularly for relatively short-term construction loans, and they also purchase many mortgages from mortgage bankers and brokers.

The mortgage banking and mortgage brokerage industries also play large roles in the financing of real estate. Mortgage bankers do not collect deposits from savers and have only a small amount of their own capital to lend. After originating loans to borrowers, mortgage bankers sell the loans in the secondary mortgage market, but continue to service (collect payments, mail late notices, etc.) the loans for a fee. Mortgage brokers do not originate loans themselves, but instead bring lenders and borrowers together in exchange for one-time fees. Both mortgage bankers and brokers are essential parts of the financial mechanism that shifts funds from capital surplus to capital deficit areas.

Appraisal

Estimates of value are needed in almost every aspect of real estate and development. Sellers need to know what their properties can bring in the marketplace, and buyers need to know what their potential purchases are worth in comparison with other properties in the market. Mortgage lenders need estimates of value (**appraisals**) before they make lending decisions. Appraisals also are essential for tax assessors, insurance adjusters, right-of-way agents and other government officials. Accordingly, many appraisers are employed by financial institutions, other private firms and government organizations, while many others work as independent fee appraisers—that is, they offer their services to the public for a fee.

Counseling

Closely related to real estate appraising is real estate counseling. The real estate appraiser makes estimates of value, while the real estate counselor advises individuals and firms regarding their real estate investments. Though the two specialties require similar kinds of knowledge, the counselor must have even more extensive knowledge than the appraiser of all phases of real estate, tax laws and other aspects of investment.

Development and Construction

Real estate development certainly is one of the most fascinating aspects of real estate and one that offers greater potential return—and greater potential risk—than perhaps any other field within the industry. Real estate development involves the subdivision of land and the construction of improvements such as roads, utilities and buildings ranging from individual homes to multimillion-dollar office buildings and shopping centers.

Although not generally considered part of the real estate industry, construction is tied closely to development and the real estate field in general.

Asset Management

Although real estate makes up a large portion of corporate assets, most corporations have not placed adequate emphasis on managing these assets efficiently. Increasingly, however, firms are establishing corporate real estate departments, and this has led to many new opportunities in the real estate field. As might be expected, utilities and other firms with very large percentages of their assets in real estate have been leaders in the field, and other companies as well are realizing that efficient management of their real estate can add significantly to corporate profits.

Land-Use Planning

Also closely related to real estate development is land-use planning. This is a diverse field: many planners are engaged in physical design, others are concerned primarily with the economic and investment aspects of development, while still others are employed by governmental agencies concerned with land-use policies and regulations.

THE REAL ESTATE INDUSTRY: THE PUBLIC SECTOR

In addition to those located in the private sector, many real estate–related jobs are found at the various levels of government. Such jobs generally are related

Real Estate Today   *Close-Up*

Real Estate Periodicals and World Wide Web Sites

Many sources provide information about current issues in the real estate market. Most general business publications, such as *The Wall Street Journal, Business Week, Forbes* and *Fortune,* often provide insight into the ongoing activities in the real estate industry. A number of specialized real estate publications also help keep industry participants informed. In addition, the World Wide Web is becoming an increasingly important information source in the business community, with individuals, firms and organizations preparing web sites designed to distribute information to the general public. The list of periodicals and web sites provided below is not meant to be exhaustive, but provides a good starting point for students who want to learn more about current issues in the real estate market.

Periodicals

Appraisal Journal, published quarterly by the Appraisal Institute, Chicago, Illinois. Includes articles related to appraisal and real estate investment analysis.

Journal of Property Management, published bimonthly by the Institute of Real Estate Management. Articles focus on topics related to the management of income properties.

Real Estate Review, published quarterly by Warren Gorham Lamont, Boston, Massachusetts. Includes articles on a variety of real estate–related topics, including law, taxation, investment analysis, lease negotiations and brokerage.

Today's REALTOR®, published monthly by the National Association of REALTORS®. Articles generally focus on real estate brokerage.

World Wide Web Sites

Appraisal Institute: http://www.realworks.com:80/ai/

Building Owners and Managers Association: http://www.boma.org/

Fannie Mae (Federal National Mortgage Association): http://www.fanniemae.com/

Institute of Real Estate Management: http://www.irem.org/

NAREIT (National Association of Real Estate Investment Trusts): http://www.nareit.com/

National Association of Home Builders: http://www.nahb.com/

National Association of REALTORS®: http://www.realtor.com/

Real Estate Education Company®: http://www.real-estate-ed.com/

Society of Industrial and Office REALTORS®: http://www.sior.com/

U.S. Department of Housing and Urban Development: http://www.hud.gov/

Women in Real Estate: http://www.hia.com/hia/wire/ ■

---

to acquisition and management of property, real property taxation, land-use planning, and land-use and housing policy.

Federal, state and local governments acquire real property for public buildings, parks, transportation projects and other government functions. Such land acquisition requires the services of many real estate specialists, including appraisers and right-of-way agents.

Many appraisers are engaged in valuing real property for taxation purposes. Most such appraisers are property tax assessors at the local government level, but many are employed by other levels of government.

Land-use planning has grown in importance with the increase in both urbanization and concern for the environment. Planners are employed by local government planning agencies, multicounty planning districts and state development offices. In addition, various federal agencies—in particular those in the U.S. Department of Housing and Urban Development and the U.S. Department of Commerce—employ planners to help formulate economic development, land-use and housing policies.

Many real estate specialists also work in government and in quasi-government financial agencies, such as the Federal Housing Administration, the Government National Mortgage Association, the Federal Home Loan Mortgage Corporation and the Federal National Mortgage Association.

Chapter Review

1. The five broad categories that compose the real estate "body of knowledge" considered in this text include real estate market analysis, the legal framework of real estate, real estate services, the real estate transaction process and investment analysis.

2. Simply defined, real estate is land and buildings.

3. The special economic characteristics are (1) fixed location, (2) uniqueness, (3) interdependence of land uses, (4) long life, (5) long-term commitments, (6) large transactions and (7) long gestation period.

4. The characteristic of real estate that distinguishes it from all other types of economic resources is its fixed location.

5. Fixity of location means that every parcel of real estate is unique, and this factor can create large differences in property values.

6. Land is indestructible, and real estate improvements generally have long lives. Thus, investment decisions are by their very nature long-term decisions.

7. Because real estate purchases involve large expenditures committed for long periods of time, outside financing is essential for most transactions.

8. The use of land depends greatly on (1) the provision of public services, (2) nearby land uses and (3) the general economic vitality of the neighborhood and community.

9. The gestation period for real estate improvements—that is, the time between conception of a real estate project and its actual completion and subsequent entry into the available supply—may be several years. This long gestation period makes the supply of real estate slow to respond to increases in demand.

10. Land and structures make up approximately two-thirds of the national wealth of the United States, with the remainder consisting of equipment and inventories. Expenditures for housing and household operation constituted 26 percent of all personal consumption expenditures in 1995, while investment in structures and related furniture and fixtures accounted for 49 percent of gross private domestic investment.

11. Five principal classifications of real estate exist in the private marketplace: (1) owner-occupied residential, (2) renter-occupied residential, (3) commercial, (4) industrial and (5) farm and other open land.

12. The general objective of the real estate property manager is to maximize the income flowing to the owners from income-producing property.

13. Mortgage loans now total about $4.6 trillion and have led to the development of a major sector of the real estate and finance industries. Major employment opportunities related to real estate are found in savings banks, commercial banks, mortgage banking and mortgage brokerage firms and life insurance companies.

14. Real estate appraisers estimate the value of real property. Their services are used by buyers and sellers, financial institutions, tax assessors and many others.

15. Real estate counselors advise individuals and firms about their real estate investments. They must have extensive knowledge of all aspects of real estate, tax law and investment.

16. Real estate development offers greater potential return and greater potential risk than perhaps any other field within the real estate industry. Although not strictly a part of the real estate industry, construction is tied closely to development and to real estate in general.

17. Land-use planners are engaged in physical design, economic and investment aspects of development, and land-use policies and regulations.

18. Many real estate specialists are employed at various levels of government in property acquisition, tax administration, land-use and housing policy development, and other operations of government.

Key Terms

appraisal an estimate of value.

gestation period the time between conception of the idea for a development project and its completion and entry into the available supply.

personal property movable items such as cars, clothing, books, etc.

real estate   land and structures that are attached to it.

real property   the legal interests associated with the ownership of real estate.

Study Exercises

1. What is the primary difference between real property and personal property?

2. What characteristic of real estate makes each parcel unique?

3. Why are real estate investment decisions by their very nature long-term decisions?

4. What is meant by "long gestation period" for real estate developments?

5. What is meant by "interdependence of land uses"?

6. Why is the provision of public services important to real estate development?

7. What is the importance of real estate to the national economy?

8. What are the five principal classifications of real estate in the marketplace?

9. What is the primary objective of the property manager?

10. What is the function of a real estate appraiser?

For Further Reading

Miles, M. E., R. L. Haney, and Gayle Berens. *Real Estate Development: Principles and Process*, 2d ed. (Washington, D.C.: Urban Land Institute, 1996).

Poorvu, W. J. *The Real Estate Challenge: Capitalizing on Change* (Upper Saddle River, N.J.: Prentice-Hall, 1996).

Wills, R. K. and H. I. Daniel. *Case Studies in Real Estate* (Englewood Cliffs, N.J.: Prentice-Hall, 1990).

PART ONE

Real Estate Market Analysis

CHAPTER 2
Understanding Real Estate Markets

In many urban markets, demand for property exceeds the existing supply. In response, developers are converting abandoned warehouses and factories into residential lofts or upscale commercial space.

Real Estate Today

- *Close-Up*
  Japanese Investors
  Learn a Painful Real
  Estate Market
  Lesson

- *Close-Up*
  Adaptive Use of
  Four Railroad
  Stations

Chapter Preview

THE KEY TO becoming a successful real estate investor, developer or other real estate professional is to gain a clear understanding of the economics of real estate markets. This is central to all aspects of real estate—sales, investment decisions, mortgage lending decisions, determination of value, and development of land-use and housing policies.

In our quest to understand real estate markets, we look to this chapter's objectives:

- Explain why the traditional supply and demand model must be modified when analyzing real estate markets because of the special economic characteristics of real estate resources.
- Describe the major factors that influence supply and demand in real estate markets.
- Analyze the factors involved in the location of cities and people and the influence these various factors have on the local demand for real estate.

THE IDEALIZED SUPPLY AND DEMAND MODEL

Courses on the principles of economics teach us how the mechanism of supply and demand works in idealized markets. The general characteristics of such markets are as follows:

- There are many buyers and sellers, each operating on too small a scale to affect the marketplace materially.
- All participants have excellent knowledge of the products concerned and the conditions of supply and demand. This knowledge is simple and easy to obtain.
- The products are homogeneous; that is, they are identical or very similar.
- The supply is flexible and may be expanded or reduced in a relatively short period of time.
- Purchases are relatively small and frequent.
- Space is not a factor in the analysis.

Although these exact conditions are never found in the real world, they approximate those of markets for certain agricultural commodities and financial securities. In somewhat more complex and realistic forms, they also approximate those conditions of many other market situations. Because of the special economic characteristics of real estate resources, the real estate market does not fit this ideal structure, however. Let us examine why real estate markets differ from these idealized ones.

REAL ESTATE RESOURCES: SUPPLY FACTORS—IMPROVEMENTS

Several characteristics distinguish the supply of real estate improvements (buildings and other structures) from resources in the simple supply and demand model:

- The supply is fixed in the short run.
- As opposed to the supply of properties, the supply of property services is somewhat more responsive to changes in demand because the properties can be used more or less intensively.
- The additions to supply in any one year are usually a relatively small proportion of the total inventory.
- Most additions to the supply are based on anticipations of future demand.
- The cost and availability of financing are vital in determining the volume and timing of new additions to the supply.

Short-Run Inelasticity of Supply

The supply of real estate improvements is fixed in the short run because of the lengthy gestation period for real estate investment and the long lives of improvements. Economists refer to this relatively fixed supply as *inelasticity of supply*. If an increase in demand creates shortages of hotel rooms or warehouse space, for example, the number of rooms or the square footage of space cannot be expanded quickly. In fact, it probably will take several years to increase the supply materially.

Conversely, if an excess of supply of certain types of real estate exists, the total inventory will not contract quickly. If too many hotel rooms are available, for example, many will just sit there vainly waiting for customers. If the imbalance continues for a long period, however, marginal hotels may be torn down or perhaps converted to other uses, thereby reducing the supply.

Elasticity of Supply of Property Services

Even though the physical supply of buildings changes slowly, the supply of real estate property services expands and contracts rapidly in response to demand conditions as the degree of use of properties varies. That is, existing properties will be used more intensively in periods of excess demand, causing vacancy rates, the percentage of space that is unoccupied, to fall to relatively low levels. Conversely, the first indication of a softening of demand will be an increase in vacancy rates.

Additions to Total Inventory and the Accelerator Effect

Another consequence of the long life of real estate improvements is the fact that net additions to the supply of real estate in any year usually constitute only a small percentage of the total stock. For example, the annual number of housing starts over the past 30 years has ranged from lows of 1.1 million in 1982 and 1 million in 1991 to a high of 2.4 million in 1972—increases of only 1.5 to 3 percent. In local markets, however, new additions, particularly of specialized types of property, may represent a much larger portion of the total.

Because new construction generally constitutes a small part of the total real estate inventory, relatively small changes in total demand can generate large percentage increases in new construction. Suppose that the total supply of housing in a community is 10,000 units and that net additions during the past year were 300 units (400 new housing units less 100 demolitions and other removals). If the number of demolitions remains the same and if total demand increases from 10,000 to 10,600 units, an increase of only 6 percent, the number of new housing starts will increase by 75 percent, from 400 to 700 (the figures for total, not net, additions). This is a real estate market application of the accelerator effect, a familiar economic principle from macroeconomics: a relatively small percentage increase in total demand will result in a much larger percentage increase in new investment.

Additions in Anticipation of Demand

New investment in income-producing real estate improvements depends on anticipations of future demand. Current market conditions are important, but only as they influence such anticipations. For example, high demand for hotel rooms in a city and resulting low vacancy rates probably indicate that future demand will support new development.

Even so, the market must be analyzed carefully to determine whether the factors underlying the demand actually will provide a solid basis for additional capacity. Furthermore, it is vital to determine the plans of other potential investors. If several groups respond to the same market stimulus, the result will be a serious oversupply upon completion of the projects, a distressingly common occurrence in real estate markets.

The Influence of Financial Factors

Because of the large size and long life of real estate investments, the cost and availability of financing are vital factors in determining both the volume and the timing of new additions to the real estate supply. Historically, housing starts and other real estate developments have been curtailed sharply during periods of tight money and have expanded during periods of monetary ease. In fact, housing starts usually run counter to general business cycles due to the influence of financing terms. When the general demand for money increases as businesses seek to borrow for expansion, rising interest rates force many developers and homebuyers to curtail or halt their activities.

Many income-producing real estate investments have been financed almost wholly with outside borrowed funds, with very little actual equity on the part of the developer entrepreneurs. These projects often are developed through separate corporations organized for this purpose, further insulating the developers from adverse financial effects if the projects fail. Thus, entrepreneur developers have had great incentive to build almost any project they could get financed. If financial institutions are eager to lend money and do not adequately analyze the economic and financial feasibility of a potential project, the result often is a poorly conceived investment that probably will result in a financial loss to the developer and to the financial institution. Unfortunately, such cases have been common and have reached alarming levels during the severe real estate recession of the early 1990s.

The Impact of Uniqueness

While the simple supply and demand model assumes homogeneous products, real estate resources are in fact heterogeneous. In other words, one parcel of real estate is not a perfect substitute for another because of each parcel's unique characteristics. Therefore, real estate market analysis requires careful consideration of the features that distinguish one property from another.

Defining Real Estate Markets

In addition to the importance of considering the special characteristics of real estate resources and transactions, realistic real estate market analysis depends on accurate identification of the real estate market to which it is applied. Real estate markets are identified in terms of geographic location, property type, tenant or use type or some combination of these descriptions.

Geographic Location   Because real estate is fixed in location, real estate markets are dramatically influenced by changing economic conditions in the surrounding communities. For this reason, identification of a specific real estate market requires careful consideration of the factors that influence activity in that market. For example, the market for luxury resort hotels depends greatly on economic conditions all over the world, while the market for convenience stores is influenced primarily by economic activity that occurs in a localized area near to site. The common term used to describe the geographically defined market is *neighborhood*. While this term has many interpretations, real estate appraisers and analysts often define a neighborhood as a geographic area containing properties whose values are affected by the same set of economic factors.

Property Type While there are many shared influences across geographic locations, the markets for office buildings, shopping centers, housing, warehouses and vacant land can rarely be thought of as being influenced identically by the same sets of economic circumstances. Therefore, it is useful to refer to property type when identifying a specific market. Many categories are used to define property-type markets, with the broadest categories being commercial, industrial, agricultural and residential. Within each of these categories, many other identifying characteristics can be used to further define a specific market. For example, office and retail properties are both considered commercial land use, but many types of office buildings and shopping centers exist. Industrial properties include such land uses as warehouses, manufacturing plants and oil refineries. Similarly, residential uses include multifamily and single-family property, as well as condominiums and mobile homes.

The term *district* combines the concepts of geographic location and property type as a means of identifying a specific market. A district is defined as a contiguous geographic area containing similar land uses, such as a section of a city that is dominated by highrise office buildings or lower-income single-family homes. A neighborhood, as defined above, can be thought of as a collection of properties or districts of properties whose values are influenced by the same set of economic factors.

Use Type Because real estate market activity is determined by real people, consideration of their characteristics further defines the parameters of a specific market. Understanding user characteristics is critical in real estate market analysis. For example, owner-occupied, single-family home markets may respond differently to changes in economic factors in comparison to tenant-occupied, single-family home markets. An increase in interest rates may make it more difficult for people who desire to own a home to obtain a mortgage, thereby increasing demand for rental properties while decreasing demand for owner-occupied residences. Similarly, small-business owners do not typically compete for office space with large conglomerates, and the demand for office space from each of these user types is separate to large degree.

Degree of Competition

Another limitation of the idealized supply and demand model when analyzing real estate markets is the degree to which prices are established by free and open competition between market participants. In idealized markets, the competition is defined as "perfect," with no one participant having any more influence on prices than any other participant. In real estate markets, however, some participants may have both better information and stronger influence on markets. For example, if potential investors know that a property owner faces imminent foreclosure due to default on a mortgage debt, they may be able to buy the property for less than its market price. If a developer has superior knowledge of a market, he or she may be able to recognize opportunities that others do not see. Thus, astute real estate investors constantly improve their awareness of current market conditions and enhance their knowledge of real estate fundamentals to gain a competitive advantage.

REAL ESTATE RESOURCES: SUPPLY FACTORS—LAND

Unlike real estate improvements, the supply of land is basically fixed. The surface of the globe is a constant, even considering that the amount of land area may vary slightly over time as volcanoes create islands, land falls into the sea, swamps are drained and lakes are filled. But though the physical amount of land is fixed, a particular piece of land may not be economically scarce. The economic scarcity of land is a function primarily of demand for land in a given geographical area and the productivity of that land.

An acre of arid land in the rural American West probably will bring very little in the marketplace because it can be put to little productive use. But if the land happens to contain deposits of valuable minerals, its value will be quite large. Or suppose the acre was located on Las Vegas's Strip or Phoenix's Miracle Mile. The scarcity of land relative to the demand in those particular locations would cause the land to be quite valuable.

National Land Supply

The major uses of land in the United States are shown in Table 2.1. Perhaps the most striking aspect of these data is the very large proportion of land that is undeveloped or in agricultural use. Approximately three-fourths of the total area is devoted to crops, grazing or woodlands, and another 11 percent consists of "miscellaneous land" of little economic value—marshes, swamps, bare rock, deserts. Slightly more than 1 percent is used for rights-of-way for rural highways, railroads and airports. Only 1.6 percent of the total land area is located within the limits of cities and towns with populations of more than 2,500, but this area contains more than 70 percent of the nation's total population. Although this figure does not include all urbanized areas and is made smaller by the inclusion of the vast, undeveloped Alaskan lands, the portion of land devoted to urban and other developed uses in the United States is still relatively small. The supply of land in the United States is ample; the supply of land for certain localized needs, however, may be quite scarce.

Local Land Supply   Many factors may restrict the supply of land available for development at the local level. Some of the same geographical attributes that lead to the founding of cities, such as harbors, rivers, lakes, wetlands and mountain passes, also restrict the supply of land that can be used for the cities' expansion. Similarly, urban growth requires large amounts of land for parks, railroads, highways, airports and other public facilities. Past use of private land also may create barriers to future development in the form of blighted neigh-

Millions of Acres of Land in Major Uses in the United States

Table 2.1

Land Use	Millions of Acres	Percentage of Total Area
Total land area	2,265	100.0
Type of ownership		
Public ownership	885	39.1
Indian lands	51	2.2
Private ownership	1,329	58.7
Type of use		
Cropland	404	17.8
Grazings, forest and woodland	1,317	58.2
Special uses	299	13.2
Urban	37	1.6
Transportation	27	1.2
Recreation	116	5.1
Wildlife areas	95	4.2
National defense and industrial	24	1.1
Miscellaneous land*	245	10.8

*Includes areas not inventoried, such as marshes, swamps, bare rock and deserts.

Source: Bureau of the Census, United States Department of Commerce, *Statistical Abstract of the United States 1995,* 115th edition.

borhoods and fragmented patterns of land ownership that make it difficult to assemble large tracts.

The lack of utilities and transportation facilities may restrict development, particularly on the urban fringe. Such problems have been intensified in recent years by the limited growth policies of some communities, which deliberately have slowed or halted the expansion of services necessary for development.

National, state and local land-use policies sometimes have a great effect on the amount of land available for development. Regulations designed for the protection of wetlands and floodplains may be very desirable in reducing urban impact on the environment, but they also tend to restrict the supply of available land in the urban marketplace. Conversely, a positive public attitude toward economic growth can greatly expand the supply of developable land by leading to the extension of needed public services and by removing zoning and other legal impediments to development.

REAL ESTATE RESOURCES: DEMAND FACTORS

The national demand for real estate is determined largely by the same factors that influence the demand for other goods and services. Because real estate is fixed in location and markets are largely local, however, regional and local

Real Estate Today

Japanese Investors Learn a Painful Real Estate Market Lesson

Real estate markets are local—and prices don't always keep going up. Japanese investors in U.S. real estate learned these facts in a very painful way. Between 1985 and 1991, they invested an estimated $77 billion in U. S. real estate, primarily in California, New York and Hawaii. Typically, they bought "trophy properties" at the top of the market, and they often were forced to sell at fire-sale prices.

For example, Mitsubishi Estate Company bought 80 percent of famed Rockefeller Center. When rents failed to rise following the real estate recession of the early 1990s, Rockefeller Center was unable to cover its debt and other costs and finally declared bankruptcy, with Mitsubishi losing more than $1 billion.

Sanwa Bank foreclosed on the $340 million mortgage it held on Financial Square in New York. It then sold the property for $130 million.

Japanese real estate developer Minoru Isutani lost $340 million after purchasing Pebble Beach Golf Club in 1990. He sold the club two years later to two Japanese investors.

In Hawaii, Japanese investors spent $18 billion to buy and build luxury hotels, condominiums, resorts and golf courses. Mitsubishi reportedly spent $400 million to build the Hyatt Regency Waikoloa on the Big Island; the company sold it for approximately $55 million. The Daichi Kango Bank sold the Ritz-Carlton Mauna Lani resort for $75 million; it originally cost $200 million. A breathtaking 219-acre golf course that cost $100 million to build was auctioned for $30 million.

Real estate markets are local, and investors who do not fully understand them often get burned—sometimes severely. Investors who believe that prices always go up discover that real estate is subject to fluctuations, particularly in markets that have been subjected to speculative fever. Unfortunately, the experience of Japanese investors and financial institutions in recent years confirms the truth of these assertions. ∎

---

growth factors are of critical importance. If investors fail to fully grasp this fact, they may make unwise real estate investments, as we see in the above Close-Up.

The principal determinants of demand for real property are national levels and regional distributions of income, employment and population. Let us examine these in turn.

Income

A high level of income is of vital importance in creating demand for all goods and services, but especially for durable and investment goods, as their purchase can be postponed more easily. Thus, during a recession and period of low consumer confidence, as occurred in the early 1990s, real estate demand is weak, particularly for commercial real estate. Conversely, general business expansion creates profitable real estate investment opportunities, and high levels of family income lead to increased demand for housing.

As mentioned earlier, the availability and cost of mortgage funds can offset demand trends. Low interest rates can increase home purchases during a recession, and high rates can decrease demand during a general business expansion.

Of course, if a recession is severe enough to cause mortgage lenders to retreat from the market, financial trends can make a real estate recession even worse. This happened to commercial real estate markets during the early years of this decade.

Employment

The overall national level of employment is important first as a determinant and an indicator of total income. Periods of rising employment are accompanied by high levels of income that lead to high levels of demand for real estate.

Changing employment characteristics also have important implications for real estate markets. Shifts away from manufacturing toward service and other white-collar employment have influenced demand for industrial parks and office buildings. The increasing number of married women in paid employment has been a major factor in the growing popularity of dining out and the consequent demand for restaurant facilities.

Of greatest importance for real estate markets, however, are shifts in industrial locations, which bring about regional shifts in employment and population migration. Such regional movements create demand for all types of real property and lead to many development opportunities. Unfortunately, structural economic changes that result in downsizings and plant closings have affected many communities adversely.

Population

Several aspects of population are major determinants of real estate demand; these include the total level of population, the population growth rate, population characteristics (particularly age distribution) and regional population movements.

Total population, population growth rate and income of the population are the major factors that create demand for housing and influence types of housing construction. For example, the baby boom following World War II created a large demand for housing, particularly for houses with three or more bedrooms. Conversely, the more recent decline in the birth rate and the increase in single-person households have increased the demand for smaller dwelling units and decreased the demand for larger homes.

Migration, determined largely by regional employment opportunities, has a great impact on local real estate demand. The expansion of a community's employment base often leads to the migration of people to that area, which expands demand for housing and other types of real estate development. Conversely, little or no real estate development occurs in communities where population is declining.

Changes in Demand

How does the real estate market react to changes in demand for property services? Examining the probable impacts of both expansion and contraction of demand may provide some answers.

The first effect of an increase in demand for real estate property services probably will be an increase in the use of existing properties. If the market has been depressed in the immediate past and substantial vacancies exist, this may be the only effect, at least for some time.

As vacancies diminish and more people bid for the fixed supply, the next effect will be increases in prices and rents. Such increases can sometimes be dramatic, especially in an atmosphere of inflationary expectations. For example, lease rates for office space in New York's midtown Manhattan doubled and even tripled as demand expanded in the 1980s after the depressed markets of the mid-1970s and firms desiring space bid for the practically fixed supply.

The profit potential of new projects rises as prices and rents rise due to the decrease in vacancy rates and as investors are attracted to new construction projects. This is a critical phase in the real estate cycle. If developers and financial institutions overreact to the economic stimulus, excessive building can result. This occurred during the 1980s, and the oversupply "hangover" in the 1990s caused the real estate recession and severe troubles for many financial institutions.

The appearance of additional supply in the marketplace tends to slow or reverse the rise in prices and rents and to increase vacancy rates. If investors have overreacted or if demand increases more slowly than anticipated or even falls, vacancy rates will rise swiftly, prices and rents will fall and many projects will be unprofitable. The drop in prices may encourage an expansion in the use of space, which will eliminate some of the excess supply; but the real estate market is likely to remain depressed until demand again increases.

PRICE-DISTANCE RELATIONSHIPS

Why is a certain parcel of land used for a particular purpose? Why are certain parcels of land worth more than others? The answer is embodied in the concept of price-distance relationships. The classical economists included land as one of the three elements of production: land, labor and capital; and rent is the return on or price of land. In theory, a particular parcel will be used in the way that yields the highest return to the owner.

The inclusion of space in the analysis of land prices first appeared more than 150 years ago. It was recognized that the value of a particular parcel was influenced not only by its fertility and topography, but also by its location in relation to other land uses. This conception of land use, which was based on a primarily agricultural economy, consisted of a series of concentric circles surrounding a central point. Commercial uses would occupy the center because of the importance of access, and those wanting to make such uses of the central area would bid the highest prices for the land. Homes, which require access to the central facilities, would surround the core; they would not occupy the central area because they could not bid as much for that land as could commercial users. Intensive agricultural activities requiring frequent attention by farmers and transport to the center population would be located farther out. Nonintensive agricultural activities, such as grazing and timber production, would be located even farther out. Figure 2.1 shows how land would be allocated among the competing uses based on these hypothetical price-distance relationships.

Theoretical Price-Distance Relationships **Figure 2.1**

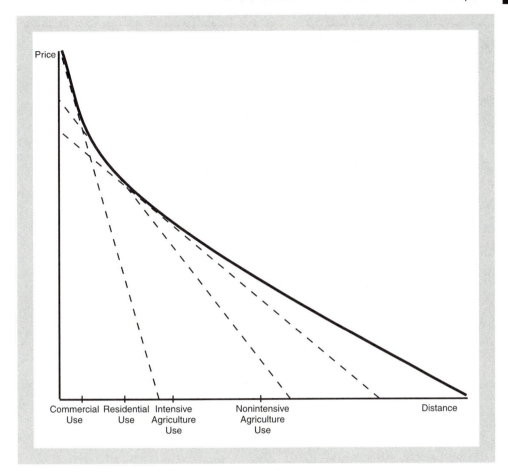

Although like the idealized supply and demand model, this model is somewhat simplistic, it offers insight into community form and the location of land uses. Others have built on the model to develop more realistic views of land-use change in the modern world. We will examine several of these models in the next chapter.

HIGHEST AND BEST USE

All the fundamentals of real estate market analysis, including the concept of price-distance relationships, come together in the concept of the **highest and best use** of land, defined as that use of land most likely to produce the greatest long-term economic return to the owner. (A more precise definition is: that use of land, among the reasonable and alternative uses that are physically practical, legally permissible, market supportable and economically feasible, that provides the highest residual land value.) The concept recognizes that most land can be used for a variety of purposes. A particular tract may be physically

Real Estate Today *Close-Up*

Adaptive Use of Four Railroad Stations

With the growing appreciation of older buildings, there has also been an increasing adaptation of obsolete buildings to new uses. Some adaptive-use projects are quite modest—a former service station to a florist shop, for example—while others are quite grand. This close-up examines four adaptive-use projects that rehabilitated historic railroad stations and returned them to productive use.

Washington's Union Station
One of the most spectacular and successful of adaptive-use projects is Washington's Union Station. When it opened in 1907, it was the world's largest railroad terminal and certainly one of the grandest. Union Station was built in the magnificent Beaux Arts style, with life-sized statues of Roman legionnaires standing guard over the main hall, which was enclosed by its 96-foot-high, barrel-vaulted, coffered ceiling. Union Station saw presidents, kings, queens and other foreign dignitaries come and go, as well as about 40,000 ordinary travelers a day during its heyday in the 1930s. As rail travel dwindled, however, the great station slipped into decline. By 1981, it had been closed completely for seven years, the roof leaked, the marble was crumbling and the building seemed destined to become just another pile of formerly elegant rubble.

Fortunately, however, a public-private partnership financed a $160 million restoration that included more than $500,000 spent just for gold leaf. In addition to returning the station to its role as a railroad terminal, the restoration provided 200,000 square feet of retail space with more than 100 shops, a nine-screen cinema complex, six restaurants and a number of fast-food establishments. Since opening in 1988, the building has been teeming with people—workers and residents from the Capitol Hill area, as well as tourists—and business volumes have exceeded expectations.

The Salisbury Station
A bit more modest adaptation of a railroad station is the Salisbury, North Carolina railroad depot. When completed in 1908, it was considered one of the finest sta-

tions on the entire Southern Railway. Constructed in the Spanish mission style, it thrived for many years. But like similar facilities, by the early 1980s, it was abandoned, neglected and facing the prospect of early demolition. Then a local preservation group, the Historic Salisbury Foundation, came to the rescue. It purchased the station from the railroad in 1981 for $130,000. But then the Foundation had to find a use for it—and the money to restore the station.

First, the foundation awarded a two-year, long-term lease option to a developer, but the developer was unable to secure potential tenants and let the option expire. The foundation tried to attract other developers but finally realized that the envisioned restaurant and retail complex was not economically viable. Instead, the group decided to develop the building itself as a community conference and event center.

In one of the largest preservation and redevelopment projects ever successfully accomplished by a small city, the Historic Salisbury Foundation secured private contributions to restore and convert the building at a cost of almost $4 million. The completed project has a large conference and banquet hall in the restored waiting room; several conference rooms; offices for the foundation and a local securities firm; and, rather appropriately, a small Amtrak station.

The Danville Rail Passenger Station and Science Center
Danville, Virginia's nearly 100-year-old rail passenger station had fallen on hard times. Although it was still used as a passenger rail station, passenger complaints about its poor condition had led Amtrak to consider abandonment.

In 1993, Danville received an award of nearly $1 million in "transportation enhancement" funds under the Federal Surface Transportation Act which was combined with $500,000 from the city to purchase and renovate the station. In addition to continued use as a passenger terminal, the building now contains a satellite facility of the Science Museum of Virginia which attracts about 30,000 visitors annually. Additional grants were used to purchase the adjoining Freight Depot and convert it to a new community market and to renovate a historic railroad trestle across the Dan River as a centerpiece of a pedestrian path system.

The station renovation has also served as a catalyst for redevelopment of the surrounding Tobacco District Historic District. The conversion of an abandoned tobacco warehouse to an import showroom and warehouse and a vacant railroad office building into a restaurant were two of the first projects.

The Lafayette Depot

Transportation enhancement funds were also used to relocate and renovate the 1902 Big Four Depot in Lafayette, Indiana. The city had been working for many years to relocate rail lines in order to eliminate numerous hazardous crossings. The depot was moved two blocks to serve as the focus of a new intermodal civic plaza overlooking the relocated railroad tracks, the Wabash River and the Wabash Heritage Trail. Another part of the project was renovating the nearby historic Main Street bridge to extend the Heritage Trail across the river to West Lafayette.

The Lafayette Depot is again serving as a transportation facility. In addition, however, the Plaza project provided a focal point to help in the revitalization of the downtown area. ∎

---

suitable for the growing of soybeans or the grazing of cattle, for single-family or multifamily home sites, for a shopping center or for an industrial plant. The highest and best use of the site will be determined by many factors, including the past and present use of the land, nearby land uses, the availability or absence of utilities and transportation facilities, and recent or anticipated economic growth in the area. The determination of the highest and best use generally is easier for vacant land than for land with improvements.

Vacant Land

Suppose that a 50-acre tract of land has been planted in soybeans for some years. The value of the land in this agricultural use is $5,500 per acre. In the past, farming represented the highest and best use of the tract because the site was located several miles from a small city. But now the city has begun expanding because increased manufacturing activity there has led to population growth. These factors, combined with road improvements and the extension of water and sewer lines, have led to a change in the highest and best use of the site. In fact, there now may be several possible uses for it. One developer believes there is demand for a low-density, single-family residential subdivision and is willing to pay $15,000 per acre. Another developer wishes to build an apartment complex and is willing to pay $40,000 per acre. A speculator believes that in a few years, the site will be suitable for a shopping center and is willing to bid even higher. In this case, the highest and best use of the land is probably the apartment complex, but the speculator may be willing to pay more than the value of this use in hopes that the potential use, and thus the value, will increase even more in the future. Obviously, the determination of highest and best use requires extensive knowledge of the area and good judgment regarding probable future growth trends.

Land with Improvements

In the case above, the determination of highest and best use was simplified by the fact that the land was vacant. Suppose, however, that a one-acre lot and the house on it are worth $125,000. If this land were vacant, its highest and best use would be for a commercial activity, and it could be sold for $75,000. Even so, the highest and best use still is residential because the value of the land and improvements in their current use still is greater than the value of the vacant land in an alternative use. As the value of the site for commercial use increases, however, it may be advantageous to tear down the existing house and shift to commercial use, particularly if the value of the improvement begins to decline as a result of age or other factors. This is particularly true for transitional neighborhoods.

Interim Use

Interim use is the temporary use of real property until such time that conditions are favorable to convert it to another use intended to be permanent. Even when economic analysis and the marketplace indicate a change in highest and best use, the existing use may be retained for an interim period, or there may be some temporary interim use. For example, suppose a vacant tract is purchased for a shopping center, but, for various reasons, actual construction is delayed for several years. During this period, part of the site could be farmed, or existing residences could be converted to short-term office or limited commercial use. In cities, parking lots often serve as interim uses.

Adaptive Use

Land is converted from one use to another as economic and demographic conditions change. In urban areas, such conversion usually has involved the demolition of existing improvements, but several factors, including growing interest in preservation of historic landmarks and the rising cost of new construction, have led to a growing development phenomenon—adaptive use. **Adaptive use** involves the conversion of a building from the use for which it originally was designed to a different and contemporary use.

Returns to the Owner versus Returns to Society

As the term normally is used by appraisers, *highest and best use* is the legal use of property that will yield the greatest economic return to the owner. It is not necessarily the use of the land that will yield the greatest social benefit or result in the greatest economic return to the community as a whole. This conflict is at the heart of many land-use policy questions, not because property owners are opposed to the public welfare, but simply because what is best for the individual and what is best for society may differ. Suppose, for example, that a developer desires to build a shopping center on a particular tract. This development represents the highest use of the land in terms of return to the owner, but the owner's application for a zoning change to permit its construction may be denied because the community perceives that the development will have adverse impacts on the neighborhood—traffic congestion that would cause accidents and bring a need for costly road improvements, increased noise levels and potential lowering of property values in nearby residential neighborhoods.

Should the community have the right to control the use of a private individual's or firm's land, or should owners be able to use their property in any way that does not cause actual harm to surrounding landholders? These questions concerning limitations on ownership and land-use conflicts will be discussed in Chapters 5 and 6.

The value of a particular tract to the community as a whole may be so great that the community will acquire it for public use despite the highest economic value the land would have if used otherwise. Central Park in New York City would be worth billions of dollars if it were converted to high-density commercial and residential use, but the community obviously has decided that the land has greater value to society when used as a park. Similar though less dramatic examples can be cited in almost every community.

Chapter Review

1. The supply of real estate improvements is characterized by several factors:

    - The supply is fixed in the short run.
    - The supply of property services is somewhat more responsive than the supply of properties because the properties can be used more or less intensively.
    - The additions to supply in any one year usually are a relatively small proportion of the total inventory.
    - Additions to the supply are based largely on anticipation of future demand.
    - The cost and availability of financing are vital factors in determining the volume and timing of new additions to the supply.

2. Some of the factors that may restrict the supply of land available for development at the local level are (1) geographical characteristics, (2) lack of utilities and transportation facilities and (3) land-use policies.

3. The real estate market usually reacts to an expansion in demand with (1) a decline in vacancy rates, (2) increases in prices and rents and (3) the attraction of investors to new construction projects.

4. The principal determinants of demand for real property are national levels of (1) income, (2) employment and (3) population, as well as regional distributions of those factors.

5. The expenditures of households, businesses and governments create demand for residential, commercial, office and industrial real estate improvements.

6. Highest and best use is defined as the use of land that will produce the greatest long-term economic return to the owner. The highest and best use of a site is determined by many factors, including (1) the past and present use of the land, (2) nearby land uses, (3) the availability or absence of utilities and transportation facilities and (4) recent or anticipated economic growth in the area.

7. The highest and best use of land is not necessarily the use that will yield the greatest social benefit or result in the highest economic return to the community as a whole. This conflict between private and public goals is at the heart of many land-use policy questions.

Key Terms

adaptive use   use of a building in a manner different from the use for which it was originally designed.

highest and best use   that use, found to be legally permissible, physically possible and financially feasible, that results in the highest land value; that use of land most likely to result in the greatest long-term economic return to the owner.

interim use   temporary use of a property until such time that conditions are favorable to convert it to another use intended to be permanent.

Study Exercises

1. Define the concept of highest and best use.

2. Why is it considered easier to determine the highest and best use for vacant land as opposed to land with improvements?

3. What is the difference between interim use and adaptive use?

4. What determines the economic scarcity of land?

5. What characteristics distinguish the supply of real estate improvements?

6. Why is the supply of real estate improvements considered inelastic?

7. Why is the supply of property services considered elastic?

8. What are the principal determinants of demand for real property?

━━━━━━━━━━━━━━━━ **For Further Reading** ━━━━━━━━━━━━━━━━

O'Sullivan, Arthur. *Urban Economics,* 3d ed. (Chicago: Irwin, 1996).

DiPasquale, Denise, and William C. Wheaton. *Urban Economics and Real Estate Markets* (Upper Saddle River, N.J.: Prentice Hall, 1996).

CHAPTER 3
The Economics of Regional and Community Growth

The shift of urban populations throughout a metropolitan area results in new commercial and residential construction projects.

Real Estate Today

- *Close-Up*
  The Piedmont
  Crescent of North
  Carolina

- *Close-Up*
  A Tale of Two Cities

Chapter Preview

OWNERS AND DEVELOPERS of real estate are concerned primarily with the market for their own property or projects. Why, then, should we study factors that influence demand at the national, regional, community and neighborhood levels? The answer, of course, is that such factors vitally affect the value and marketability of the individual parcel.

In the previous chapter, we examined some of the national factors that influence demand for real estate. But changes at the national level are not the only factors that property owners and investors should consider. Local demand for real estate is also greatly influenced by the level of regional and local economic and population growth or decline and changes in neighborhoods. In short, there is a hierarchy of influences, from the national through the regional and local levels to the individual parcel, that determines the market value of a property.

In this chapter, we will examine the following:

- Factors influencing the location of cities, including (1) transportation facilities, (2) other factors in the created environment, (3) natural resources, (4) climate and (5) labor force
- Factors influencing the growth and decline of regions and cities
- Why people locate where they do
- Models of urban growth
- The importance of public facilities in the growth process, including (1) transportation facilities and (2) water and sewer facilities
- A synthesis of urban form
- The dynamics of neighborhood change, including (1) the process of neighborhood change and (2) neighborhood stabilization and rehabilitation

ECONOMIC FACTORS INFLUENCING THE GROWTH AND DECLINE OF CITIES

Why does one region or locality develop into a center of trade or industry while others do not? Why do the economy and population of a city or region grow or decline? What factors determine the economic growth rate of an area? The answers to these questions are closely linked to the concepts of comparative advantage and economic base.

Community Growth Factors

Rapid economic and population growth generally results because one locale has a **comparative advantage** over another. This advantage may result from several factors. A city may grow because it has advantages in transportation facilities or in the quality or quantity of other factors in the created environment, or because of natural resources, a favorable climate or the quality or quantity of its labor force.

Transportation Facilities   Perhaps the most important factor that gives a community comparative advantage is transportation facilities. Almost all colonial cities in the United States developed around ports, either on natural harbors or along rivers. Most of the latter ports were located at important river junctions or at fall lines (the points at which rivers cease to be navigable because their waters, descending from the uplands to the lowlands, form rapids and falls).

These initial natural advantages were often aided by further transportation improvements. For example, New York became the dominant port on the eastern seaboard and a world city largely because of the initial advantage it enjoyed after the completion of the Erie Canal in 1825, which provided easy access to the developing West.

Later, the advent of the railroad led to the "railroad town." A community located on a railroad enjoyed a distinct economic advantage over a town that was not, and communities at important rail junctions gained even greater comparative advantages. The best example is Chicago, which developed into one of the nation's largest cities primarily because of its dominance as a rail center between East and West. Another example is discussed in the Close-Up on page 38.

Because major highways have tended to follow the paths of major railroads, rail centers have also become highway centers. Similarly, many have become major air-traffic transfer points. Two of the busiest airports in the United States are those in Chicago and Atlanta, two cities that serve as transfer points, one between East and West and the other for the Southeast.

Educational Facilities   In today's technological and service-oriented economy, the quality of educational facilities is of great importance, both in providing centers for technological development and in increasing the educational quality of the labor force. These factors undoubtedly will become even more important in future years.

Other Factors in the Created Environment   The created environment consists of such things as utilities, public services and tax levels, housing, cultural activities, and transportation and educational facilities. The quality and quantity of such factors may give a region or community a comparative advantage or disadvantage. If a community has an industrial park, for instance, it may attract additional industrial employment. Conversely, an industrial firm will not locate where adequate utilities and other services are not available.

Natural Resources Another important factor in the location of cities is the existence of various natural resources. Denver owes its origins to the discovery of gold and silver in the nearby mountains; ample deposits of coal and iron ore greatly aided the development of Birmingham and Pittsburgh. After the resources that led to its formation have been depleted or become less of a comparative advantage, and if it is to continue to prosper, a resource-based city must develop other advantages as a center of trade and industry.

Climate Other cities and regions owe much of their comparative advantage to their favorable climates; for those whose economies are based on tourism, this factor may be dominant. Climate has been an extremely important factor in the development of cities in Florida and California and is cited as one of the major comparative advantages of the Sunbelt. As a greater percentage of the population reaches retirement age over the coming decades, the advantage of these communities as retirement locations will also rise in significance.

Labor Force Another important factor that may give an area a comparative advantage is the quality or quantity of the labor force. For example, the textile industry, for the most part, deserted the cities of New England for those of the Southeast following World War II, largely because the Southeast offered an ample supply of labor who would work for relatively low wages. Conversely, New England cities—particularly those in Massachusetts—were able to attract a substantial portion of the expanding electronics industry because their labor forces possessed relatively high levels of education and skill.

Leadership An intangible but critical factor in community growth and in a community's becoming a quality place to live is community leadership. In fact, many feel this is *the* most important factor in regional and area growth and quality development. Some communities have many comparative advantages but languish; others prosper though they possess few natural advantages. The difference, in most cases, is the caliber of local leadership.

The Concept of an Economic Base

Specialization is both a fundamental economic concept and the primary reason for the existence of cities. In a developed economy, and even in most primitive societies, neither the individual nor the family nor the community can be wholly self-sufficient. Even solitary trappers occasionally must emerge from the wilds to sell pelts and purchase necessary supplies. Similarly, a community or region is not self-sufficient, but must sell goods and services outside its borders to pay for the imports it needs.

The pelts trapper Joe sells are "exports" for his economy, and the proceeds can be used to purchase needed supplies ("imports"). Similarly, a community tends to specialize in certain activities in which it has a comparative advantage and to sell those goods and services to the rest of the world. The income from those exports can be used to import goods and services from outside the community.

Real Estate Today

The Piedmont Crescent of North Carolina

Access to improved transportation facilities was particularly important in the development of the Piedmont Crescent of North Carolina, an area that now contains nearly half of the state's urban population. There are no distinct geographical differences between the Crescent area and the remainder of the Piedmont, so what caused this pattern of urban development?

Because North Carolina has a somewhat treacherous coastline, no major ports and no rivers flowing from west to east, the state's Piedmont region was populated in colonial days largely by settlers who traveled overland along an Indian trading path. Several small towns, including Hillsborough, Salisbury and Charlotte, grew near Indian villages along the path. Other towns and villages sprang up in the region, but by the 1840s, the area still was very poor, its economy committed almost wholly to subsistence agriculture. Governor William A. Graham lamented the lack of adequate transportation:

The man who is obliged to transport on wagons over no better roads than ours, a distance varying from 60 to 250 miles, at a speed of 25 miles per day, can no more contend for profits with him who has the advantage of railroads or good navigation, than can the spinning wheel with the cotton mill.

Railroads had been built from the seaport of Wilmington to the small town of Weldon and from the state capital of Raleigh (located, like Washington, D.C., by a political decision) to connect with Virginia railroads. A great clamor arose for a railroad to aid development in the Piedmont, and the North Carolina Railroad Company finally was chartered by the legislature in 1849, funded with $3 million in state funds and $1 million of required private stock subscriptions. This last feature was introduced by legislators from eastern North Carolina in the hope that it would block the construction of the project, but it had some unforeseen consequences.

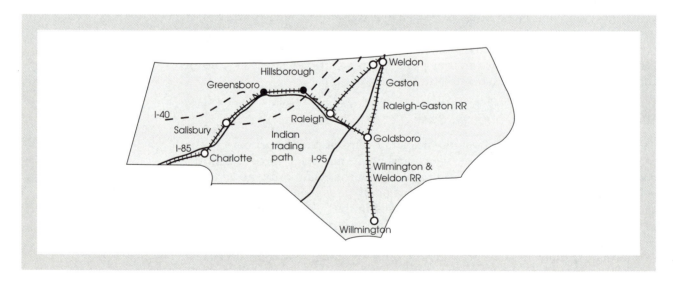

The charter had specified that the railroad would begin at a junction with the Wilmington & Weldon Railroad, near the present-day city of Goldsboro, and proceed westward to Raleigh, Salisbury and Charlotte. It did not specify the route between Raleigh and Salisbury, but simply stated it should be the "most practical."

Former governors John M. Morehead of Greensboro and William A. Graham of Hillsborough were convinced that the most practical route was by way of their own towns. They led a group that purchased most of the stock, hired a surveyor and directed him to determine whether the longer route by way of Hillsborough and Greensboro, "all things considered, is not the most practical." To no one's surprise, the surveyor decided that it was, and the railroad was built along that crescent-shaped path.

The railroad gave the Crescent an initial competitive advantage over the remainder of the Piedmont that it has retained to this day, even though railroads were extended to other portions of the Piedmont within a few years. Towns and cities whose economies were based primarily on industrial development sprang up along the North Carolina Railroad. In the automobile era, the main highways were built in the same general locations, often alongside the railroad. Today, I-85 and I-40 traverse the same general path.

Because of its excellent access to transportation, Charlotte became a distribution center and one of the leading cities of the Southeast; Greensboro is the second largest city in the state and boasts a viable and diversified economy. Hillsborough, whose people had little desire to encourage growth, remains a rather sleepy but pleasant town of approximately 1,500 people. ■

In examining local economies, analysts often classify employment into two general categories: (1) **export activities,** also called *basic activities,* which produce goods and services for sale or consumption outside an area's borders, and (2) **population-serving activities,** also called *nonbasic activities,* which produce goods and services for sale or consumption within a community itself. Although it is difficult to determine with any exactness which of a community's activities are for export, they usually include most of those in the fields of agriculture, mining, manufacturing and wholesale trade.

The population-serving activities generally include those undertaken by the construction industry, public utilities, the retail trade, financial institutions, service industries and government. Sometimes, however, population-serving activities are also export in nature. A regional shopping center may draw customers from far beyond the local area; a city may serve as headquarters for financial institutions serving a large region; and a large university usually attracts students far from the local area.

If export activity in a region or city expands, so will employment in the population-serving industries. Suppose that Amalgamated Whitzadidle opens a new manufacturing plant in Lower Swampville that employs 500 workers. The economic impact of the new plant will go far beyond this direct employment increase. Construction workers will be needed to build the facility and homes and apartments for individuals and families who may move to the area. Purchases of various goods and services by the manufacturing workers will give rise to additional employment in the trade and service industries. The new residents also will purchase and finance homes and buy insurance, thereby creating new jobs in those fields. In the same fashion, the impact of the new plant will spread throughout the local economy so that the total employment and income created will be far greater than the direct impact.

In the past, many regional analysts, planners and appraisers have tried to quantify the relationship between changes in employment in industries that bring income into a region from beyond its borders—that is, changes in the **economic base**—and changes in total employment, income and population. Although the use of these models as precise, predictive tools generally has been discredited, the concept of an economic base is still valid. To understand the potential market for real property in a community, it is essential to understand the community's industrial structure and the probable changes that will occur. If the economic base is likely to expand, demand for real property also is likely to expand. Conversely, of course, if the economic base is expected to contract, demand for real estate also is likely to contract.

THE LOCATION OF PEOPLE

Cities tend to develop in places that offer firms a comparative advantage, and exploitation of that advantage leads to growth of the economic base. People also tend to locate where they can achieve a comparative advantage, and although there are exceptions, most people live where they do because of economic opportunities. When jobs are plentiful, other factors come into play as well—personal preferences for a particular type of climate or landscape, big-city attractions or small-town tranquility, and closeness to or distance from relatives. When jobs become more scarce, such considerations tend to lose their force; people go where they can find work.

The growth of Social Security and other retirement benefits in recent years has created a large group of retirees who are relatively free to follow their locational preferences. This group has been a major factor in the population growth of such warm-weather states as Florida and Arizona. Most interstate migrants in this age group move for family or retirement reasons. Even in this age group, however, nearly 14 percent of the moves in a recent census study were made for reasons of employment.

It follows that demand for housing in a locality is very closely related to employment demand—that is, to the community's economic base. Indeed, most real estate activity occurs as a result of changes in the economic base. For example, industrial construction is a direct result of such changes. And indirectly—through increases in the demand for population-related activities—changes in the economic base lead to the development of shopping centers, the construction of schools and the like.

ANALYZING LOCAL REAL ESTATE DEMAND

How do these regional and community growth factors influence the local demand for real estate? The real estate analyst must have an understanding of both the current changes in the industrial structure of the community and the factors that might lead to economic changes that attract new people or cause residents to leave. Demand for existing properties is tied to the current industry mix and expected short-run changes. Long-term demand for existing properties and for new developments is related to the long-run vitality of the community's economy, which can be assessed only by an analysis of potential change.

Analysis of Short-Run Demand

In the previous chapter, we saw that although completion of new construction may add to the supply of real property improvements, the supply is largely fixed in the short run. Changes in demand in the short run largely affect vacancy rates, sales of existing properties, prices and lease rates.

The real estate analyst attempting to ascertain possible short-term changes in local real estate markets must ask these questions:

- What are the current supplies of various types of real estate improvements?
- What is the industrial structure of the community?
- What changes have occurred in the local economy in the recent past?
- What is likely to happen to the economy in the near future?

Suppose, for example, that a city's economy depends heavily on the automotive industry. A decrease in demand for automobiles would have an immediate impact on employment, which would lead to a decrease in consumer spending. If these conditions persist, and particularly if a major firm closes its local manufacturing facility, housing and other real estate markets would be quite adversely affected.

Analysis of Long-Run Demand

Suppose that a potential investor has been considering building a new resort facility in a community or that a developer is considering building a shopping center in a city where the dominant manufacturing employer has been forced to begin massive layoffs. In such a situation, the prospects obviously would be poor in the short run. But the proposed improvement would not actually come onto the market for some time, and demand could then be quite different and favorable for the new project. In this situation, the analyst must examine additional questions:

- What are the long-run prospects for the economy of the community?
- What national or regional trends are likely to affect employment in the area?
- Are new firms likely to locate in the area, bringing additional employment?

Projecting and forecasting future employment trends is an interesting exercise that often involves sophisticated modeling techniques. In the final analysis, however, the real estate investor must carefully evaluate the assumptions that lie behind population and employment projections. Sophisticated techniques are no substitute for informed judgment.

| Figure 3.1 | Concentric-Circle Growth |

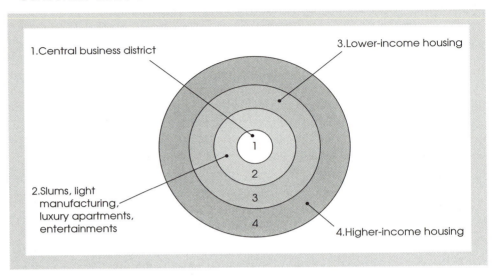

MODELS OF URBAN GROWTH PATTERNS

A city may grow in several ways: vertically, by replacement of smaller structures with taller ones and by use of air rights to construct new buildings over existing ones; by **in-filling** of open spaces between existing structures; and by extension of settled areas.

Of these forms of growth, the first two apply to already established urban areas, while the last describes the process of urban expansion. Several models have been used to explain these growth patterns, including the concentric-circle, axial, sector and multiple-nuclei models of growth. Each model describes aspects of modern urban growth in simplified model form, and observed growth patterns contain elements from several models.

Concentric-Circle Growth

One model of urban growth patterns resulted from a 1920s study of land uses in Chicago. The **concentric-circle model** postulates that from a central business district, several concentric zones radiate outward. (See Figure 3.1.) In this model, the zone immediately bordering the central business district was one of transition, consisting primarily of slums occupied by recent immigrants, who remained there until they were financially and socially prepared to move to better-quality residences farther from the center. The study found that this zone also contained widely contrasting development, including luxury apartment buildings, elegant restaurants, nightclubs and theaters. Light-manufacturing facilities were located at its outer edge.

The next zone was occupied mostly by workers employed in the manufacturing activities located in zone 2. Most housing consisted of older single-family dwellings converted into multifamily use. The passage of older housing to less affluent families as it ages is referred to as **filtering,** and it is an important element in neighborhood change.

Higher-income families who could afford better housing on larger lots occupied the fourth zone. This zone also contained specialized commercial activities serving the affluent group. Still farther out was the limit of the commuter zone, consisting of satellite cities and suburban developments. The area beyond was given over to agricultural activities.

The concentric-circle model basically follows the price-distance relationship described in Chapter 2. Users that are able to pay higher rents are located closer to the center. When considering the realism of the concentric model, we must remember that it was developed in the 1920s, when the central business district was *the* business district because the automobile had not yet influenced the creation of alternate shopping nodes. The model is also more realistic when its assumption of uniform topography is dropped.

Rivers, lakes, mountains and other geographical features may constrain growth or make it impossible in certain directions. For example, Chicago cannot grow to the east because of Lake Michigan; and the growth of Colorado Springs to the west is constrained by Pikes Peak. Growth in the San Francisco area has been southward, down the peninsula, and largely restricted to the eastern side of the peninsula because of the coastal mountain range. Urban development in the east Bay area is constrained by San Francisco Bay on the west and the Diablo Range on the east. Similarly, the form of most other urban areas has been shaped by geographical features and barriers.

Axial Growth

Transportation is a critical factor not only in the location of cities, but also in the way they develop. We know that cities are often located at transportation nodes—that is, at the junctions of major transportation routes. They may originate near ocean or river ports, at junctions of major railroads or highways or where various modes of transportation interconnect. These cities have a competitive edge over communities that do not enjoy such transportation advantages.

Similarly, land within an urban area that is well served by transportation facilities has a comparative advantage over land that is not. Thus, land tends to develop along major transportation routes. The result, according to the **axial model** of growth, is a star-shaped city with growth extending outward along transportation lines. (See Figure 3.2.)

The axial growth model was developed in the 1930s, before most workers had automobiles to commute to work and before trucks freed industrial facilities from dependence on railroads. These factors, plus the construction of major beltway highways, have reduced the impact of radial transportation routes on urbanization, but they are still important factors in urban development.

Sector Growth

Extensive studies in the 1930s of residential neighborhood change also led to the development of the **sector model** theory of urban growth. The studies found that particular types of development tended to extend in wedge-shaped sectors

Figure 3.2   Axial Growth

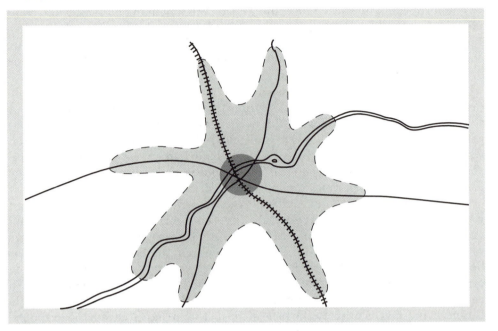

from the center of the city, as illustrated in Figure 3.3. For example, if expensive homes were first built in the western sector of a city, their development tended to continue outward in the same direction. The older houses in the sector would be occupied by successively lower-income groups through the filtering process and eventually might be converted into multifamily dwellings. Lower-income groups were not able to commute long distances and tended to live near their work. Thus, lower-income housing usually was located near manufacturing activities, but also tended to develop in wedge-shaped patterns.

Most people's experiences verify the sector model. Consider your own hometown and how it has developed. While it won't follow the model precisely, you probably will be able to identify a number of sectors that conform to this model of urban growth.

Multiple-Nuclei Growth

The **multiple-nuclei model** of city growth takes the sector theory another step toward describing the actual growth process. It emphasizes that many commercial activities occur in clusters and that, in most cities, more than one center of commercial activity exists. (See Figure 3.4.) This theory of urban growth was formulated in the 1940s, after the automobile's impact on land-use dispersion had more fully developed. It holds that these clusters developed because (1) certain activities require specialized facilities, (2) many similar activities benefit from close proximity to one another, (3) certain dissimilar activities are detrimental to each other and (4) some activities must seek less desirable, lower-priced sites.

Many factors, particularly highway and communications improvement, have led to the further fragmentation of most cities' commercial activities in recent

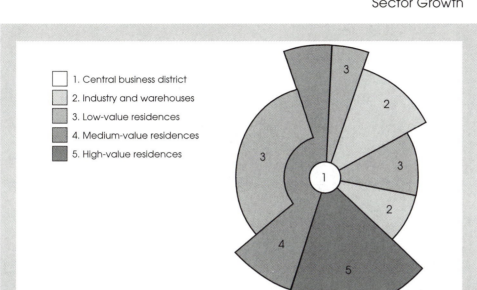

Sector Growth   **Figure 3.3**

1. Central business district
2. Industry and warehouses
3. Low-value residences
4. Medium-value residences
5. High-value residences

decades. Generally, the importance of the central business district has greatly declined with the growth of major suburban shopping centers and office parks. The development of such subcenters has led to a serious deterioration in the central business districts of many communities, and the question "What can we do to save the downtown?" has occupied the attention of many planners and public officials.

Some downtowns, however, have experienced a revival recently as a result of concern with urban sprawl, a lessening of inner-city tensions and public policies designed to encourage such development.

THE IMPORTANCE OF PUBLIC FACILITIES IN THE GROWTH PROCESS

Investments in public facilities, often called **infrastructure,** play a critical role in the local development process. Transportation improvements figure prominently in the theories of urban form, but other public investments in such facilities as sewerage and water lines also are important in the local development process. Infrastructure development or the lack of it is often used as a policy tool to encourage or discourage growth. The effects of public investments in infrastructure are clearly seen in the development of Boston and Los Angeles, discussed in the Close-Up on pages 48–51.

| **Figure 3.4** | Multiple-Nuclei Growth |

1. Shopping and offices
2. Industry and warehouses
3. Low-value residences
4. Medium-value residences
5. High-value residences

Transportation Facilities

Until about 1870, urbanized areas were almost exclusively pedestrian cities, with commuting limited to the distance one could travel on foot or in a horse-drawn vehicle. The introduction of the streetcar and electric rail transit greatly extended commuting ranges during the next 50 years and led to axial-type development along the transit lines. The automobile era (which began around 1920), when cheap, mass-produced cars became available, expanded the size of the city even more. The automobile tended to bring more concentric-type growth, for it was not limited to a few axial routes. Freeways and other highways, however, did promote development along their routes.

Figure 3.5 illustrates the process of development that often occurs when a major freeway is constructed at the rural fringe of an urban area. In the first drawing, the land is used primarily for farming, but scattered residences and some minor commercial activity are located at one road junction. In the second stage, the highway is under construction, and developers have recognized the area's heightened potential. Much of the farming activity has ceased, and this land has been purchased for possible future development. In the third picture, intense development occurs. In addition to several subdivisions, commercial strips have formed along the road near the freeway interchange. Some apartments have been constructed, and still another tract awaits development.

The beltways constructed around many large cities as part of the interstate highway program have also had a great effect on urban form. Beltways have reduced the star-shaped growth tendencies of their cities, making many areas highway program have also had a great effect on urban form. Beltways have

The Impact of Freeway Construction on Urban Development   **Figure 3.5**

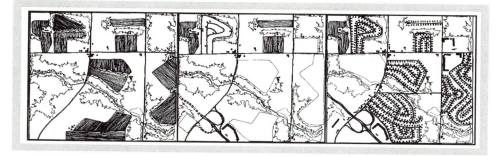

reduced the star-shaped growth tendancies of their cities, making many areas more accessible, and have encouraged large amounts of residential and industrial development. They have also served as the sites of many shopping malls and office parks, thereby furthering the development of multiple nuclei and greatly weakening the importance of the central business district. Figure 3.6 shows the influence of freeways and beltways on the development of major shopping centers in Atlanta and Houston.

Water and Sewer Facilities

Water and sewer facilities are not glamorous, but they are essential to urban growth. Even in areas that have ample water, access to a municipal water system is necessary for any type of concentrated growth. In more arid regions, where wells are often impractical, almost any type of urban development is impossible without access to a municipal water system. Similarly, if soil and other conditions are adequate, it may be possible to serve low-density developments with septic tanks, but public sewerage is essential to high-density developments. The growth potential of a particular parcel can be influenced dramatically by its access to such facilities.

Figure 3.7 shows how the construction of a major sewer line can enhance the development potential of a particular site. The first drawing shows scattered residences along rural roads in the watershed of a creek at the edge of an urban region. The building of the sewer system paralleling the stream enables subdivisions to be built within this area. Because no sewers exist in the adjoining areas, intensive development cannot occur there.

URBAN FORM: A SYNTHESIS

The development of urban form may, at first, appear of interest only to city planners and public officials. To the contrary, the real estate investor or analyst must understand the factors that direct city growth to assess the potential development of a certain piece of real estate. The various theories of urban growth describe particular aspects of the growth process. Let us synthesize and summarize some of the critical growth factors so we can better understand the impact of potential urban change on the economics of the individual parcel.

Real Estate Today

Close-Up

A Tale of Two Cities: The Effects of Public Expenditures on Infrastructure on the Development of Boston and Los Angeles

Boston and Los Angeles offer the extremes of urban form in the United States. Boston's core dates back to the early colonial period; it later expanded along streetcar lines, but remains an area of relatively high population density. Los Angeles developed in the inter-urban and automobile eras and has a relatively low population density.

Boston

In 1630, the Massachusetts Bay Company established a new town as capital of the colony of Massachusetts Bay on the Shawmut Peninsula, a hilly area barely connected to the mainland by a marshy, narrow neck of land. By 1722, when the map shown here was drawn, the city had a population of 15,000 and had become the center of trade for the New England area. Later, textile and footwear manufacturing became the dominant regional industries. In recent years, these activities have declined and been replaced by electronics firms and various types of service and finance activities.

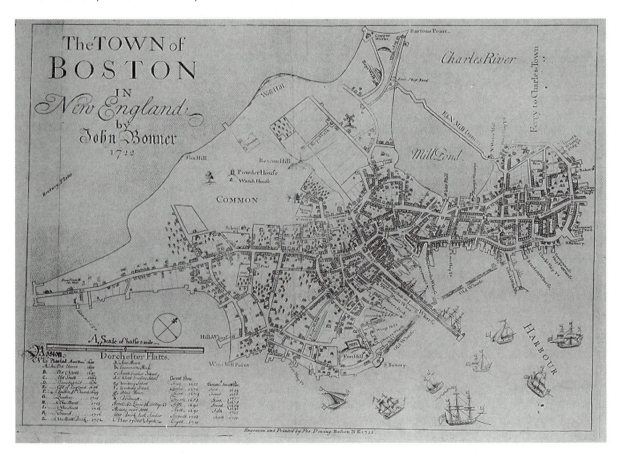

The colonial city developed a medieval type of street pattern that still confounds drivers in the older section of town. As it grew, Boston expanded outward, but also in-filled to create a tighter urban mass. Much of the in-filling required the swampy areas to be drained and filled to create more usable land. (See the map below.)

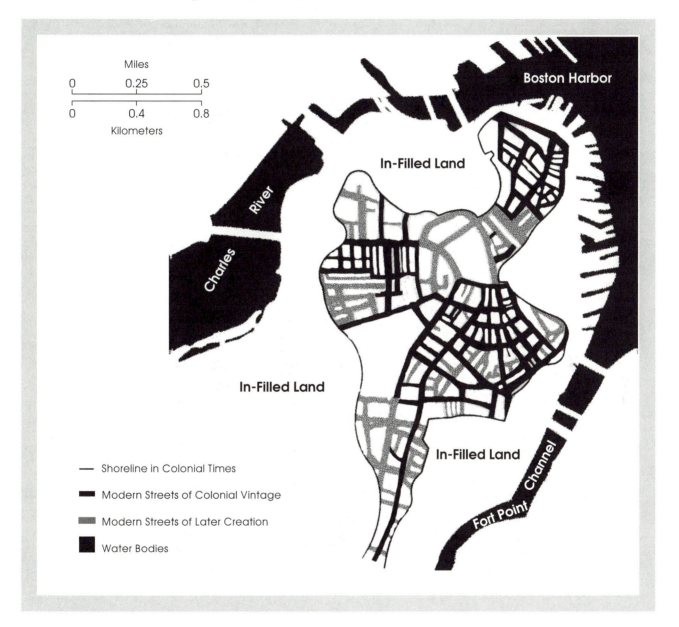

By 1850, the city's population of 200,000 was located almost entirely within a two-mile radius of city hall—that is, within pedestrian range. During the next 30 years, streetcars pulled by horses stretched out the existing city to an approximate four-mile radius. The 20 years between 1880 and 1900 was a period of rapid growth in the Boston area. Electric street railroads extended the city dramatically, and subways also were developed. By 1900, the population of approximately 1 million stretched in a ten-mile radius from the center of town. Boston had developed into two distinct sections: an industrial, commercial and communications center packed tightly against the port and an outer suburban ring of residential, commercial and industrial sub-centers.

During this century, commuter railroads, heavy-rail transit and highways have extended the urbanized area almost to the semicircular I-495, approximately 25 miles from the old port. The 46 square miles contained in the city of Boston now constitute only 7 percent of the total urbanized area.

Los Angeles

Los Angeles was founded in 1781 by Spanish priests as part of their effort to colonize California. With water for irrigation available from the Los Angeles River, the settlement was to serve as an agricultural village (pueblo) to furnish food to other missions and fortified settlements (presidios). The community retained its primarily agricultural orientation for more than 100 years; by 1850, it had a population of only 1,600.

The next 30 years saw Los Angeles transformed from a Mexican pueblo to a U.S. town and trade center with a population exceeding 11,000. The transcontinental railroads reached the city in the 1880s, bringing thousands of migrants and an economic boom. Population totaled more than 50,000 in 1890 and 102,000 in 1900.

Several reasons explain the subsequent geographical expansion of Los Angeles as the city's population grew. Although ringed by mountains, the Los Angeles basin is essentially flat, with few natural barriers to expansion. The Los Angeles River provided an adequate source of water for the early settlement, but by the turn of the century, it proved inadequate, and an aqueduct was built to the Owens Valley, 250 miles to the north. The availability of this water enabled the city to grow from 107 square miles to 440 square miles within the next 15 years. More recently, southern California has tapped the Colorado River and the northern California area for water to serve its burgeoning population.

The city's period of rapid population growth following the arrival of the steam railroads coincided with the beginning of the trolley age. The first interurban line was built to Pasadena in 1895, and over the next two decades, the Pacific Electric Railway Company built a system of more than 1,000 miles of track that covered the entire basin. (See the map on page 51). The Big Red Cars made it possible to commute long distances and helped create a metropolis of numerous communities and single-family detached homes. New lines, sometimes subsidized by land developers or by the development activities of the transit company, were often built in advance of population—a classic example of axial growth.

The process of population dispersion was furthered by the automobile. The number of automobiles registered in the Los Angeles area mushroomed from fewer than 20,000 in 1910 to more than 800,000 in 1930. In the 1940s, freeways began to replace the interurban railroads, and by 1965, the transit system had been abandoned completely. The freeway system soon grew to more than 600 miles of roadway, and the Los Angeles urban area population totaled more than 8 million.

Los Angeles sometimes is described as a collection of suburbs in search of a city, and one observer commented, "There's no there there." Also, fear of earthquakes restricted building heights to 150 feet until 1957 (the only exception was the city hall). But in recent years, a "there" has developed in the central city, which serves as a center of finance and commerce.

Population densities also are increasing, with much of the recent residential construction consisting of multifamily dwellings. Los Angeles has also begun a new transit system, but it remains to be seen whether it can be successful in a city with such low population densities. ■

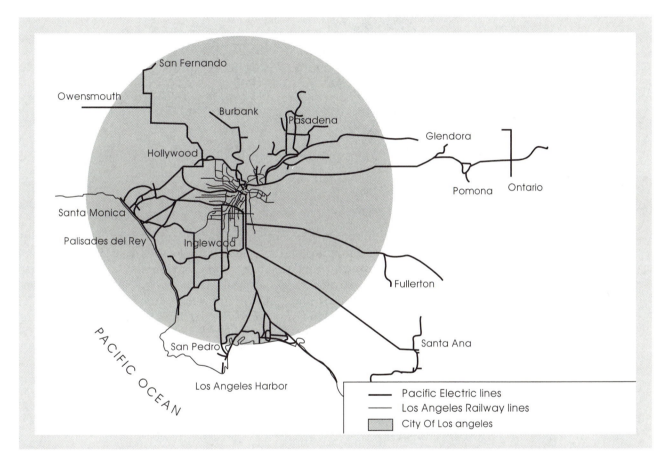

Sources:

Boston: Sam Bass Warner, Jr., *Streetcar Suburbs: The Progress of Growth in Boston, 1870–1900* (Cambridge, Mass.: Harvard University Press, 1978); Michael P. Conzen and George K. Lewis, *Boston: Geographical Portrait* (Cambridge, Mass.: Ballinger, 1976).

Los Angeles: Howard J. Nelson and William A. V. Clark, *Los Angeles: The Metropolitan Experience* (Cambridge, Mass.: Ballinger, 1976); Robert M. Fogelson, *The Fragmented Metropolis: Los Angeles, 1800–1930* (Cambridge, Mass.: Harvard University Press, 1967); Spencer Crump, *Ride the Big Red Cars: How the Trolleys Helped Build Southern California* (Costa Mesa, Calif.: Ivans-Anglo Books, 1970).

Figure 3.6   Location of Major Shopping Centers in Atlanta and Houston

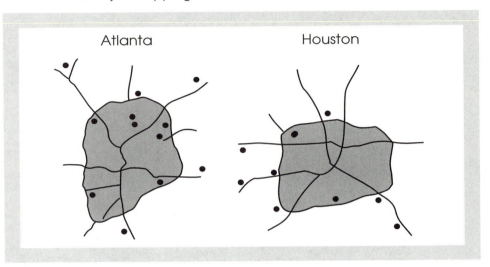

Commercial Growth

Because access is so important to commercial developments, major commercial projects like regional shopping centers are usually located near freeway interchange nodes or other major road junctions. Smaller commercial developments also depend on transportation access and the customer traffic it brings; therefore, they usually are located along heavily traveled roads and streets.

Because of improvements in transportation, particularly the development of the automobile and the attendant growth of highways, cities have spread out, and many commercial subcenters have been created. As a result, the central business district has declined in importance and, in many communities, has become a blighted area. Office buildings have also been moving from the central city to outlying subcenters, often in suburban office parks.

Industrial Growth

Like commercial development, industrial growth has tended to move away from the central city to the suburbs or to rural areas. Most small and medium-sized plants, along with warehousing and other distribution facilities, are often found in industrial parks where transportation and other necessary public facilities are available. Major manufacturing facilities often locate in more rural areas, where land for expansion is more readily available but major highways or railroads provide accessible transportation.

Residential Growth

Residential development is also strongly influenced by the location of public facilities. High-density development is impossible without the provision of public water and sewerage facilities. Commuting access is important, but

The Impact of a Major Sewer Line on Urban Development   **Figure 3.7**

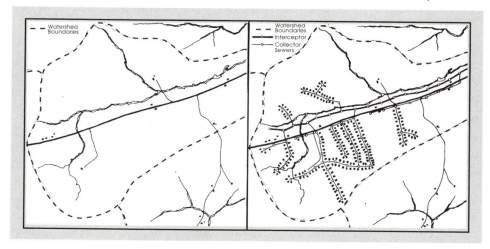

individuals have demonstrated that they will endure long commutes to enjoy a suburban or rural lifestyle and to escape some of the central city problems. In addition, the dispersion of employment to suburban locations in recent years has encouraged the dispersion of residential development to these areas.

THE DYNAMICS OF NEIGHBORHOOD CHANGE

Thus far, we have seen that the value of individual parcels of real estate depends, to a large extent, on national changes in demand, regional and community growth, and urban growth patterns. The final factor that influences property values is neighborhood change.

What Is a Neighborhood?

Location is perhaps the most important single factor in determining the value of real property. The selling prices of identical houses built in different locations within an urban area almost always vary with the character of the surrounding neighborhoods.

A **neighborhood** can be defined in several ways: as an area in which types of property are similar; as a distinct geographical area or one distinguished by a conspicuous physical feature; as a social unit—that is, a community with religious or ethnic ties; and as a group of people with the same general level of income. All these factors work to create housing submarkets in which the values of properties are influenced by the same general set of outside influences.

Neighborhood Change

As do humans, neighborhoods go through a life cycle consisting of several stages: (1) gestation, (2) youth, (3) maturity, (4) incipient decline, (5) clear decline,

(6) accelerating decline and (7) death or abandonment. Unlike the human situation, however, the process of change in neighborhoods is not inevitable. It can be arrested or reversed, and a declining neighborhood can be restored to vigorous health.

Gestation, Youth and Maturity   In the early stages of a neighborhood's life cycle, both property values and residents' incomes generally are rising. Turnover usually is relatively low, and new residents are economically and socially similar to those already living in the neighborhood.

Incipient Decline   At some point in the process of neighborhood change, those who leave the neighborhood are replaced by less affluent families and individuals, and over time, the housing may filter down to still less affluent groups. In this stage of the life cycle, housing prices and rentals decline as more affluent families leave the neighborhood.

The process of decline may be caused by several factors. The houses simply may have reached an age where the costs of maintenance are greater than the residents can afford. There may be outside influences, such as construction of a new freeway, which make living conditions in the area less desirable and competing areas more accessible. The decline of the neighborhood may be caused by various changes in the socioeconomic characteristics of its residents or by their aging and deaths. Likewise, construction of more desirable dwellings in other neighborhoods may lead to a drop in demand for property in a certain area.

Clear Decline   As the housing in a neighborhood ceases to provide a reasonable return to the owners and becomes substandard by most definitions, the neighborhood enters a period of clear decline. Owners make only minimal repairs, and properties deteriorate noticeably. Financial institutions may avoid investing in the area, making rehabilitation and the introduction of new owners even more difficult. As owners try to squeeze additional income from their declining investments, housing densities and the consequent need for public services increase dramatically, though those services (schools, police protection, sanitation) may not be provided.

Accelerating Decline and Abandonment   The demise of a neighborhood often occurs quickly. Those who are able to move elsewhere do so. Only the lowest-income residents remain, and unemployment rates and the percentage of families on welfare are high. Landlords cease making repairs and often abandon their buildings when they are no longer profitable. At the terminal stage, the neighborhood may be virtually abandoned—as are portions of the South Bronx in New York City—or the buildings may be demolished, allowing the neighborhood to enter a new cycle.

Neighborhood Stabilization and Rehabilitation

It must be emphasized that the process of neighborhood deterioration and decline is not inevitable. Values in many mature neighborhoods remain strong over long periods of time if the areas remain competitive in housing markets. Other neighborhoods may, as a result of a conscious public policy effort or natural market forces, reverse their declines and become healthy once again.

The first people who attempt to renovate deteriorated dwellings usually are young, middle-income individuals or families who desire to live in town, cannot afford housing in the established, higher-income neighborhoods and are willing to spend the time and effort to rebuild the dwellings and social fabric of the declining neighborhood. If the process is successful, values may rise dramatically as the neighborhood becomes a desirable location for middle-income or upper-income groups.

A negative aspect is the displacement of low-income families, who often can no longer afford to live in their neighborhood.

Chapter Review

1. The reason one locality rather than another will develop into a center of trade or industry is because that community enjoys a comparative advantage, which can result from transportation facilities or other factors of the created environment, natural resources, climate or the quality and quantity of the local labor force.

2. A community's export activity produces goods and services for sale outside its borders. Population-serving activities produce goods and services sold within the community itself.

3. Almost all real estate market activity and development depends directly or indirectly on the location of people, and the location of people depends largely on the location of employment.

4. Because the supply of real estate is largely fixed in the short run, changes in demand largely affect vacancy rates, sales of existing property, prices and lease rates. Over the long run, the supply can, of course, be increased, and the potential investor in a new development must carefully analyze the long-run prospects for the community's economic base.

5. Nothing is more essential to the determination of real estate values than the process of community development and neighborhood change.

6. A city may grow in several ways: (1) vertically, by replacement of smaller structures with taller ones and by use of air rights to construct new buildings over existing ones; (2) by in-filling of open spaces between existing structures; and (3) by extension of settled areas.

7. Some models that have been used to explain the peripheral growth patterns of urban areas are (1) concentric-circle growth, (2) axial growth, (3) sector growth and (4) multiple-nuclei growth.

8. Investments in public facilities, often called the *infrastructure,* play a critical role in local development. The infrastructure includes transportation improvements, sewer systems and water lines.

9. Because access is so important, major commercial growth tends to occur near transportation nodes, such as freeway interchanges and junctions of other major roads.

10. Industrial growth tends to occur along major highways or railroads, or both.

11. A neighborhood can be defined in several ways: (1) as an area in which types of property are similar; (2) as a distinct geographical area or one that is distinguished by a conspicuous physical feature; (3) as a social unit—that is, as a community with religious or ethnic ties; and (4) as a group of people with the same general level of income.

12. Neighborhoods tend to go through a life cycle, from gestation to maturity to decline, but this process can be arrested or reversed, and a declining neighborhood may be restored to economic health.

Key Terms

axial model   a model of urban growth patterns based on transportation routes.

concentric-circle model   a model of urban growth patterns based on concentric zones surrounding a central business district.

economic base   employment in industries that bring income into a region from beyond its borders.

export activities   activities that produce goods and services for sale or consumption outside an area's borders.

filtering   the passage of housing to less affluent families as the housing ages.

infrastructure   investment in public facilities such as roads, schools, etc.

multiple-nuclei model   a model of urban growth patterns that emphasizes more than one center of commercial activity.

population-serving activities   activities that produce goods and services for sale or consumption within an area's borders.

Study Exercises

1. What is meant by the concept of comparative advantage?

2. What are some of the factors that may give a community a comparative advantage in attracting new employment?

3. Why do people locate where they do?

4. Discuss the concept of an economic base. What are export activities, and what are population-serving activities?

5. How do local real estate markets react to changes in short-run demand? To changes in long-run demand?

6. What steps might a community take when faced with declining industry or a plant that closes?

7. Discuss the concept of price-distance relationship, and explain how it tends to allocate land resources.

8. Why would we not expect to find someone growing corn on a lot in Midtown Manhattan in New York City?

9. Discuss some of the models that have been used to explain growth patterns in urban areas.

10. What is meant by infrastructure?

11. Suppose a new freeway is completed in a relatively undeveloped suburban area. What would be some of the probable developmental impacts?

12. A new interceptor sewerage line is completed in an area that previously could be served only by septic tanks. How would this likely change residential development?

13. Discuss how improvements in public facilities influence the local development process.

14. Why have American cities tended to develop in a more multinucleated form during the past several decades?

15. Where does major commercial growth tend to occur within a community?

16. Where does industrial growth tend to occur?

17. Describe the life cycle of neighborhoods.

PART TWO

Real Estate Legal Framework

CHAPTER 4
Property Rights and Ownership Interests

The St. Louis Arch, a monument rising high above the city, holds rights not only to the land on which it is located but also to the air space that it occupies.

Chapter Preview

PERHAPS YOU OWN some real estate. But what exactly do you own, and what is the nature of that ownership? These may seem rather simple questions, but often real estate ownership interests can be quite complex. Real estate ownership rights can be divided in many ways, with one party owning the right to use the surface of the land, another holding the right to subsurface minerals, and perhaps another holding the right to use the water that flows across or under the land. This chapter will examine several questions:

- What is real property?
- What are estates in land?
- What are the different types of real property ownership?
- How can real property be owned jointly?

WHAT IS REAL PROPERTY?

Although the term *property* can be used in several ways, people generally think of objects that can be owned or possessed—buildings, boats, books or bonds, for example. Legally, the concept of property can be divided into two broad classes: real property and personal property. **Real property** consists of legal interests in land and things permanently attached to the land, such as buildings (the term *real estate* refers to the physical land and structures on the land). **Personal property** includes legal interests in all other types of property. Stated simply, real property is real estate—land and things attached to that land—while personal property is movable property, such as automobiles, furniture, clothing and business equipment.

An important difference exists between the two types of property, particularly when ownership is transferred. The requirements for transfer of personal property are much less complex than those for real property.

Most personal property is exchanged or sold informally, and a bill of sale may or may not be given to conclude the transaction. But with only a few exceptions (such as short-term leases in a few states), whenever rights in real property change hands, a written agreement signed by both buyer and seller is required.

Title to real property, or legal ownership, is transferred by a formal legal document called a *deed*. All deeds must be properly signed, witnessed, acknowledged, delivered and accepted before title to real estate actually passes to the new owner. Chapter 7 discusses the specific requirements of a valid deed.

FIXTURES

Whether a particular item of property is considered real or personal property cannot always be readily determined. An air-conditioning unit that clearly is movable personal property at the time it is purchased may become so attached to the land as part of a building that it is treated as part of the real estate. This type of item is a **fixture,** personal property that becomes part of the real property when it is attached to the land or a building.

If, for example, you hang the antique chandelier you inherited from Aunt Matilda in your dining room, it becomes a fixture and part of the house. Unless it is specifically excluded when the house is sold, the new buyer becomes the proud owner of the chandelier. Other items generally considered fixtures include yard plantings, appliances installed in the home (such as dishwashers and air conditioners) and television antennas. It is important to remember that if you sell a home and want to retain ownership of Aunt Matilda's chandelier or your prize rose bushes, you must specifically exclude them from the transaction in the contract. Other important aspects of real estate sales contracts are discussed in Chapter 11.

Tests for Fixture Status

Whether an item of personal property has become a fixture can be critical in determining (1) the value of real property for tax purposes, (2) whether a real estate sale includes the item, (3) whether the item is part of the security given to the mortgagee and (4) whether the item remains with the landlord or can be removed by the tenant when the lease is terminated.

Intent of the Parties   The most crucial test used to determine whether something is a fixture or personal property is the parties' intent. The best way to indicate this, of course, is by a written agreement at the time of sale or lease that states clearly which items are to remain as part of the real estate and which are personal property. For instance, a sales contract for a house might specify that the satellite television antenna may be removed by the seller; a lease agreement for a factory or warehouse might state that the tenant may attach such **trade fixtures** (personal property used in a trade or business) as machinery, office equipment and counters to the building without losing the right to remove these items at the termination of the lease.

Other Tests of Fixture Status   Often, unfortunately, the intent of the parties is unclear, so other tests of fixture status must be applied. If an item of personal property becomes attached to the real estate, it usually is considered a fixture, and the damage caused to the land or building by the item's removal is a crucial element in the *test of attachment*. For example, while a window air conditioner would be personal property, one that was built into a wall would be a fixture. Because the building would be damaged if the air conditioner were removed, the unit is considered an attachment. Another method for determining whether an item is a fixture is the *test of adaptability*. Under this test, items that have been specifically adapted to the real estate are generally considered fixtures. The issue considered in this test is whether removal of the item would substantially alter the usefulness of the remaining real estate. For example, kitchen cabinets and a built-in entertainment center would probably be considered fixtures, while freestanding, noncustom cabinets would be classified as personal property.

Because the law of fixtures does not necessarily provide clear-cut distinctions between real and personal property, the parties involved always should indicate their clear intent by a written agreement. This, of course, helps avoid disputes in *all* business matters.

MINERAL AND AIR RIGHTS

Real property rights are not limited to the surface of the earth; they also include the space above the earth's surface (**air rights**) and the space below it (**mineral rights**). Originally, a landowner's real property interests were conceptualized as pie-shaped, beginning at the earth's center and extending through the surface boundaries indefinitely into outer space. In modern thought, the property rights associated with the surface of the land, minerals that exist under the land and airspace above the land are often separated among several owners. Similarly, the rights to water that may flow over the land or adjacent to the land are sometimes considered separately from the land itself.

Today, ownership of airspace is limited to a reasonable distance above the earth's surface. Obviously, an airplane flying over a property at an altitude of several thousand feet rarely interferes with the owner's use or enjoyment of the land. But when aircraft fly so low that a reasonable use of the land is prevented (for example, near a lengthened airport runway), the owner of the land may be entitled to compensation.

Mineral rights and air rights may be owned by someone other than the owner of the surface. It is common, for example, for a surface owner to sell to a third party the rights to any oil, gas, coal and other minerals that may be located below the surface. The air rights, likewise, may be transferred to persons other than the owner of the surface. For example, office buildings and parking decks have been constructed over the tracks of railroads, with the owners of the buildings and decks owning only the air rights.

A developing area of real estate law concerns a landowner's right to sunlight. This right has become especially important to those who depend on solar energy. People have questioned the legality of building a tall structure on a lot if that building will partially or totally block the adjoining landowner's use of sunlight. This matter is currently unresolved and, in many jurisdictions, undoubtedly will be the subject of future litigation and legislative attention.

WATER RIGHTS

Who has the right to withdraw water from land is a question of considerable importance, particularly in the more arid western states—and increasingly in the eastern states. These rights vary from state to state and depend primarily on what type of water the land touches.

Littoral Rights

The owner whose land joins a navigable body of water, such as an ocean, a sea or certain rivers, generally owns the land to the high-water mark (the government owns the water and the land underneath). The owners of such adjoining lands are called **littoral proprietors.** Disputes about their use of water from these waterways seldom occur because usually there is sufficient water to be shared. The principal issue involving navigable waters has been pollution. Laws regulating the pollution of these waters exist at both the federal and state levels.

Riparian Rights Theory

The rights of a landowner to use water from a nonnavigable lake or stream that flows across the land are much more complex. If an upstream owner uses too much water, for example, there may be none left for landowners downstream. How should these waters be allocated? The laws that answer this question have developed in a way that reflects the abundance or scarcity of water within the geographical area. For example, two theories with regard to an owner's rights to nonnavigable bodies of water have been used. In the eastern United States, the dominant theory is that of the **riparian rights doctrine.** Under this theory, all owners whose land underlies or borders the water have equal rights to the water. This concept allows all riparian landowners to use all the water needed as long as the use does not deprive other landowners who are also entitled to some of the water.

Real Estate Today   *Close-Up*

The Last Chance Ditch

As engineering structures go, the Last Chance Ditch is not very imposing, but it has provided the economic lifeblood to part of the Truckee Meadows area near Reno, Nevada, for more than a century. It also provides an example of just how important water rights can be in the arid western states.

The Last Chance Ditch was begun by land developers in 1874 and extends approximately ten miles southward from the Truckee River in Reno. Under a 1943 court decree that clarified area water rights, the ditch company can draw 8,644 acre-feet each year from the river (an acre-foot is enough water to cover an acre of land with one foot of water). The company can draw this amount of water from the river *if it is available* after the Pioneer Ditch and the Steamboat Ditch companies, which have priority because they started earlier, have received their allocations.

The Last Chance Ditch's share is then suballocated to property owners holding agricultural water rights along its length, most having the right to about four acre-feet of "consumptive" water per acre. This means that shareholders normally receive this much water flowing on their properties during a year. They cannot dam up the water; any "waste," about one-third of the flow, returns to the ditch for use downstream. These rights provide a benefit to the landowner that can be sold separately, recently bringing about $2,500 per acre-foot, or $10,000 per acre, for shareholders in the Last Chance Ditch.

If agricultural land is developed for residential use, additional water rights are required, usually from a utility company that holds water rights and provides water services. For homes on one-third-acre lots, about 6.5 acre-feet are needed per acre. For land that holds no water rights, it costs around $16,250 per acre just to acquire water rights. For shareholders in the Last Chance Ditch, the cost would be reduced to $6,250 because they already have rights to four acre-feet. Yes, the Last Chance Ditch is not a very impressive structure, but it provides quite impressive economic benefits to those holding rights to its water. ∎

The Last Chance Ditch

Prior Appropriation Theory

Many states west of the Mississippi are extremely arid and consequently have rejected the theory of riparian rights. Instead, they have adopted the **prior appropriation doctrine.**

Under this concept, the first person to use a body of water for some beneficial economic purpose has a right to use all the water needed, even though landowners who later find a use for the water may be precluded from using it. This "first-come, first-served" concept is based on the premise that there is an insufficient supply of water to satisfy everyone's needs; therefore, the first landowner(s) who use the water for some worthwhile purpose should be allow to use all of the water. Prior appropriation states usually establish a permit system whereby a governing authority can control the water's use. The Close-Up describing the Last Chance Ditch on page 65 provides a real-life example of the prior appropriation concept.

Underground Water

Underground water is of two types. That flowing in a definite channel is called an *underground* or a *subterranean* stream, while water in pockets not clearly located is called *percolating* water. Issues involving underground streams generally are resolved by applying the same principles that would be used if the bodies of water existed on the earth's surface. In the case of percolating waters, states generally apply a reasonable-use test. A landowner may use the water beneath the land for industrial, agricultural or other purposes necessary to the beneficial use of the land. But if withdrawing the water depletes the underground water supply of adjoining landowners, the courts may restrict such action.

ESTATES IN LAND

Ownership interests in real property often are described as **estates in land.** These are divided into two basic types: **freehold,** or ownership; and **leasehold,** or the right to use and possess (but not own) the property for a period of time. Homebuyers normally purchase freeholds; renters have leaseholds. Figure 4.1 summarizes the different types of estates. When discussing estates in land, the terms **grantor** and **grantee** often are used. The grantor is the party who transfers (by sale or gift) a real property interest; the grantee is the party who receives the interest. In the case of a leasehold estate, the landlord is known as the **lessor,** and the tenant is known as the **lessee.**

Freehold Estates

Freehold estates are separated into presently possessed interests and those that may be possessed in the future. Presently possessed interests are classified as either fee simple absolute estates, qualified fee estates or life estates. Future interests, which accompany qualified fee and life estates, include possibility of

Types of Estates in Land **Figure 4.1**

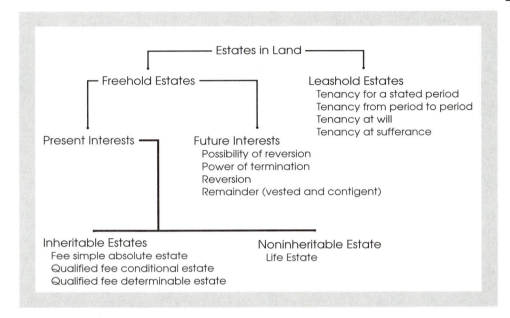

reversion, power of termination, reversion and remainder. We discuss each of these ownership interests below.

Fee Simple Absolute Estates The **fee simple absolute estate** is the fullest and most complete set of ownership rights one can possess in real property. Also known as a *fee estate* or a *fee simple estate,* this estate is the one most commonly associated with owning real estate and is the type of estate acquired in a typical residential transaction.

The property owner receiving a fee simple absolute title has an unlimited right to transfer the property to another during his or her lifetime or at death. Legally stated, the fee simple absolute estate is alienable, devisable and descendible. **Alienable** means the owner can transfer any interest owned in the property while living. **Devisable** means the interest can be transferred by will. **Descendible** means the interest passes to the owner's legal heirs if he or she dies without a valid will.

In addition to the ability to transfer a fee simple absolute estate without restriction, the owner has the right of unlimited use and even abuse of the land, constrained only by liens and other encumbrances, public land-use controls and restrictive covenants. These restrictions are discussed in Chapters 5 and 6.

Qualified Estates In a **qualified** (or defeasible) **estate,** the owner's rights can be defeased, or lost, in the future should an event or a stated condition come to pass. For example, the University of Georgia holds a qualified estate in an old rock house located on the campus in the midst of its modern buildings. Many years ago, the Lumpkin family donated a large tract of land to the university with the qualification in the deed that the family house had to be retained. If the university were to destroy the building, a large portion of the campus would revert to the donors' heirs.

Although qualified estates are present interests in real property, each qualified estate must also be accompanied by a future interest in the property. The **qualified fee determinable** and **qualified fee conditional** are two of the most common types of qualified estates. The qualified fee determinable is accompanied by a future interest known as **possibility of reversion.** If the condition specified is ever violated, such as the removal of the Lumpkin House, ownership in the property automatically reverts to the grantor (or the grantor's heirs). In a qualified fee conditional estate, the grantor (or the grantor's heirs) must seek a court order to terminate the qualified estate if the condition is ever violated. The future interest associated with the qualified fee conditional estate is known as the **power of termination.**

Many qualified estates are set up to protect a seller's or donor's wishes. A will might state that a parcel will transfer to Al, provided he marries before he is 25 years old; if not, then to Bob. If Al wants the property, he had better marry before he lights 25 candles on the cake. In this case, Al holds a qualified estate in the property, while Bob holds a future interest in the property that may or may not become a present interest.

Life Estates   The noninheritable estate, or **life estate,** is an ownership interest of indeterminable length that normally ends upon the death of a named person, but may be terminated by some other stated condition. In most cases, the person who receives the life estate is the named person, but a life estate can also be held by someone other than the person whose death terminates the estate. In the latter situation, the estate is known as an *estate pur autre vie* (estate for the life of another). The future interests associated with life estates include **reversion** and **remainder.**

Suppose, for example, that a woman remarries after the death of her husband and wants to ensure that in the event of her death, the new spouse will have a home to live in for the rest of his life. On the other hand, she wants the home ultimately to pass to her four children. In this case, her will might state that the home will be transferred to "my husband Alan for life." Alan has a life estate in the property, which gives him the right to possess the property until his death. During his lifetime, he can sell, lease or mortgage his life estate, but at his death the property reverts back to the grantor. The future interest retained by the grantor is known as *reversion*. Because the grantor is deceased when the reversion occurs, the property passes to her four children.

Alternatively, the grantor could give Alan a life estate and name only two of her children, Ivy and Nell, as remaindermen. In this case, the future interest is known as *vested remainder*. Upon Alan's death, Ivy and Nell automatically become the owners of the property. Future interests following a life estate can also take the form of *contingent remainder*. Suppose the original grantor's will states that the home will be Alan's "for life, then to my daughter Ivy, provided she is married at the time of his death, otherwise to Nell." In this case, both Ivy and Nell hold contingent remainders. If Ivy is married when Alan dies, she receives the property, and Nell's future interest is terminated. If Ivy is not married, Nell receives the property.

The life estate is a useful technique in estate planning. John might, for example, put the family home and farm in trust for his children Sue and Sally, but give his wife Mary a life estate. Estate taxes have to be paid upon John's death.

Mary may use the property during the remainder of her lifetime, but at her death, no additional taxes are due because she possessed only a life estate. This can reduce taxes greatly, particularly if the property has risen appreciably in value since John's death.

Leasehold Estates

A **leasehold estate** is a possessory interest created by the establishment of a landlord-tenant relationship. Such an estate may last for a definite time period or for as long as the parties are willing to continue their relationship. For the duration of a lease, the tenant possesses or occupies the land or building with the understanding that the landlord retains full ownership of the real property. In other words, the landlord has a reversionary interest often referred to as the *right of reentry.*

Leases, or tenancies, can be divided into the following four categories:

1. Tenancy for a stated period
2. Tenancy from period to period
3. Tenancy at will
4. Tenancy at sufferance

A **tenancy for a stated period** occurs when a landlord and a tenant enter into an agreement for a specified term. The stated period may be six months, a year, ten years or any mutually acceptable time. In most states, all leases must be written and signed by the parties if the lease period exceeds one year. Of course, it is advisable to always have a written agreement even if the law does not require one.

A **tenancy from period to period** is created when landlord and tenant agree to continue their relationship from year to year or month to month. The agreement may establish an original term of one year, for example, with the provision that the lease is to continue yearly unless terminated with proper notice by either party. The method of giving proper notice should be set forth in the lease agreement. It is common to require notice of termination 30 to 60 days prior to the expiration of a period, depending on state law.

Should a lease term be unspecified, it is likely that the parties have entered into a **tenancy at will.** As the name implies, this lease lasts as long as both tenant and landlord desire. The tenancy at will can be treated as a lease from month to month. The required termination notice is provided by state statute. A 30-day notice is most typical for the tenant; some states require, however, that the landlord give 60 days' advance notice of termination. Although the tenancy at will might last more than one year, the original agreement does not have to be in writing because there is the possibility that it will end within one year. It generally is unwise to enter into a tenancy at will.

A **tenancy at sufferance** occurs when a tenant refuses to re-lease the premises at the termination of the lease. The landlord must decide whether to evict the holdover tenant or to negotiate a new lease agreement. A tenancy at sufferance also might occur when a homeowner has the existing mortgage foreclosed and sold at public auction. Until the original mortgagor moves out, a tenancy at sufferance is established, and the purchaser at the foreclosure sale is considered the landlord.

The lease transaction and the landlord-tenant relationship are discussed in more detail in Chapter 9.

CONCURRENT ESTATES

The preceding discussion of property interests was based on the assumption that only one person owns each interest. These interests are known as **estates in severalty**—that is, estates "standing alone." Nevertheless, most of the real property interests discussed above may be owned simultaneously by more than one person. Perhaps you want to buy a house with your spouse, another relative or even an unrelated person. Or your Aunt Matilda may leave you and your sister Bess a farm to be owned jointly. Or you may want to make a real estate investment with business associates. All these interests in property owned simultaneously by two or more persons are examples of **concurrent estates,** or, more simply, joint ownership. The most common types of concurrent estates are

- tenancy in common;
- joint tenancy;
- tenancy by the entirety; and
- community property.

(Although the word *tenancy* is used here, it should not be confused with the tenant's relationship with a landlord.)

Tenancy in Common

The traditional form of multiple ownership is **tenancy in common.** Each of the joint owners holds an undivided proportional interest in the entire property. For example, if Jack and Jill Jones own their home as tenants in common, each owns one-half of the entire property. Each owner can dispose of his or her share through sale or will.

Tenants in common who become unhappy with the joint relationship can demand a *partition* of the property. Voluntary partitions result when cotenants agree how to divide the property. If they cannot agree, however, a court will determine a compulsory partition.

Joint Tenancy

Joint tenancy is similar to tenancy in common except it carries with it the **right of survivorship.** If two parties own a property in joint tenancy, and one owner dies, the other owner automatically receives the share owned by the deceased. If more than two parties are joint tenants in the property, the surviving owners divide the share owned by the deceased. This type of ownership often is used to ensure the continued operation of an investment property should one of the owners die. The joint tenancy ends if any tenant sells his or her share of the property to a third party. The joint tenancy then converts to a tenancy in common.

Historically, to establish a valid joint tenancy, the four unities of time, title, interest and possession had to be present. To satisfy the unity of time, the joint tenants' ownership had to be created at the same time by the same conveyance. The unity of title exists when the owners have the same estate in the land, such as a fee simple estate, a life estate or another estate discussed in this chapter.

Joint tenants meet the unity-of-interest requirement only when they have the same percentage interest in the real estate. For example, two joint tenants must each own 50 percent of the undivided property, three must own 33.3 percent each, four must own 25 percent each and so forth. Finally, joint tenants have unity of possession only when each owner has the right to possess all of the real estate subject to the other owners' rights of possession.

Originally, due to the unity-of-time requirement, a grantor who was the sole owner of real estate could not create a joint tenancy with the right of survivorship between himself or herself and another person. To get around this problem, the grantor had to deed the property to a friendly third party, known as a *straw man,* who would then transfer that property to the grantor and the other party (or parties) as joint tenants.

Some states have abolished the need to use a straw man in the above situation. In other words, these states have relaxed the unity-of-time requirement under these particular circumstances.

Tenancy by the Entirety

A **tenancy by the entirety** is a specialized type of joint tenancy that can be created only between husbands and wives. The spouses share ownership equally, shares automatically pass to the surviving spouse and individual interests cannot be sold without the consent of the other spouse or without division by a court in case of divorce. Many states do not recognize tenancy by the entirety.

Community Property

Nine states (Arizona, California, Idaho, Louisiana, Nevada, New Mexico, Texas, Washington and Wisconsin) recognize a system of property rights between husbands and wives generally called **community property.** In these states, all property, whether real or personal, acquired during the marriage, is considered property of the "marital community." In other words, property ownership is divided equally between husband and wife. This division disregards the financial contribution each spouse actually made to the property's acquisition. Real property in community-property states cannot be transferred without the consent of both parties. Thus, a purchaser of real community property must obtain the signatures of both husband and wife on the sales contract and deed.

It is possible for married couples in one of these community-property states to acquire property not subject to a spouse's interest. Examples of this separate property include property owned prior to the marriage or property received by one of the spouses as a gift or an inheritance. Generally, any income derived from a spouse's separate property is also separate property.

CONDOMINIUM OWNERSHIP

In addition to the traditional forms of concurrent ownership, the condominium and cooperative are two other ways to own real estate jointly. In a **condominium** (condo), all owners have fee simple titles to their personal units, while common areas such as sidewalks, yards, entrances, hallways, pools, tennis courts and other recreational facilities are jointly owned in a tenancy in common. A condominium association maintains these common areas, and each unit pays a mandatory association fee for this purpose.

All states have laws governing the formation of condominiums. These statutes require that three basic documents be filed—the condominium declaration, the bylaws and a deed conveying the individual unit. The purchase of a condominium interest is legally more complex and potentially more demanding than the typical single-family home purchase. In most states, this complexity and past abuses have led to more rigorous disclosure of information to prospective buyers of condominium homes.

Condominium Declaration

The condominium declaration describes the individual units and all common areas, assigns a specific share of the common areas to each unit, creates an association to govern the project and maintain the common areas and sets forth restrictions on use. These restrictions usually are quite extensive and often deal with such details as the color of curtains visible in windows and whether pets must be kept on leashes.

The declaration may also grant the association the right of first refusal to help it screen prospective purchasers. If an individual property owner locates a willing buyer, the association has a limited time either to approve of the purchaser or to purchase the unit under the same terms. This right of first refusal cannot be used to exclude prospective purchasers on the basis of race, creed, color or national origin, although this type of discrimination often is hard to prove.

Bylaws

The bylaws represent a private contract among property owners regarding how the condominium shall be operated. They provide for the selection of the board of directors, the powers and duties of the directors, meetings, regulations for the common areas, assessment and collection of association fees, and other relevant matters.

Individual Unit Deed

Deeds for condominium units are similar to other deeds conveying real property. These deeds are described in Chapter 7.

COOPERATIVE OWNERSHIP

In the **cooperative** form of ownership, the land and building usually are owned by a nonprofit corporation; individual residents own stock in the corporation and have the right to live in a particular unit. Rather than fee simple ownership, residents have leasehold interests in specific units.

The tenants run the cooperative through their stock interests in the corporation. They are assessed periodic amounts (according to their proportionate interests) for mortgage payments, maintenance, repairs, taxes and other operating costs. Cooperatives, the majority of which are located in New York City, are often accused of being the last bastions of housing discrimination. A tenant usually needs approval from the board of directors to sell to a new tenant, and approval has sometimes been withheld for reasons that appear to have a racial or religious motivation. Or the directors may withhold approval because they simply feel the buyer is incompatible for some reason. For example, former President Nixon was turned down as a tenant in a expensive New York cooperative because the board members felt he would attract too much attention to their building.

TIME-SHARING

Time-sharing, or interval ownership, is a type of concurrent estate that splits ownership further by time. Most of the activity in the time-share is vacation oriented, with several large companies such as Disney and Marriot expanding into this market. Two basic categories of time-sharing interests include a fee interest and a right-to-use. A **fee interest time-share** divides the ownership of a unit, usually a resort condominium, into 52 separate intervals. Owners receive fee simple title to their particular ownership periods. A **right-to-use time-share,** on the other hand, basically is a lease arrangement with no ownership interest and often with more restrictions regarding resale.

───────────────● **Chapter Review** ●───────────────

1. Real property consists of the legal rights related to land and things attached to that land. Personal property consists of everything a person owns that is not real property. It is important to distinguish between real and personal property because the law treats these classes of items differently regarding inheritance, formality of transfer and applicability of the statute of frauds.

2. Fixtures are the middle ground between real and personal property. Items that once were movable personal property and now are attached to real estate are called *fixtures*. Three tests help to determine an item's fixture status: (1) the parties' intention, (2) whether removal will cause damage and (3) whether the item was specifically adapted to the property.

3. Ownership interests in real property often are called *estates in land*. Such estates can be subdivided broadly into freehold and leasehold estates. Freehold estates refer to ownership interests in real property, while leasehold estates refer to a tenant's right to use and possess a property as defined in the lease contract.

4. Freehold interests in land can be divided into present and future interests. Not all present interests are absolute, and the grantee whose interest is qualified may lose it. Therefore, future interests were created so that the total ownership interest could be identified at all times.

5. Present estates in land are classified as inheritable or noninheritable. Inheritable interests are those estates that can be passed to another upon the owner's death. Such interests include absolute and qualified fee simple estates. A holder of noninheritable interests cannot transfer them to another person at death because the future interest (reversion or remainder) is already specified. In such life estates, the life tenant's ownership interest ends with his or her death.

6. Ownership interests in land can be held by one or more persons. Multiple ownership interests often are referred to as *concurrent estates*. Tenancy in common is the form most frequently created when two or more persons own the same property. Joint tenancy and tenancy by the entirety are special forms that include the right of survivorship if the four unities of time, title, interest and possession are satisfied. Several states have adopted the concept of community property, which provides that husband and wife hold property acquired during their marriage in equal shares.

7. Today, two other methods of jointly owning real property exist—condominiums and cooperatives. Owners of condominiums have fee simple absolute title to their individual units and hold a tenancy in common for public areas. Cooperative owners possess shares in a corporation, and they lease their units from the corporation.

Key Terms

air rights   property rights associated with the space above the surface of the earth.

alienable   a property owner's right to transfer interests owned in a property during his or her lifetime.

community property   theory under which all property acquired during a marriage is considered to be equally owned by the husband and wife, regardless of the financial contribution each spouse actually made to the property's acquisition.

concurrent estate   ownership interests held jointly by two or more owners.

condominium   a form of joint ownership whereby the property owners own their individual units separately but share ownership of common areas; a building owned in this manner.

cooperative   a form of joint ownership whereby the property owners own shares of stock in a corporation that owns the property and are entitled to occupy space within the building.

descendible   a property owner's right to transfer interests owned in a property to legal heirs should the owner die without a valid will.

devisable   a property owner's right to transfer interests owned in a property via a will.

estate in land   legal interests in real property.

estate in severalty   term used to describe ownership interests without regard to the number of owners.

fee interest time-share   a type of concurrent estate that splits ownership of a property over time across joint owners.

fee simple absolute estate   the fullest and most complete set of ownership rights one can possess in real property.

fixture   an item that was once personal property but has become part of the real estate.

freehold estate   ownership interests in real property.

grantee   the party who receives a freehold estate in real property from a grantor.

grantor   the party who transfers a freehold estate in real property to a grantee.

joint tenancy   joint ownership in which all owners have an equal, but undivided, interest in a property.

leasehold estate   a possessory interest in real property created by a lease agreement.

lessee   the person who receives a leasehold interest in a property from the lessor.

lessor   the person who gives a leasehold interest in a property to a lessee.

life estate   an ownership interest in real property that normally ends upon the death of a named person.

littoral proprietor   owner of land that adjoins navigable bodies of water.

mineral rights   ownership rights associated with minerals that may be located below the surface of the earth.

personal property   movable items such as cars, clothing, books, etc.

possibility of reversion   the future interest that follows a qualified fee determinable estate.

power of termination   the future interest that follows a qualified fee conditional estate.

prior appropriation doctrine   theory which states that the first person to use a body of water for some beneficial economic purpose has the right to use all the water needed, even though landowners who later find a use for the water may be precluded from using it.

qualified estate   an estate that can be lost should an event or stated condition come to pass.

qualified fee conditional estate   an estate that a court may rule has been terminated should some condition be violated.

qualified fee determinable estate   an estate that terminates automatically should some condition be violated.

real property   the legal interests associated with the ownership of real estate.

remainder   the future interest associated with a life estate that is held by someone other than the grantor.

reversion   the future interest associated with a life estate that is held by the grantor.

right of survivorship   the right of surviving joint owners to automatically divide the share owned by a deceased owner.

right-to-use time-share   a form of leasehold estate that permits the holder to use a property for a certain period each year.

riparian rights doctrine   theory that permits landowners whose land underlies or borders nonnavigable bodies of water to use all the water needed as long as the use does not deprive other landowners who are also entitled to use some of the water.

tenancy at sufferance   a tenancy created when a holder of a lease continues to occupy the property after the expiration of the term.

tenancy at will   a lease that may be terminated by either party at any time.

tenancy by the entirety   a form of concurrent estate in which a husband and wife can own property jointly.

tenancy for a stated period   a leasehold estate that has definite starting and ending dates.

tenancy from period to period   a leasehold estate that continues to automatically renew each period unless terminated by either party.

tenancy in common   a form of concurrent estate in which each owner has an undivided interest in the property.

time-sharing a form of concurrent estate that splits ownership of a property across owners and across time.

trade fixture personal property used in a trade or business.

Study Exercises

1. Define the following terms: real property, personal property, joint tenancy, tenancy by the entirety, freehold estate, leasehold estate, qualified fee conditional estate, qualified fee determinable estate, condominium, cooperative, remainder, power of termination, possibility of reversion, and reversion.

2. What is a fixture, and what are the three tests used to determine fixture status?

3. Fred Ford leases a building from George Wood to house his restaurant. To increase business, Fred installs an antique bar in the center of the restaurant, complete with a wet bar and drain. A year later, Fred's business is so successful that he wishes to move to a larger building. He plans to remove the bar. George Wood protests that the bar is a fixture and cannot be removed. Does Fred have the right to remove the bar? Why or why not?

4. What is meant by *littoral rights?* By *riparian rights?*

5. Distinguish between the reasonable-use and prior appropriation theories of water usage.

6. If Jenny sells her land to Ivy and the deed states, "To Ivy, her heirs and assigns," who is the grantor? Who is the grantee?

7. After Ivy receives the property (see question 6), she tells a friend that her interest is alienable, devisable and descendible. What does Ivy mean by each of these terms?

8. Explain how life estates can be used in estate tax planning.

9. Mabel, a senior citizen, has a life estate in the home in which she lives that was willed to her by her husband. She wishes to move to a warmer climate, so she offers her interest in the house to a neighbor for $10,000. The house has a total value of $100,000. Under what circumstances would the neighbor buy Mabel's interest?

10. If the neighbor declines to purchase her property (see question 9), Mabel will offer it to her grandson, who has the remainder interest. Would he be likely to buy her estate?

11.   If Mabel's grandson declines to purchase her property (see question 10), Mabel plans to leave it to her friend Betty in her will. What interest will Betty have upon Mabel's death?

12.   Lisa and Anne were business partners who owned real estate as joint tenants, not as tenants in common. At the time of Lisa's death, a dispute arose between Lisa's heirs and Anne as to who was the rightful owner of Lisa's one-half interest in the property. Who is entitled to the property interest that Lisa owned?

13.   Madeline has an opportunity to invest in either a cooperative or a condominium. What are the differences between these types of ownership?

14.   Dick agrees to rent a two-bedroom house from Larry for a two-year period. What type of leasehold interest is involved in this transaction?

15.   Charles rents a home from Woodley on a month-to-month basis. On June 15, he gives notice that his new home will be ready on July 15, and he will move at that time. On July 22, he still has not moved. Under what kind of tenancy does Charles now hold possession?

For Further Reading

Gibson, F., J. Karp, and E. Klayman. *Real Estate Law* (Chicago: Real Estate Education Company, 1992).

Reilly, J.W. *The Language of Real Estate,* 4th ed. (Chicago: Real Estate Education Company, 1993).

CHAPTER 5
Private Restrictions on Ownership

Property ownership does not necessarily mean total control. Historic business districts, such as this one in New Orleans, often require property owners to preserve the architectural style of their buildings.

Real Estate Today

- *Legal Highlight*
  Prescriptive
  Easement
- *Legal Highlight*
  Adverse Possession
- *Legal Highlight*
  Validity of
  Restrictive
  Covenants

Chapter Preview

EVEN THOUGH SOMEONE owns the entire fee simple ownership rights in a piece of real estate, this interest is limited by certain restrictions placed on the property by other private entities or by a government. These restrictions and limitations, known collectively as **encumbrances,** generally run with the land; in other words, they are binding on anyone who gains a subsequent interest in the property. In some cases, encumbrances may adversely affect both the use and the value of the property. In extreme cases, the land may be so encumbered that it would be valueless for a potential purchaser. Conversely, some public or private land-use restrictions may enhance the value of a property by protecting it from detrimental actions by others.

Several forms of private restrictions on ownership are discussed in this chapter. These include

- liens;
- easements;
- licenses;
- profit a prendre;
- adverse possession;
- encroachments; and
- restrictive covenants.

The next chapter will examine public restrictions on ownership, including

- property tax;
- tax liens;
- eminent domain;
- zoning and other land-use controls under the police power; and
- escheat.

LIENS

A **lien** is a claim on a property as either security for a debt or fulfillment of some monetary charge or obligation. For example, an owner might give a mortgage on a property in order to borrow money, thus creating a lien on the property. The lien does not represent right of ownership for the creditor; rather, it amounts to a financial security interest in the property, a claim the creditor holds against the property to help make sure the debt will be repaid. If the creditor is a private individual or business, the mortgage lien creates a private restriction on ownership; when the property is sold, the creditor receives payment before any money is turned over to the seller. If the creditor is a government, the resulting encumbrance is a public restriction on ownership. The property tax lien is a common example of a public restriction.

Real estate liens may be either voluntary or involuntary. A voluntary lien is one placed on property by the owner, usually in the form of a mortgage to secure repayment of long-term debt. An involuntary lien protects the interests of persons who have valid claims against the owner of real property—such as a lien resulting from a judgment in a lawsuit, from not being paid for some service or from unpaid taxes.

Liens are also classified as special or general. A **special lien** is created to secure debts that arise from ownership of real estate. A **general lien**—for example, a judgment lien or an income tax lien—is placed on all the property that might be owned by an individual, including real estate.

Special Liens

The two types of special liens that are created specifically to protect creditors using real estate as their security for repayment of debts are mortgages and mechanics' liens.

Mortgages   Because few people are able to buy real estate without borrowing money, a **mortgage** is the most common encumbrance on an owner's title. In return for a loan to buy real property, a purchaser normally mortgages the property. This creates a lien in favor of the lender, and the mortgage represents a limitation on the purchaser's ownership interest. The borrower who gives real estate as security or collateral against a loan is the mortgagor; the lender that receives the benefits of this lien is the mortgagee. (A helpful hint for keeping the "ors" and "ees" straight in all real estate terms: the "ors" give and the "ees" receive.) Although a mortgage lien puts a restriction on a mortgagor's ownership interest, the lien makes it possible for the purchaser to obtain long-term financing for a relatively large real estate purchase.

A mortgage lien acts as a private restriction to ownership in that if the loan is not repaid on schedule, or if other requirements of the loan contract are not met, the mortgagee may instigate foreclosure proceedings. By satisfying the legal requirements of foreclosure, the mortgagee can have the encumbered land sold to the highest bidder at a public auction to satisfy the debt. Mortgage lending and the foreclosure process will be discussed more fully in Chapter 13.

Mechanics' Liens   **Mechanics' liens** protect those who provide labor or materials for real estate improvements, including suppliers, architects, engineers, landscapers, carpenters, plumbers and similar workers. Any such supplier of materials and labor who is not paid can file a mechanic's lien on the property. If payment still is not made, foreclosure proceedings can result, with the property being sold to satisfy the debt.

Mechanics' liens are not just a concern to persons who fail to pay for work done to their real property; they also can create problems for subsequent purchasers. Suppose, for example, that Marty and Carole Teem purchase a home from Potts Development. Some weeks after closing on the house, they are dismayed to learn that several subcontractors have filed mechanics' liens on the home because they were not paid by the general contractor. Even though Marty and Carole have already paid for the house, they may have to pay twice for the same work if the claims are valid. Needless to say, it is vital to see that all suppliers of material and labor are paid before the general contractor is fully paid or the house purchase completed.

General Liens

Like special liens, general liens do not represent property ownership; they are, however, creditors' claims against a property owner's title. Unlike special liens, general liens normally may be filed on either personal or real property.

A common general lien is a judgment lien. If the winner in a lawsuit has not been paid, he or she may collect the debt by claiming an interest in the loser's property, including any real estate. If the judgment debt still is not paid, the real estate can be sold to satisfy the creditor's claim. Such a sale, commonly referred to as a *judicial sale,* is conducted as an auction by a sheriff or another legal authority. In some states, the debtor-owner of the real property may redeem ownership interest within a year of the sale by reimbursing the purchaser for the sales price and paying all of the costs of the sale.

Other general liens that could result in similar ownership limitations are public liens for delinquent taxes: federal income, federal estate, state income, and state estate or inheritance. As in a court-awarded judgment, such unpaid tax debts can be levied on real property. Ultimately, if the lien is not satisfied and removed, the land can be sold at public auction.

EASEMENTS

An **easement** is a right given to one party by a landowner to use the land in a specified manner. The landowner does not have to give up the land, but rather coexists with the holder of the easement. For example, a property owner may grant a utility company the right to run a power line across the land, or one landowner may allow an adjoining owner to build a driveway across the property.

Types of Easements

Two types of traditional easements exist: an easement appurtenant and an easement in gross. An **easement appurtenant** exists when an easement is legally connected to an adjoining property. Suppose, for example, that Bill pays Susan to grant him an easement to run a sewer line from his house across her property

Figure 5.1   Easement Appurtenant Created by a Joint Driveway

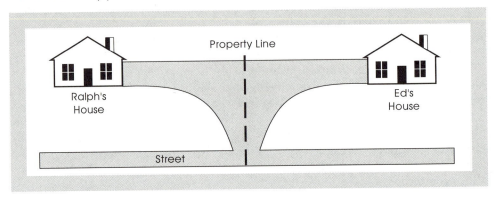

to the city's trunk sewer line. In this case, Bill's land is being served or benefited by the easement and is known as the **dominant estate.** Susan's land, on the other hand, is burdened by the easement and is known as the **servient estate.** Susan can continue to use her land, but cannot do anything that would interfere with Bill's use of the sewer line.

As with almost all easements, this easement runs with the land—in other words, continues when ownership changes. Even though the new owners of Susan's land may not want Bill's sewer line to remain on their property, they have no choice in the matter.

In some cases, adjoining properties are both dominant and servient. Suppose that Ralph and Ed are neighbors, and each wants a paved driveway. To save money, they decide to share the building costs of one driveway that will serve both lots, as shown in Figure 5.1. Each grants the other an easement appurtenant to use the portion of the driveway on each other's land. Both lots are simultaneously the servient estate and the dominant estate.

With an **easement in gross,** there is no dominant estate, only a servient estate. For example, a utility company that acquires an easement to run its power line or pipeline across a property, or the highway department that acquires an easement for a road right-of-way, has acquired an easement in gross. The easement has been granted to the utility company or the highway department, not to a parcel of land. The land over which the utility line or road crosses is the servient estate, and the easement binds all future owners of the property.

Creation of Easements

Both easements appurtenant and easements in gross may be established in a number of ways. The most common method is by an express grant or reservation, but easements also may be established by implication and by prescription.

Express Grant or Reservation   Most easements are created by either express grant or express reservation. Suppose Scott sells half of his ten-acre lot to Darlene. If the property Darlene purchases has no road frontage, Scott may expressly grant her the right to use a portion of his remaining property for a driveway. In this case, Scott owns the servient estate, and Darlene owns the dominant estate. The deed Scott gives Darlene should specify the easement appur-

Easement Created by Express Grant **Figure 5.2**

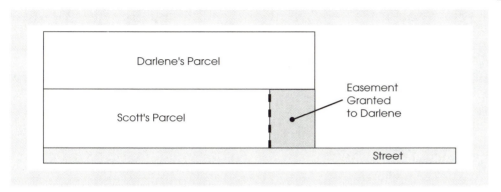

tenant that has been created. This easement by **express grant** is shown in Figure 5.2.

An easement also may be established by an **express reservation.** If Sam were to sell the front half of his land to Bob, the remainder of Sam's property would be landlocked because it does not front on a public road. In the deed that transfers ownership of the frontage land to Bob, Sam could reserve a right-of-passageway through Bob's newly acquired land. Sam owns the dominant estate, and Bob owns the burdened estate. By this express reservation in the sale of land, an easement appurtenant has been created, as shown in Figure 5.3.

Implication   Sometimes, when one or more parcels are severed from a larger tract under common ownership, the right to use the land may be implied from the factual circumstances even when an easement is not created expressly. The easement supposedly reflects the intentions of the parties and is called an **easement by implication.**

Suppose no mention of an easement was made in the previous examples. If Scott sold the land illustrated in Figure 5.2 to Darlene, and he allowed her to use the road on the property he retained, an easement by **implied grant** probably would be established. Likewise, as depicted in Figure 5.3, Sam's continued use of the passageway over the land granted to Bob would create an easement by **implied reservation.**

In both of these situations, the implied easement is called an **easement by necessity** — that is, a court-ordered easement that permits the owner of a landlocked parcel to continue crossing a portion of land of which the easement formerly was a part. In the absence of the easements, the properties would have no access and virtually no value. Of course, even when an easement can be implied, it is best that all easements be stated expressly in writing.

Prescription   An **easement by prescription** may be created when someone other than the owner uses the land "openly, hostilely and continuously" for a statutory time period. To use the land openly means that the user comes onto the land and acts entitled to be there. Such a user does not use the land secretly, as if to hide the use. Hostile use means the user treats the land as if he or she is the true owner of an easement. If the landowner has given specific permission for the use of land, hostility does not exist. To be continuous, the use must be

| **Figure 5.3** | Easement Created by Implied Reservation |

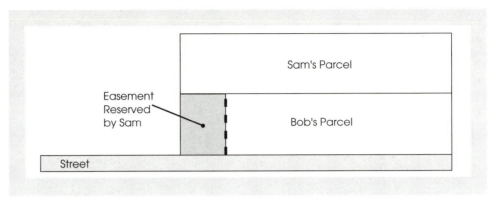

uninterrupted for the time period provided by the applicable statute, usually between 7 and 20 years. These elements of prescription are very similar to those required for gaining title by adverse possession, a topic discussed later in this chapter.

Suppose, for example, that college students begin driving across kindly farmer Wilhelm's land to reach a swimming hole on the river. Being a good fellow, he says nothing about it, and the use continues for many years. Later, when Wilhelm attempts to close the road, he is sued successfully to keep it open because of the prescriptive easement. This may be unfair, but it is the law.

The lesson of all this for property owners is clear: they should not allow anyone to use their property without specific permission, and they should make certain the use is interrupted at intervals. Otherwise, these property owners may find that an easement has been created.

Nature of Easements

Easements are considered to be permanent in nature. That is, easements *run with the land* from owner to owner. Under an easement appurtenant, both the benefit to the dominant estate and the burden on the servient estate are transferred to the new owner if either of the properties is transferred. The owners represented in Figures 5.2 and 5.3 own their respective lots subject to easements of passageways over the northern land. If ownership of these lots were to change, the easements would still exist, as the passageways would continue to be necessary for the southern landowners to have access to the street.

The burden on the servient estate also runs with the land under an easement in gross. If Susan grants a utility company an easement to use her land for its electrical lines, then sells her land to Wilbur, the transfer does not destroy the utility company's right to use the land. The easement, therefore, is just as valid under Wilbur's ownership as it is under Susan's. In addition, the utility company normally could pass this right to another organization, as long as the burden on the servient estate is not increased. For example, an electric company could permit a cable television company to run its cable alongside those of the utility.

Real Estate Today   *Legal Highlight*

Prescriptive Easement

Not all disputes about prescriptive easements involve roads across relatively undeveloped lands; some involve valuable urban properties. Such was the case in a dispute between the owners of two abutting commercial properties, the Powers Ferry Square Shopping Center and the Boston Sea Party restaurant.

The shopping center had a main parking lot and a little-used north parking lot that was reached by using a one-lane drive around one corner of the building. There was no clearly defined dividing line between the shopping center and restaurant property, and the center actually paved the disputed small part of the restaurant's land in 1986.

No conflict occurred until 1994, when Harry's In A Hurry moved into the corner space in the shopping center, shifting its main entrance to the north parking lot. To provide better access, the center extended the sidewalk alongside the building between the two parking lots and widened the driveway to two lanes. The Boston Sea Party restaurant's owners pointed out that the driveway crossed their land, and they threatened to put a fence across it unless they were paid for the land by the shopping center's owner, Metropolitan Life. Metropolitan sued, claiming it had used the disputed property as a driveway for more than the required seven years and was entitled to a prescriptive easement. Metropolitan lost.

Not only did the court hear witnesses regarding the use or nonuse as a driveway of the disputed land, the court actually inspected the site. It found that although old pavement markings had been painted over after the construction for Harry's, the old markings were still visible. The markings clearly showed that two parking spaces for the center blocked cars from traveling over the disputed restaurant land, and other markings directed traffic to the north lot by way of the narrow driveway on the shopping center property. Thus, the land had not been used for the requisite seven years as a driveway, and the center was not entitled to a prescriptive driveway easement. ■

Source:
Metropolitan Life Insurance Company v. Popescu, 172 Bankr. 691 (1994).

Termination of Easements

Even though easements are considered permanent and pass from owner to owner, the rights and restrictions of an easement may be terminated under certain circumstances. Methods of terminating an easement include agreement, merger and abandonment.

Agreement   Parties affected by an easement may expressly agree to terminate their respective rights in the easement. Such an agreement should be written and recorded so that notice is given to everyone interested that a prior easement no longer exists. Because easements are valuable, convincing the owner of the dominant estate to terminate the easement can be quite expensive. If an easement is created by an express grant or reservation that specifies it will last for a limited term only, the easement automatically ceases at the end of that term.

Merger   An easement can also be terminated by the merger of the dominant and servient estates. If Bill's land is burdened by an easement that permits Sarah, the adjoining landowner, to travel across a portion of his property, Bill could persuade Sarah to sell him the land and thereby terminate the easement. Bill could then sell the land to another party without granting an easement, provided the property has another access route. Such a strategy is used when an agreement to terminate an easement cannot be reached.

Abandonment   A third method of terminating an easement is abandonment. If the benefited party does not exercise his or her rights to use the servient estate over an extended period of time, the easement may be terminated. The length of time an easement may remain in effect without being used varies from state to state and from case to case. Some states require that the holder of a servient estate perform some act to block the easement's use before any abandonment is possible. In essence, these states say that the easement must be terminated by the burdened owner's prescriptive use or adverse possession.

LICENSES

A **license** is a revocable personal privilege to use land for a particular purpose. Whereas easements are created by express grants, prescription or implication, licenses are established by verbal or written grants of permission. A landowner might, for example, rent parking spaces by the hour, the right to park evidenced only by a ticket stub. Licenses can generally be revoked at will by the owners. The benefits under a license and the burdens to the grantor's land are temporary in nature and do not pass to successive owners.

PROFIT A PRENDRE

A profit, more correctly known as a **profit a prendre,** is a nonpossessory interest in real property that permits the holder to remove part of the soil or produce of the land. It is similar to an easement, although the holder of a profit has the right to remove specified resources, such as soil, produce, wild animals, coal or other minerals, or timber, while the holder of an easement does not.

ADVERSE POSSESSION

Perhaps nothing in real estate law is so upsetting to property owners as **adverse possession,** which allows individuals to acquire title to land they do not own because they have openly possessed it for a statutory period of time, usually 7 to 20 years.

For title to be transferred by adverse possession, such possession must be "actual and exclusive, open and notorious, hostile, and continuous" for a statutory period of time. The phrase *actual and exclusive* does not require that the adverse possessor physically occupy the land at all times. Improving the land with a residence would constitute actual possession. So would clearing the land, building a fence along its boundaries or farming it. Allowing other people to use the land without express permission would prove that the possession was not exclusive. The possessor must maintain possession in the manner of a reasonable owner. The terms *open and notorious, hostile* and *continuous* have the same meanings in the case of adverse possession as they do in the case of a prescriptive easement.

Another important prerequisite for adverse possession in some states is that the possessor be under a "claim of right." This means that the adverse possessor must have a basis for believing he or she owns the real estate claimed. A tenant who takes possession of a house while acknowledging the landlord's ownership cannot adversely possess the leased property. If a claim of right is based on a written document, such as an invalid deed, the claim is said to be made under "color of title." Some states require the possessor to have color of title to possess land adversely, while other states reduce the number of years required for continuous possession if written color of title is present. Still other states treat all claims of right in the same manner, whether or not they are based on documents.

At times, it is hard to imagine how anyone could become confused about land ownership unless a mistake has been made in the deed's property description. Adverse possession today is much more common in connection with boundary disputes than with possession of entire tracts. Boundary disputes involving adverse possession are of particular importance in residential areas, as can be seen in the Legal Highlight on page 90.

ENCROACHMENTS

An **encroachment** is an unauthorized invasion or intrusion of a fixture, a building or another improvement onto another person's property. Examples are a fence that strays across the property line and a driveway or patio constructed partially on the adjoining property. Although most of these intrusions are the results of carelessness or poor planning rather than intent, they should not be taken lightly. The owner of the property being encroached upon has the right to force the removal of the encroachment; but if that owner fails to force removal, the other party may claim the legal right to continue encroaching by adverse possession or easement.

Before making a loan, almost all lending institutions require a survey of the property primarily to reveal any encroachments, as they can adversely affect the value of a home or other real estate.

RESTRICTIVE COVENANTS

Restrictive covenants, also called *deed restrictions,* are promises made by a landowner or predecessor in title that the land will or will not be used in certain ways. These covenants are found in the deeds or plats (plans or maps) of real property and are recorded as part of the deeds or plats in the public records. For example, the developer of a single-family residential subdivision wants to estab-

Real Estate Today *Legal Highlight*

Adverse Possession

The Cappuccios purchased a lot in the town of Narragansett, Rhode Island, for the purpose of building a home. Unfortunately, they did not have the lot surveyed before completing the purchase, and when they finally did, they received quite a shock.

Twenty-five years earlier, the Fortunes purchased the adjoining lot. They also did not have their lot surveyed, but cleared it to what they believed was the side property lines perpendicular to Winterberry Road. The Fortunes then built a house with a septic tank and drainage field in the back of the lot and also constructed a driveway along what they thought was the side lot line.

The Fortunes lived in the house for five years. It then passed through a succession of owners and renters who maintained the same area, cutting the grass and even planting a garden along the assumed side boundary. According to his later testimony, when James Walsh purchased the property, the real estate agent told him the side lot line was marked by a line of rocks, and he cut the grass to the apparent property line established many years earlier.

The Cappuccio survey revealed that the platted lots were laid out at a 57 degree angle to the road, not a perpendicular angle, as the Fortunes had assumed 13 years earlier. Because of the Fortunes' mistake, a portion of Walsh's home and most of the rear yard, including the septic system, encroached on a substantial portion of the Cappuccios' lot. In fact, the encroachment occupied approximately half of the land.

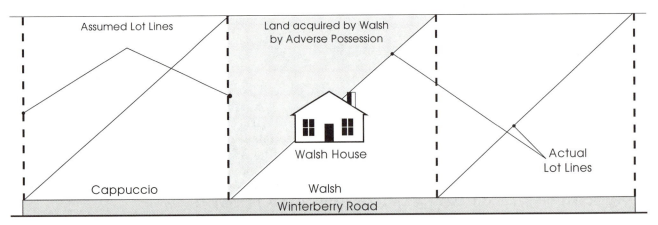

Walsh sued to have the disputed portion of the Cappuccios' lot declared his property through adverse possession. He won. The court ruled that possession by Walsh and his predecessors was "actual, open, notorious, hostile, under claim of right, continuous, and exclusive" for a period in excess of the statutory ten years, clearly establishing adverse possession of the property.

The Cappuccios then sued the seller for indemnification. The result of that dispute is not yet settled, but obviously the Cappuccios are now much sadder and—we hope—much wiser.

The lesson of this saga is quite clear: never purchase property without having it surveyed before closing. It also shows why lenders require a survey before loaning mortgage monies. ■

Source:
Walsh v. Cappuccio, Supreme Court of Rhode Island, 602 A.2d 927.

lish an aesthetically pleasing neighborhood that will increase the value of all owners' property, and he wants to be able to assure purchasers that they will be protected in the future. Protection against many property abuses can be achieved through restrictive covenants.

Typical covenants restrict property to single-family uses, require that a house be a certain minimum size and prohibit business enterprises, domestic animals or large antennas. Covenants also can be much more specific, requiring the approval by an architectural committee of all buildings and landscaping plans, prohibiting the use of certain building materials and even mandating the painting of a home at regular intervals and the approval of paint colors.

Covenants cannot, however, create unreasonable or unlawful limitations on an owner's use of land. For example, restrictions preventing the sale of property to a person of a particular ethnic or racial group clearly are unenforceable because they violate the laws and Constitution of the United States.

Restrictive covenants are important particularly to the owners of attached condominium dwellings. Suppose, for example, that the owners of a town house paint their unit in their college's colors—a brilliant orange and green. Or suppose they decide that dozens of plastic flamingos would be just the thing for the front yard. Not only would these actions have definite detrimental aesthetic impacts, they would have economic impacts on fellow property owners and therefore could be prevented through restrictive covenants (stating, for instance, that outside paint colors must meet the approval of a homeowners' committee and that no statuary or furniture can be placed in front yards).

Because a restrictive covenant is a type of contractual agreement, parties to the original agreement may enforce it. To recover damages or obtain an injunction, the nonbreaching party must be able to show that some damage has been suffered. In other words, to be justified in enforcing a covenant, the party must be able to show how the intended benefit has been denied.

Suppose, for example, that Mary violates the covenants in the deed to her home by erecting a 12-foot satellite dish antenna in her front yard. Either the developer or other property owners could secure a court injunction to force the removal of the offending antenna. If the covenant violation were even more severe, they could seek monetary damages.

Covenants generally run with the land from owner to owner. They may exist only for a stated period of time—say, 20 years—or they can be terminated by the agreement of all affected parties should the right of enforcement be waived or abandoned or if the restricted land is condemned for a public use. Alternatively, an owner could place a permanent restriction on the land. Restrictive covenants can supersede zoning regulations if the covenants are more restrictive, and they generally offer more protection to property owners, as the following Legal Highlight illustrates.

Chapter Review

1. Restrictions and limitations on ownership interests in real property take many forms. A private restriction is a claim on the owner's title by

Real Estate Today   *Legal Highlight*

Validity of Restrictive Covenants

Salima Worthington purchased a home in the Mains Farm subdivision near Sequim, Washington, for the purpose of establishing an adult care facility. She knew restrictive covenants limited use in the subdivision to "single-family residential purposes only," but contended that the proposed use did not violate the covenants. She and her daughter moved into the home with four elderly residents. The homeowners' association sued to enforce the deed restrictions and won.

The court held that Worthington's use of her home was not for single-family residential purposes only because of the business elements involved. Because Worthington provided 24-hour care for fees of $500 to $1,000 per person per month, the property's use was essentially commercial, a use that was inconsistent with a residential purpose.

Worthington also contended that even if her use violated the restrictive covenants, the covenants could not prevent a home care facility because the state legislature had adopted legislation permitting such facilities in all areas zoned for residential or commercial purposes, including areas zoned for single-family dwellings. She contended that this enactment established the fact that maintaining disabled persons outside institutions is of greater value to the public than is the right to restrict the use of land through restrictive covenants.

Again, the court disagreed, holding that unlike covenants that might attempt to restrict ownership by race, creed, color, national origin or handicap, the covenants in question served the legitimate public purpose of protecting residential neighborhoods from the effect of business uses. Although the legislature had restricted local governments from zoning adult family homes out of residential areas, it did not limit the right of private homeowners to adopt restrictive covenants that prohibit certain uses of land in residential areas. ■

Source:
Mains Farm Homeowners Association v. Worthington,
   824 P. 2d 495 (Washington Appeals, 1992).

---

some private individual or business. An encumbrance created by a governing body or public authority is a public restriction.

2.   A common ownership restriction is the lien. A lien is a claim on property held by a creditor as security for repayment of a debt or another obligation. It does not represent an ownership interest in the property. Some liens are created to secure debts that arise out of real estate ownership. Mortgages and mechanics' liens are examples of special liens. Other claims, such as judgment liens, are more general in that they can be attached to real or personal property. If a debtor fails to satisfy a specific or general lien, his or her property may be auctioned at a judicial sale, and the title will then pass to the highest bidder.

3.   Easements and licenses are restrictions on a landowner's title. They also represent ownership interests in real property held by another person. An easement is one person's right to use someone else's land. When an

easement is granted, the land where the easement is located becomes the servient estate. An easement appurtenant exists when the easement's benefits are tied to another piece of property—the dominant estate. If such benefits are held by an individual or a business without regard to the location of that individual or business, an easement in gross exists. A license is created by the landowner's grant of permission to use his or her property. Generally, licenses can be revoked at the landowners' whims; therefore, they are less permanent than easements.

4. Restrictive covenants, also called *deed restrictions,* are restrictions in the deed for a property that restrict how the property may be used. Restrictive covenants in residential subdivisions and condominiums protect and enhance property values by preventing uses that would be incompatible with other properties.

Key Terms

adverse possession   the acquisition of property as a result of "actual and exclusive, open and notorious, hostile and continuous" possession under a claim of right for a statutory period of time.

dominant estate   the property benefitted by the existence of an easement appurtenant.

easement   a right given to another party by a landowner to use a property in a specified manner.

easement appurtenant   an easement with clearly identifiable dominant and servient estates.

easement in gross   an easement with only a servient estate.

easement by prescription   method of creating an easement as a result of "actual and exclusive, open and notorious, hostile and continuous" use for a statutory period of time.

encroachment   an unauthorized invasion of a fixture, a building or another improvement on a person's property.

encumbrance   any restriction that limits ownership interests in real property.

express grant   method of expressly creating an easement on a grantor's property.

express reservation   method of expressly creating an easement on a grantee's property.

general lien   a security interest on all property owned by an individual.

implied grant   a method of implicitly creating an easement on a grantor's property.

implied reservation a method of implicitly creating an easement on a grantee's property.

license a revocable personal privilege to use land for a particular purpose.

lien a claim on a property as security for a debt or fulfillment of some monetary charge or obligation.

mechanic's lien a claim on a property held by a supplier of materials or labor for nonpayment of a debt.

mortgage a contract by which real property is pledged as security for a loan.

profit a prendre a nonpossessory interest in real property that permits the holder to remove specified natural resources from a property.

restrictive covenant limitations placed on a property by a landowner or previous landowner that prevents the property from being used in certain ways.

servient estate the property burdened by the existence of an easement appurtenant or easement in gross.

special lien security interest that relates only to real estate.

Study Exercises

1. What is the difference between a general lien and a special lien?

2. Suppose that Charlie decides he will cheat Harry out of the money Charlie owes him for installing a new air-conditioning system in Charlie's house. What steps might Harry take to collect the debt? (Do not include breaking Charlie's legs.)

3. Why would someone voluntarily put a mortgage lien on his or her property?

4. Define the following terms: *easement, license* and *encroachment*.

5. What is the difference between an easement appurtenant and an easement in gross?

6. Suppose that David sells Joan an easement to run a water line across his property to her property. Who has the dominant estate, and who has the servient estate? Is this an easement appurtenant or an easement in gross?

7. Suppose that David sells his property (see question 6) to Tamara. She tells Joan to remove the water line from her property. Can she force Joan to remove the line?

8. What are the differences between creating an easement by grant, by reservation and by implication?

9. What is meant by an easement by necessity? By an easement by prescription?

10. List three methods for terminating an easement.

11. What is the difference between an easement and a license? Between an easement and a profit a prendre?

12. Suppose that Cindy purchases a house and discovers that her neighbor Eleanor has several roses bushes that encroach on her lot. When Cindy asks Eleanor to move the bushes, Eleanor becomes indignant and accuses Cindy of being unfriendly and a poor neighbor. Can Cindy legally insist that the bushes be moved? Why or why not?

13. Suppose that Jack inherits his grandmother's house. He finds that the deed, which was granted many years ago, contains a restriction that the property can be sold only to someone of the Caucasian race. Could this restriction be enforced?

14. When Claudia decides to sell her house, she discovers that a restriction in her deed prohibits putting up a For Sale sign in her yard. "This violates my free speech," she fumes. "I'm going to sue the community association." Will she win? Why or why not?

15. Tim makes the argument: "Even though restrictive covenants limit what a property owner can do with his land, they may increase property values." Is Tim right? Why or why not?

For Further Reading

O'Sullivan, Arthur. *Urban Economics,* 3d ed. (Chicago: Irwin, 1996).

Kaiser, E. J., D. R. Godschalk, and F. S. Chapin, Jr. *Urban Land Use Planning,* 4th ed. (Champaign, Ill.: University of Illinois Press, 1994).

CHAPTER 6
Public Restrictions on Ownership

Local governments can control the density, height and appearance of property through the enforcement of zoning laws.

Chapter Preview

IN ADDITION TO the private restrictions discussed in the previous chapter, governments also have the power to create limitations on the ownership of real estate. These powers include

- the power of taxation;
- the power of escheat;
- the power of eminent domain; and
- zoning and other land-use controls under the police power.

After reviewing the four powers governments have over real property, this chapter will discuss some of the techniques and tools of public land-use control and examine a few of the controversies surrounding land-use policy issues. The specific topics covered are

- the history of land-use controls;
- the public land-use planning process;
- zoning and other land-use control methods; and
- the takings issue.

THE PROPERTY TAX

The first power of government over private property to be considered is the power of taxation. The government exercises this power by levying both property taxes and income taxes. We will consider the impact of income taxes later in this text and focus our attention on the property tax in this chapter.

The property tax is an important source of revenue for state and local governments. On average, property taxes account for about 75 percent of state and local government tax revenues in the United States. These revenues are used to fund education, police and fire protection and other government services. Governments often find that property taxation provides a stable source of revenue that is not greatly affected by short-term fluctuations in business activity. And because it is tied to property that is largely immobile, the property tax is relatively easy to administer and very difficult to evade.

The Property Taxation Process

The property tax is an **ad valorem tax;** that is, it is levied as a percentage of value. It is a tax on the value of property as opposed to a tax on the income earned from property. From the government's perspective, the three steps involved in taxing property are

1. property value assessment;
2. development of a budget and tax rate; and
3. tax billing and collection.

Property Value Assessment   The first step in the property taxation process is to value for tax purposes all properties within the jurisdiction, a process known as *assessment*. The government official responsible for doing so, usually called the *assessor* or *tax assessor*, must discover, list and value all taxable properties. An efficient assessor needs a complete set of maps that show each parcel of land and its measurements, as well as a system of continuing inspection of deeds and building permits to keep up with new construction and changes in property ownership.

After all properties have been identified, the assessor must accomplish the most difficult part of the job, that of estimating the value of the properties within the jurisdiction. Valuation generally is based on an estimate of fair market value—the price a property probably would bring in the market, given knowledgeable and willing buyers and sellers who act under no abnormal pressure and who have a reasonable time to complete the transaction. Many states use mass appraisal techniques, or statistical models, to assess the value of all properties in a jurisdiction each year.

After estimating a property's market value, or some legally authorized fraction thereof (such as 40 percent), the assessor arrives at the **assessed value,** the value of the property established for the purpose of computing property taxes. This value is subject to review, and the results of the review process may be appealed by the taxpayer before an appeals board or court.

Development of a Budget and Tax Rate   The next step in the property taxation process is the development of a budget and tax rate by the city council, the county commission or another governmental body. The amount of revenue coming from other taxes and from nontax sources is subtracted from the total budget; the remainder must be collected in property taxes. This amount then is divided by the total of assessed valuations to obtain the tax rate. For example, suppose that the local government needs to raise $10 million in property taxes, and the total assessed value of all properties in the jurisdiction, known as the *tax digest,* is $500 million. The tax rate needed to raise these revenues is therefore

$$\frac{\$\,10,000,000}{\$500,000,000} = .02$$

The tax rate usually is expressed as the rate per thousand dollars of assessed value—the **millage rate.** One **mill** equals $.001, or 1/1,000 of $1. In the example above, 20 mills equal $20 tax per $1,000 assessed valuation, or 2 percent.

As a matter of practice, of course, the local governing body does not merely decide what it would like to spend and then set a corresponding tax rate. It may feel constrained not to raise the present tax rate at all, to raise it only slightly or even to lower it. In many areas, tax rate adjustments require a vote on the issue by the people in the jurisdictions.

After the tax rate is set, the assessed values are multiplied by the tax rate to obtain individual tax bills. If a house in our hypothetical locality were assessed at $50,000, for example, the property tax would be $1,000 (20 mills × $50,000).

Tax Billing and Collection   Tax billing and collection procedures vary widely among the states. In some, property tax bills are payable annually; in others, taxes are payable semiannually or quarterly. Some states have special taxing districts that send their tax bills at different times of the year.

If property taxes are not paid when due, the government to which the taxes are owed can place a lien on the real estate for the unpaid taxes, plus a penalty and interest. If the taxes remain unpaid for a period of time that varies from state to state, the property may be sold at public auction to satisfy the tax lien. In essence, the tax sale is similar to a foreclosure sale that follows default on either a mortgage or a mechanic's lien. Failure to pay other public assessments also may create liens. For example, nonpayment of utility services provided by a government or a special assessment for roads or sidewalks can result in a lien and possible sale of the property to satisfy the debt.

ESCHEAT

The second power governments have over private property is known as the *power of escheat.* In the event a landowner dies without leaving either a valid will or living relatives, the state government becomes the new owner of the property. This power prevents real estate from simply becoming "unowned." The right of the government to land under these limited circumstances is called **escheat,** a concept that dates back to the medieval feudal system. The king gave land to his barons, but if they died without surviving sons, the king would reclaim the land. If a knight or servant had no male heirs, that person's land would escheat to the next higher tier in the feudal order. Today, of course, the presence of any heir, even if not a relative of the deceased landowner, will prevent the state from asserting its right of escheat.

EMINENT DOMAIN

Under the power of **eminent domain,** a government can acquire property for a public use, even if the owner doesn't want to sell, when it pays just compensation—that is, the property's market value. This power comes from the Fifth Amendment to the U.S. Constitution, which, among other things, states that property shall not be taken from any person for public uses without the payment of just compensation. Although this provision applies specifically to the federal government, it has been extended to the states through the due process clause of the Constitution's Fourteenth Amendment.

In an eminent domain proceeding, also known as a *condemnation proceeding,* the government must establish that the land is needed for a public use or benefit and that the amount of money offered to the landowner is the reasonable value of the land being taken.

The concept of public use is quite broad. It has been extended to include the condemnation of private land for resale to other private individuals or firms for urban renewal, as well as the enforced breakup of old Hawaiian estates to extend land ownership more widely. The concept also has been broadened to include quasi-public organizations, such as utility companies, railroads and pipelines.

Whether the taking is for a public use is generally not the major issue, however. Of utmost concern, rather, is the question of adequate compensation. If the condemning authority and the owner fail to agree on the property's value, the owner can request a jury trial to determine the amount of just compensation. If property is condemned for a highway, a school, a utility plant or another similar public purpose, the government will, of course, take complete fee simple absolute title to the land. Certain situations, however, require that only an easement be acquired. For example, consider VORTAC stations, which transmit radio signals that airplanes use to track their positions. Although such a station physically takes up only a portion of an acre, the area around the station must not contain any object more than six feet high for a radius of approximately one-half mile. In other words, the government has no need for the actual land surrounding VORTAC stations; it needs only the assurance that no physical obstructions will be constructed. In this situation, the government would condemn both the title to a station's physical location and an easement surrounding the building. The landowner could continue to use the land for farming purposes right up to the VORTAC building. Of course, the owner is entitled to just compensation for both the easement restriction and the land that is taken completely.

Inverse condemnation occurs when a property owner, seeking to force the purchase of the property, starts condemnation proceedings against the government, contending that a governmental action has destroyed or reduced the value of the property. For example, suppose a highway department announces plans for a new road, but delays purchasing the necessary rights-of-way. A property owner in the path of the proposed road could sue to force the highway department to purchase the land, contending that the announced plans have made it impossible to sell the land for private purposes. Or a property owner near an airport might bring legal action to force a condemnation and collect payment for damages caused by the noise of low-flying aircraft.

POLICE POWER

Under **police power,** governments have the power of regulation, which gives them the ability to protect the public health, safety, morals and general welfare. In addition to obvious actions such as protecting against crime and health hazards, governments have relied on these police powers to enact a variety of controls over the way landowners can use their properties.

The use of a particular parcel of land is affected greatly by other nearby land uses and depends heavily on public investments and the economic vitality of the surrounding neighborhood and community. It is this interdependence of land uses that creates the need for public land-use controls. Generally speaking, the use of land affects the owners of other property more than the use of any other type of private property. Conversely, financial returns for the real estate developer or investor may be greatly affected by the land uses permitted by governments or by the allowable intensity of land use. Consequently, the issue of public land-use controls is vital to all concerned with real property.

The concept of planning and control of land use is not new. In fact, in this country, it dates back to the colonial era. Many early American cities were carefully planned and developed under a variety of land-use controls. One of the early controls still valid today is the English common-law concept of **nuisance,** the use of property in such a way as to harm the property of others. Most of the prohibited land uses were hazardous or noxious practices, such as the operation of a slaughterhouse or the manufacture of bricks near a residential area. In such a case, the offending activity might be declared a nuisance. The injured parties could seek an injunction to force the polluter to stop the offending activity, or they could seek monetary damages.

The nuisance doctrine provided some relief to individual property owners from the worst types of injurious land uses, but it was not well suited for public land-use control because a substantial injury has to be proved before any relief can be given. As the United States rapidly urbanized around the turn of the century, municipalities increasingly turned to police power controls to regulate land uses. Most cities have found that a comprehensive general plan is necessary to effectively implement land-use controls.

THE COMPREHENSIVE GENERAL PLAN

To ensure that urban areas develop in an orderly fashion, many local governments have formulated and adopted **comprehensive general plans** that serve as statements of policies for the future development of the communities. These policies provide a basis for the land-use control methods employed by a municipality. The policies should reflect a long-range plan that examines closely the community's physical needs for 15 to 25 years in the future. It usually contains the following elements:

Real Estate Today

Close-Up

The Impact of Environmental Hazards on Real Estate Values

Environmental legislation can have a significant effect on real estate values, but perhaps no piece of environmental legislation has as great or more general impact than the Comprehensive Environmental Response, Compensation, and Liability Act of 1980 (CERCLA), commonly called the *Superfund Act*. In contrast to almost all other environmental legislation that seeks to prevent harmful acts in the future, the purpose of CERCLA is to clean up environmental pollution that occurred in the past.

Under the act, the current owner of a contaminated property may be held responsible for the costs of cleanup even though the owner did not cause the contamination and had no knowledge of it when he or she purchased the site. Even financial institutions have been held liable when they have become the "owners" of contaminated properties through foreclosure. The cost of a cleanup may far exceed the cost of the property. For example, one purchaser bought a property at a tax sale for $200, but was later forced to spend more than $250,000 in cleanup costs.

Because of the potential liability, lenders and insurers, as well as many purchasers, require an environmental site assessment when possible environmental contamination exists. A Phase I environmental assessment is performed by an environmental professional to determine whether there may be potential environmental hazards on the site. If so, it may be necessary to move to a Phase II assessment, which involves soil, water and other testing. If these tests confirm contamination, an extensive Phase III environmental assessment will be required to determine the horizontal and vertical extent of the contamination. If it is determined that major site contamination exists, the cleanup costs may greatly reduce the property's value or make it worthless. ■

Source:
Robert V. Colangelo and Ronald D. Miller, *Environmental Site Assessments and Their Impact on Property Value: The Appraiser's Role* (Chicago: Appraisal Institute, 1995).

- Analysis of projected economic development and population change
- Transportation plan to provide for necessary circulation
- Public-facilities plan that identifies such needed facilities as schools, parks, civic centers and water and sewage-disposal plants
- Land-use plan
- Official map

The comprehensive plan may also include other elements, such as housing, redevelopment and historic preservation. It should not be a static document, but must be revised continually as conditions change.

Implementing the Comprehensive Plan

The comprehensive plan and its land-use component are implemented through several tools of land-use control. The most prominent of these is comprehensive zoning, but the controls also include building codes, mandatory dedication,

Real Estate Today   *Close-Up*

Shaping the Skyscrapers of Manhattan

Although the office skyscraper has become symbolic of New York City, it was not until almost the turn of this century that a secular building rose above Manhattan's church steeples. Then, within a few years, a number of monumental towers were constructed, climaxed by the 792-foot Woolworth Building. Although tall, all of these early skyscrapers featured relatively slender towers rather than tremendous bulk. All this changed with the construction of the Equitable Building at 120 Broadway, a 1.2-million-square-foot, 42-story monolith that rose 340 feet straight up from the lot lines. The building was overpowering, casting a huge shadow that denied direct sunlight to both the street and the building's neighbors. The city's 1916 zoning law, the United States's first comprehensive zoning, was largely a response to the excesses of this building.

The zoning law established height and setback regulations that led to "wedding cake" architecture, which stacked buildings in layers, like a wedding cake. Instead of happy couples perched on the tops, however, towers shot up from these buildings. These towers often were rather short and dumpy, but sometimes, as in the case of the Empire State Building, the towers fairly soared to the heavens. By the late 1950s, reaction to the wedding cake style led to changes in the zoning law to promote "towers in a plaza." This movement was fostered by the completion of the landmark Seagram Building, which consisted of an elegant 38-story tower situated in a large plaza.

Thus, New York turned enthusiastically to incentive zoning in 1961. A "sky exposure plane" standard replaced height districts to govern establishment of setbacks, while the floor-area ratio (FAR) concept was introduced to govern bulk. To promote the construction of plazas and other amenities, a 20 percent floor-area bonus was offered if these features were included in a new building. It also was possible for a developer to increase density by acquiring air rights. Through the compounding of bonuses and air rights, it was possible to construct buildings that made a mockery of the regulations designed to protect the openness of the streets. The incentive system also led to an era of zoning negotiations for almost every major new building and to a maze of special districts and zoning amendments.

The zoning law recently was modified with two strategic goals. The first was to simplify the zoning process and give it more certainty and predictability. The number and amount of development bonuses were reduced in the new regulations and made less subject to negotiation. New bulk regulations provide for daylight and openness while offering architectural latitude without the necessity of obtaining variances or entering into other zoning negotiations. Second, the new zoning law attempts to shift growth from the overheated East Side to the West Side and the south through higher allowable floor-area ratios in the growth-incentive areas.

Will the new zoning ordinance achieve the desired effects? The regulations definitely are simplified, and the bulk regulations provide greater flexibility in design. Some observers have expressed fears that a multitude of "ski-slope" buildings will result from the daylight requirements and will supplant wedding cake architecture as the new standard of urban banality. It is hoped these fears will not be realized. It is comforting to note that the highly acclaimed Citicorp Center, for example, scores quite well under the new daylight requirements.

The second goal of the modified zoning law is the more difficult. Although strong market forces still favor the East Side, the zoning and tax incentives have steered a much greater percentage of recent growth toward the west and south. ■

impact fees, zoning for planned unit development, performance or impact zoning, incentive zoning and transfer of development rights. We will consider each of these methods in turn.

COMPREHENSIVE ZONING

Comprehensive zoning divides a community's land into districts to regulate the use of land and buildings and the intensity of various uses. The first comprehensive zoning ordinance was passed in New York City in 1916 to restrict the use and height of buildings in various districts of Manhattan. Zoning gained increasing acceptance during the 1920s, and after the constitutionality of the concept was upheld in 1926, zoning ordinances and related land-use controls were adopted in most urban areas and many rural communities of the United States. The Close-Up on page 103 describes how the zoning ordinance in New York City helped shape the city's skyline.

Zoning

The most widely employed method of regulating the use of land is zoning, which divides land within the local jurisdiction into zones and prescribes regulations relating to the type and intensity of use. Provisions also are made to deal with changes in zoning and the phasing out of nonconforming uses.

Type of Use   The three main kinds of districts classified by use are residential, commercial and industrial. Each such district usually is divided into several subcategories. For example, generally there are several single-family districts with varying minimum sizes of lot and house. Other residential districts may permit multifamily housing. Similarly, commercial and industrial districts usually are subcategorized as neighborhood shopping districts, highway commercial districts, light industrial districts and so on. Most zoning ordinances contain, in addition to the three main categories, such special-purpose districts as agricultural, floodplain and historic preservation.

Intensity of Use   Intensity of use, also referred to as developmental density, is the extent to which the land within a given district may be used for its permitted purposes. The government can regulate intensity of use in several ways, including placing restrictions on building height and bulk, specifying minimum lot size and establishing setback requirements.

Height and bulk limitations.   Height limitations regulate the maximum height of buildings in feet or stories. **Bulk regulations** control the percentage of lot area that may be occupied by buildings. Both control the volume of a structure on the land and therefore the intensity of use.

Floor-area ratio.   Another measure by which building volume may be controlled is the **floor-area ratio.** The FAR is the relationship between the total floor area of a building and the total land area of the site. For example, an allowable ratio of four to one would permit a 4-story building to occupy the entire area of its lot; an 8-story building would be permitted to occupy only half of the site's

Examples of Floor-Area Ratios   **Figure 6.1**

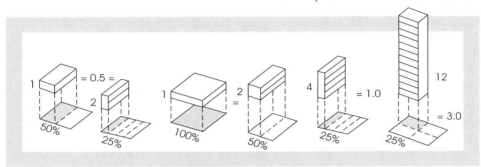

surface area; a 16-story building could occupy only one-fourth of the land area. Other floor-area ratios are illustrated in Figure 6.1.

Minimum lot size and setback regulations.   The most common method of regulating development density is through provisions for minimum lot size. Relatively large lots may be necessary for public health reasons if public sewer and water systems are not provided. However, requirements of very large minimum lot sizes may run into court challenges on the basis that they deprive owners of reasonable use or are designed to exclude various groups.

Zoning ordinances generally provide for **setback** of buildings from the street and minimum size of side yards in residential districts. Such restrictions also may be applied to commercial and industrial districts, but this is less common.

Zoning Changes

For various reasons, a property owner may seek a change in zoning or relief from some provision of the zoning ordinance. This can be accomplished through legislative, administrative or judicial means.

Legislative Relief   If a property owner seeks a change in the property's use, he or she can request a change in zoning-use classification from the local zoning authority, usually the city council or county commission. A zoning amendment generally requires review by a planning commission, an advertised public hearing and some type of justification from the applicant demonstrating that changed conditions justify the zoning change. Because zoning changes often are quite controversial, the hearings often are quite controversial also, with spirited and sometimes acrimonious public debate.

Administrative Relief   If a property owner seeks a relatively minor change, it sometimes can be accomplished administratively through a **variance** or special-use permit granted by a board of adjustments, a zoning appeals board or some such body. A variance permits use to deviate slightly from a strict interpretation of the zoning ordinance to avoid placing undue hardship on an owner. For example, for a house to be constructed on an oddly shaped lot, some relief from minimum side-yard requirements may be needed.

A zoning ordinance often permits special uses within certain districts if certain conditions are met. For example, a public utility substation, church, school

Real Estate Today   *Legal Highlight*

The Strange Case of the Incredible Shrinking Building

In New York City, developer Laurence Ginsberg applied for a building permit to construct a 31-story apartment building on Park Avenue at 96th Street. The city had established a special zoning district 150 feet on each side of Park Avenue that limited new buildings to 210 feet (18 floors), but Ginsberg based his application on a zoning map that erroneously showed the special district to extend only 100 feet from Park Avenue. He received the building permit and began construction. Later, however, the city discovered the error, canceled the permit and issued a stop-work order on the top 12 floors. Ginsberg appealed the order and kept on building—all the way to the 31st floor.

New York's highest court turned down Ginsberg's appeal, ruling that "reasonable diligence would have readily uncovered for a good-faith inquirer the existence of the unequivocal limitations of 150 feet in the original binding metes and bounds description of the enabling legislation, and that this boundary has never been changed by the (City)." The court ordered the top 12 floors removed. Ginsberg then applied, after the fact, to the city for a variance for the additional height, but this was also denied.

Finally, eight years after construction began, a 7,000-pound, hammer-wielding robot began pounding away, reducing the 31-story apartment building to 18 stories, at an estimated cost of $1 million. The developer's total losses were approximately $14 million. ■

Source:

Parkview Associates v. City of New York, 519 N.E.2d 1372 (1988).

or recreational facility may be permitted in a residential district if the board determines that the required conditions have been satisfied.

Variances and special-use permits can make a zoning ordinance much more reasonable and less burdensome to property owners. If not carefully controlled, however, these permits also can completely undermine the community's land-use planning efforts. Variances that change the essential character of land use within a district often are granted with little justification. The powers of the board must be spelled out carefully to prevent such happenings.

Judicial Relief If a property owner is unhappy because the legislative or administrative relief sought was not granted, the owner may appeal to the courts. An appeal is based on a contention that zoning regulations are in some way unconstitutional or that the owner was deprived of the property without due process of law because a decision was arbitrary, unreasonable or capricious. Even with the increased aggressiveness of the judicial branch, courts generally are reluctant to substitute their judgment for that of legislative bodies, and zoning ordinances usually are upheld unless they involve clear abuses of power or are unduly restrictive.

Real Estate Today   *Legal Highlight*

The Case of the Costly Permit

In 1990, a Boynton Beach, Florida, building code inspector observed Andre St. Juste performing extensive repairs to the roof of a residential rental house St. Juste owned. The inspector ordered St. Juste to stop work until he obtained a permit and later sent him an official notice that he was violating city codes.

St. Juste ignored the notice, and several weeks later, the Code Enforcement Board began fining him $200 per day. Four months later, St. Juste finally applied for a building permit, but when he told the building department that the repairs would cost only $21.80, the building department told him he didn't need a permit because the repairs cost less than $500. When the code inspectors learned that the repairs would actually cover more than 25 percent of the roof and cost con-

siderably more than $500, they again ordered St. Juste to get a permit. Again, he ignored them.

In 1992, the city made St. Juste an offer: get a permit, fix the roof and ask the Code Enforcement Board to reduce the fines. He refused.

In 1994, the circuit court ruled that the city had made every effort to help St. Juste pass the building code and that he owed $316,000 in fines and $20,000 in court costs. St. Juste attempted to declare bankruptcy to avoid the fines, but the judge refused to approve the bankruptcy.

Finally, in 1995, the city commissioners voted unanimously to auction off St. Juste's house to pay the fines. It was sold on the courthouse steps. ■

Zoning restrictions are of great importance to real estate developers. Those who disregard them do so at their peril, as the developer in the Legal Highlight on page 106 found to his chagrin and financial loss.

Nonconforming Uses A **nonconforming use** is a continuing use that was legal before a zoning ordinance was passed, but that no longer complies with the current zoning regulation. Such a use generally is allowed to continue for some period of time unless the nonconforming structure is substantially destroyed or abandoned. Regulations concerning nonconforming use usually do not permit the existing structure to be enlarged or substantially changed in use. They also may require that the nonconforming use be discontinued after a stated period of time, a process known as **amortization.** Most amortization periods for buildings are relatively long, perhaps 50 years. Most controversy has centered around more minor uses, such as nonconforming signs and billboards.

Although the courts have not been unanimous in their approval of the amortization concept, most have regarded relatively long phase-out periods, such as three to seven years, as reasonable compensation for nonconforming signs.

Building Codes

Another tool used in implementing a comprehensive land-use plan is the set of ordinances known as **building codes.** Such codes establish detailed standards for the construction of new buildings and the alteration of existing ones. Their primary purposes are to protect health and provide safety, and the codes are related primarily to fire prevention, quality and safety of construction and public health safeguards.

Building codes also may be used to promote energy conservation and other public purposes. A building permit is required before construction can begin, and this procedure enables local officials to ascertain that the proposed construction complies with applicable building codes, zoning regulations and subdivision regulations and that the site plan has been approved.

Property owners who ignore building code requirements do so at their peril, as the owner of the rental property interest in the Legal Highlight on page 107 discovered.

Subdivision Regulations

Subdivision regulations, another tool for implementing the community planning process, establish the standards and procedures for regulating the subdivision of land for development and sale. Their purpose is to protect both the community and future residents from poorly planned and executed developments.

The local planning board or another planning agency determines the standards that must be met for subdivision approval. Standards are provided for the design and construction of new streets, utilities and drainage systems. The planning board also establishes an approval procedure, usually consisting of three distinct steps: a preapplication conference, approval of the preliminary plat and approval of the final plat.

Preapplication Conference   The purpose of the preapplication conference is to allow the developer to meet informally with the planning board before going to the expense of preparing a formal plat. Working with a sketch plan, the planning staff can review the proposal with the developer and make suggestions for changes that may be necessary to meet the subdivision regulations. The developer also may benefit from general planning efforts of the board that may affect the development.

Approval of the Preliminary Plat   The next step is for the developer to prepare and submit a *preliminary plat* for approval. The term preliminary plat is misleading because all construction and mapping of the lots will be done on the basis of this plat. Detailed information is required therefore, usually including topographic data regarding existing boundary lines, utilities and ground elevations. Also required is the layout of the proposed subdivision, including streets, other rights-of-way or easements, lot lines and numbers, sites of special uses and minimum building setback lines. A preliminary plat is shown in Figure 6.2.

Approval of the Final Plat   After receiving approval of the preliminary plat, the developer can stake the lots and construct streets and other required improvements. After these tasks are completed, or with the posting of a certified check or bond to guarantee completion, the developer can prepare a final plat and related documents.

A Preliminary Plat   **Figure 6.2**

The Preliminary Plat Shall Show:

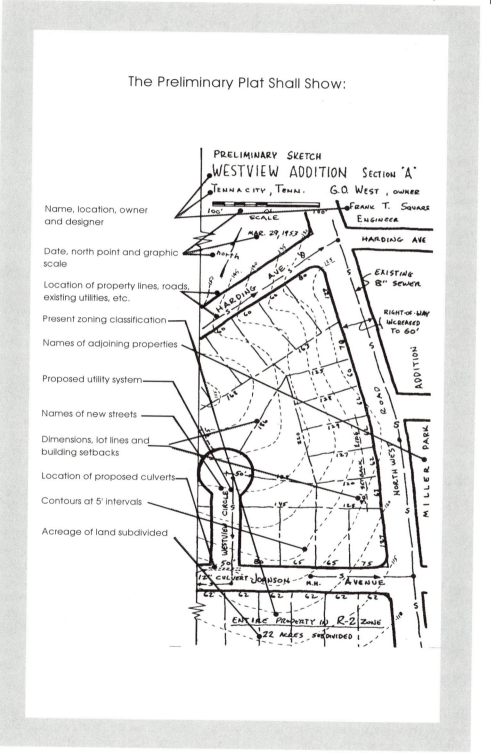

Name, location, owner and designer

Date, north point and graphic scale

Location of property lines, roads, existing utilities, etc.

Present zoning classification

Names of adjoining properties

Proposed utility system

Names of new streets

Dimensions, lot lines and building setbacks

Location of proposed culverts

Contours at 5' intervals

Acreage of land subdivided

The final plat is intended to be filed in the registry of deeds and must contain all information necessary for land titles, such as exact lot lines, street rights-of-way, utility easements and surveying monuments. A final plat is shown in Figure 6.3. The required accompanying documents usually include a certification by a licensed engineer or surveyor regarding the accuracy of the details of the plat, plans concerning utility improvements within the subdivision and certification that the improvements have been constructed in accordance with the approved plans.

After approval by the planning board, the final plat will be recorded, and the developer then will be permitted to sell the lots in the subdivision.

Mandatory Dedication

Another method used to shape city growth is referred to as **mandatory dedication.** To obtain approval for a project, the developer often is required to dedicate parts of the property to such public purposes as rights-of-way for streets, utilities and drainage. In some communities, he or she also may be required to dedicate land for parks, open space and schools. If the development is small, payments in lieu of dedication sometimes are required.

The mandatory dedication of land for parks and schools understandably is controversial. One view is that the need for such facilities is created by the new subdivision, while the opposing view holds that parks and schools are general governmental responsibilities that should be borne by the public at large. The courts are divided on the issue as well, in some cases upholding mandatory dedication of land for such purposes and in other cases holding that the denial of the right to subdivide land on the condition that the developer donate land for parks and schools violates of due process. In some jurisdictions, the developer is required to reserve the land only for a stated period of time, during which the municipality may purchase the property. If the land has not been purchased by the end of the period, the developer no longer is bound by the reservation.

Impact Fees

In addition to mandatory dedications, a community may enact **impact fees** on new development to help raise the funds necessary for the expansion of public facilities. These fees are specific assessments on development—for example, $2,500 per dwelling unit or $2,000 for each 1,000 square feet of new commercial or office space. As might be expected, these fees are quite controversial, but their use by local governments is spreading rapidly.

Recent court decisions and legislation in many states have made it a necessity for governments imposing impact fees to tie them directly to the need created by the development. Otherwise, the fees may be regarded as illegal extortion.

INNOVATIVE LAND-USE CONTROL METHODS

Traditional zoning has been criticized for being inefficient, subject to poor administration and even corruption, and for having little relationship to planning goals. Some attack it for its flexibility, charging that true separation of uses

A Final Plat

Figure 6.3

The Final Plat Shall Show:

Streets, lots, setback lines, lot numbers, etc.

Sufficient engineering data to reproduce any line on the ground

Dimensions, angles and bearings

Monuments

Name of adjoining properties

Date, title, name and location of subdivision

Graphic scale and true north point

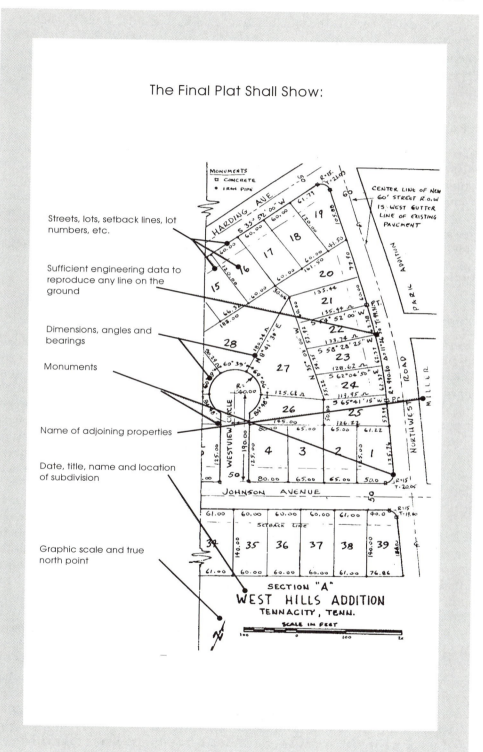

seldom is achieved because zoning boards submit to developer pressure to grant extensive rezonings. Others attack zoning for its rigidity, charging that its inflexible requirements stifle good design and foster inefficiency and rising costs. A few have come to the conclusion that zoning controls should be abolished, while others have attempted to improve the zoning process. The latter movement has led to some innovative techniques, including zoning for planned unit development, performance or impact zoning, incentive zoning and transfer of development rights.

Planned Unit Development

Zoning for planned unit development (PUD) can avoid some of the failings of traditional zoning practices. Generally, many bulk and use regulations may be waived to permit greater flexibility of design. For example, lot sizes may be reduced to permit greater densities, and setback and side-yard requirements may be waived to permit attached housing. Convenience shopping also may be permitted within the development. In return, the community should receive the advantages of preservation of natural features, community recreation and open space, greater housing choice, safer streets and pedestrian ways, reduced need for automobile travel and lower costs.

Performance Zoning

Performance zoning, often known as *impact zoning,* is a technique to relate permitted uses of land to certain performance standards, usually to protect the environment. Such performance standards, particularly industrial-use standards related to noise, smoke, smell and the like, sometimes are quite detailed.

Adoption of performance zoning generally results in simplified land-use controls. The performance standards relate land-use demands to land-use capacity, and they can be used to achieve better design and to reduce the cost of regulation, as well as to protect the environment. The standards used usually are related to density, open-space ratio, impervious-surface ratio (surface-water runoff) and number of vehicle trips generated by the site.

During the past several decades, a number of municipalities in Bucks County, Pennsylvania, have adopted performance zoning ordinances that reduce the number of residential zoning districts to only one or two. A variety of housing densities is possible, however, because the number of units permitted is related to the environmental carrying capacity of each site. Although, at first glance, these rules seem somewhat complex, developers generally have favored the innovation because the performance standards are not subject to varying administrative interpretation and permit much greater variety in design.

Breckenridge, Colorado, has abolished zoning altogether and regulates all development through a comprehensive permit system based on performance standards. A small Victorian mining community in the Rocky Mountains, Breckenridge has become a major ski area in recent years, with attendant development pressure. The performance standards establish architectural guidelines to ensure that new development is compatible with the existing Victorian character of the town, prohibit certain features in a development and require others, and assign positive or negative scores for other features related to environmental impact. The development must achieve a total score of zero or better to receive a permit, but can receive significant density bonuses if it achieves a higher score. As in Bucks County, developers generally have been pleased with the permit system because its highly structured nature reduces uncertainty and processing time.

Performance zoning also can aid redevelopment of an area. For example, South Pointe, a deteriorated, 250-acre, multifamily residential district on the southern tip of Miami Beach, was originally platted in small 50-by-100-foot lots and sold to individual buyers in the 1920s. Attempts to redevelop the area had met with little success until a new performance zoning ordinance was enacted that increased the minimum lot size and minimum width of lots. The ordinance required 60 to 70 percent open space, yet increased the allowable floor-area ratio. These changes have encouraged the aggregation of the small lots and already have led to substantial development.

Incentive Zoning

Closely related to performance zoning is **incentive zoning,** which encourages developers to provide certain publicly desired features in return for various incentives. For example, the San Francisco City Planning Code permits increased floor area if the developer provides a pedestrian plaza or arcade. New York City has provided similar incentives, although they have been reduced in the new zoning code. Other communities permit higher densities for residential developments that provide such a feature as open space.

Transfer of Development Rights

A relatively recent technique of land-use regulation that has received increasing attention and seems to hold considerable promise involves **transfer of development rights.** Under a transfer system, landowners can sell part of their bundles of rights to other landowners, who then can use their own land more intensively. For example, suppose that Elena Johnson owns a ten-acre wooded tract that she wishes to preserve as it as. Nearby, Alan Hite owns another ten-acre tract that he wishes to develop. Existing regulations require minimum one-acre lots in the area, so Alan could build only ten houses on his land. Elena, having no interest in developing her property, could sell her development rights to Alan, who then could build 20 houses on his ten acres, while Elena's land remained in its wooded state. Proponents of this system contend that it is more equitable than one that does not permit such transfer of development rights; it enables communities to preserve floodplains, open space and historic structures without wiping out their property values because development rights can be sold to other property owners.

The use of transfer of development rights still is limited, but is growing in application. Several communities in New Jersey and California are experimenting with the system in their efforts to preserve open space. A number of cities, including New York, Chicago, Denver and Washington, are using the transfer mechanism as a means to preserve historic landmarks. Floor-area ratios on such properties can be transferred to other properties to allow denser development on those sites. For example, Tiffany's sold development rights over its 5th Avenue building to Donald Trump to enable him to add more space to his Trump Tower development.

THE TAKINGS ISSUE

If a governmental unit acquires property for public use under the power of eminent domain, this action is a taking that requires the payment of compensation, whether it involves acquisition in fee simple or only partial property rights, such as an easement. Regulation of land use under police power, on the other hand, normally does not constitute a taking. The courts have ruled, however, that if the regulation is so severe that it deprives an owner of any beneficial use of his or her property, it may then constitute a taking and thus be invalid. The problem is that the courts have never defined the exact point at which regulation goes too far and becomes a taking. The increasing magnitude of land-use regulation has made this a very real issue for many property owners.

Land-use regulation generally is not ruled unconstitutional simply because it reduces the value of a parcel of land. It is only when a regulation deprives the landowner of the entire use and value of the property, or does not allow a reasonable return, that the regulation is held unconstitutional as applied to that particular parcel. As discussed in the Legal Highlight on pages 115–117, exactly how far regulation can go without becoming a taking, however, has not been fully resolved by the U.S. Supreme Court. Some states have passed property rights laws that entitle landowners to compensation if government regulations significantly reduce their property values. The question of whether a property owner is entitled to compensation as a result of a government regulation undoubtedly will continue to be debated for many years.

Real Estate Today *Legal Highlight*

The Supreme Court Grapples with the Takings Issue

Although the general rule is that actual or potential losses resulting from police power regulations do not require compensation, the U.S. Supreme Court has ruled that if a restriction goes "too far," it will be considered a taking. Unfortunately, the Court has provided little guidance as to how far is too far. Recent decisions offer some guidance, however.

The Euclid Decision

Sometimes, the Supreme Court issues a decision that is truly momentous in a particular area. *Village of Euclid v. Ambler Realty Company* in 1926 was such a case, upholding the constitutionality of comprehensive zoning regulations.

Euclid, a suburb of Cleveland, adopted a comprehensive zoning ordinance in 1922. The Ambler Realty Company owned a 68-acre tract of land that it hoped to sell for industrial development. Because industrial use was precluded by the ordinance, which zoned part of the tract for single-family residential use only, Ambler Realty attacked the ordinance on the ground that it was a taking of the company's property without compensation. The district court agreed and declared the ordinance null and void. The village appealed to the U.S. Supreme Court, which reversed the lower court by a five-to-four decision. The victory was a narrow one, with one justice changing his mind in favor of upholding the ordinance after an opinion striking down the principle of zoning had been written, but not made public. In its final decision, the Court ruled that the community was not taking or destroying Ambler Realty's property for public use, but was invoking a general power over private property, which was necessary for the orderly development of the community.

For better or worse, the *Euclid* decision changed the course of urban development in the United States. The zoning ordinances of more than 400 municipalities were upheld, and hundreds of others were soon passed. Now, almost every city of more than 10,000 population has enacted a comprehensive zoning ordinance, as have many smaller municipalities and counties. It is interesting to speculate what might have happened to the course of urban development in the United States if the one justice had not changed his vote.

Upholding Historic Preservation Regulations

Following the *Euclid* decision and two related cases in the 1920s, the U.S. Supreme Court did not accept another zoning case for 50 years, when the Court upheld New York City's landmarks preservation law. Not only was this an important victory for preservationists; it was also a landmark takings decision.

New York enacted a landmarks preservation law in 1965 to establish a citywide program of identification and preservation of historic structures and sites. Designation barred any construction or alteration of a building's exterior appearance without the approval of the Landmarks Preservation Commission. Grand Central Terminal, a monumental building in the beaux-arts style that was completed in 1913, was designated as a landmark under the law. Later, the Penn Central Railroad leased air rights over the terminal for a proposed skyscraper. The Landmarks Preservation Commission rejected the plan, reasoning: "To balance a 55-story office tower above a flamboyant Beaux-Arts facade seems nothing more than an aesthetic joke which would reduce the Landmark itself to the status of a curiosity."

Penn Central challenged the constitutionality of the landmarks law, contending it resulted in the taking of private property without compensation. The Court disagreed, concluding that

the submission that appellants may establish a "taking" simply by showing that they have been denied the ability to exploit a property interest that they heretofore had believed was available for development is quite simply untenable.

Even so, the Court made it clear that preservation laws could not deprive the owner of a reasonable return from the property, but that the return need not be the highest possible return.

Preservation of Open Space

In 1980, the Court upheld Tiburon, California's, open-space zoning ordinance against a takings claim. The Agins owned five acres of unimproved land overlooking San Francisco Bay that they considered "the most valuable land in California." The city subsequently enacted a zoning ordinance that restricted density on the tract to between one and five single-family residences, and the Agins sued, asserting that the city had effectively taken the property, preventing its development for residential use and completely destroying "the value of the property for any purpose or use whatever." They also sought $2 million in damages for inverse condemnation—the taking of private property by a governmental unit through an inference of property rights without actually seizing the property. In other words, the Agins felt the rezoning was a taking that required compensation. The U.S. Supreme Court did not agree.

In upholding the ordinance, the Court held that a zoning ordinance would constitute an unconstitutional taking only if (1) legitimate governmental interests are not substantially advanced or (2) the landowner is denied any economically viable use of the property. The Court considered the preservation of open space and the promotion of orderly development to be legitimate state interests and noted that the effects of the ordinance fell on numerous property owners, not just on the Agins. It also found that although the ordinance restricted the density of development, it did not deny the Agins "economically viable use" of the land because it could still be developed for residential purposes, though perhaps not at the density they desired.

Limits on Mandatory Dedications

Property owners commonly are required to dedicate land or make infrastructure improvements as a condition to obtaining developmental approvals. Another Supreme Court decision dealt with the question of how far these developmental regulations can go in requiring such exactions—to the question of the limits and relevance of "legitimate state interests."

The Nollans wanted to replace a small bungalow on their beachfront lot with a larger house. As a condition to granting a building permit, the California Coastal Commission required the donation of a ten-foot walkway easement along the beach in front of the Nollan property. The commission contended that the easement was necessary to offset the reduced "visual access" caused by the construction and to help prevent congestion of the public beaches. The Nollans contended the exaction was not related to any need to which their project contributed directly and was therefore a taking.

The Supreme Court reaffirmed the constitutionality of developmental controls and exactions, stating that the commission could have legitimately imposed conditions to protect the public's ability to see the beach, such as height and width restrictions or a ban on fences, could have required the dedication of a "public viewing spot" on the Nollans' property or even could have prohibited the new construction altogether. However, the Court agreed with the Nollans that the requirement to dedicate the public walkway easement was not sufficiently related to the problems supposedly created by the new construction:

> The lack of nexus between the condition and the original purpose of the building restriction converts that purpose to something other than what it was. The purpose then becomes, quite simply, the obtaining of an easement to serve some valid governmental purpose, but without payment of compensation. . . . Unless the permit condition serves the same governmental purpose as the development ban, the building restriction is not a valid regulation of land use but an out-and-out plan of extortion.

This need to tie any dedication requirements more closely to the actual impact of the proposed development was made clearer in the Supreme Court's decision, *Dolan v. Tigard*. The Dolans owned a plumbing and electrical supply store in the city of Tigard, Oregon. They wanted to double the size of their building and add parking spaces. The planning commission approved the plans with the requirement that the Dolans dedicate about a tenth of their land for flood control for the adjacent creek and about an additional 15 feet for a bike path.

The Dolans challenged the dedication requirement. The Supreme Court in 1994 decided by a five-to-four vote that requiring a dedicated easement as a condition of permission to build or expand is an unconstitutional taking unless the government can show a "rough proportionality" between the regulation and impact of the development. Do these decisions mean that local governments can no longer require mandatory dedications from developers? No, but the Court has made it clear that any required dedications must be closely related to the regulatory objective.

The Lucas Decision

In its latest land-use decision, the Supreme Court made it clear that regulation that rendered land virtually valueless definitely went too far. Lucas had bought two residential lots in 1986 on the Isle of Palms, a South Carolina barrier island, for $975,000. He intended to build single-family homes on the lots, as the owners of adjacent lots had done. To his dismay, however, the South Carolina legislature passed the Beachfront Management Act in 1988, which prohibited building on Lucas's lots. He sued, contending that the regulation had taken his property because he was left with no economically viable use of his land. The Supreme Court agreed and ruled as follows:

> Total deprivation of beneficial use is, from the landowner's point of view, the equivalent of a physical appropriation. . . . We think, in short, that there are good reasons for our frequently expressed belief that when the owner of real property has been called upon to sacrifice all economically beneficial uses in the name of the common good, that is, to leave his property economically idle, he has suffered a taking.

Although this ruling seems to settle the issue for extreme cases—a property owner must be left with some economic use of his or her property unless the use constitutes a public nuisance—the Court still has not adequately defined the dividing line between a regu-

lation that reduces property value, but does not result in a taking, and one that does result in a taking, requiring compensation. Uncertainty will be the rule for all involved in land-use development and planning until the Supreme Court more clearly defines exactly what is permissible in land-use regulation and what is not.

The Takings Battle in the Legislatures

Recently, the takings battle has moved into the legislatures and the Congress, with takings assessment bills and compensation laws being introduced in many states. The takings assessment laws would require that an assessment be made for land-use regulations to analyze their impact on private property values. The compensation bills would require that private property owners be compensated if regulations reduced the value of their property by some percentage, often 25 percent. At this writing, the fate of these bills is uncertain, as they will undoubtedly be challenged through the court system.

The Takings Issue

The takings controversy boils down to the basic question of the nature of private property rights. Do private parties own property subject to regulations, or do they have the unlimited right to use their property as they choose? Where is the proper middle ground? This is an issue that promises to be a lively one for many, many years to come. ■

Sources:

Village of Euclid, Ohio v. Ambler Realty Co., 272 U.S. 365, 47 S.Ct. 114 (1926); *Penn Central Transportation Co. v. City of New York,* 438 U.S. 104 (1978); *Agins v. Tiburon,* 447 U.S. 255 (1980); *Nollan v. California Coastal Commission,* 483 U.S. 825 (1987); *Dolan v. Tigard,* 114 S.Ct. 2309 (1994); *Lucas v. South Carolina Coastal Council,* 112 S.Ct. 2886 (1992); John Tibbetts, "Everybody's Taking the Fifth," *Planning,* January 1995, personal property, 4–9.

1. Government has four basic powers that affect real estate owners: (1) the power of taxation, (2) the power of escheat, (3) the power of eminent domain and (4) police power.

2. Property taxes are an important source of revenues for state and local governments. They provide a relatively stable source of revenue that is not subject to wide fluctuations in short-term business activity, and they are very difficult to evade because they are tied to property that is largely immobile.

3. The steps involved in the property taxation process are (1) property value assessment, (2) development of a budget and tax rate and (3) tax billing and collection.

4. In the event that a property owner dies without heirs or a valid will, the government, through the power of escheat, becomes the owner of the property.

5. The government's right to condemn land is founded on the power of eminent domain, as granted by the Fifth Amendment to the U.S. Constitution. Once the government establishes the right to take title to or place an easement on property for society's needs, the major issue of concern is the determination of just compensation.

6. The police power is the power of government to regulate activities to promote the public health, safety and general welfare.

7. The interdependence of land uses—that is, the impact that the use of land has on other property and on the public as a whole—eventually necessitates land-use controls.

8. A comprehensive general plan is a statement of the community's long-range policies covering its physical needs for 15 to 25 years in the future. It usually contains the following elements: (1) an analysis of projected economic and population developments, (2) a transportation plan, (3) a public-facilities plan, (4) a land-use plan and (5) an official map.

9. The most widely employed method of regulating the use of land is comprehensive zoning. This divides land into zones and prescribes regulations relating to the type and intensity of use. Relief from zoning regulations can be sought through legislative rezoning, through administrative variance or special-use permit or through the courts.

10. Developers often are required to dedicate rights-of-way for public streets, utility and drainage, and in some communities, they also may be required to dedicate parks, open space and schools.

11. Building codes establish detailed standards for the construction of new buildings and the alteration of existing ones.

12. Under a system of planned unit development (PUD), many regulations are waived to permit greater flexibility of design. Lot sizes may be reduced, for example, if community open spaces are provided.

13. Performance zoning is a technique to relate permitted uses of land to certain performance standards. Such standards usually are intended to protect the environment.

14. Incentive zoning, which is closely related to performance zoning, is any type of zoning provision that encourages developers to provide certain publicly desired features in return for such an incentive as increased density of land use.

15. Under the concept of transfer of development rights, a landowner can sell part of his or her bundle of rights to another landowner, who then can use his or her own land more intensively.

16. Regulation of land use under the police power normally does not constitute a taking unless the regulation is so severe as to deprive the owner of any beneficial use of the property. Land-use regulation generally is not held to be unconstitutional simply because it reduces the value of a parcel of land.

Key Terms

ad valorem tax   a tax that is levied as a percentage of the value of the taxed item.

amortization   the process of gradually retiring a loan or other asset; also, the requirement that a nonconforming use be discontinued after a stated period of time.

assessed value   the estimated value of a property for tax purposes.

building codes   regulations that establish standards for the construction of new buildings and the alteration of existing ones.

bulk regulations   regulations that control the percentage of the lot area that may be occupied by buildings on a site.

comprehensive general plan   a statement of land-use policies that shape the future development of a community.

comprehensive zoning   division of a community's land into specific land-use districts to regulate the use of land and buildings and the intensity of various uses.

eminent domain the government's power to take private property for public use upon payment of just compensation.

escheat the government's right to own real estate following the owner's death in the absence of a valid will or legal heirs.

floor-area ratio relationship between the total floor area of a building and the total area of a site.

impact fees fees charged to developers to raise funds for expansion of public facilities needed as a result of the new development.

incentive zoning a practice used by communities to encourage developers to provide certain publicly desired features in their developments in exchange for relaxed enforcement of the zoning code.

inverse condemnation a lawsuit initiated by a property owner to force the government to purchase a property whose value has been diminished by a governmental action.

mandatory dedication a requirement that developers donate property to the community for public use as a condition for obtaining development approval.

mill one one-thousandth, or 0.001.

millage rate the tax rate imposed on property owners, expressed as the dollars of tax for each $1,000 of property value.

nonconforming use a use of land that does not conform to the current land-use controls imposed by the government.

nuisance the use of property in such a way as to harm the property of others.

performance zoning regulations that restrict land-use based on the environmental carrying capacity of the site.

police power the government's power to regulate the way private property is used to protect the health, safety, morals and general welfare of the public.

setback a common land-use regulation that requires a certain amount of space between improvements on a property and the property lines.

subdivision regulations the standards and procedures that regulate the subdivision of land for development and sale.

transfer of development rights a system whereby landowners can sell their development rights to other property owners so the other property owners can use their property more intensely.

variance permission granted by a government for a landowner to use the property in a manner not ordinarily permitted.

Study Exercises

1. What are the desirable features of the property tax for local governments?

2. What is the tax digest?

3. Suppose a local government has a tax digest of $500 million and feels it must raise $15 million for the operation of its schools and general government. What would be the millage rate?

4. Why is the government's power of escheat so seldom used?

5. By what authority does the government have the power of eminent domain?

6. What is meant by public use?

7. What characteristic of real estate leads to the need for public land-use controls?

8. Contrast police power and the power of eminent domain.

9. Discuss the history of the takings issue.

10. Describe the elements usually contained in a comprehensive general plan.

11. How is zoning used to control land use and intensity of use?

12. What are mandatory dedications?

13. What is incentive zoning? Performance zoning?

14. Describe the transfer of development rights process.

15. Suppose that Mack owns 25 acres of land on the edge of town on a major road that is now zoned for residential use. He decides he would like to develop this land as an office park and a shopping center. What steps would he have to take to secure approval of his project?

16. Suppose Mary owns a lot on which she wishes to build her dream house. To her consternation, she finds that if the house is placed on her rather narrow lot, the lot will fail to meet the side-yard setback requirements by three feet. What can she do?

For Further Reading

Callies, D. L., ed. *Takings: Land-Development Conditions and Regulatory Takings after Dolan and Lucas* (Chicago: Section of State and Local Government Law, American Bar Association, 1996).

Platt, R. H. *Land Use Control: Geography, Law and Public Policy* (Englewood Cliffs, N.J.: Prentice Hall, 1991).

Stein, J. M., ed. *Classic Readings in Real Estate and Development* (Washington, D.C.: Urban Land Institute, 1996).

Wright, R. R. *Land Use in a Nutshell,* 3d ed. (St. Paul: West Publishing Company, 1994).

CHAPTER 7
Deeds and Legal Descriptions

In order to transfer ownership of any parcel of property, a deed containing the exact legal description of the property must be conveyed. This discription involves much more specific information than property name or street address.

Chapter Preview

THE PREVIOUS CHAPTERS in this section have described the concept of real estate ownership, including the legal rights held by real estate owners and the public and private limitations on those ownership rights. In this chapter, we consider deeds, which are the legal documents used to convey ownership from one party to another, and the various systems used to legally identify parcels of real estate.

Under the topic of deeds, we will examine

- the necessary elements of a deed and
- types of deeds, including the (1) general warranty deed, (2) special warranty deed, (3) bargain and sale deed and (4) quitclaim deed.

Under the topic of legal descriptions, we will consider

- the metes-and-bounds system;
- the rectangular survey system; and
- references to plats.

DEEDS

Centuries ago in England, any person who possessed land generally was considered to be the legal owner, as possession and ownership essentially were synonymous. In the presence of witnesses, an owner could transfer his **title,** or legal ownership, to another person simply by going on the land and handing the new owner a clod of earth while announcing that title was transferred. This symbolic transfer of title by delivery caused great confusion because no written records existed. The potential for fraud or forcible seizure was limitless. Therefore, in 1677, Parliament enacted a statute of frauds, which required that all title transfers of real property be in writing. This provision has been adopted by every state in the United States, with the goal of limiting the opportunities for fraudulent transactions. Thus, when title to real estate is to be transferred today, a written document called a **deed** must be given by the grantor to the new owner, the grantee.

Once the deed is written, title to real property is transferred by delivery of the deed to and acceptance by the buyer. The delivery can be made by the seller or a person acting on behalf of the seller. Delivery of a signed deed can even be made after the seller's death if that was the seller's intent. When ownership is to be transferred, a deed must be drafted, signed by the grantor and delivered to and accepted by the new owner. Several elements are necessary for a deed to be valid. In addition to the basic requirement that a deed must be in writing, a valid deed must include

- designations of the parties;
- consideration given for the conveyed interest;
- legal description of the property;
- specification of the interests conveyed; and
- signatures of the proper parties.

After the deed has been written properly, it must be delivered to and accepted by the new owner.

Necessary Elements of a Deed

All deeds begin by identifying the parties involved in the transfers of title. In general, the seller is the grantor, and the buyer is the grantee. The grantee must give up something in return for the interest conveyed, generally the purchase price. Sometimes the exact amount of this consideration is stated, but often a nominal amount (such as $10) is mentioned in the deed as the consideration paid. This tends to keep the actual purchase price a secret known only to the parties.

Next, the property being transferred must be described accurately so that the precise boundaries can be determined. A mere street address is an insufficient description in the deed because the address does not establish the exact property boundaries and is subject to change. A buyer frequently discovers that the street number by which his or her new property is known (and where mail is delivered) is not the number stated in other documents; at some time in the past, the number was changed. To describe the real property's precise location, the metes-and-bounds system, the rectangular survey or a reference to plats should be used. We will consider each of these systems later in this chapter.

The legal description is followed by the words that actually convey the property interest. Recall from Chapter 4 that interests in real property can include several estates in land, such as fee simple or life estates. The words of conveyance must make it clear what interest is being transferred. The grantor then must sign the deed. Before a deed can be recorded, most states require that the grantor sign in the presence of one or more witnesses (who also sign the document).

Once the deed is properly signed, it can be said to have been *executed,* or subjected to all requirements that establish its validity.

Finally, the deed must be delivered to the grantee. Title to the property is not actually transferred from the grantor to the grantee until delivery has been completed. Of course, it is assumed for the purposes of this discussion that the grantee accepts the deed. Refusal to accept the deed results in an ineffective delivery. Although a transfer of title need not be recorded in the public records to be valid, the grantee must record the new deed in the county's record or deed office to be assured of protection against a claim that the grantor later transferred his or her title to someone else. The public records system will be discussed in more detail in Chapter 15.

Additional Elements

Although the elements just described are the only ones essential to a valid deed, the most common types of deeds contain additional elements called **covenants** and **warranties.**

A covenant is any agreement or promise, and a warranty is a guarantee that the statements made are true. Traditionally, there are four covenants and one warranty: (1) covenant against encumbrances, (2) covenant of seisin or ownership, (3) covenant of quiet enjoyment, (4) covenant of further assurances and (5) warranty forever. Whether all, some or none of these items exists in a deed depends on the type of deed required to be given by the grantor. In some states, the five items are not expressly stated in the deed, but are incorporated by reference to statute.

Types of Deeds

Many kinds of deeds exist, each having its own special characteristics. The more common types are general warranty deeds, special warranty deeds, bargain and sale deeds and quitclaim deeds.

General Warranty Deed   The warranty deed is the broadest type of all deeds. In a **general warranty deed,** the grantor makes promises that cover the traditional covenants and warranty. The grantor assures the grantee that no liens or encumbrances other than those on public record exist against the property (**covenant against encumbrances**), that the grantor has a fee simple interest in the property and that he or she is in full possession of the interest being conveyed and thus has the right to convey it (**covenant of seisin**). (The covenant against encumbrances does not mean that there are no encumbrances on the property, but rather that if there are encumbrances, they will be listed in the

Figure 7.1	General Warranty Deed

I THIS DEED, made this 20th day of December, 1996, between Harold J. Stewart and Gladys Atwater Stewart, husband and wife, of St. Joseph, Missouri, hereinafter referred to as "Grantors," and Frank L. Barr and Elizabeth McKenna Barr, husband and wife, St. Joseph, Missouri, hereinafter referred to as "Grantees."

II WITNESSETH, that Grantors, in consideration of the sum of ten dollars ($10.00), receipt whereof is hereby acknowledged, do grant, sell and convey unto Grantees, their heirs and assigns, all that tract or parcel of land with improvements thereon located in Buchanan County, Missouri, described as follows:

Part of SW¼ of the SE¼ Section 14, T. 57 N., R. 35W., of the 5th P.M., Buchanan County, State of Missouri, beginning at a point being 202 feet East of the SW corner of the SE¼ of said Section 14; running thence North 8 degrees East 200 feet to an iron pin; running thence due East 100 feet to an iron pin; running thence South 8 degrees West 200 feet to an iron pin; running thence due East 100 feet to the point of beginning. This property is that described as Lot 3, Block G, of the Harris Billups Estate, as recorded in Plat Book 8, page 37, in the Office of the Clerk of the Circuit Court of Buchanan County, Missouri.

III TO HAVE AND TO HOLD the premises hereby granted to Grantees, their heirs and assigns in fee simple forever.

IV The Grantors warrant that the premises are free from all encumbrances except for the following:
   (a) The underground gas line easement running along the eastern boundary within five feet thereof
   (b) All other restrictions of record

V The Grantors, having a fee simple interest and the right to convey such interest, warrant that Grantees, their heirs and assigns shall enjoy quietly and peaceably possession of the premises.

VI It is further warranted that Grantors shall procure and execute any further assurances of the title to the premises and that Grantors will forever defend the title to the premises against all claims.

IN WITNESS WHEREOF, Grantors have set their signatures and seals, the day and year first written above.

_____ (Seal)

Harold J. Stewart

_____ (Seal)

Gladys Atwater Stewart

Signed, sealed and delivered in the presence of

_____

_____

Notary Public, Buchanan County, Missouri

_____

*This form is intended for instructional purposes only and should not be relied on in practice, as it may not satisfy all existing circumstances. In most states, warranty deeds must be prepared by lawyers.

deed. In many states, encumbrances that are open and visible and that benefit the land are also excluded.) The grantor also promises that the grantee's enjoyment of the property will not be disturbed by some party claiming to own or to have a lien on it (**covenant of quiet enjoyment**). These covenants relate to the present condition of the grantor's title.

A general warranty deed further assures the grantee that the grantor will execute any future documents needed to perfect the grantor's title (**covenant of further assurances**). Finally, the grantor promises to always defend the title conveyed (**warranty forever**). These latter two items relate to the grantor's duties as they might arise in the future.

In the typical residential sales transaction, the buyer should insist that the sales contract require the seller to transfer title by warranty deed. Figure 7.1 presents a sample warranty deed for a single-family home transaction.

The traditional warranty deed is not divided by section headings, as shown in Figure 7.1. The Roman numerals are used only to facilitate the explanation that follows. Section I identifies the parties as "Grantors" and "Grantees." Section II discloses the consideration paid in return for the deed, states that the property is being conveyed and describes the property's boundaries. Section III actually indicates that the grantees now hold the property in a fee simple absolute estate. These first three sections plus the grantors' signatures satisfy the necessary elements of a deed.

Because Figure 7.1 is a general warranty deed, the remaining paragraphs contain the covenants and warranty previously discussed. For example, Section IV provides the grantors' promise that no encumbrances exist against the property other than those clearly stated. Section V includes the grantors' statement that they have a fee simple interest and the right to convey this interest to another person. This provision also contains the covenant of quiet enjoyment. Section VI includes the covenant of further assurances and the warranty forever. This latter covenant and warranty create the grantors' duty to provide any documents of title needed in the future to give the grantees clear title. For example, the grantors have promised that if this deed is defective for any reason, they will sign a new deed free of all defects.

When the deed has been signed, or executed, by the grantors and the witnesses, it is ready to be delivered to the grantees. Remember that title to real property actually passes only when the deed is delivered and accepted.

A warranty deed provides some protection to the purchaser concerning the acquisition of "good title." This protection, however, may not extend to "marketability" of the title. If, for example, a neighbor has obtained an unrecorded easement by prescription (as described in Chapter 5) over the land being transferred, the grantee under a warranty deed can successfully sue the grantor for the amount by which this encumbrance has diminished the property. In this situation, the grantor would have breached the covenant of quiet enjoyment and the covenant against encumbrances. Some states have interpreted the covenants and warranties of a deed as being breached only if the grantee loses possession to another party. Obviously, under this interpretation, the existence of a prescriptive easement would not breach the covenant of quiet enjoyment or the covenant against encumbrances.

| **Figure 7.2** | Language of a Quitclaim Deed |

The Grantors, their heirs and assigns, convey all the interests, if any, they might have in the premises hereby grant Grantees, their heirs and assigns, in fee simple forever. The Grantors, their heirs and assigns, shall not hereafter claim or demand any right or title to the aforesaid premises or any part thereof, but they and every one of them shall be excluded and forever barred.

Special Warranty Deed   A **special warranty deed** limits the extent of the seller's warranties to events that occurred during the seller's period of ownership. It does not protect the grantee against encumbrances that may have arisen before the grantor took title. The grantor's warrants cover only title defects that occurred during the grantor's ownership. For example, a corporation might give a special warranty deed to protect itself against any potential liabilities resulting from a foreclosure that happened before it owned the property. This type of deed is similar to the grant deed, which is commonly used in California. Title insurance, discussed in Chapter 15, is highly recommended if a general warranty deed is not obtained.

Bargain and Sale Deed   A deed that implies the grantor has title to the property and the right to convey it, but does not contain any express covenants as to the title's validity, is called a **bargain and sale deed.** This deed is also called a *warranty deed without covenants.*

In essence, the bargain and sale deed simply specifies that the grantor "does hereby grant, sell, and convey" some interest in real property to the grantee. If the sales contract fails to specify what type of deed must be delivered, the bargain and sale deed may be the only one required. If the buyer wants to make certain he or she receives a warranty deed, this must be clearly stated in the sales contract.

Quitclaim Deed   A **quitclaim deed** transfers any interest that the grantor may have in the property described, but does not imply that the grantor has any valid interest in it. The quitclaim deed is most commonly used to clear defects in the title to property. For example, suppose Bob wished to sell land he allegedly owned to David, but Clare, Bob's sister, claimed to own a one-fourth interest in the land. Before David would be willing to purchase the land, he would want a quitclaim deed from Clare. That deed would indicate that Clare had relinquished her claim to her one-fourth interest, but she would not be liable for any defects in the title. If David wished to get full clear title to the land, he typically would insist on receiving a general warranty deed from Bob, as well as the quitclaim deed from Clare.

Similarly, a quitclaim deed is also used to release marital interests in a property. If Bob and Jane divorce, and Jane is awarded ownership of the family home, Bob may be required to sign a quitclaim deed that releases any interest he may have in the property to Jane. The quitclaim deed would serve as evidence that Bob no longer holds an interest in the property after the divorce.

The grantee who takes property under a quitclaim deed must understand that he or she may receive nothing of value. A person could give a quitclaim deed

Principal Meridians and Base Lines in the United States   **Figure 7.3**

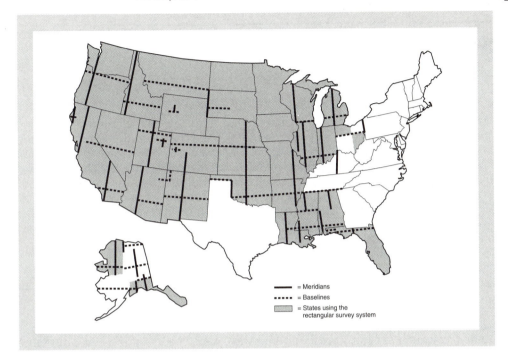

= Meridians
= Baselines
= States using the rectangular survey system

describing a neighbor's land, or even a university's football stadium, for that matter. Under a quitclaim deed, the grantor conveys all the interests possessed without any assurances that any rights of ownership exist. If the grantor has no rights in the property, nothing is transferred.

A sample of the language used in a quitclaim deed is shown in Figure 7.2. This language would be substituted for Sections III through VI of Figure 7.1.

Degree of Protection   It is important to understand the degree of protection each type of deed gives to the grantee. The order in which these types of deeds were discussed is also the order of the amount of protection provided. The general warranty deed contains the greatest assurances by the grantor that the grantee will have security for nearly all potential claims. The special warranty deed (and the grant deed) limits the grantor's liability to title defects that occurred during the grantor's ownership. The bargain and sale deed simply states that the grantor has the right to convey the title involved, but all other assurances are missing. Finally, the grantor who gives a quitclaim deed does not even promise that he or she has any rights in the land at all.

Deeds for Special Uses   Several other kinds of deeds have specific purposes. Each of these specialized deeds is named for the signer, and the warranties given, if any, depend on that signer's capacity. An **executor's deed** is an example. An executor of an estate seldom promises that the title being transferred is free of all defects. Therefore, the executor covenants only that he or she conveys the title held by the deceased person and that the executor has not encumbered the property in his or her capacity as executor. A grantee taking property

Real Estate Today   *Legal Highlight*

How Did an Acre Get To Be an Acre?

Unlike the rational metric system, the English system of land measurement that the United States inherited doesn't seem to make much sense. It does, however, but only if related to experience rather than to mathematics. Village farmland in medieval England was laid out in long rows so that plows drawn by oxen would not have to turn around often. A strip of land a furrow long and wide enough to be plowed in a day was called an *acre.* Its actual size varied from one part of the country to another, however, until a standard measure was introduced by Edmond Gunter during the time of King James I. Gunter defined a chain as 66 feet and a furlong (the length of furrow for an ox-drawn plow) as ten chains. An acre was defined as the length of a furlong by the width of one chain (660 feet by 66 feet, or 43,560 square feet). Eight furlongs stretch 5,280 feet, or a mile, and 640 rectangular acres fit in a square mile. It's all very logical, but only if your frame of reference is medieval England. ■

under any such special deed must be aware that the grantor's covenants and warranties are very limited or nonexistent.

LEGAL DESCRIPTIONS

A proper description of the property involved is essential in all documents that affect title to real estate. When it comes to the actual transfer of title to real estate through a deed, a precise legal description is necessary. Specification of the exact boundaries of the land being conveyed is essential for a valid transfer. In the United States, three methods commonly are used to obtain a precise legal description of land—the metes-and-bounds system, the rectangular survey system and reference to official plats.

Metes and Bounds

The original way to achieve a formal legal description of the exact boundaries of any piece of land was to refer to **metes and bounds.** Metes are the distances used in a description, and bounds are the directions of the boundaries that enclose a piece of land. A metes-and-bounds description starts at a designated point of beginning and, through specific distances, directions and reference points, locates the outlying boundaries of the land. Today, particularly in residential subdivisions, such reference points commonly are iron stakes or pins that were driven into the ground at the corners of each lot.

A typical modern metes-and-bounds description might start as follows: "Beginning at an iron pin on the western side of Westella Street 95 feet south

Quandrangles Divided into Townships   **Figure 7.4**

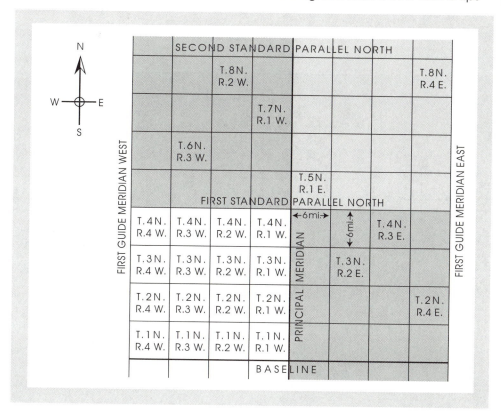

from the southwestern corner of the intersection of 6th Avenue and Westella Street, as measured along the western side of Westella Street." This language describes simply the beginning point of the measurement. Thereafter, each boundary is detailed—its length, its direction and the points where it begins and ends. It is vital that the boundaries described actually enclose the property involved. In other words, each boundary must begin at the preceding boundary's end and end at the next boundary's beginning. The description of the last side always must conclude at the original point of beginning.

By now, it should be obvious that reference points are crucial to the metes-and-bounds description. Before developers began to use iron pins to mark these points, natural monuments often were used. Such a monument might be "the large oak tree," "the spring-fed stream" or "the old Indian rock mound." Although reference to such natural objects could cause some confusion because they are subject to change over time, they still are used today to describe some rural land. The following land description, found in an old deed in North Carolina, demonstrates an interesting use of natural monuments as reference points in a standard metes-and-bounds description:

Beginning at an ash bush on the North bank of Withrow's Creek above the bridge, corner to the lands of R. N. Barber, and running thence North 14 degrees West 17.50 chains [one chain equals 66 feet] to a stone pile, in the

Figure 7.5   A Township Divided into Sections

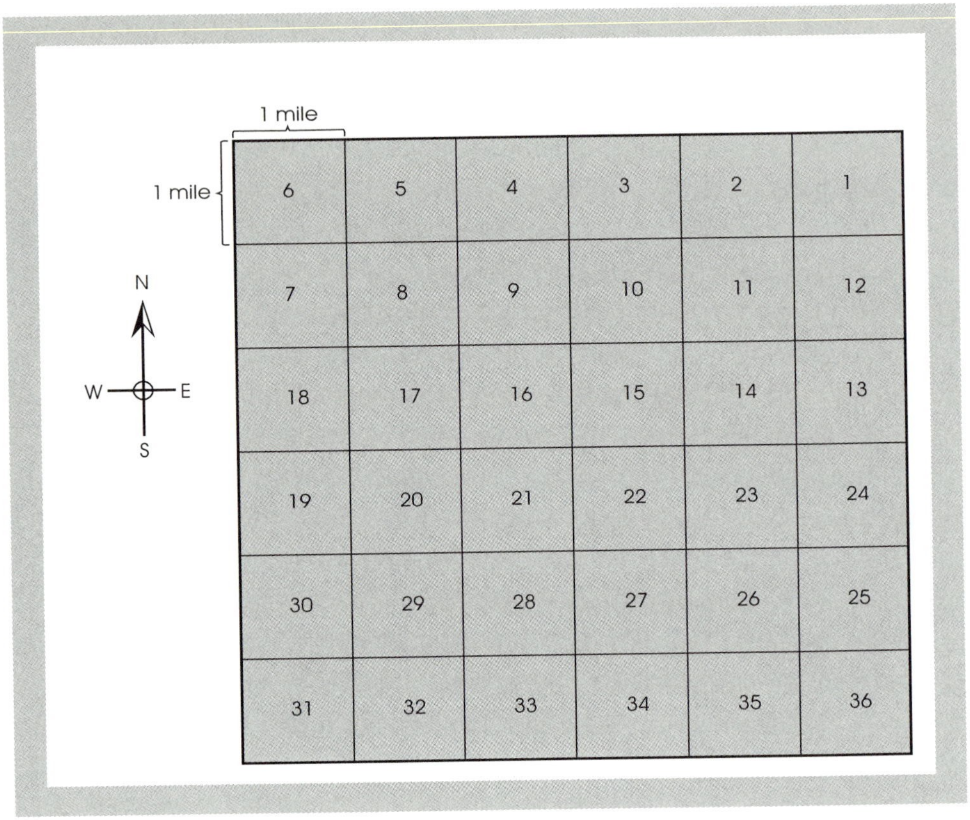

line of Mrs. E. M. Summerell; running thence North 68 degrees East 6.56 chains to a post oak, corner to the lands of Elias Barber; running thence South 27 degrees East 8.80 chains to a hickory on the North bank of Withrow's Creek, corner to the lands of Jane Barber; running thence Southwesterly up said creek 13.75 chains to the point of beginning, containing 12 $\frac{1}{10}$ acres, more or less.

A legal description does not describe "the side of the hill"; it defines a flat plane that may or may not have a mountain in it. In mountain states, many a seller will tell you he or she has, say, 20 fenced acres, thinking he or she is really selling 20 acres—not the actual smaller number of surveyed acres. For example, suppose a tract of land measures 1,000 feet by 1,000 feet, or approximately 23 acres. If the property contains a steeply sloped hill within its boundaries, the actual ground area of this tract could be much more than 23 acres.

Rectangular Survey System

Shortly after the end of the Revolutionary War, when the westward movement from the original states began, a method of describing wilderness land was required. The U.S. Congress approved a description method known as the

Subdivision of a Section (640 Acres) | **Figure 7.6**

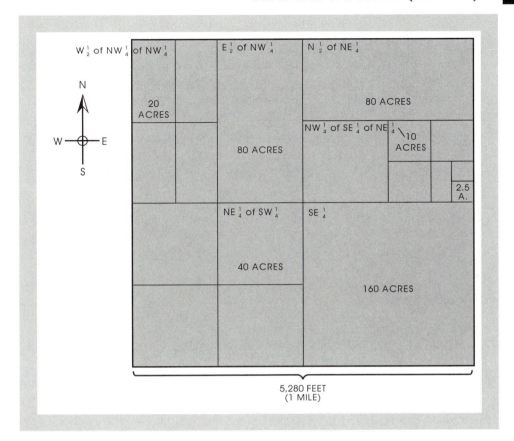

5,280 FEET
(1 MILE)

rectangular survey system. With the exception of Texas, land descriptions in all states west of the Mississippi, the five states formed from the Northwest Territory and most of Alabama, Florida and Mississippi are based on this method.

Principal Meridians and Base Lines The rectangular survey system is based first on **principal meridians** running north and south and **base lines** running east and west. Placement of these meridians and base lines generally coincides with an established landmark, such as the mouth of the Ohio River. The principal meridian was drawn north-south through the river's mouth, and the base line was drawn east-west to intersect the meridian at the landmark. The principal meridians and base lines are shown in Figure 7.3.

Townships The land on each side of a principal meridian is divided into six-mile-wide strips known as *ranges,* which are numbered consecutively east or west of the principal meridian. Lines running east and west parallel with a base line and six miles apart are called **township lines.** The range and township lines form the basic unit of the rectangular survey, the **township,** an area of land approximately six miles square.

Figure 7.7   Aerial Photograph of Land Surveyed under the Metes-and-
                                  Bounds System

To identify a specific township, reference is made to the intersection of the principal meridian and the base line. For example, the shaded township in Figure 7.4 is Township 3 North, Range 2 West, indicated as T. 3 N., R. 2 W.

Townships are not only the basic unit of the rectangular survey system; they often are the basis of political subdivisions as well. Somewhat confusingly, however, the term is also used to describe political subdivisions in states that were not surveyed under the rectangular system.

Sections   The rectangular survey system divides each township into 36 equal **sections.** Within any given township, sections were numbered beginning in the northeast corner, moving westerly, then southerly one section, and back easterly. The process continued until all sections were numbered. Figure 7.5 demonstrates this numbering process. Each section consists of one square mile, or 640 acres.

In the states covered by the rectangular survey, rural land generally is sold in patchwork pieces. Of course, farms in these states may be smaller than the sectional size of 640 acres. For example, farms claimed under the Homestead Act were one-quarter section, or 160 acres. For another example, a buyer might purchase the land indicated in the shaded portion of Figure 7.6, the northwest quarter of the southeast quarter of the northeast quarter of Section 14 of Township 2 North, Range 4 West (T. 2 N., R. 4 W.). How many acres did the buyer purchase? The answer is ten.

Figure 7.8

Aerial Photograph of Land Surveyed under the Rectangular Survey System

Aerial photographs clearly show the effect a particular method of land survey has on rural areas. Under the metes-and-bounds survey system, farmlands are laid out in the random pattern illustrated in Figure 7.7, a photograph of farmland in the eastern United States. A comparable rural area surveyed under the rectangular system, with its even patchwork pattern, is shown in Figure 7.8. This photograph of land in Kansas is typical of the midwestern and western United States.

Combined Use of Metes-and-Bounds and Rectangular Survey Systems

The rectangular survey system describes very accurately the extensive acreage involved in farmland. It becomes difficult to use, however, when one wishes to describe the small subdivision lots found in most communities. Subdividing a section of 640 acres into lots of one-half acre or less is an all but endless task. Therefore, metes-and-bounds descriptions become vital to clear legal descriptions.

For example, it will be of the utmost necessity to have a precise legal description of the half-acre lot transferred in the general warranty deed presented earlier in Figure 7.1. Because the Stewarts' land is located in St. Joseph, Missouri,

Figure 7.9   Location of the Stewarts' Lot in the Southwestern Quarter of the Southeastern Quarter of the Section of the Township Described in Their Sales Contract

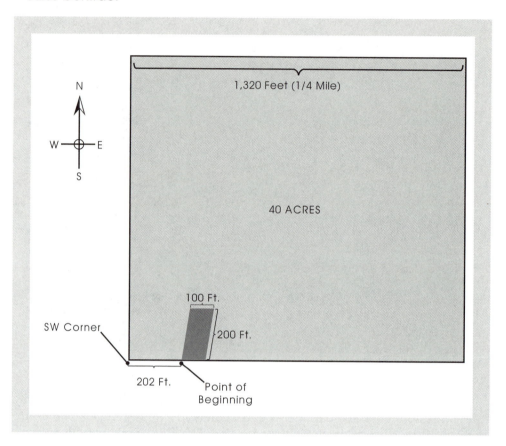

a combined type of land description is most appropriate. The description of the Stewarts' lot could appear as follows:

> Part of the SW¼ of the SE¼ of Section 14, T. 57 N., R. 35 W., of the 5th P.M., Buchanan County, State of Missouri, beginning at a point being 202 feet East of the SW corner of the SE¼ of said Section 14; running thence North 8 degrees East 200 feet to an iron pin; running thence due East 100 feet to an iron pin; running thence South 8 degrees West 200 feet to an iron pin; running thence due West 100 feet to the point of beginning.

Figure 7.9 represents the southwestern quarter of the southeastern quarter of Section 14 in Township 57 North, Range 35 West, of the fifth principal meridian. The Stewarts' lot appears near the southwest corner.

Figure 7.10 shows a residential development that has grown up in and around farmland that was surveyed under the rectangular survey system. Here, we see the combined use of the metes-and-bounds system applied on the rectangular survey system.

Aerial Photograph of Land Surveyed by the Combined
Metes-and-Bounds and Rectangular Systems

Figure 7.10

References to Plats

A common alternative and supplement to these methods of legally describing
real estate is to refer to land surveys, called **plats,** that have been recorded as
part of the official public record. Plats or similar documents include the streets,
blocks and lots as they actually exist. A plat of a subdivision appears in Figure
7.11. Land can be described simply by reference to the number of the lot as it
appears in the plat of the block of the subdivision in which the lot is located. For
example, the general warranty deed in Figure 7.1 also described the Stewarts'
property as "Lot 3, Block G, of the Harris Billups Estate, as recorded in Plat Book
8, page 37, in the Office of the Clerk of the Circuit Court of Buchanan County,
Missouri." Although reference to a plat constitutes an accurate legal description
by itself, such references generally are used in conjunction with other types of
descriptions.

Figure 7.11   Plat of a Subdivision

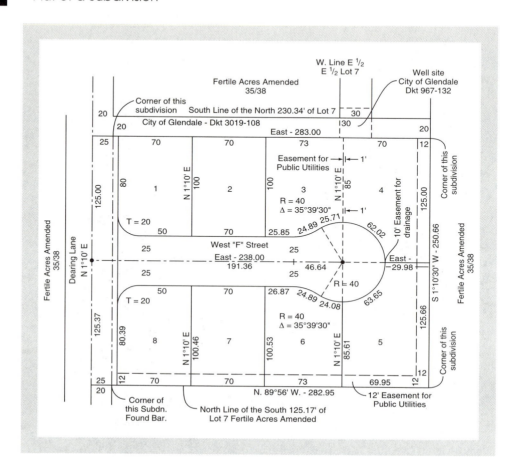

In the case of a condominium, each individual unit of the complex is described separately by referring to a previously recorded plat of the complex. In addition, a condominium description includes a reference to the fractional share (based on the number of units) of the common areas within the complex.

A different problem of legal description arises when the property does not actually touch the ground—for example, an apartment condominium on the 32nd floor, air rights above a railroad line or subsurface mining rights below the surface of the earth. In these cases, vertical distances are measured from a point of known vertical height called a *datum*. The most common vertical reference is mean sea level, but official bench marks have been established all over the United States by the Coast and Geodetic Survey that can be used as reference points for both horizontal and vertical distances. Thus, the air lot of the 32nd-floor condominium might be described by identifying the parcel of land underneath and the vertical measurements of the airspace above this ground lot.

Preparing the Legal Description

A proper legal description of a property often can be obtained from the tax office or other public records. However, an original description should probably be prepared by an attorney. This avoids potential risks for buyer, seller and broker that can result from an improperly drafted legal description. A correctly drafted legal description is important particularly in deeds, mortgages and other instruments directly affecting title to land.

Chapter Review

1. A deed is a legal document that conveys title, or ownership, from one party to another. A valid deed must be written formally to include (1) identification of the parties, (2) a legal description of the property, (3) language of conveyance in return for the consideration named and (4) signature of the grantor. It then must be (5) delivered to and accepted by the grantee.

2. Deeds are differentiated by the covenants and warranties that the grantor makes regarding the title being transferred. Such assurances may include (1) covenant against encumbrances, (2) covenant of seisin, (3) covenant of quiet enjoyment, (4) covenant of further assurances and (5) warranty forever. The general warranty deed, special warranty deed, bargain and sale deed and quitclaim deed are the most common deeds used in real estate transactions. Each has a special purpose, with which the parties involved should be familiar.

3. Accurate legal descriptions of land are essential to the transfer of real estate titles. All parties must know the precise boundaries of the land being transferred or encumbered. Legal descriptions refer generally to the metes and bounds of the property, to the rectangular survey system, to applicable plats or to some combination thereof.

4. A metes-and-bounds description is made up of the exact distances (metes) and directions (bounds) of the property's boundaries. Starting at a beginning point, the description traces the outline of the land involved. The beginning point, as well as each corner, is marked by an iron pin or some natural monument. Natural monuments still referred to in descriptions of rural land might include "the big maple tree," "the mound of granite" or "the stream known as Wilson's Creek." References to iron pins are most common in descriptions of residential lots by the metes-and-bounds method.

5. Shortly after the United States gained its independence, the federal government began to sell undeveloped land west of the original states. A new method of describing this wilderness land, known as the *rectangular survey system,* was approved by Congress. Principal meridians were

drawn in a north-south direction, intersected by base lines running east and west. From the point of intersection, townships measure six miles by six miles established in each direction. Townships are subdivided again into 36 sections. Each section contains one square mile, or 640 acres. An acre contains 43,560 square feet.

6. A plat is an official survey of a real estate subdivision showing streets, blocks and lots. Often, a reference to the lot, block and name of the subdivision, as found in the specified plat book, is used to describe a parcel of land.

Key Terms

bargain and sale deed   a deed which simply states that the grantor has title to the property and the right to convey it, but does not contain any express covenants or warranties to the title's validity.

base lines   east-west lines used as reference points in the rectangular survey system.

covenant   a promise or guarantee made by a grantor in a deed.

covenant against encumbrances   an assurance made by the grantor that there are no encumbrances against the property other than those of public record.

covenant of further assurances   an assurance made by the grantor that the grantor will execute any future documents needed to perfect the grantee's title.

covenant of seisin   an assurance made by the grantor that he or she is in full possession of the interest being conveyed by a deed and thus has the right to convey it.

covenant of quiet enjoyment   an assurance made by the grantor that no other party will disturb the grantee claiming to own the property or to have a lien on it; a promise from the lessor that the tenant has the right of exclusive possession of the property during the term of the lease.

deed   a written document that evidences ownership.

executor's deed   a special use deed used by the executor of an estate to transfer ownership without any assurances regarding the quality of title being transferred.

general warranty deed   the deed that offers the most protection to the grantee, complete with all relevant covenants and warranties.

metes and bounds   a legal method for describing the exact boundaries of a property; metes refer to the distances and bounds refer to the directions of the property's boundaries.

plat   a detailed land survey drawing, usually prepared by a professional surveyor, that shows the features of a property and its legal description.

principal meridians   north-south lines used as reference points in the rectangular survey system.

quitclaim deed   a deed used to transfer any interest a grantor may or may not have in a property, without implying that the grantor has a valid interest to convey.

rectangular survey system   a grid-based system used to legally describe the location of a property.

section   a grid-based system used to legally describe the location of a property.

special warranty deed   similar to a general warranty deed, except the covenants and warranties apply only to events that occurred during the grantor's period of ownership.

title   legal ownership.

township   a 36-square mile area formed by township and range lines in the rectangular survey system.

township lines   east-west lines that run parallel to base lines in the rectangular survey system.

warranty   a promise or guarantee made by a grantor in a deed.

warranty forever   an assurance made by the grantor to always defend the title conveyed to the grantee.

Study Exercises

1.   What are the essential elements of a deed?

2.   Describe the covenants and warranty contained in a general warranty deed.

3.   What are the differences between a general warranty deed and a special warranty deed? Between a general warranty deed and a bargain and sale deed?

4.   What is a quitclaim deed, and when might it be used?

5.   Name the three most common methods of describing real estate.

6.   According to the rectangular survey, if a buyer purchases the south half of the northeast quarter of a section of land, how many acres has he or she purchased?

7. How many square feet are in an acre? How many acres are in a section? How many sections are in a township?

8. Use a simple sketch to show the location of T. 5 S., R. 6 E. Label the principal meridian, base line and each of the range and township lines appropriately.

9. Use a simple sketch to show the location of Section 17 in a township.

10. Use a simple sketch to show the location of the parcel described as "the NW¼ of the NE¼ of the SE¼ of the SE¼" of a section. How many square feet does the parcel contain?

For Further Reading

Gibson, F., J. Karp and E. Klayman. *Real Estate Law,* 3d ed. (Chicago: Real Estate Education Company, 1992).

Reilly, J. W. *The Language of Real Estate,* 4th ed. (Chicago: Real Estate Education Company, 1993).

PART THREE

Real Estate
Services

CHAPTER 8
Real Estate Brokerage

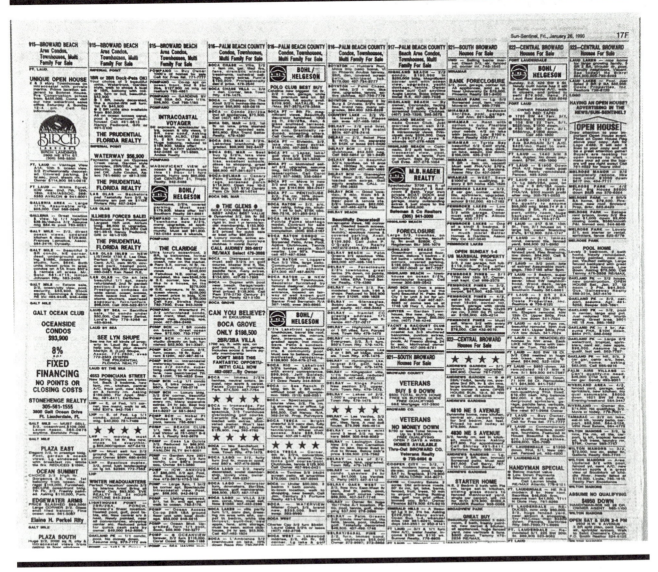

Each year, there are nearly 4 million sales of existing homes in the United States—a $70 billion business. Brokerage firms are a key part of the real estate industry, helping people buy and sell properties every day.

Real Estate Today

- *Close-Up*
  Marketing Real
  Estate on the
  World Wide Web

- *Legal Highlight*
  Seller's Agent's
  Obligations to the
  Buyer

- *Legal Highlight*
  Enforcement of
  Fair Housing Laws

Chapter Preview

THE LARGE SIZE (in terms of capital required) and long-term nature of real estate make transactions relatively complex. Because most individuals sell or purchase real property infrequently, trained specialists are often helpful in overcoming the complexities of real estate transactions. These specialists include real estate brokers, property managers and appraisers. The three chapters in this section evaluate each of these service activities in turn.

The objective of this chapter is to describe the typical real estate sales process, then consider numerous aspects of the real estate brokerage business, including

- the difference between real estate brokers and salespersons;
- state licensing and regulation of brokers and salespersons;
- the legal nature of agency relationships;
- the role of real estate brokers in real estate transactions;
- types of listing agreements, namely the (1) open listing, (2) exclusive-agency listing, (3) exclusive-right-to-sell listing and (4) net listing;
- the buyer representation agreement;
- duties and rights of brokers, sellers and buyers;
- the termination of agency relationships;
- types of real estate brokerage firms and their characteristics; and
- issues relating to broker and salesperson compensation.

THE REAL ESTATE SALES PROCESS

When a property owner decides to sell a property, or a potential buyer decides to purchase one, real estate brokers can often provide useful assistance. The primary functions of the real estate brokerage industry are to match properties and customers and guide buyers and sellers through the complexities of real estate transactions. Both buyers and sellers of real estate need to understand the sales process, which typically involves the following steps: (1) listing, (2) marketing the property and qualifying buyers, (3) presentation and negotiations, (4) contracts and (5) settlement or closing.

Listing Agreement

The **listing agreement** is the contract that defines the relationship between the property owner and the real estate broker. This agreement authorizes the broker to begin searching for a buyer for the property. Perhaps the most critical point in the listing agreement is the determination of an offering price. Most sellers do not have adequate market information to determine the value of their property. If the offering price is too high, the property probably will not sell within a reasonable period of time, if at all; if it is too low, the owner will not receive as much as he or she should. Usually, the broker will have enough market data to suggest an asking price, but on a larger or more complex property, it may be necessary to obtain a professional appraisal.

Marketing the Property and Qualifying Buyers

With the listing agreement in place, the broker begins marketing the property to potential buyers. Marketing techniques include a For Sale sign on the lawn, newspaper advertisements, special television advertisements, open houses and even a home page on the World Wide Web (see the Close-Up on page 150). As responses to these advertisements are received, the broker deals with potential prospects directly.

In the process of searching for a buyer, the broker provides an important service for the seller: separating true prospects from casual shoppers or those who really do not have adequate financial resources to buy the property. For example, a family earning $30,000 a year and having little available equity may be quite ready and willing to buy a $175,000 house, but they probably will be unable to pay for it. The process of examining prospective buyers' ability to purchase the property is known as *qualifying the buyers*. Mortgage lenders also use this phrase when they determine a borrower's creditworthiness.

Presentation and Negotiations

After the broker has found a qualified and interested buyer, a period of presentation and negotiation begins. This period can last for a few hours or many months, depending on such factors as the complexity of the transaction, the extent to which the property actually meets the potential buyer's perceived needs and, of course, price. The buyer should remember that in these negotiations, the broker generally is employed by the seller and is obligated to represent the seller's interests. Accordingly, in any complicated transaction, the buyer may want to employ the services of a broker to represent his or her interests.

Contracts and Closing

If the parties agree, a contract that spells out the details of the agreement is drawn up and signed by both seller and buyer, a process discussed in Chapter 11. Though the broker cannot provide legal advice unless he or she is a licensed attorney, the broker can assist the parties in negotiating an agreement and committing that agreement to paper. After insurance is obtained, financing is arranged and the deed and other necessary legal papers are prepared, the transaction can be closed. At the closing, or settlement, of the transaction, ownership is formally transferred to the buyer. Real estate closings are described in Chapter 15. With this general discussion of the real estate sales process in mind, we now turn our attention to more specific aspects of the real estate brokerage business.

REAL ESTATE BROKERS AND SALESPERSONS

In general terms, a **broker** is an intermediary who brings together buyers and sellers, assists in negotiating agreements between them, executes their orders and receives **commissions** (or brokerage) in compensation for services rendered. The broker does not take ownership of the item being transferred from seller to buyer, but merely negotiates a transaction between the parties. A **real estate broker** is a specialized type of broker—an intermediary licensed by the state in which he or she operates, who arranges real estate sale or lease transactions for fees or commissions. A **real estate salesperson** is also a broker in the general sense, but, under the laws of the state, is authorized to act only under the direction of a licensed real estate broker. In other words, salespersons can carry out only those responsibilities assigned to them by their supervising brokers.

LICENSING OF SALESPERSONS AND BROKERS

Although you need not hold a real estate license to conduct real estate transactions on your own behalf, a license is required if you engage in real estate activities on behalf of someone else. The license and educational requirements imposed by states generally do not constitute serious obstacles to most people who want to enter the field, and the number of brokers and salespersons in the industry tends to expand or contract with swings in demand for real estate.

All states and the District of Columbia require that real estate salespersons and brokers obtain licenses. The license requirements vary from state to state and also depend on whether the applicant wishes to become a salesperson or a broker. Typically, an applicant for a salesperson's license must have completed high school and a basic real estate course. In addition, the applicant must pass a written test given by the state real estate commission. The prospective salesperson usually needs no previous experience if educational requirements have

Real Estate Today

Marketing Real Estate on the World Wide Web

Although many feel it is still in its infancy, the World Wide Web has great promise of becoming a valuable resource for the real estate industry. A search on the words *real estate* using any of the popular search engines (Infoseek, Lycos, etc.) and a web browser such as Netscape results in hundreds of web sites to explore. Many of these sites allow real estate brokers from across the country and around the world to use the web to market all types of properties. Potential homebuyers, apartment renters and investors can use the web to search for the properties that match their criteria, then view photographs of the properties. These sites also make it simple to contact the listing broker via electronic mail.

One popular World Wide Web site with an emphasis on residential property is located at this address, http://www.america-homes.com/. It takes you to the home page of the World-Wide Real Estate Network. The site permits licensed real estate brokers to include their current listings in the database, complete with photographs and text-based descriptions of the homes. Potential buyers can search the database for their dream homes by browsing the listings or by specifying the features they desire in a home. If a particular home catches the eye, a click of the mouse sends an electronic mail request for the listing broker to provide more information. Undoubtedly, the World Wide Web will become an increasingly important marketing tool for real estate brokers and a great time-saver for potential buyers. ■

---

been met satisfactorily. To obtain a brokerage license, however, the applicant usually must work for several years as a licensed salesperson, complete additional real estate educational courses and pass a more comprehensive written test.

About half of the states now have continuing education requirements for both salespersons and brokers. The intent of these requirements is to ensure that those involved in real estate brokerage keep abreast of current developments in the field. Successful completion of the required course is a prerequisite for license renewal.

Because real estate licensing laws and regulations change from time to time, readers interested in obtaining real estate licenses should contact their local realty boards or state real estate commissions for full details on current licensing requirements.

REAL ESTATE BROKERAGE REGULATION

In addition to licensing salespersons and brokers, the state real estate commission or a similar body is responsible for ensuring that licensees obey laws designed to protect the public from unscrupulous business practices. These include misrepresentation, fraud and failure to comply with fair housing laws.

If the commission finds a licensee guilty of an infraction, it may revoke or suspend that person's license or invoke similar penalties.

In more severe cases, a legal judgment may be brought through a lawsuit by the injured party against a licensee or firm. Because these judgements sometimes are uncollectible due to a defendant's poor financial status, roughly 40 states either require that real estate brokers be bonded or, more commonly, maintain a state-sponsored recovery fund. A portion of each real estate license fee goes into the recovery fund, available to pay uncollectible judgments against licensees.

LEGAL ASPECTS OF THE BROKER-CLIENT RELATIONSHIP

Because people have neither the time nor the knowledge to accomplish everything they want or need to do, they hire other people to assist them. This certainly is true in real estate transactions, where a specialized knowledge of markets, law and financing is vital to the success of a transaction.

The law recognizes the relationship between an employer and an employee as that of principal and agent. The **principal** (employer) is the person who authorizes the **agent** (employee) to act on his or her behalf. The agent is a **fiduciary** of the principal, which means the agent is in a position of confidence and must perform his or her duties in the best interest of the principal. In addition to fair dealings, the principal owes the agent compensation for services, and the agent owes the principal the duties of good faith, diligence and loyalty.

The legal relationship known as **agency** applies to real estate transactions in several ways. First, a seller of real estate may authorize a broker to help locate a buyer. Second, a potential buyer may engage the services of a broker to search for available properties. Third, many brokers hire salespersons to assist in locating buyers and properties. These three relationships are created from written or oral contracts. In each case, one party is the principal, and the other is the agent. The broker is the agent in the relationship with the client (either seller or buyer), and the broker is the principal in the relationship with a salesperson. The salesperson is an agent of the broker and a **subagent** of the broker's principal.

THE ROLE OF REAL ESTATE BROKERS

Real estate brokers and salespersons play important roles in many real estate transactions. Traditionally, real estate brokers have been hired by property owners to help locate buyers for their properties. The broker's role is to advertise and market a property and assist the seller in finalizing the transaction once a buyer is found. In this situation, the broker is an agent of the seller (**seller's agent**). Brokers may also represent property owners who wish to lease their properties to tenants. Property management and leasing are discussed in the next chapter.

Many real estate transactions involve more than one broker. Frequently, one broker (called the **listing broker**) obtains a listing agreement with the property owner, while another broker (called the **selling broker**) actually locates a buyer. The selling broker in such a transaction may represent either the buyer or the seller. If the selling broker represents the seller, he or she is an agent (subagent) of the seller. If the selling broker represents the buyer, the broker is an agent of the buyer.

Increasingly, potential buyers hire brokers to assist them in locating properties for purchase. As a **buyer's agent,** the broker identifies properties that meet the buyer's specifications, then assist the buyer in negotiating a transaction for the desired property. In some cases, a single broker is employed by both the seller and the buyer to assist in the completion of a transaction. When this broker has fiduciary duties to both parties simultaneously, the broker is known as a **dual agent.** If the broker acts as a third party in the negotiations between the buyer and seller, the broker is known as a *transaction broker.* Most states' laws require that the broker disclose the nature of his or her agency relationship to all parties involved in the negotiations as soon as possible to avoid confusion and possible violations of the fiduciary responsibilities. The next section examines the creation of agency relationships between (1) sellers and brokers and (2) buyers and brokers.

THE CREATION OF AGENCY RELATIONSHIPS

Before a principal is bound by the acts of an agent, the agent must have actual or apparent authority to transact business on the principal's behalf. In other words, there must be evidence that the principal has hired the agent. Real estate brokers can act as agents for either sellers or buyers because a broker may be employed by either. A listing agreement refers to the agreement between the seller and the broker when the broker is an agent of the seller. A buyer representation agreement defines the agency relationship between the buyer and the broker when the broker is an agent of the buyer. We will examine each of these agency relationships in turn.

The Broker-Seller Relationship (Seller's Agent)

Property owners generally give real estate brokers authority to sell their property using a written document called a *listing agreement.* Because listing agreements are contractual in nature, the essential elements of a binding contract must be present. These elements are discussed more fully in Chapter 11. Only about 20 states actually require listing agreements to be in writing, but as in any transaction, a written contract always is preferable to an oral agreement to clarify the relationship established and the duties owed.

A listing agreement describes the property and states the asking price, the duties of the broker, the extent of authority granted and the rights of the broker to a commission. Various forms of listing agreements exist, and each has its own legal impact. The more common types of agreements are the open listing, the exclusive-agency listing and the exclusive-right-to-sell listing. These listing agreements create certain obligations between the broker and the seller, and the extent of the obligations depends on the type of agreement.

Suppose, for example, that Harold and Gladys Stewart are being transferred and want to sell their home in St. Joseph, Missouri. They have decided to hire Smith & Smyth Realty Company to assist them in this sale. The following paragraphs outline how the various types of listing agreements would affect the terms of this agency relationship.

Open Listing   If the Stewarts sign the document that appears in Figure 8.1, they grant an **open listing** to Smith & Smyth Realty Company. Such a listing begins with a paragraph identifying the parties to the agreement and their relationship as owner and broker. Section I describes the property to be sold. The description must be precise enough to identify exactly the property involved. Section II establishes the sales price for the property. Section III sets forth the broker's commission as a percentage of the purchase price. Section IV specifies the type of listing agreement and the conditions under which the broker is entitled to collect the commission.

By signing an open listing, the Stewarts authorize Smith & Smyth to find a willing buyer. Nevertheless, it is clear that the owners reserve the right to authorize another broker to locate a potential buyer. In addition, the Stewarts may sell their property without the aid of any broker. Under the open listing agreement, Smith & Smyth Realty is entitled to the stated commission only if it successfully brings a buyer to the Stewarts. Smith & Smyth will not receive any commission if either another broker or the Stewarts themselves sell the property.

The open listing has both advantages and disadvantages for the sellers. Because they are not limited to one broker, they have greater flexibility. On the other hand, the broker does not have as much incentive to concentrate on selling their property because the broker has no assurance of actually earning a commission. For this reason, the open listing agreement is seldom encouraged by brokers.

Exclusive-Agency Listing   If the Stewarts had signed an **exclusive-agency listing** agreement, the contract would be similar to the one in Figure 8.1 except that section IV would be replaced with the language shown in Figure 8.2. This listing differs from the open listing in that the Stewarts cannot authorize another broker to find a buyer as long as the exclusive-agency agreement is effective. Despite the limit placed on the Stewarts' use of brokers, they reserve the right to sell their property without becoming liable to pay Smith & Smyth a commission. This type of agreement may seem most beneficial to the sellers because they have one broker acting as their exclusive agent and can sell their property themselves without becoming liable for the commission. The broker may not be totally dedicated to marketing the property, however, because he or she could lose all rights to the commission on a sale-by-owner transaction.

Exclusive-Right-to-Sell Listing   An **exclusive-right-to-sell listing** is the most common type of listing agreement used in residential sales. Had the Stewarts signed this type of agreement with Smith & Smyth, section IV of the document would look like Figure 8.3. By that language, the listing broker is guaranteed a commission if the house is sold, whether by the listing broker, by another broker or by the owner. Of course, this exclusive right to sell lasts only as long as the listing agreement states, typically three months, as in our example. Under this relationship, the listing broker has the greatest incentive to promote the availability of the property. Often, the exclusive-right-to-sell listing

| **Figure 8.1** | Open Listing Agreement [*] |

Agreement made this *3rd* day of *October, 1996,* between *Harold and Gladys Steward, of 1097 Timbers Crossing, St. Joseph, Missouri,* herein referred to jointly as "Owner," and *Smith & Smyth Realty Company, of 243 South Thompson Street, St. Joseph, Missouri,* herein referred to as "Broker."

I   This listing agreement is for the real estate described as follows: *That lot and two-story, single-family residence located at 1097 Timbers Crossing in St. Joseph, Missouri. Such property is more accurately described as Lot 3, Block G, of the Harris Billups Estate, as recorded in Plat Book 8, page 37, in the Office of the Clerk of the Circuit Court of Buchanan County, Missouri.*

II   The selling price on the above-described property, herein referred to as the "property," shall be *One Hundred Twenty Five Thousand dollars ($125,000),* or such other price as Owner may agree to accept.

III   In consideration for the services provided by Broker, Owner agrees to pay Broker a commission equal to *seven percent (7%) of the purchase price of the property* as long as all the duties and conditions of this agreement are satisfied.

IV   Owner and Broker understand and agree that this is an open listing agreement, and Owner reserves the right to sell the property himself or through any other broker without payment to Broker of the commission established herein. Broker shall be entitled to such commission only in the event that

   (a)   Broker procures a prospect ready, willing and able to purchase the property on the terms established herein;

   (b)   Broker procures a buyer who does in fact purchase the property; or

   (c)   the property is sold, by Owner or any other person, at any time during this listing agreement or within *two (2) months* after its termination, to a prospect first submitted, directly or indirectly, to Owner by Broker.

Owner and Broker understand this agreement is to continue from *noon on October 3, 1996,* until *noon on January 4, 1997.*

IN WITNESS WHEREOF, the parties execute this agreement on the day and year first written above.

_____   _____
Smith & Smyth Realty Company   *Harold C. Stewart, Owner*

BY: _____   _____
    Thomas F. Smith, Broker   *Gladys Q. Stewart, Owner*

[*]This example and the three following are intended solely for instructional purposes and should not be relied on in practice, as they may not meet all particular circumstances. The portions printed in italics are left blank in the printed form, to be filled in at the time the agreement is made with the seller.

Exclusive-Agency Listing Agreement   **Figure 8.2**

IV   Owner and Broker understand and agree that this is an exclusive-agency listing, and Owner reserves the right to sell the property personally without payment to Broker of the commission established herein. Broker shall be entitled to such commission in the event that

   (a)   Broker procures a prospect ready, willing and able to purchase the property on the terms established herein;

   (b)   Broker procures a buyer who does in fact purchase the property;

   (c)   the property is sold by any broker during the term of this agreement; or

   (d)   the property is sold, by Owner or any other person, at any time during this listing agreement or within *two (2) months* after its termination, to a prospect first submitted, directly or indirectly, to Owner by Broker.

---

also is the most advantageous to the owner because the broker is encouraged to locate a willing buyer as quickly as possible.

Multiple-Listing Service Clause   Frequently, an exclusive-right-to-sell listing will be obtained by a broker who is a member of a **multiple-listing service** (MLS), an arrangement in which participating brokers make their listings available to all other members. If Smith & Smyth Realty Company were a member of the St. Joseph, Missouri, MLS, the language of the exclusive-right-to-sell agreement of Figure 8.3 would be followed by that in Figure 8.4. Under the multiple-listing service clause, Smith & Smyth typically must make the Stewarts' listing available to all other MLS members within a specified period from the time the listing agreement is signed. (This time period ranges from 48 hours to one week.) Through an MLS, sellers' properties get the greatest exposure, and potential buyers usually have access to the bulk of properties for sale.

Under an exclusive-right-to-sell listing distributed through the local MLS, Smith & Smyth, as listing agent, typically will receive 50 percent of the total sales commission. If a broker other than Smith & Smyth assists the buyer, that broker receives the remainder of the commission. Suppose the agreed-upon commission is 7 percent of the property's sales price. Thus, if the commission split is 50-50, and the seller and the buyer have different agents, each will receive 3.5 percent of the selling price. For example, if Acme Realty Company finds a buyer for the Stewarts' house at the asking price of $125,000, Smith & Smyth—as the listing agent—and Acme—as the selling agent—would receive $4,375 each of the $8,750 total commission.

Of course, Smith & Smyth may find a buyer for the Stewarts' property. In that case, it would be the listing agent and the selling agent at the same time and would receive the entire 7 percent commission.

Net Listing   A type of listing used very infrequently today, and illegal in many states, is the **net listing.** In this agreement, the seller is guaranteed a specified amount of money, while the broker receives the remainder of the sales price. The net listing obviously invites fraud because the broker has an incentive to deceive

| **Figure 8.3** | Exclusive-Right-to-Sell Listing Agreement |

IV   Owner and Broker understand that this is an exclusive-right-to-sell listing. Broker shall be entitled to the commission established herein in the event that

(a)   Broker procures a prospect ready, willing and able to purchase the property on the terms established herein;

(b)   Broker procures a buyer who does in fact purchase the property;

(c)   the property is sold by anyone, including Owner, during the term of this listing; or

(d)   the property is sold, by Owner or any other person, at any time during this listing agreement or within *two (2) months* after its termination, to a prospect first submitted, directly or indirectly, to Owner by Broker.

the seller about the fair market value of the property and thus obtain a larger commission.

The Broker's Right to a Commission

To be eligible to collect a commission, a broker must be hired by a principal. As discussed earlier, the seller's broker usually is hired when a written listing agreement is executed. An important purpose of the listing agreement is to make clear when a broker has earned a commission. Typically, a commission is payable to the broker when he or she either (1) procures a ready, willing and able buyer or (2) sells the property. (Section IV in Figures 8.1 through 8.3 demonstrates these conditions.)

Listing agreements also usually contain a clause protecting the broker from losing the commission when the buyer waits to purchase until the listing agreement expires. Under this clause, the broker is entitled to a commission if the property is sold within some reasonable time period, usually two to six months, after the expiration of the agreement to a prospect introduced to the property by the broker.

Thus, if the Stewarts were to sell their home on March 15 to a buyer who was shown the property by a salesperson from Smith & Smyth Realty (termination of the listing agreement was January 4), the real estate brokerage firm would be entitled to the 7 percent commission. If, however, the same person bought the property two years later, no commission would be due.

The Broker-Buyer Relationship (Buyer's Agent)

When a potential buyer hires a broker to assist in locating a property for purchase, the relationship between the broker and buyer should be clearly specified in a written document referred to as a **buyer representation agreement.** As in the case of listing agreements, buyer representation agreements must contain the essential elements of a contract. In addition, the document should specify the type of property desired, the duties and obligations of the buyer and seller

---

Multiple-Listing Service Clause | **Figure 8.4**

V It is understood that Broker is a member of the *St. Joseph Board of REALTORS®
multiple-listing service,* and it is understood further that Broker shall file this
listing with the multiple-listing system to be referred to its members. Such
members will act as subagents in procuring or attempting to procure a
purchaser in accordance with this agreement. If a sale or an exchange shall
be made through any subagent, all the terms of this agreement shall apply to
such transaction.

---

and the terms by which the broker will be paid for services rendered. A sample
buyer representation agreement is provided in Figure 8.5.

Types of Buyer Representation Agreements Similar to the different types of
listing agreements discussed above, buyer representation agreements may
specify that the broker has an exclusive right to represent or that the arrangement is an open one. Under an exclusive right to represent, the broker is entitled
to a commission if the potential buyer purchases a property with or without the
assistance of the broker. In an open arrangement, the broker is entitled to a commission only if the buyer purchases a property identified and suggested by the
broker. If the buyer finds a property without the broker's assistance, no commission is due.

Compensating the Buyer's Broker Structuring the compensation to a buyer's
broker properly is an important aspect of the buyer representation agreement.
In many cases, the agreement calls for a retainer fee at the time the contract is
signed, with a commission due if a property is purchased. The commission is
either a fixed fee or is calculated as a percentage of the transaction amount. If
the property is identified through the MLS, the buyer's broker will receive a commission split from the listing agent. Typically, the compensation due from the
buyer is reduced by this amount. Because the compensation due the broker is
calculated as a percentage of the purchase price, one might question whether
the broker will negotiate aggressively for the lowest price possible on behalf of
the buyer. Fortunately, the fiduciary responsibility owed to the principal pre-
cludes the agent from engaging in this type of behavior.

DUTIES AND RIGHTS UNDER AGENCY RELATIONSHIPS

Once any principal-agent relationship is established, each party owes the other
the duties of loyalty, good faith and diligence in fulfilling the conditions promised. These duties are not a matter of choice, but are created by state laws that
govern the agency relationship. In addition to their legal responsibilities, real
estate brokers and salespersons know that ethical business practices are critical
to continued professional success. For example, the National Association of
REALTORS®, the largest trade organization for real estate brokers and salespersons, holds its members to high ethical standards. In general, these standards
require fair dealings with clients, customers and the public.

| **Figure 8.5** | Buyer Representation Agreement* |

I   Parties:_____ ("Buyer") appoints_____ ("Broker") as Buyer's exclusive agent and grants Broker the exclusive right to represent and assist Buyer in locating and negotiating the acquisition of suitable real property as described in part III below.

II   Term: This agreement will begin on the __ day of __, 19__, and will terminate at noon on the __ day of __, 19__. If Buyer enters into an agreement to acquire property that is pending on the termination date, this agreement will be in effect until the transaction has closed or otherwise terminated.

III   Property: Buyer desires to acquire real property described as follows, or as otherwise acceptable to Buyer.

   (a)   Type of property _____
   (b)   Location _____
   (c)   Price range _____
   (d)   Terms and conditions _____

IV   Broker's Obligations: Broker will use his or her best efforts to (a) identify suitable properties, (b) assist Buyer in negotiating a contract for the chosen property and (c) monitor the transaction through the closing.

V   Buyer's Obligations: Buyer agrees to cooperate with Broker in accomplishing the objective of this agreement, including (a) conducting all negotiations through Broker and (b) being available to meet with Broker at reasonable times to view properties recommended by Broker.

VI   Retainer: Upon execution of this agreement, Buyer will pay to Broker a nonrefundable retainer fee of $_____. This fee will be credited to Buyer in the event compensation is earned by Broker as defined in the following paragraph.

VII   Compensation: Broker's compensation is earned when Buyer contracts to acquire real property meeting the requirements of section III above or will be responsible for paying Broker $__ or __ percent of the total purchase price for the acquired property. Buyer will be credited with any amount paid to Broker by the seller or seller's agent.

VIII   Early Termination: Buyer may terminate this agreement at any time, but will be held responsible for Broker's compensation until the original termination date if Buyer contracts to acquire any property that, prior to early termination, was found by Buyer or submitted to Buyer by Broker or any other person. Broker may terminate this agreement at any time, in which event Buyer will be released from all further obligations.

IX   Acknowledgment: The parties execute this agreement on the_ day of_ ,19_.

_____   _____
Broker   Buyer

                                                                 _____
                                                                 Buyer

*This example is intended solely for instructional purposes and should not be relied on in practice, as it may not meet all particular circumstances.

Real Estate Today   *Legal Highlight*

The Seller's Agent's Obligations to the Buyer

The Strassburgers owned a 3,000-square-foot home in Diablo, California, located on a one-acre lot and complete with a swimming pool and large guest house. They listed their home with Valley Realty, which sold the property to the Eastons for $170,000. Unfortunately for the Eastons, however, they were not aware that part of the property was on filled land that had been subject to earth slides.

Shortly after moving in, the Eastons became painfully aware of this fact when massive earth movement cost them a portion of their driveway and caused the foundation of the house to settle, the walls to crack and the doorways to warp. Estimates to repair the damage and avoid recurrence ranged as high as $213,000. The Eastons sued the Strassburgers and Valley Realty for damages, charging misrepresentation. In a landmark decision that has had lasting implications for the real estate brokerage industry, they won.

The court held that although there was no evidence that the broker intentionally misled the buyers by deliberately giving false information, he had an "affirmative duty" to the buyers to conduct "a reasonably competent and diligent inspection of the property listed for sale and to disclose to prospective purchasers all facts materially affecting the value or desirability of the property that such an investigation would reveal." Because the broker did not do this, he was liable for part of the assessed damages of $197,000. As a result of this case, brokers are held responsible for disclosing information about the condition of property to buyers. ∎

Source:
Easton v. Strassburger, 199 Cal. Rptr. 383 (Cal. App. 1 Dist., 1984).

The Broker's Duties

Real estate brokers and salespersons assume fiduciary roles when they are hired by either sellers or buyers. A fiduciary occupies a position of trust and confidence in relation to another person or that person's property. Therefore, brokers must protect their clients' best interests at all times. A breach of a fiduciary's duties may occur as a result of negligence, fraud, misrepresentation or failure to follow instructions. **Fraud** is present if a broker, (1) with the intention to mislead, (2) makes a false statement material to a transaction that (3) is justifiably relied on by a client, resulting in (4) injury to the client. The elements of **misrepresentation** are the same as for fraud except that the intention to mislead need not be present.

Seller's Agent's Duties to Sellers   After a listing agreement is signed, the broker's job is to locate a ready, willing and able buyer. Of course, the broker must do so honestly, diligently and in good faith while following any instructions given by the owner and looking out for the owner's interests. The broker must also keep the seller informed at all times and communicate any and all offers received to the seller.

Seller's Agent's Duties to Buyers   When the broker is an agent of the seller, the broker must look out for the seller's best interests. Even so, the broker must be careful not to misrepresent the property to a potential buyer, and courts increasingly hold that the broker must go further, having a responsibility to disclose any negative factors that might adversely affect the property's value. Suppose, for example, that the foundation of a house has settled, necessitating repairs. In addition, the basement has been subject to flooding in extremely wet weather. The broker has the responsibility to inform any interested buyer that these problems exist and that additional repairs to correct them may be necessary in the future. The Legal Highlight on page 159 illustrates the liability brokers may face if they do not furnish adequate information to a prospective buyer.

If a buyer gives a broker any money as a deposit on a potential purchase, these funds must be kept separate from the broker's personal funds and cannot be used for the broker's benefit. For example, any use of earnest money by the broker for anything other than the buyer's instructed purposes is improper and illegal. The money must be deposited in an escrow account for the benefit of the buyer.

Fair housing.   The broker also must be careful not to violate **fair housing laws,** which prohibit housing discrimination based on sex, race, color, religion, national origin, disabilities or familial status. In the past, some brokers have engaged in the practice of **steering**—that is, channeling minority prospects only to minority neighborhoods. Other unscrupulous brokers have engaged in **blockbusting**—using scare tactics to drive down home prices when minority owners begin moving into an area.

The Civil Rights Act of 1866 provides that "all citizens of the United States shall have the same right, in every State and Territory, as is enjoyed by white citizens thereof to inherit, purchase, lease, sell, hold and convey real and personal property." In 1968, the U.S. Supreme Court ruled that this law prohibits "all racial discrimination, private as well as public, in the sale or rental of property." More recently, the Fair Housing Act of 1988, enforced by the U.S. Department of Housing and Urban Development (HUD), was enacted to, among other things, provide civil penalties ranging from $10,000 to $50,000 plus actual and compensatory damages against individuals who engage in discriminatory practices. Americans who feel their rights have been violated should file complaints immediately with the Office of Fair Housing and Equal Opportunity at HUD. The law means what it says, as the broker in the Legal Highlight on page 162 discovered.

Buyer's Agent's Duties to Buyers   When a buyer representation agreement is in place, the broker is a fiduciary of the buyer. The broker must act diligently and in good faith to find a property that matches the buyer's criteria. Failure to attempt to locate a property for the buyer would violate the terms of the buyer representation agreement. Although normally obtaining a commission paid by the seller, the buyer's broker's loyalties must lie with the buyer. The broker has the responsibility of advising the buyer, negotiating the lowest price and otherwise assisting the buyer in closing the transaction.

Buyer's Agent's Duties to Sellers   Even though a buyer's broker is a fiduciary of the buyer, the broker must treat sellers fairly, honestly and with due care. Failure to do so violates the fair dealings requirement imposed on state-licensed real estate agents.

Disclosure of Agency Relationship

Most states have enacted laws and regulations that require real estate brokers and salespersons to disclose the nature of any agency relationships at the first substantive contact with clients and customers. In many states, this disclosure must be made in writing and acknowledged by the parties involved. In the past, many buyers have purchased property with the mistaken belief that one of the brokers involved in the transaction represented their best interests. Unless a buyer representation agreement is executed, buyers should assume that brokers work for sellers.

It is legally permissible for a broker to represent both sides of the negotiation in a real estate transaction. With full consent and permission of both the buyer and seller, a single broker could serve as a dual agent. In the absence of informed consent, however, the broker must be careful not to attempt to represent both the buyer and the seller at the same time. Unless both parties specifically agree to be represented by the same broker, the broker is subject to violating the basic tenets of the agency relationship for one or both parties.

TERMINATION OF AGENCY RELATIONSHIPS

In the typical agency relationship in real estate, the relationship ends when a transaction occurs as specified in the listing agreement or buyer representation agreement. For example, if an open listing created the relationship, the relationship terminates on a sale, whether that sale is completed by the listing broker, another broker or the owner. In an exclusive-agency listing, it is understood that the agreement ends with the sale, whether the real estate is sold by the listing broker or by the owner.

If a transaction does not occur, the time period provided in the agency agreement governs the duration of the agency relationship. At the expiration of that term, the relationship terminates. If such a term is not stated, the agency relationship lasts for a reasonable time. A "reasonable" time is generally considered to be three months for residential property and six months for commercial property. The determination of a reasonable time period often must be made by a court; therefore, absence of a specific term in the agency agreement may result in expensive litigation.

A third way the agency relationship between a broker and owner ends is by mutual agreement. Some circumstances make it more beneficial to all parties to relieve the broker of his or her duties to locate a buyer and to relieve the owner of his or her duties to the broker. Such an agreement may occur before the expi-

Real Estate Today   *Legal Highlight*

Enforcement of Fair Housing Laws

Gordon Blackwell, a licensed real estate broker, owned a rental house, which he listed for sale with another real estate agent. An African-American couple, the Herrons, were shown the house by their broker. They liked the house, and after offer and counteroffer, a contract for sale was signed by both parties. Later, however, after Blackwell learned that the Herrons were black, he refused to close on the property. He changed the locks and would not discuss the matter with his broker. He also signed a lease on the property with an option to purchase with the Coopers, whom Blackwell described as "some really good white tenants."

The Herrons filed a housing discrimination complaint with the U.S. Department of Housing and Urban Development, alleging that Blackwell had discriminated against them because of their race, in violation of the Fair Housing Act. After an investigation by HUD, a federal district court issued an injunction restraining Blackwell from selling or leasing the property except to the Herrons and requiring him to notify the Coopers that they would have to vacate the property. Blackwell still failed to close on the property, and eventually, the Herrons decided they no longer wanted the house.

An appeals court found that the record supported the determination that

- the Herrons were qualified buyers;
- they had obtained a mortgage loan commitment;
- Blackwell rejected the Herrons on the basis of race; and
- Blackwell made the property available to others after he repudiated his contract with the Herrons.

The court ordered Blackwell to pay the Herrons $4,592 for economic losses and $40,000 for "embarrassment, humiliation and emotional distress." It awarded the Coopers $594 in damages and $20,000 for their emotional distress. Blackwell was also assessed a civil penalty of $10,000. ∎

Source:

Herron v. Blackwell, 908 F.2d 864 (U.S. Court of Appeals, 11th Circuit, 1990).

---

ration of the agency agreement's term. Provisions for early termination should be specified in the agreement.

Even without the consent of the agent, many states allow the principal to revoke at any time the listing agreement that established the agency relationship. Revocation of an open or exclusive-agency listing is looked upon less harshly than revocation of an exclusive-right-to-sell listing. Of course, the principal who breaches the agreement is liable to the broker for damages, although the determination of an agent's damages may be difficult.

Of course, if either party to the agency relationship breaches his or her duties, the other party is relieved of further liability under the listing agreement. For example, if a broker fails to keep the seller fully informed of negotiations, the seller can list the property with another broker or sell it without a broker even if the original listing agreement was an exclusive right to sell. The owner's revocation of the listing agreement releases the broker from all duties to locate a buyer.

Because the agreement that creates the principal-agent relationship is a contract between the parties, loss of contractual capacity by either party terminates the relationship. Such loss of capacity may occur as the result of the death or insanity of either the principal or the agent. Destruction of improvements on the listed property or the property's seizure by the government under the power of eminent domain also terminates the agency relationship. A broker is under no obligation to seek a buyer for a house that has been destroyed in a hurricane, for example, and a seller is not obligated to pay a commission for one that has been condemned for a highway right-of-way.

In summary, the broker-owner agency relationship can be terminated by several means:

- A transaction occurs.
- The term of the agreement expires.
- The parties agree to termination.
- One party breaches his or her duties.
- One party becomes contractually incapacitated.
- A listed property's improvements are destroyed.
- A listed property is taken by the government under the power of eminent domain.

TYPES OF BROKERAGE FIRMS

Real estate markets, particularly markets for single-family homes, are local in nature, and real estate brokerage firms traditionally have been small, one-office businesses that operated only in their local markets. For the most part, the real estate brokerage industry is still made up of small firms. Increasingly, however, the real estate brokerage market in most larger communities is dominated by large, multioffice firms, often part of regional or national organizations.

Many real estate brokers and brokerage firms specialize in one type of real estate transaction. Some brokers, for example, act only as buyer's brokers, while others serve only as seller's brokers. Many brokers limit their activities to the owner-occupied residential market, apartment leasing, vacant land sales, or commercial, industrial or retail properties. Concentrating their efforts on smaller market segments allows some brokers to finely tune their skills to the needs of their clients and customers and to ultimately increase their productivity.

Franchises

One way the smaller real estate brokers compete with the large regional and national firms is by becoming part of a franchise chain, such as Century 21 or Better Homes and Gardens. Franchisees pay an initial fee plus a percentage of their annual gross. For this, they receive the advantages of sales and management training programs, a referral network and, perhaps of most importance, name recognition. Just as families moving to an area recognize McDonald's and

Kentucky Fried Chicken, they also often recognize real estate franchise chains. Consumers should realize, however, that most of these firms are independently owned and operated, and the quality of service can vary.

Desk Fee Arrangements

Increasingly, brokerage firms organize the brokers and salespersons who work in the firms in desk fee arrangements. Brokers who wish to work with other members of a firm pay a monthly fee for the right to occupy space in the office. The firm provides phone service, cooperative advertising and other resources that are shared by the members of the firm. In some cases, the members must also share portions of their commissions earned with the other members of the firm.

Multiple-Listing Services

Another way the smaller broker is able to compete with larger firms is by becoming part of a multiple-listing service. If another broker sells a property, the listing broker still receives a portion of the commission. While the multiple-listing service is particularly valuable to the small broker, who otherwise might not have enough properties to sell, the service is also usually an advantage to the seller because all members of the MLS offer the property for sale, and it may reach many more potential buyers.

BROKER AND SALESPERSON COMPENSATION

As discussed above, a real estate broker or salesperson receives a commission for services rendered in connection with a transaction. Normally, the commission is determined by a percentage of the gross transaction amount, though it can also be a flat fee. Usually, no commission is paid until the transaction is completed. In some cases, however, the broker may receive an advance fee, or a fee may be paid for performance of specific services, such as consultation and advice or appraisal of property. The commission amount varies with the type of property sold. Commissions on single-family homes typically range from 5 to 8 percent. Large commercial properties usually carry lower percentage commissions, in the range of 3 to 6 percent, while commissions on unimproved land generally range from 6 to 10 percent.

Of course, real estate brokerage commissions cannot be set by agreement among brokers, but must be negotiated between brokers and clients. Even discussion between brokers concerning the level of commissions is an antitrust violation and a criminal offense. Even so, like other prices, commission rates tend to be relatively uniform, although lower rates can be negotiated, particularly in a "sellers" market.

When more than one broker is involved in a transaction, the commission usually is split among the selling broker, the listing broker and the firms that employ the brokers. Each broker typically receives half of the commission amount specified in the listing agreement. The brokers may then be obligated to split their commissions with their respective firms and possibly their salespersons. Of course, if the selling and listing agent are the same person, he or she collects both commissions.

Compensation for Salespersons

As discussed above, state laws require that salespersons work under the direction of a broker. Compensation for salespersons is based on a percentage of the commissions earned for the broker. The actual percentage varies from firm to firm and from salesperson to salesperson on the basis of such factors as the prevailing practice in the area, the degree of advertising and other support provided by the broker and the sales record of the agent. In general, the portion of the total commission going to the salesperson increases with his or her level of sales.

Chapter Review

1. Two characteristics of real estate markets—the complexity of transactions and buyers' limited knowledge of the markets—have led to the establishment of various real estate service activities, including real estate brokerage, property management and appraisal.

2. The steps in the real estate sales process are (1) listing, (2) marketing the property and qualifying prospective buyers, (3) presentation and negotiations, (4) contracts and (5) settlement or closing.

3. A real estate broker is an intermediary who arranges real estate sale or lease transactions for fees or commissions. A real estate salesperson must work through a broker and can carry out only those responsibilities assigned by the broker.

4. All states and the District of Columbia require brokers and salespersons to be licensed and meet mandatory education or experience requirements. Failure to obtain the proper license prohibits the collection of any commission.

5. The primary functions of the real estate brokerage industry are to match properties with buyers and to guide buyers and sellers through the complexities of real estate transactions.

6. Real estate brokers' relationships with sellers and buyers are governed by the law of agency. The broker or salesperson serves as an agent for the seller or buyer, who is the principal. A principal authorizes his or her agent to perform certain functions on behalf of the principle. In a typical real estate transaction, the principal (seller) grants the agent (broker) express authority as stated in the listing agreement.

7. The broker-seller relationship is created upon the establishment of a listing agreement, usually written. Such an agreement specifies the par-

ties, describes the property, states the asking price and provides the governing terms. The traditional types of listing agreements include (1) the open listing, (2) the exclusive-agency listing and (3) the exclusive-right-to-sell listing. Net listing agreements are used infrequently today because of the possibility of fraud.

8. The broker-buyer relationship is created upon the establishment of a buyer representation agreement, usually written. Such an agreement identifies the parties, describes the property desired and establishes the broker's right to compensation. These agreements can be open or exclusive.

9. A broker or salesperson has the duty to act honestly and diligently on the principal's behalf. Complete loyalty is owed to the party the agent represents.

10. Fair housing laws prohibit housing discrimination based on a buyer's or lessee's sex, race, color, religion, national origin, disabilities or familial status.

11. A commission is earned when the conditions of an agreement have been satisfied. In a listing agreement, the commission is due when the broker procures a ready, willing and able buyer or when the transaction is actually completed. In a buyer representation agreement, the commission is due when the buyer contracts to purchase a property.

12. The agency relationship terminates when a transaction occurs, when the term provided in the agreement expires, when both parties consent to termination, when either party breaches its conditions, when either party becomes incapacitated, when the property is destroyed or heavily damaged or when the property is condemned by the government under the power of eminent domain.

13. A real estate broker or salesperson normally receives a commission when the transaction is completed successfully, but no salary or other fee until that time. The commission normally is stated as a percentage of the gross sales price, and it varies with the type of property sold.

Key Terms

agency a legal relationship between a principal and an agent.

agent the party authorized to conduct business on the principal's behalf.

blockbusting the illegal practice of encouraging property owners to sell their homes when minorities begin moving into an area.

broker an intermediary who brings together buyers and sellers, assists in negotiating agreements between them, executes their orders and receives compensation for services rendered.

buyer representation agreement the legal agreement between a buyer and a broker hired to represent the buyer's interests.

buyer's agent a broker who is legally obligated to represent a buyer's interests.

commission the compensation received by a broker for services rendered.

dual agency a legal relationship that exists when an agent is legally obligated to represent the best interests of two competing principals.

exclusive-agency listing a listing agreement that guarantees the broker's right to a commission if the property is sold by any licensed real estate broker or salesperson.

exclusive-right-to-sell listing a listing agreement that guarantees the broker's right to a commission if the property is sold by the seller or any licensed real estate broker or salesperson.

fair housing laws laws that protect the rights of certain citizens in housing transactions.

fiduciary a person who is obligated to act in the best interest of another.

fraud a false statement made with the intention to mislead that is material to a transaction that is justifiably relied upon by a client and that results in injury to the client.

listing agreement the legal agreement between a broker and a property owner that authorizes the broker to attempt to sell the property.

listing broker the broker who negotiates the listing agreement with the seller.

misrepresentation a false statement that is material to a transaction that is justifiably relied upon by a client and that results in injury to the client.

multiple-listing service an arrangement in which brokers share their listings with other brokers in exchange for a share of the commission generated by a transaction.

net listing a listing agreement in which the broker is entitled to receive as commission any amount above a base price.

open listing a listing agreement in which a broker is entitled to receive a commission only in the event the broker procures a buyer for the property.

principal the person who authorizes an agent to conduct business on his or her behalf.

real estate broker an individual licensed by a state to represent others in real estate transactions in exchange for compensation.

real estate salesperson   an individual licensed by a state to assist real estate brokers in arranging real estate transactions in exchange for compensation.

seller's agent   a real estate broker who is obligated to represent the best interest of the seller.

selling broker   the broker who actually locates a buyer for a property.

steering   the illegal practice of steering potential home buyers into certain areas to influence the racial or ethnic composition of the areas.

subagent   an agent of an agent of a principal.

Study Exercises

1. What characteristics of real estate have led to the establishment of the real estate brokerage industry?

2. Discuss the difference between the function of a real estate broker and that of a real estate salesperson.

3. What is the difference between an open listing and an exclusive-agency listing? How does an exclusive-agency listing differ from an exclusive-right-to-sell listing?

4. What is a net listing? Why is it illegal in most states?

5. What is the difference between fraud and misrepresentation?

6. What are blockbusting and steering? Why are these practices illegal?

7. What are the advantages of a multiple-listing service to real estate brokers? Are there any advantages for sellers?

8. Joe desires to sell his house. He lists the property with Johnny White, a real estate broker. In this case, who is principal, and who is the agent? What duties does Johnny owe to Joe? What duties does he owe to any potential buyer?

9. Suppose that Johnny (see question 5) shows the house to Janice, who asks him to negotiate on her behalf with Joe. If he does so, what is he guilty of? What must he do to protect his right to a commission on this sale if he grants her request?

10. Sylvia listed her house for sale at $105,000 with Keg Realty Company, and Keg began to show the property. A prospective buyer looked at Sylvia's house, liked it and gave a written offer for her asking price— $105,000. Having some second thoughts about selling, Sylvia claimed that this particular buyer could not afford her house and refused to

accept the offer. If there is no evidence that the buyer is in financial difficulty, does Keg Realty have any claim against Sylvia?

11. Real estate broker Molly Smith has listed a house for sale that is located in a floodplain and has flooded on several occasions. Does Molly have an obligation to make these facts known to prospective buyers?

12. Suppose that Molly knows about the potential floodplain problem (see question 11), but tells a potential purchaser that the house is not in the floodplain. Of what is she guilty? Would the buyer have a claim against her?

13. Suppose that Molly fully informs the potential buyer about the floodplain problem (see question 12), but he still buys the house. Later, his house floods, and he sues Molly for not telling him that houses in floodplains can flood. Does he have a legitimate claim?

For Further Reading

de Heer, R. *Realty Bluebook,* 31st ed. (Chicago: Real Estate Education Company, 1996).

CHAPTER 9
Property Management and Leasing

A property manager's responsibilities include selecting tenants, collecting rent and keeping the building in good repair.

Real Estate Today

- *Close-Up*
  Green Acres
  Shopping Center

- *Close-Up*
  The Empire State
  Building

- *Case Study*
  Jill Jewell Rents an
  Apartment

Chapter Preview

AS DISCUSSED THROUGHOUT this text, the characteristics of real estate resources and transactions imply that specialized knowledge is needed for successful decision making regarding real estate. Just as real estate brokers and salespersons provide a valuable service to buyers and sellers, property managers also provide an important service to property owners. This chapter will explore several issues related to the business of property management, including the

- role of the property manager in investment real estate;
- functions of the property manager;
- property management agreement and manager's compensation; and
- role and functions of the corporate real estate asset manager.

Because of its importance to the property manager's duties, we will also consider the topic of leasing, including

- requirements of a valid lease;
- different types of leases and lease clauses; and
- the relationship between landlord and tenant in a residential lease.

THE ROLE OF THE PROPERTY MANAGER

Many owners of real estate find they have neither the ability or the desire to cope with the complexities of managing rental properties. Day-to-day operating decisions for most income-producing properties require specialized skills that many real estate investors do not have. Professional property managers are trained to manage properties efficiently, with the objective of securing the highest net returns for the property owners over the properties' useful lives. A **property manager** acts as an agent for a property owner in respect to the leasing, marketing and overall operation of the property. In many cases, the property manager is also a licensed real estate broker.

Consider an investor who purchases a small shopping center. Unless that investor is experienced in shopping center management, a property manager may be required to handle the center's operations. For example, the property manager will be responsible for marketing space in the center to potential tenants, negotiating the lease agreement, collecting rents, addressing tenant concerns, coordinating the property maintenance program bookkeeping and paying the property expenses such as utilities, property insurance, property taxes and employee salaries. Having a trained professional to handle these tasks improves the likelihood that the investment will prove successful.

Property managers may be hired by property owners as employees, or property managers may work for property management firms that contract with property owners to provide management services. Many successful property managers hold designations such as the Institute of Real Estate Management's Certified Property Manager (CPM) or Accredited Resident Manager (ARM) designations. Managers can be awarded these designations only after meeting the education and experience requirements established by the awarding organization. Some states regulate the property management profession by requiring managers to obtain licenses from the states after completing educational and experience requirements.

FUNCTIONS OF A PROPERTY MANAGER

The property manager may be involved in virtually all aspects of the operation of a rental property. The functions of a property manager include (1) administrative management, (2) marketing and (3) physical management.

Administrative Management

Administrative management—the collection of rents, the keeping of records and the preparation of reports—is one of the vital, if not very glamorous, functions of a property manager. It is, of course, impossible for a rental project to be successful unless the rents are collected. Fortunately, most tenants pay their rents when due, but sometimes there are problem cases. Such cases can be minimized, however, if the management establishes a firm but fair collection policy. Generally, a tactfully worded reminder should be sent to the tenant if the rent is not paid within five days of the due date. If the payment still is not forthcoming, further action is necessary. Such action may include a personal interview to determine why payment has not been made. If the tenant suffers from some temporary financial difficulty, the manager may gain goodwill by granting a time extension. Such an extension may avoid the cost of renting the property again, though it may lead to additional lost rent. As a last resort, it may be necessary to ask the tenant to leave or even to bring eviction proceedings.

Accurate records and accounts are vital to the efficient management of income property. The manager needs such records to report receipts and disbursements to the owner, to file tax and other reports required by governmental agencies and as a source of data on which to base management decisions and reports.

Marketing

Leases are perishable commodities: they expire. Rental space therefore must be merchandised continually so that new tenants can be found to take the place of those who leave. Lease periods range from one day for hotel and motel rooms to several years for commercial property. (Apartment complexes may be leased for perhaps six months or a few years.) The general objective of marketing is to maximize income. This usually means to maximize occupancy rates and rental price schedules. The two obviously are in conflict, however, and a balance must be found to maximize income. One can ensure a rental unit's occupancy for three years, for example, by granting a three-year lease, but the income derived from the unit may be greater if it is rented to three successive tenants for one year each—if, at the end of each year, market conditions provide a tenant willing and able to pay a higher rent. The property manager must know the market in which he or she operates to make the right decision. We will consider the lease transaction in more detail later in this chapter.

Marketing Strategy   Choosing the correct marketing strategy is important to the success of any rental project. This is an area where the property manager's experience and expertise can be of tremendous value to the owners. A clear marketing strategy is essential. What type of tenant is sought? Will the project attempt to stress some price advantage, location, design or other marketing feature? Unless a clear strategy is carried over into tenant selection, rent schedules and the physical character of the project, it will be impossible for the property to reach its maximum potential.

Tenant Selection   A general rule in residential projects is to seek tenants with similar characteristics and interests. For example, a combination of families with small children, young singles and retirees rarely is a harmonious one—nor does it lead to high occupancy rates. Tenants also must be screened for their financial status, particularly their creditworthiness. The property manager must be careful, however, that fair housing laws are not violated. It is against the law to refuse to rent to anyone on the basis of age, sex, marital status, race, religion or national origin.

The tenant mix is also important for commercial projects. In contrast to the homogeneity sought in residential projects, the objective usually is to achieve a variety that will complement and enhance the image the project seeks. For example, a coin-operated laundry would not be a desirable tenant in an up-scale shopping center where relatively expensive goods are sold in boutiques, but it might be quite complementary to other stores in a small neighborhood shopping center.

Rent Schedules   The establishment of rent schedules is a continuing function of marketing that requires extensive knowledge of market conditions. If rents are set too low, the project may achieve full occupancy, but still not maximize income. If rents are set too high, vacancies may increase to such an extent that total income will be reduced.

Physical Management

Physical management is divided into two categories: (1) maintenance designed to conserve the property and (2) rehabilitation and renovation designed to make the project more competitive in a changing market. A program of continuing maintenance is essential to continued economic viability. Owners and managers who fail to give proper attention to landscaping, redecorating and other items of general maintenance soon find their projects no longer competitive in the marketplace. Even if a project is well maintained, it may be necessary, after a time, to conduct extensive renovations to keep it viable. For instance, an older shopping center may benefit greatly from a new facade and redesigned landscaping and parking areas. The Close-Up on the following page gives a vivid example of how good property management can revive an aging shopping center and create value for its owners.

THE MANAGEMENT AGREEMENT

The **management agreement** establishes an agency relationship between the owner of a property and the property manager. To clarify each party's duties and responsibilities, this agreement should be written. The document should specify the powers and obligations of the manager and the compensation he or she will receive and should set the term of the agreement.

Powers of the Manager

As the agent of the owner, the property manager has the power to set rents; to execute, extend and cancel leases; to make settlements with tenants; to collect rents; to spend money on behalf of the property (a power generally limited to some maximum dollar amount beyond which the owner's approval is necessary); and to hire, fire and supervise personnel to operate the property.

Just as the manager has the power to act on behalf of the owner, he or she also has the obligation to carry out those functions in a professional manner. Because the manager has a fiduciary relationship with the owner, many management agreements require that the agent and his or her employees be bonded.

Compensation

If the property manager is employed directly by the property owner, the most common form of compensation is a fee based on a percentage of the property's

Real Estate Today

Close-Up

Green Acres Shopping Center—A Property Management Success Story

When Frank Bookings took over the management of the Green Acres Shopping Center, it was in real trouble. Built 20 years earlier in typical neighborhood strip shopping center style, the center was showing its age. Two-thirds of its approximately 60,000 square feet were vacant, and the main tenant, a grocery store, had just moved out, leaving its 16,000-square-foot space empty. The tenant mix was less than desirable. For example, a "game room" had become well known to local police for the drug activity that allegedly occurred there. The center obviously was not generating an acceptable return for its owners, and its marketability was low.

Frank's first task was to improve the appearance of the center. He was helped by a storm and the local government. The storm tore the outdated turquoise facade off the building, and the insurance settlement provided the monies to replace it and repaint the center. The local government bought right-of-way for widening the road in front of the center, and these monies paid for a new sign with a time and temperature display to give the center some identity. The ugliness of the blacktop parking lot was broken by the construction of islands filled with shrubs and trees. Although these improvements were relatively inexpensive, they vastly improved the attractiveness of the center.

The next task was to improve the tenant mix and to fill the empty spaces. The key was securing a tenant for the black hole formerly occupied by the supermarket. Frank learned that the state's nursing school was unhappy with its current location. Although this would be a somewhat unconventional tenant for a neighborhood shopping center, the 100 students would provide a ready market for restaurants and other potential tenants. The catch was that the state required the owner to provide building improvements equal to about three years' rent, although the school would sign only a one-year lease. Even so, the owner took the plunge.

With the nursing school as an anchor, two restaurants and other stores soon followed, one replacing the game room, whose lease was not renewed. Currently, the center is fully leased, and it generates three times the gross income it did just five years earlier, with consequent increase in value.

"Successful property management depends on constant attention to detail," explains Frank. "Every morning, I am there making sure the parking lot is clean, the plants maintained and that the center is ready for customers. That's what keeps tenants happy, creates value for the owners and provides good commissions for me." ■

---

gross income. The fee ranges from approximately 4 to 10 percent, depending on such factors as the size of the project, the responsibilities of the manager and the competitiveness of the local market. If the property manager is an employee of a property management firm, the manager's compensation is usually a fixed salary. The management company contracts with the property owner to provide management services for a fee. In the past, fee schedules often were established by local real estate associations, but this practice now would be considered a violation of antitrust laws.

THE ROLE AND FUNCTION OF ASSET MANAGERS

The preceding discussion focused on the role of the property manager when the property is operated as income-producing real estate. Another type of property manager, known as the **asset manager,** is increasingly common in the real estate market.

Almost every business firm must own or lease real estate as part of its operation, even if the firm's primary line of business is not real estate related. Often, the company's exposure to the real estate market is quite substantial, and a professional real estate manager is needed to manage the company's real estate assets. In this situation, persons assigned to the task are known as *corporate real estate asset managers.* The tasks of an asset manager are often more complicated than those of a traditional property manager because the asset manager must operate within the framework of meeting the company's overall objective in its primary line of business. Corporate real estate asset managers are real estate specialists who provide a wide range of real estate services for their companies, even though the companies may not be in the real estate business.

The asset manager has four major functions: (1) management, (2) acquisition, (3) financing and (4) disposition of corporate real estate assets.

Management

The management function of the real estate asset manager goes beyond facility management to include the strategic decisions involving the real estate needs of a firm. The asset manager can aid operating units in planning, acquiring and financing facilities, often improving the return on the firm's real estate that might otherwise be underutilized.

Acquisition

Few top business executives possess the specialized skills needed in planning for their real estate needs or in site selection. A professional real estate asset manager can assist in targeting space requirements and design features. He or she also might aid in the site selection process, considering the complex factors involved in locating various types of facilities. The asset manager also can serve as a firm's negotiator in reaching a final agreement when it comes to leasing or buying additional space.

Financing

The first issue in financing a new facility is the question of whether it is in a company's best interests to lease or purchase the property. This decision involves many factors, including the general financial status of the firm and whether the facility required is a special-purpose building. The firm might decide to build the structure needed, then immediately sell it to an investor and simultaneously lease it back. This strategy, known as **sale-leaseback,** frees up the firm's capital for use in its primary line of business. If ownership is the chosen alternative, the asset manager assists in deciding what type of financing will best fit the objectives of the firm.

Real Estate Today

Close-Up

The Empire State Building

Want to buy a historic American icon building cheap? You could have several years ago. The Empire State Building, for four decades the world's tallest, with its 2.24 million square feet of space 95 percent occupied, is worth somewhere between $600 million and $800 million. Why then did the building sell for only $40 million?

Here's a hint. A partnership has a leasehold on the building that controls every aspect of the property through the year 2075. The fee owner receives less than $2 million each year in lease payments, while the owners of the leasehold currently receive about $35 million in rentals from the firms that actually occupy the space. The fee owners will not gain control of the Empire State Building for more than 80 years. It will then be more than 145 years old. In other words, most of the value of the building is in the leasehold interest; the leased fee interest is worth comparatively little.

This unusual situation arose when a partnership bought the building in the 1960s for $68 million. Prudential Insurance Company provided $29 million in financing and was given ownership of the fee interest to transfer tax advantages to the company that reduced the cost of financing for the partnership. After these tax advantages were exhausted, the insurance company sold the building, but fee ownership is worth relatively little—unless the lease can be broken. At this writing, a group headed by Donald Trump is trying to do just that, charging that the owners of the leasehold are not properly maintaining the building, but the group's chances of success appear less than bright. ■

Disposition

Another important part of the corporate asset manager's job is to redeploy or divest property that is no longer needed by a firm. This may occur because of reduced operations and consolidations or because facilities have been made surplus by the acquisition of new ones. Disposition may involve a property's sale or lease to another firm, renovation for another use or exchange for another property. The Close-Up above describes the role of the corporate asset manager in a modern corporation.

LEASES

One of the most obvious tasks of a property manager is to negotiate leases with tenants. A **lease** is a type of contract, and its basic requirements are the same as the general requirements for contracts. Through the lease contract, the landlord conveys use and possession of the property in return for the tenant's agreement to pay rent. The lease also defines the rights, duties and liabilities of both landlord and tenant and contains the following elements:

- Names of the **lessor** (landlord) and **lessee** (tenant), who must have contractual capacity to enter into the lease agreement
- Description of the premises
- Conveyance of the premises
- Term or duration of the lease
- Amount of rent and manner of payment
- Duties and obligations of the parties
- Signatures of the parties

As in all contracts, a lease becomes valid when it is delivered and accepted. If the lease is for a term of one year or longer, it must be in writing to be enforceable in court.

Classification of Leases

Leases can be classified in several ways. Generally, they are classified by duration of term, type of use and method of rental payment.

Duration of Term   The duration of the term of a leasehold determines whether it is a tenancy for a stated period, a tenancy from period to period, a tenancy at will or a tenancy at sufferance. A **tenancy for a stated period** conveys the property to the tenant for a stated period of time, called the *term*. The term may be for any length of time from one month to many years, although in most states, a lease for longer than 99 years is regarded as a fee simple transaction. Possession of the property reverts to the landlord at the end of the term, subject to any right of renewal set forth in the lease. Many states require that long-term leases, usually for more than one or three years, be recorded in the public record to be enforceable as contracts.

A **tenancy from period to period** is of indefinite duration. The tenancy does not terminate until proper notice is given by either party. It commonly exists from month to month and is renewed automatically at the end of each month provided the tenant has paid the rent.

A **tenancy at will** may be terminated by either party at any time. Tenant-protection statutes, however, generally require reasonable notice on the part of the landlord—usually 30 days.

A **tenancy at sufferance** is created when a tenant continues to occupy property after the expiration of the lease period. The tenant has no right to the property and remains there at the sufferance of the landlord. Even so, many states require that the tenant be given notice to quit the premises before eviction proceedings can be instituted.

Type of Use   Leaseholds are used for either commercial or residential purposes. A commercial lease permits the tenant to use the property for income-producing retail, manufacturing or office activities. The purpose of the residential lease is to provide housing for the lessee, not to produce income. A commercial lease is generally of longer duration and more complicated in its terms than is a residential lease.

A **ground lease** is a long-term (usually 50 years or longer) lease involving unimproved land. The leased land is usually developed by the tenant for commercial, residential or agricultural purposes. At the end of the lease, the land

and any improvements revert to the landowner. Because such a lease makes it possible to separate the ownership of the land from the ownership of the improvements, the ground lease frequently is used as a financing device in the development of major office buildings.

For example, many Manhattan office buildings are built on leased land. Because the land often constitutes 30 to 40 percent of the cost of such a project, a ground lease can greatly reduce the amount of money the developer must raise. The ground lease can also offer substantial tax advantages to the lessee because lease payments are fully deductible from taxable income as an ordinary expense, whereas the cost of land cannot be depreciated; that is, the owners cannot reduce their taxes by stating on their tax returns an amount by which the value of the land has decreased with age, as one can do in the case of buildings.

Method of Rent Payment or Adjustment   Arrangements for rental payments between tenant and landlord can take many forms, and rental arrangements are far from uniform.

Two rental factors that determine the form of the lease are the degree of overhead cost that the tenant assumes and whether the amount of rent is fixed or variable. Under a **gross lease,** the landlord agrees to pay the real estate taxes, utilities, insurance and all other operating expenses in connection with use of the premises.

Under a **net lease,** the tenant pays the operating expenses in addition to rent. Such a lease transfers uncertainty regarding the future cost of operating expenses to the tenant and leaves the landlord with a more definite net return. Occasionally, the tenant assumes responsibility for other costs as well, leading to net-net leases and net-net-net leases. Under a **net-net lease,** the lessee pays not only operating expenses, but insurance premiums as well. Under a **net-net-net lease,** also known as the *triple-net lease,* the lessee pays operating expenses, insurance premiums and real estate taxes.

Under a **fixed-rent lease,** the amount of the rental payment is fixed for the term of the lease. This type of rental payment is most common for short-term residential leases.

In the **graduated-rent lease,** also known as a *step-up rent lease,* the rental payment is fixed for the initial term of the lease and then is increased by specified percentages at designated intervals. This type of lease provides some protection against inflation for the landlord and also may be used for a new business or property whose income-producing ability is expected to increase in the future. This type of lease is seldom used for rental terms of longer than ten years.

The **reappraisal lease** is similar to the graduated-rent lease except that the level of each rent increase is determined by a reappraisal of the property. Such leases are used most often for the long-term rental of entire buildings. For example, if a tenant leases an entire warehouse for $10 per square foot, and the property value increases by 10 percent, the rent in the following year would be $11 per square foot.

The **percentage lease** is a lease of a property used for commercial purposes under which the rent payments are based on some percentage of sales made on the premises. Usually, the stated percentage of gross sales is combined with a flat minimum rent. Such leases are found predominantly in shopping centers, particularly in the larger malls. For example, a toy store in a mall may be charged a base rent of $1,500 per month plus 2 percent of gross sales exceeding $50,000. If the store's December sales are $90,000, the rent is $1,500 plus 2 percent of $40,000, for a total of $2,300. If January's sales are only $25,000, the store pays only the base rent of $1,500.

The percentage of gross sales charged as rent varies depending on whether the store is a low-margin/high-volume or high-margin/low-volume outlet and on its relative importance to the shopping center. For example, an anchor department store almost always can negotiate more favorable lease terms than can a small merchant.

Another type of lease is known as the **index lease.** In this arrangement, lease payments are "indexed" to some measure of the cost of living, such as the Consumer Price Index. Rents are adjusted periodically to account for changes in the value of the dollar. The adjustments provide protection for the landlord against inflation and rapidly changing prices in the economy.

THE LANDLORD-TENANT RELATIONSHIP IN A RESIDENTIAL LEASE

Much of the above information regarding lease terms relates to commercial leases. A residential lease can be on a month-to-month or fixed-term basis. On a month-to-month basis, either the landlord or the tenant has the right to terminate the lease after giving the other party 30 days' notice. With a tenancy for a stated period, the tenant has the right to occupy the property for a specific period of time, such as six months or two years. At the end of that time, the tenant can move out, the lease can be renewed for another stated period or the parties can agree to continue the relationship as a tenancy from period to period.

Many leases contain a **renewal option,** a provision that protects the tenant against large increases in rent. The renewal option specifies what the rent will be if the lease is renewed, usually at a higher level to protect the landlord against rising costs. Without the renewal option, the landlord can raise the rent to any level desired. The tenant then has the option of paying the higher rent or moving out.

Expenses

The lease should state clearly who pays for expenses in connection with the property, including maintenance, property taxes, insurance and utilities. Generally, the landlord is responsible for normal maintenance to the building, taxes and insurance on the real estate. Utilities usually are the responsibility of the tenant, as is breakage or other damage caused by the actions of the tenant.

Assignment and Subleasing

It often is desirable to a tenant to be able to assign a lease or sublease to another tenant if plans change before the end of the lease term. **Assignment** means that all of the tenant's rights under lease are transferred to the new tenant, although the lessee still is liable unless released by the landlord. **Subleasing** means transferring a portion of rights under a lease. For example, a tenant could sublease an apartment for only six months of a two-year lease term. Under a sublease clause, the landlord may reserve the right to approve of any sublessee, generally for reasons of creditworthiness. Unless the landlord consents, the tenant is not relieved of his or her obligation to pay the rent.

If rents are rising, it may be possible to sublease to another tenant at a profit, receiving rent from the sublessee and then paying the required rent under the original lease to the landlord. In a long-term commercial lease, this leasehold interest may be worth literally millions of dollars. If the lease contains a clause against subleasing, subleasing violates the lease agreement and can result in eviction.

Security Deposits

The lease may require the tenant to provide a **security deposit** prior to occupancy. The security deposit is intended to give the landlord protection if the tenant damages the property, moves out early or fails to pay the rent. The landlord may also require the tenant to pay a cleaning fee at the termination of the lease; this is usually withheld from the security deposit due to the tenant. Deposits make it essential that both landlord and tenant inspect the property *before* occupancy and note any damages that may exist.

Improvements

If a tenant makes improvements to a rented dwelling, the tenant must recognize that unless they can be removed easily, these improvements normally become part of the real estate (fixtures) and remain with the property when the lease expires. If built-in bookcases were added, for example, these would become fixtures and part of the property. Before making any improvements, it is wise to reach an agreement with the landlord, preferably written, as to who will own them at the termination of the lease.

The following Case Study illustrates the provisions of a typical residential lease. After identifying the parties and the property, the agreement states that the property is rented only for the purpose of a single-family residence. If Jill should open some type of business in the apartment, for example, she would be in default, and Virginia would have the right to immediately take possession of the premises. Jill also agrees to pay $850 per month rent in advance and to pay a late payment fee if the rent is not paid on time. This agreement does not allow subletting or assignment of the apartment without the consent of Virginia.

Jill needs to be certain the apartment is in good repair before signing the agreement because she agrees to accept the premises in their present condition. If she thinks the apartment needs painting, for example, it is too late after the agreement is signed unless a written notation is made on the agreement that Virginia will paint the apartment. Jill also agrees to keep the premises in good repair, to pay for damages, including repair to plumbing caused by freezing, and to pay all utility bills on the property. The agreement contains no renewal provisions. If Jill wants to renew the lease after the first year, she must agree on new terms with Virginia. Because this leaves her vulnerable to future price increases or other changes in lease conditions, she might seek the inclusion of some sort of renewal provision that would specify renewal terms.

Real Estate Today   *Close-Up*

Jill Jewell Rents an Apartment

Jill Jewell had just graduated from college and moved to Charlotte, North Carolina, to take a job with Amalgamated Whitzadiddle Corporation. She needed a place to live and decided to rent a duplex apartment in a nearby suburb. Let's look at the rental agreement to see what Jill agreed to do and what was promised by the landlord, Virginia Wells.

RENTAL AGREEMENT

(The underlined portions are entered on a standard rental agreement form.)

STATE OF NORTH CAROLINA, MECKLENBURG COUNTY.

This agreement, made the 21st day of May, 1996, between Virginia M. Wells of the County of Mecklenburg, hereinafter known as "Lessor," and Jill J. Jewell, of said county, hereinafter known as "Lessee":

WITNESSETH; That said Lessor has this day rented to said Lessee the following: two-bedroom duplex apartment situated on the easterly side of Harden Mill Road between High Shoals Road and U.S. 21 Highway in High Shoals, Mecklenburg County, North Carolina and known as 149 Jarnigan Drive for the purpose of single-family residence and for no other purpose.

The duration of said rental shall be 12 months commencing on the 1st day of June, 1996, and ending on the 31st day of May, 1997.

Payment of Rent

For the rental of said premises, Lessee is to pay the sum of $850.00, Eight Hundred Fifty and 00/100 Dollars, per month, payable in advance; rent payments are due promptly on the first day of each month, and a late fee of 5 percent of rent for 5 days late and 10 percent of rent for 10 days late shall be paid.

Subletting and Assignment

Should Lessee fail to pay said rent promptly when due, or sublet said premises or assign this lease without the consent of Lessor in writing, or use said rented premises for any other purpose than that specified, or otherwise violate any of the terms of this contract, then Lessor may at her option terminate this contract, cancel the same and take immediate possession of the rented premises, without waiving any rent that may have accrued at the time of cancellation, or any claim for damages for breach of the contract on the part of Lessee.

Inspection and Repairs

Lessee hereby certifies that said premises have been examined by Lessee, and agrees to accept them as they now stand, and agrees that Lessor shall make only such repairs to said premises during the term of this contract as seem to Lessor advisable, but Lessor reserves the right to enter upon said premises for the purpose of making repairs or improvement upon the same or upon adjoining property of Lessor.

Utilities and Damages

Lessee agrees to repair at her own expense any damage to the plumbing on said premises caused by freezing, and to pay the water, gas and electric expenses on said premises, and to deliver said premises to Lessor at the expiration of the term of rental in as good order as when received, ordinary wear and tear with careful usage excepted. Lessee further agrees to pay for all breakage or loss occurring to said premises.

Habitability

Lessor agrees that if the premises should be destroyed by fire or act of God or so damaged as to become untenable, due not to the fault or neglect of Lessee or her employees or family or guests or other persons on said premises with Lessee's consent or knowledge, the rent on said premises shall cease until the same are restored to tenable conditions, Lessor having the option to rebuild, repair or make any other disposition of said premises that she may deem proper.

Claims for Damages

No claims for damages shall be made by Lessee nor delay in payment of rent for the want of repair in these premises or any other premises of Lessor.

For Rent Signs

Lessor reserves the right to place a card For Rent or For Sale on said premises at any time within 60 days prior to the termination of this contract of rent.

Renewal

It is agreed between the parties to this contract that neither shall be bound by any verbal statement or agreement or any subsequent contract relating to the above described property during the period covered by this contract unless endorsed hereon and signed by the parties hereto.

Keys

Upon termination of this agreement, Lessee agrees to leave floors of the premises broom clean, to close all windows, lock all outside doors and return all keys to Lessor or her agent.

Special Stipulations

1. Lessor acknowledges receipt of an $850.00 damage deposit.
2. Lessee agrees that no pets are allowed in the apartment.

_____   _____
Jill J. Jewell   Virginia M. Wells

Date _____   Date _____

The Rights and Obligations of Tenant and Landlord

The fundamental right of the landlord is to receive rents, while that of the tenant is to use, enjoy, occupy and possess the leasehold premises. The tenant has the right of exclusive possession of the property during the period of the lease, known as the **covenant of quiet enjoyment,** and can use the property in any legal manner that is agreed to in the lease document. Unless exceptions are made in the lease, the landlord cannot enter the property except to abate some nuisance or prevent destruction of the property. For example, a landlord could enter a tenant's apartment without securing permission to repair a burst water pipe, but not to make alterations or improvements without the tenant's prior consent. Conversely, the tenant cannot alter the leasehold premises without the permission of the landlord. The tenant has the obligation to pay the rent when due and not violate any of the lease provisions. If the tenant fails to pay the rent or violates other provisions of the lease, the landlord can move to have the tenant evicted from the premises.

Under the implied **warranty of habitability** principle, the landlord also has the obligation to maintain the premises in reasonable condition. Should a landlord fail to do so, many states have granted tenants of residential property the right to repair minor defects and deduct the cost of such repairs from rent payments. Local ordinances also require landlords to meet city and county health and safety codes.

Landlords also have the obligation to maintain common areas, such as elevators, hallways and grounds, in safe conditions. If they do not, they may be liable for injuries that result from any defects or lapses in security.

The landlord's responsibility to protect tenants against criminal acts committed by third parties is still a murky area; nevertheless, courts increasingly award tenants damages when landlords are held partially responsible because of some type of negligence (such as not repairing locks).

Many leases contain provisions giving the tenant the option of renewing the lease before its expiration. As mentioned above, this does not necessarily mean, however, that the lease can be renewed with the same terms as in the old lease, and rental rates often are raised at this time.

A lease may contain one or two distinct types of renewal clauses. If, by its terms, a lease is renewed automatically if neither party gives notice of termination, a **negative renewal clause** is involved. A lease that provides for renewal only when the tenant gives notice to the landlord that renewal is desired contains a **positive renewal clause.** In accordance with this latter provision, if no notice of renewal is given properly, the landlord-tenant relationship terminates at the end of the original lease period.

Most leases have a specific time period within which notice to terminate (under a negative renewal clause) or notice to renew (under a positive renewal clause) must be given. Although the landlord and tenant always may agree to whatever time period they desire, one to two months prior to the expiration of the lease is very common.

Chapter Review

1. Professional property managers are trained to manage properties efficiently, with the objective of securing the highest net returns for the property owners over the properties' useful lives. The property manager acts as an agent for a property owner in respect to the leasing, marketing and overall operation of the property.

2. Property management encompasses several functions: (1) administrative management (the collection of rents, the keeping of records and the preparation of reports); (2) marketing (the leasing of rental space in the manner most profitable for the owner in the long term); and (3) physical management (maintenance designed to conserve the property and rehabilitation and renovation designed to make the project more competitive in a changing market).

3. The management agreement identifies the powers and obligations of the property manager and the compensation he or she is to be paid. The agreement also specifies the time period for which the relationship will exist.

4. The usual form of compensation for property managers is a fee based on a percentage of gross income from the property.

5. Corporate real estate asset managers are real estate specialists who provide a wide range of real estate services for their companies, even though the companies may not be in the real estate business. The asset manager

has four major functions: (1) management, (2) acquisition, (3) financing and (4) disposition of corporate real estate assets.

6. A lease is a contract that conveys use and possession of a property from the landlord to the tenant in return for the tenant's agreement to pay rent.

7. The four types of leasehold estates in regard to duration of term are (1) tenancy for a stated period, (2) tenancy from period to period, (3) tenancy at will and (4) tenancy at sufferance.

8. A ground lease is a lease of land to the exclusion of any improvements. Such leases frequently are used as financial devices in the development of major office buildings.

9. In a gross lease, the landlord agrees to pay the overhead expenses that arise in connection with the use of the premises. In a net lease, the tenant pays the operating expenses.

10. Rental payments can be fixed or variable under a lease. In a graduated-rent lease, the payment is increased by specified percentages at stated intervals, while under a reappraisal lease, the level of each rent increase is determined by a reappraisal of the property. A percentage lease is a lease of property used for commercial purposes under which the rental payments are based on some percentage of sales made on the premises.

Key Terms

asset manager   a company executive charged with management of the firm's real estate facilities and activities.

assignment   the act of passing all of one's rights and responsibilities under a legal agreement to a third party.

covenant of quiet enjoyment   an assurance made by the grantor that no other party will disturb the grantee claiming to own the property or to have a lien on it; a promise from the lessor that the tenant has the right of exclusive possession of the property during the term of the lease.

fixed-rent lease   a lease contract that stipulates a fixed rent amount for the period of the lease.

graduated-rent lease   a lease contract that stipulates scheduled rent increases over the period of the lease.

gross lease   a lease contract which stipulates that the landlord will pay all operating expenses, taxes and insurance for the property during the period of the lease.

ground lease   a long-term lease for vacant land.

index lease a lease in which rent payments are adjusted based on changes in the cost of living.

lease a legal agreement between lessor and lessee.

lessee the person who receives a leasehold interest in a property from the lessor.

lessor the party who transfers a leasehold estate to a lessee.

management agreement a legal agreement authorizing a property manager to conduct business on behalf of the landlord.

negative renewal clause a clause in a lease contract that automatically renews the lease in the event neither party desires to terminate the agreement.

net lease a lease that stipulates that the lessee will pay operating expenses for a property during the lease period.

net-net lease a lease that stipulates that the lessee will pay operating expenses and insurance for the property during the lease period.

net-net-net lease a lease that stipulates that the lessee will pay operating expenses, insurance and property taxes for the property during the lease period.

percentage lease a lease for a property used for commercial purposes under which the rental payments are based on some percentage of sales made on the premises.

positive renewal clause a clause on a lease that states that if no notice of renewal is given properly, normally one to two months prior to the expiration of the lease, the lease terminates at the end of the lease period.

property manager a person authorized by a property owner to manage the property on his or her behalf.

reappraisal lease a lease that stipulates that the rent will be adjusted periodically as the value of the building changes, as determined by an appraisal.

renewal option a clause in a lease agreement that defines the parties agreement regarding renewal of the lease upon termination.

sale-leaseback an arrangement whereby a property owner sells the property to an investor and immediately leases the property back from the investor.

security deposit an amount required by a lessor in advance of occupancy as security against potential damages caused by the lessee.

subleasing the act of transferring a portion of the leasehold estate to a third party.

tenancy at sufferance a leasehold estate that defines a tenant's rights to occupy the property against the wishes of the lessor.

tenancy at will an informal leasehold estate of indeterminable length which may last as long as the parties agree.

tenancy for a stated period   a leasehold estate that has definite starting and ending dates.

tenancy from period to period   a leasehold estate that continues to automatically renew each period unless terminated by either party.

warranty of habitability   an assurance made by a lessor that the property is fit for its intended use.

Study Exercises

1. What is the primary objective of a property manager?

2. What are the general functions of a property manager?

3. What is the legal relationship between a property manager and an owner? What document creates this relationship?

4. Define the following: lease, lessor, lessee, tenancy for a stated period, tenancy from period to period, tenancy at will, tenancy at sufferance.

5. What is the difference between a gross lease and a net lease?

6. Define the following: percentage lease, graduated-rent lease, ground lease, reappraisal lease and index lease.

7. What is the difference between subleasing and assignment? When is subleasing desirable for the existing tenant?

8. What do the terms *covenant of quiet enjoyment* and *warranty of habitability* mean?

9. What purpose do security deposits serve from the lessor's perspective?

10. What is the difference between a negative renewal clause and a positive renewal clause?

11. What does an asset manager do? How do these tasks differ from the traditional property manager's?

12. Al's Shoe Store has a percentage lease that requires a base rent of $2,000 per month plus 2 percent of gross sales exceeding $10,000. What is the rent when the monthly gross sales are $18,000?

13. Describe the strategy known as *sale-leaseback*.

For Further Reading

Alexander, A. A. and R. F. Muhlebach. *Managing and Leasing Commercial Properties* (New York: Wiley, 1994).

Banning, K. B. *Residential Property Management Handbook* (New York: McGraw-Hill, 1992).

Brown, R. K. *Managing Corporate Real Estate* (New York: Wiley, 1994).

Lapides, P. D. and E. R. Miller. *Managing and Leasing Residential Properties* (New York: Wiley, 1993).

CHAPTER 10
Real Estate Appraisal

Because the factors that determine value vary so widely, appraisers tend to specialize in particular types of markets: commerical, residential or agricultural.

Real Estate Today

- *Case Study*
  Applying the
  Appraisal Process
  in a Single-Family
  Home Appraisal

Chapter Preview

WHAT IS THE property worth? This question is central to decision making in almost every aspect of real estate. Sellers want to know what their properties should bring in the marketplace, and buyers want to know what their potential purchases are worth in comparison with other properties in the market. Mortgage lenders want to know that the value of a property being pledged as security for a debt is at least as much as the loan amount. Tax assessors, insurance adjusters and right-of-way agents also must obtain estimates of value to collect property taxes, pay insurance claims and compensate landowners for eminent domain takings.

Arriving at reliable estimates of property values requires an in-depth understanding of the factors that influence value, as well as the methods available for estimating value. A thorough understanding of the process appraisers use to estimate value is beneficial to all real estate market participants and absolutely necessary for anyone who hopes to make a career in the appraisal profession. The objectives of this chapter are to

- discuss the regulatory environment surrounding the appraisal profession;
- define the concept of value;
- define some of the basic principles underlying the appraisal process;
- describe the steps in the appraisal process;
- review the basic techniques appraisers use to arrive at value estimates; and
- demonstrate the appraisal process for a single-family home.

UNDERSTANDING THE APPRAISAL PROFESSION

Even though almost all individuals, businesses and other organizations use real estate in their normal activities, few have the expertise necessary to evaluate real estate market conditions and arrive at sound estimates of property value. As a result, many real estate decision makers often must seek the services of real estate appraisers who possess the skills and knowledge necessary to accurately estimate property value. To ensure that people who engage in appraisal services do so in a competent and professional manner, all states have established minimum education and experience requirements for obtaining an appraisal license or certification.

Prior to 1989, few states regulated the appraisal industry, and no specific license was required to perform appraisals. In that year, Congress passed the Financial Institutions Reform, Recovery, and Enforcement Act (FIRREA). Among other things, FIRREA established a federal regulatory hierarchy for the appraisal industry in an attempt to improve the reliability of appraisals in the loan approval process. Under FIRREA, appraisals for properties involved in federally related transactions must be performed by state-licensed or state-certified appraisers. Federally related transactions include those involving any federal government agency, as well as those involving institutions that are regulated or insured by federal agencies. Because most banks, savings institutions and credit unions are federally regulated, virtually all appraisal assignments must be completed by a state-licensed or state-certified appraiser.

The Appraisal Foundation establishes minimum guidelines that states must use to issue appraisal licenses and certifications. The guidelines establish three appraiser categories that permit the license or certificate holder to perform appraisal services in federally related transactions. These categories distinguish between residential and nonresidential assignments and the size of the transactions. Generally, **licensed appraisers** are authorized to perform appraisals for commercial properties in transactions of less than $250,000 and for one-unit to four-unit residential properties in transactions of less than $1 million. **Certified residential appraisers** may perform appraisals on residential properties for transactions of any amount and any number of units. **Certified general appraisers** are permitted to appraise residential and nonresidential properties, regardless of the transaction amount. The education and experience requirements increase for each category.

WHAT IS VALUE?

The concept of value is a topic that has been dear to philosophers and economists for centuries, and the debate over a proper definition of value is frequently revisited in the real estate appraisal literature. Some of the questions considered by researchers include: What constitutes value? Is it the worth of a property to society in general or to an individual investor? Is it price in terms of money or some intrinsic characteristic of the property? Is it value in exchange, value in use or perhaps the cost to produce? For our purposes, we limit our concern to the question: What is it that real estate appraisers try to estimate? As we will see, the answer to this question is carefully defined.

Market Value

The type of value that real estate appraisers generally attempt to estimate is **market value.** The following definition, taken from the Uniform Standards of Profession Appraisal Practice, is the most widely accepted definition of market value and is the basis for most appraisal reports:

Market value: The most probable price which a property should bring in a competitive and open market under all conditions requisite to a fair sale, the buyer and seller each acting prudently and knowledgeably, and assuming the price is not affected by undue stimulus. Implicit in this definition is the consummation of a sale as of a specified date and the passing of title from seller to buyer under conditions whereby:

1. buyer and seller are typically motivated;
2. both parties are well informed or well advised, and acting in what they consider their best interests;
3. a reasonable time is allowed for exposure in the open market;
4. payment is made in terms of cash in United States dollars or in terms of financial arrangements comparable thereto; and
5. the price represents the normal consideration for the property sold unaffected by special or creative financing or sales concessions by anyone associated with the sale.

Though lengthy as a whole, each portion of this definition is important to the appraiser's estimate of value. For example, the price for which one family member might sell a particular property to another could be very different than the price that could be received if the property were offered to all prospective buyers. Similarly, because the financing terms of a transaction may affect the price, the definition of market value refers to the most probable cash or cash equivalent price. Furthermore, this definition assumes that all market participants have an opportunity to consider the property and make an informed and voluntary decision about whether to purchase it. While the implications of the above definition should be always kept in mind, we will refer to a property's market value simply as its most probable selling price.

Investment Value

Market value is what the classical economists called *value in exchange*—that is, the consensus price that would be reached in a market with many buyers and sellers. Another classical value concept is value in use, which has a modern real estate application in the concept of investment value. **Investment value** is defined as the worth of a property to a particular investor, based on that investor's personal standards of investment acceptability. Investment value refers to the value of a property to a specific buyer, while market value refers to the value of a property to the typical, but unspecified, buyer in the market. We will consider the topic of investment analysis in Chapter 17.

Price versus Market Value

As opposed to market value, which is an estimate of the most probable selling price, **price** is the amount actually paid for a property in a particular transaction. It is historical fact, not a prospective concept. Because the buyer or seller may not be well informed, may not be acting prudently or free from undue pressure or may not be engaged in an arm's-length transaction, the price actually paid for a property may not be the same as the market value estimated by an appraiser. On the other hand, price is an accurate indicator of market value if the transaction matches the conditions described in the definition of market value.

Market Value versus Cost of Production

One of the factors influencing market value is cost of production. No rational entrepreneur will keep producing a product unless it is expected to sell for a price that is high enough to cover costs and provide a profit. Unfortunately, however, this does not mean that an entrepreneur will not make a mistake and produce a product that the market values at less than the cost of production. Real estate developers occasionally make mistakes by misjudging markets and developing projects that do not sell at their desired prices. Although costs are one indication of value, market value actually may be higher or lower than cost of production.

Other Types of Value

Although appraisers usually estimate market value, they may be asked to estimate other measures of value as well. Among these are assessed value and insurable value. **Assessed value** is the value placed on a property for property tax assessment purposes. As shown in the discussion of the property tax in Chapter 6, even though assessed value is based on market value, it is seldom a valid estimate of current market value.

Insurable value represents the amount of insurance that should be carried on the destructible portion of real estate to compensate the owner adequately in case of loss. Because insurable value is measured using the concepts of actual cash value and replacement cost, it often differs from current market value. The principles of real property insurance are considered in Chapter 12.

SOME KEY APPRAISAL PRINCIPLES

A number of basic principles drawn primarily from economic thought are essential to the practice of appraisal, and they apply to every type of real estate appraisal assignment. Among them are the principles of anticipation, change, substitution and contribution.

Anticipation

The current value of a property depends on the anticipated utility or income that will accrue to the property owner in the future. This is the principle of **antici-**

pation. Because the present value of a property depends on the expected future benefits of ownership, the appraiser must be skilled in analyzing national, regional, local and neighborhood trends that will influence future income or utility. For example, a motel may have been very profitable in the past, but changing road patterns and other neighborhood factors may considerably reduce the property's income and hence its value in the future.

Change

The principle of anticipation is closely related to the principle of **change,** the notion that economic, social, political and environmental forces constantly cause changes that affect the value of real property. Real estate markets are dynamic rather than static, and appraisers must carefully analyze the direction and degree of change in factors affecting market values. For this reason, every value estimate must be made as of a specified date.

Substitution

The principle of **substitution** holds that a prudent buyer will pay no more for a property than the cost of acquiring an equally desirable substitute in the open market. This principle is fundamental to all three traditional approaches to real estate valuation—the sales comparison, income and cost approaches. It supports the premise that a buyer will not pay any more for a home or another real estate improvement than the cost of reproducing the improvement on a similar site. Suppose, for example, that a lot can be purchased in a particular subdivision and a certain size and type of house constructed for a total cost of $300,000. This will tend to set the upper limit to value for existing houses of similar size and type in the subdivision unless they have some distinguishing locational feature, such as an exceptional view or nearness to a golf course or lake.

Contribution

The principles of diminishing marginal utility and diminishing returns to factors of production are fundamental to economic theory. Their application in real estate appraisal is closely related to the principle of **contribution,** which states that the value of a component part of a property depends on the amount it contributes to the value of the whole. For example, tasteful landscaping may increase the value of a home much more than the cost of the improvement. An expenditure for extensive plantings of exotic shrubs, however, probably will not be recovered if the property is sold. In fact, certain improvements to a property can actually have a negative effect on value.

Suppose a homeowner builds an elaborate shrine to a major league baseball team in the dining room. Because the typical buyer prefers that such an item not be a part of the property, the value of the shrine equals the cost of removing it, less any salvage value. The principle of contribution is an especially important consideration for real estate appraisers. Even though a property may have an expensive feature or characteristic, the contribution to market value is often less than the cost of the feature because the typical buyer in the market does not desire that feature in the property.

THE APPRAISAL PROCESS

Over the years, appraisers have developed a formal process to collect data, analyze them to arrive at an estimate of value and present their findings. The **appraisal process** is a systematic procedure employed to arrive at an estimate of value and convey that estimate to the appraisal user. Although we present the steps of this process in their general chronological order, it is important to realize that in practice, the order of consideration of these steps may need to be adjusted to match the conditions of a specific appraisal assignment. Careful consideration of each of the following steps will lead to sound estimates of value:

1. Definition of the problem
2. Data selection and collection
3. Highest and best use analysis
4. Application of the three approaches to value
5. Reconciliation of value indications into a final value estimate
6. Report of defined value

Step 1: Definition of the Problem

The first step in the appraisal process is to define the problem at hand. The accuracy of the value estimate provided by the appraiser depends on careful specification of the appraisal assignment. The appraiser and the client must be in accord as to the type of value to be estimated, the property involved, the specific property rights being appraised and the effective date of the appraisal.

The most common purpose of an appraisal is to estimate market value, but appraisers may be asked to estimate rental value, insurable value, assessed value or investment value. The type of value to be estimated will largely dictate the type of data that must be collected and the way they should be analyzed. It is essential therefore that the purpose of the appraisal and the definition of value be stated clearly.

The description of the property to be appraised must include the location of the property, usually provided by both its street address and legal description. This description must also include any easements or encroachments that might affect value. Obviously, the physical characteristics of the property must be identified, including buildings and other improvements; the size of the parcel; and its topography, soil conditions, elevation and other physical features.

Not only the physical property but the specific property rights to be appraised must be clearly identified. These rights may be complete, as in a fee simple estate, or partial, including only such interests as air rights, the reversionary right in a leased fee, an easement or some other type of limited property interest. The description should include limitations on these property rights, such as restrictive covenants and land-use controls.

The appraiser usually is called on to make an estimate of the current value of the property, although in some cases, an appraisal is required for some date in the past. Retrospective appraisals may be required for many reasons, including determination of inheritance taxes and insurance claims. Because the value of property changes over time, specification of an effective date for an appraisal is a necessary part of defining the problem.

Step 2: Data Selection and Collection

After defining the problem, the appraiser must identify and collect data that will permit an accurate estimate of property value. In addition to general information regarding economic, social, political and environmental factors that may affect the value of the property being appraised, the appraiser must collect specific information regarding recent sales prices of similar properties, construction cost data and income and expense information for the subject property and comparable properties in the market. As we will see in the remaining steps of the appraisal process, the accuracy and appropriateness of data collected for analysis are critical to the validity of the value estimate. Estimates of value based on inaccurate or inappropriate data are not reliable.

Step 3: Highest and Best Use Analysis

After determining the data requirements for an appraisal assignment and collecting the data for analysis, the next step is to analyze the property's highest and best use. **Highest and best use** is defined as that use, found to be legally permissible and financially feasible, that results in the highest land value. As we noted earlier, market value refers to the most probable price a property would bring in an open market transaction. Because the typical buyer in such a transaction would most probably use the property in its highest and best use, value estimates are based on the assumption that the highest and best use of the property has been identified. This follows from the recognition that competition among market participants results in the most efficient and appropriate use of a property, even if that means changing its current use. Any estimate of market value must include a determination of the property's highest and best use.

The determination of the highest and best use of a property is of primary importance in any appraisal, although in many cases, it is readily apparent. For example, if the property to be appraised is a five-year-old house in an established single-family neighborhood, the highest and best use of the property is most likely a single-family home. In other cases, however, the highest and best use of a property may be dramatically different from its current use.

Highest and best use of a property is affected by many factors, including its past and present uses, land-use controls, nearby land uses, the availability or absence of utilities and transportation facilities, and recent or anticipated economic growth in the area. Analysis of highest and best use generally is easier for vacant land than for land with improvements that might require removal, so we will consider each in turn.

Highest and Best Use of Vacant Land   Suppose that a 50-acre tract of land has been planted in soybeans for some years. The value of the land in this agricultural use is $2,500 per acre. In the past, farming represented the highest and best use of the tract because the site was located several miles from a small city. More recently, the city has begun expanding because increased business and manufacturing activity there has led to population growth. These factors, combined with road improvements and the extension of water and sewer lines, have led to a change in the highest and best use of the site. In fact, there may be several legally permissible and financially feasible uses for it. One developer believes there is sufficient demand for a low-density, single-family residential subdivision and is willing to pay $30,000 per acre. Another developer wishes to build an apartment complex and is willing to pay $120,000 per acre. The second developer must believe that using the land for an apartment complex is more profitable than using it for single-family homes. Assuming both of these uses are legally permissible and physically possible, the highest and best use of this parcel is an apartment complex because it results in the highest land value.

Highest and Best Use of Land with Improvements   In the example above, the determination of highest and best use was simplified by the fact that the land was vacant. Suppose, however, that a one-acre lot and the house on it are worth $175,000 as a single-family home. Under the current zoning ordinances, if the land were vacant, it could be sold for $80,000 as a single-family home site, or $150,000 for a commercial activity. If vacant, the highest and best use of the site is clearly commercial, but because the property is worth more in its current use, its highest and best use still is residential. If the value of the site for commercial use increases above its value in residential use, however, it would be advantageous to tear down the existing house and change the use to commercial. The highest and best use of this property may change quickly if the existing improvements begin to deteriorate rapidly as a result of age or other factors. Although identifying a property's highest and best use can be a difficult task, appraisers must understand the manner in which the property would be used by the typical buyer in order to estimate its most probable selling price.

Step 4: Application of the Three Approaches to Value

In the traditional appraisal process, the appraiser normally considers three approaches to value. Each of these approaches is intended to replicate the thought processes of the typical buyer in order to estimate a property's most probable selling price in an open market transaction. Because we will consider the details of each of these approaches in the following sections of this chapter, we provide only brief descriptions here.

In the **sales comparison approach,** appraisers compare the subject property to similar properties that have been sold recently in open market transactions. The prices of these comparable properties provide an indication of the value of the subject property. Of course, every property is unique, and any differences between the comparable properties and the subject property must be taken into consideration.

In the **cost approach** appraisers arrive at an estimate of the market value of a property by estimating its cost of production. Estimating value using this approach involves (1) estimating the value of the site as though it were vacant, (2) estimating the cost to produce the improvements, (3) subtracting depreciation and (4) adding site value. Numerous techniques for estimating the value of vacant land exist, with the preferred method being the sales comparison approach. Estimating production cost requires knowledge of construction methods and current prices of materials and labor. Of course, the estimate of production cost is based on constructing a new structure, so appraisers must subtract any depreciation that exists in the subject property. Adding the site value to the depreciated cost of the improvements provides an indication of market value.

In the **income approach,** appraisers estimate market value by discounting or "capitalizing" the future income expected to accrue to the property owner. Appraisers must estimate the income that the property is expected to generate, then convert the income stream into a present value estimate. The techniques used to relate income expectations to market value estimates include gross income multiplier analysis, net income capitalization and discounted cash flow analysis.

Step 5: Reconciliation of Value Indications

Although the three approaches described above should theoretically lead to identical value estimates, the realities of real estate markets usually result in a different estimate of value from each approach. Large differences between the value indications suggest that one or more of the approaches may not be appropriate for estimating a property's market value. To arrive at a final estimate of value, appraisers must reconcile the estimates obtained from all approaches. Reconciliation of the three approaches requires considerable judgement on the part of the appraiser.

In most appraisal situations, the appraiser may feel that one of the approaches provides a better indication of value than the others and therefore gives more emphasis to that approach in the reconciliation step. For example, if an appraiser estimates the market value of a church building, the sales comparison approach might not be appropriate if sales of church buildings are infrequent in the market. Similarly, the income approach may not be appropriate because such properties are not considered income producing. The lack of data required to implement these approaches in this situation may lead the appraiser to place more emphasis on the value estimate provided by the cost approach. In all cases, the appraiser must determine the weight given to the value indicated by each approach using his or her professional judgment. The appropriate weight depends on the amount and quality of available data, as well as the relevance of the approach to the problem at hand. When all of the approaches are relevant to some degree, appraisers often use a weighted average of the three value estimates to arrive at a final value estimate.

Step 6: Report of Defined Value

After reaching an estimate of value, the appraiser must convey the information to the client, normally in a written report. This report describes the data considered, as well as the methods and reasoning used in arriving at the final value estimate. Any assumptions used in the analysis must be clearly stated and defended.

When the property involved is a single-family home and the function of the appraiser is to verify property value for loan approval purposes, the appraiser's analysis and conclusion must be reported in a format acceptable to the lender. Because lenders often sell their loans in the secondary mortgage market, the secondary market participants dictate the format of the appraisal report. Fannie Mae and Freddie Mac have jointly approved a Uniform Residential Appraisal Report (URAR) form for loans sold in the secondary mortgage market. (A example of the URAR is shown in the Case Study at the end of this chapter.) Similar forms are used for other types of property, including vacant land and small income properties. For more complex appraisal assignments, the analysis and conclusions are usually presented in narrative report formats. Narrative appraisal reports often exceed several hundred pages for large-scale income properties.

Now that we understand the general process appraisers use to estimate property value, we can take a closer look at the specific techniques used in each of the three approaches to value: the sales comparison approach, the cost approach and the income approach.

THE SALES COMPARISON APPROACH

Perhaps the best single indication of the value of any good is the price that similar goods sell for in the marketplace. This is the basis of the sales comparison approach to the valuation of real property. This technique has tremendous intuitive appeal because it closely resembles the process most buyers go through when selecting properties for purchase. The procedure involves comparing the subject property with similar properties that have sold relatively recently or are currently offered for sale, and using the sales prices of these properties to gain insight into the market value of the subject property.

Because individual parcels of real estate all have unique characteristics, close comparisons are difficult. In addition, sales data may be very sketchy or nonexistent for specialized properties. Nevertheless, when data are available, the sales comparison approach generally is considered the best method for estimating the value of real property. It is particularly valuable in appraising single-family homes in active markets.

The sales comparison approach involves two steps: (1) collection of data on sales of similar properties and (2) adjustment of the sales data to make them reflect the subject property as accurately as possible in regard to physical and locational characteristics, financing arrangements, conditions of the sale and market conditions at the time of the sale.

Comparable Sales Data

The selection of "comparables," recent sales of properties that are roughly the same as the subject property, is critical to the market value estimate. The appraiser must take great care that the sales selected are truly representative and not distorted in some way. For example, the price that results in a voluntary sale to a mortgage lender in lieu of foreclosure probably would not be representative of the property's market value, nor would the price that results from a sale from one family member to another.

Generally, three to six comparable sales are considered adequate. The information on each transaction should include the date of sale, price, financing terms, location of the property and a description of its physical characteristics and improvements. Deed records can provide information regarding location and date of sale, and where available, deed tax stamps may also give some indication of sales price. More definitive price and property characteristics may be provided by buyers and sellers, brokers, title and abstract companies, multiple-listing services or specialized financial report services.

Adjustment of Sales Data

After data on comparable sales have been gathered, they must be adjusted to reflect the subject property as accurately as possible. The appraiser may make a lump-sum adjustment by evaluating all of the differences between the comparable sale and the subject property that are considered important. For example, the appraiser may conclude that on the basis of a comparable sale of $75,000, the subject property should sell for $80,000 because of its more desirable location and better-quality construction. A refinement of this lump-sum approach is to evaluate the individual elements that may affect value. In any case, the following elements of comparison must be evaluated for potential differences between the subject property and the comparable properties.

Elements of Comparison   Six different elements of comparison must be considered in the sales comparison approach. The first two elements of comparison are *property rights conveyed* and *conditions of sale*. If analysis of these two elements identifies significant differences between the subject property and any potentially comparable property, the sales price of such a comparable provides little insight into the market value of the subject property, and it should be eliminated from further consideration.

For example, if the subject property involves a fee simple absolute estate and a comparable property was sold as a life estate, the subject property is almost certainly worth more than the comparable. Therefore, the sales price of the comparable property will not give a reliable indication of the value of the subject property. In most cases, appraisers prefer to eliminate properties with inconsistent property rights from further analysis. Similarly, if a potentially comparable property's transaction price is not the result of arm's-length negotiation between informed parties, the sales price of the comparable property will not provide a valid indication of the market value of the subject property. The definition of market value is explicit in defining the conditions of sale for the subject property. In general, appraisers assume that the subject property will be sold in a competitive and open market under all conditions necessary for a fair sale.

Another element of comparison addresses the *financing terms* in a comparable sale. As required by the definition of market value, the market value of the subject property is estimated in terms of cash or financial arrangements comparable to cash. If the transaction of a comparable property involved unique financial arrangements that may have affected the sales price, the sales price of the comparable must be adjusted to reflect this difference. For example, if a seller provides a mortgage loan with a below-market interest rate to the buyer, it is likely that the buyer would pay a higher price for the property. Because the financing terms in this transaction are more favorable than those generally available in the market, the price of the comparable must be adjusted downward to accurately reflect the value of the subject property. The amount of adjustment depends primarily on the interest savings provided to the buyer by the below-market financing.

Another important consideration is the fact that local market conditions are subject to change over time as a result of changing economic, political, social and environmental factors. This element of comparison is frequently referred to as *market conditions*. A property that sold four months ago or even a week ago may sell for more or less today as a result of changing market conditions. Therefore, appraisers must adjust the sales prices of comparable properties to reflect differences in market conditions between the time of sale and the effective date of appraisal. If conditions have improved such that a sale of a comparable property in today's market would result in a higher price, the price of the comparable should be adjusted upward to provide a valid indication of the subject property's current market value.

Yet another element of comparison involves differences between the *locational characteristics* of the subject and comparable properties. Most people are familiar with the old saying among real estate investors that the three most important factors affecting real estate values are location, location and location. Though simplistic, this statement embodies a certain amount of wisdom. Because real estate values are dramatically influenced by local market factors, properties in the same neighborhood are considered the most comparable to each other. A **neighborhood** can be defined as a geographic area containing complementary land uses. For some properties, the boundaries that define a neighborhood are quite expansive, while others are more compact. Even within the same neighborhood, one site may be preferable over another due to access and proximity to shopping and schools, traffic volume on the surrounding streets and numerous other factors. Consideration of locational characteristics is a critical step in the adjustment process.

The final element of comparison reflects differences in *physical characteristics* between the subject property and the comparable properties. Though the possibilities are endless, some commonly encountered differences include the size of the property (land area and improvements), number and size of the rooms, type of construction, quality of construction, interior design and architectural style, as well as numerous special features. If the comparable properties possess physical characteristics that differ from those of the subject property, appropriate adjustments must be made to the sale prices of the comparable properties to ensure that the prices are indicative of the subject property's market value.

When the adjustments for each of these elements of comparison are complete, the adjusted sales prices for the comparables give an indication of the value of the subject property. Again, the steps involved in this approach mirror the steps a potential buyer might go through when comparing alternative properties and making a purchase decision. The example below demonstrates the logic behind the sales comparison approach using "pair-wise" comparisons of comparable properties to determine the appropriate adjustment amounts.

Applying the Sales Comparison Approach

Consider the problem of estimating the value of a vacant, lakefront lot in a residential subdivision. The lot under consideration measures 80 feet by 120 feet. Three similar vacant lots in this subdivision have sold recently in transactions resulting from arm's-length negotiations for the transfer of fee simple absolute estates, and all sales prices reflect cash-equivalent financing terms.

Sales Comparison Market Data Grid **Table 10.1**

	Subject	# 1	# 2	# 3
		Comparables		
Sales price	—	$30,100	$32,500	$21,600
Size in square feet	9,600	10,200	11,900	9,600
Price per square foot	—	$2.95	$2.73	$2.25
Date of sale	Current	– 2 weeks	– 1 year	– 6 months
Adjustment for changing market conditions	—	+$0	+$.22	+$.11
Adjusted price per square foot	—	$2.95	$2.95	$2.36
Location	Lake	Lake	Lake	Interior
Adjustment for location				
Adjusted price per square foot	—	+$0	+$0	+$.59
	—	$2.95	$2.95	$2.95

Indicated value of subject property: 9,600 square feet × $2.95 = $28,320

The significant differences between these properties are date of sale, lot size and location of the lot relative to the lake. Comparable 1 measures 85 feet by 120 feet and is also located on the lake. It sold for $30,100 two weeks ago. Comparable 2 is a lakefront lot measuring 85 feet by 140 feet. This lot sold one year ago for $32,500. Comparable 3 sold six months ago for $21,600. It is an interior lot measuring 80 feet by 120 feet.

One way to organize and analyze sales comparison data is through a market data grid such as the one shown in Table 10.1. Because the lots differ in terms of size, we can simplify our analysis by first calculating the sales price per square foot. After adjusting the sales price of each comparable for differences in market conditions since the sale date, we can multiply the adjusted price per square foot by the size of the subject property to arrive at an estimate of value for the subject property.

To determine the adjustment necessary to account for changing market conditions, notice that comparables 1 and 2 are both lakefront properties, but comparable 2 sold approximately one year later than comparable 1. Because we eliminated the size difference by calculating price per square foot, the only difference between comparables 1 and 2 is the date of sale. The difference in price for these properties suggests that property values have increased by approximately $.22 per square foot over the past year. Because the effective date of the appraisal is today, we must estimate the price the comparables would bring if offered for sale under current market conditions. Thus, we adjust the price per square foot of comparable 2 upward by $.22. Assuming the change in property values has been constant over the past year, we can also adjust the sales price of comparable 3 upward by half of this amount, or $.11, to account for changing market conditions over the past six months.

After the adjustment for changing market conditions, the only remaining difference between the subject property and any of the comparables is location of the lots relative to the lake. Our subject property is a lakefront lot, as are comparables 1 and 2. Comparable 3, however, is an interior lot. Just as we determined the adjustment for changing market conditions by comparing the sale prices of two of the comparables that differed only in terms of their sale date, we can determine the appropriate adjustment for location by comparing the sales price of comparable 3 with the sales prices of the other comparables. The higher sales prices of the first two comparables suggest that lake frontage adds approximately $.59 per square foot to property values in this neighborhood. Adding this amount to the price per square foot of comparable 3 results in a value indication from each of the comparables of $2.95. Multiplying this amount by 9,600 square feet yields $28,320. Thus, we conclude that this amount is an estimate of the current market value of the subject property, after adjustments for differences in market conditions, lot size and location.

Although this example refers to vacant land, the same procedure can be applied to improved residential and nonresidential properties. We will apply this approach to a single-family home in the Case Study at the end of the chapter. Of course, it is unlikely that all of the comparable properties will provide identical indications of value. Also, the appropriate unit of comparison is not always price per square foot. The primary consideration in this approach to value is to correctly determine the appropriate amount and direction of adjustments for each element of comparison. In most situations, the adjustments are much more detailed than those described here. Furthermore, the data available from sales of comparable properties may be insufficient to provide a valid value estimate. Without adequate data, the sales comparison approach is not reliable.

THE COST APPROACH

In addition to existing properties to choose from, a potential buyer of a home or another real property improvement usually has the alternative of buying a similar site and constructing a new building. Generally, therefore, site value plus production costs of the improvements tend to set the upper limit to value. In this sense, the principle of substitution is the basis of the cost approach to value. The cost approach comprises four key steps, including (1) estimating the value of the site as though it were vacant, (2) estimating the cost to produce the improvements, (3) subtracting depreciation and (4) adding site value.

The indicated value of the property is the cost to produce the building, less the estimated accrued depreciation, plus the value of the site and site improvements. Subtracting accrued depreciation is necessary because the cost estimate is based on constructing a new, identically designed building using current prices for materials and labor. The subject property is most likely not new, and if it were constructed new, any design flaws would be corrected. Estimating the accrued depreciation for a property is often the most difficult step of the cost approach.

Estimating Site Value

The first step in the cost approach is to estimate the value of the site. Land values are usually estimated by the sales comparison approach as demonstrated above, though other techniques are sometimes used. The costs of site improvements such as grading, landscaping and paving must be added to arrive at a total value for the site.

Estimating Production Cost

The second step in the cost approach is to estimate the production cost of the improvements. Production cost estimates are based on either **reproduction cost** or **replacement cost.** Reproduction cost refers to the cost of constructing an exact replica of the subject property's improvements, while replacement cost refers to the cost of constructing an equally functional improvement, rather than an exact duplicate. Using replacement cost as the basis for this approach simplifies the cost-estimating procedure when the property being appraised contains design elements or materials that are out of date and would therefore not be included if the building were constructed today.

Estimating production cost requires specialized knowledge regarding construction methods, so appraisers frequently rely on engineering and architectural experts for accurate cost estimates. Professional cost-estimating companies publish cost manuals or provide computerized cost programs that assist appraisers in this task. In practice, construction costs can be estimated by obtaining actual expenditure data on the subject property, by collecting data on other similar projects in the area or through data services that collect and distribute cost data on various types of construction. Methods used in estimating production costs include the comparative-unit method, the segregated cost method and the quantity survey method. Of these methods, the quantity survey method is the most detailed.

The comparative-unit method employs the known costs of similar structures, typically measured in dollars per square foot, to derive an estimate of the cost to produce a subject property's improvements. For example, a typical warehouse might cost $32.15 per square foot to construct. If the subject property contains 50,000 square feet, its cost is estimated at $1,607,500. This approach does not separately identify the individual components that make up the building, but can be fairly accurate for properties with uniform construction.

In the segregated cost method, the unit costs for various building components are used to arrive at a cost estimate. For instance, the cost of building finished exterior walls on a warehouse is $5.52 per square foot, and the subject property has 10,700 square feet of exterior walls, the cost of this component would be approximately $59,000. The cost of each major component of the building (walls, roof, flooring, plumbing, etc.) is estimated separately, then all costs are added together for a final cost estimate. This method is more comprehensive than the comparative-unit method, but less detailed than the quantity survey method.

The quantity survey method is the most comprehensive method and therefore the most accurate. In this method, the quantity and quality of all materials and all categories of labor are identified separately, then costs for all of these items are totaled to arrive at a final cost estimate. For example, the number of sheets of plywood, gallons of paint, amount of piping and hours of electricians' labor, as well as all other materials or labor needed to construct a building, must be identified and the costs of each estimated. The quantity survey method provides the most detailed cost estimate, but it is time consuming and not used frequently in the appraisal process.

Estimating Accrued Depreciation

Structures wear out over time. They also may become obsolete or unprofitable because of technological innovation or economic change. Therefore, unless the subject property's improvements are new, appraisers must estimate **accrued depreciation**—the amount by which the value of a building has declined since it was built, as a consequence of physical deterioration, functional obsolescence and economic obsolescence.

Physical deterioration may result from ordinary wear and tear, weathering from the elements, vandalism or neglect. Physical deterioration should be minimal in new buildings and can be prevented or minimized by proper maintenance and quality construction. Appraisers often estimate the effective age of the improvements, then use the ratio of effective age to useful life to measure physical deterioration. For example, a 15-year-old house with normal maintenance might exhibit 25 percent physical deterioration if its useful life is 60 years.

Many properties suffer their greatest loss in value from the effects of obsolescence, both functional and economic. **Functional obsolescence** is a loss in value that occurs because the property has less utility or ability to generate income than a new property designed for the same use. This sort of depreciation results from factors inherent in the property itself. It may occur because of changes in technology or in tastes, which would cause a new building to be constructed quite differently from the way the existing structure was built. For example, buildings using asbestos insulation now suffer large penalties. To a lesser extent, so do outmoded, multistory factory buildings and poorly designed houses with small, dark rooms. An increasingly important issue faced by appraisers is the difficulty of estimating the value of environmentally contaminated parcels.

Economic obsolescence is a loss in value resulting from factors outside of the property that affect its income-producing ability or other degree of use. For example, suppose that a well-designed and well-constructed motel in good physical condition is located in an area bypassed by a new highway. The resulting decline in traffic may greatly decrease the income-producing ability of the property and hence its value. Economic obsolescence also may occur because of changes in consumer expenditure patterns, population movements, adverse legislation or neighborhood change.

Adding Site Value

The final step in the cost approach is to add the site value to the depreciated cost of the improvements. This step provides an estimate of total value indicated by the cost approach.

	Site Value
+	Production Cost
−	Depreciation
	Value Indicated by Cost Approach

Applying the Cost Approach

To demonstrate the steps involved in the cost approach, consider a two-year-old apartment building. To estimate its value by this approach, we must estimate the value of the site, the production cost of the improvements and the accrued depreciation resulting from physical deterioration and economic and functional obsolescence. Suppose the appraiser estimates these items as shown in Table 10.2. The land value is estimated as $150,000 using the sales comparison approach. Estimated production cost for the two-year-old building is $594,000.

Even though the buildings are almost new, the appraiser determines that some allowance for depreciation is called for. A minor roof repair is necessary ($4,680), and some miscellaneous physical deterioration requires attention ($17,820). In addition, the appraiser judges that the swimming pool has been placed too close to apartment 11, resulting in some minor functional obsolescence that could be eliminated by building an appropriate screening wall ($4,000). Because the property is relatively new, the appraiser determines that no allowance is necessary for economic obsolescence. Depreciation from all causes in the amount of $26,500 is subtracted from the estimated production cost to yield a building value of $567,500. Adding this amount to the site value provides an indication of value by the cost approach of $717,500, which the appraiser rounds to $718,000.

THE INCOME APPROACH

The income approach to value is based on the principle of anticipation, which assumes that purchasers buy properties in expectation of receiving future benefits. In general, the value of any income-earning asset can be thought of as the sum of the present value of the expected future returns to the owner, including both periodic cash flows from operations and cash flows from the eventual sale of the asset. The same logic is valid for any income-producing asset, whether it be the goose that lays golden eggs, a savings certificate from a financial institution, common stock or such income-producing real estate as an apartment complex, a shopping mall, an office complex or an industrial building. The income approach in real estate appraisal involves two basic steps: estimating future income and converting the income estimate into a present value estimate.

Appraisers employ many different techniques to convert future income into present value estimates. Each of these techniques has been developed to replicate the thought processes of the typical buyer in a market. We consider three of these techniques here: gross income multiplier analysis, net income capitalization and discounted cash-flow analysis.

Table 10.2	Summary of Cost Valuation of an Apartment Property

Estimated production cost		$594,000
Depreciation		
Physical deterioration: cost of repairs	$ 4,680	
(roof repair, painting, exterior caulking)		
Miscellaneous physical deterioration	17,820	
(3% of reproduction costs)		
Functional obsolescence	4,000	
(screen between swimming pool and		
apartment to reduce noise from pool)		
Economic obsolescence	0	
	$26,500	
Production cost less depreciation		567,500
Estimated site value		150,000
Total value indicated by cost approach		$717,500
Rounded		$718,000

Gross Income Multiplier

All techniques used in the income approach to value are based on the idea that market participants demand investment returns in exchange for purchasing income properties. Furthermore, competition between market participants results in a relatively stable relationship between income and value in most real estate markets. When this relationship can be measured or quantified, appraisers can use it to estimate market values. One rule-of-thumb measure of the relationship between gross income and market value is the **gross income multiplier** (GIM):

$$\text{Gross income multiplier } = \frac{\text{Value}}{\text{Gross income}}$$

The GIM is an estimate of the prevailing relationship between prices investors are willing to pay for properties and the income the properties are expected to produce. To calculate the GIM for a market, appraisers collect information about properties that have recently sold in the market, then divide the price of each property by its expected gross income. Of course, the properties used to estimate the GIM for a market must truly be comparable to the subject property. Gross income is defined as the total amount of revenue the property is expected to generate annually.

For example, consider a property expected to generate $10,000 per year in gross income. If that property is sold in an arm's-length transaction for $100,000, the GIM for this property is 10 ($100,000 ÷ 10,000). To use this measure to estimate the value of a similar property expected to generate $9,000 per year in gross income, we multiply $9,000 by 10 to get a market value estimate of $90,000. By observing market transactions, appraisers can measure the relationship between income and value using the GIM, then use the multiplier to estimate market value of the subject property.

Because the GIM technique ignores the expenses of operating an income property, it is most appropriate when the expenses of the comparable sales are similar to the expenses of the subject property. When expenses differ across properties, a more detailed technique is required. The net income capitalization technique described below is an alternative technique that recognizes the variability in operating expenses across similar properties.

Net Income Capitalization

The net income capitalization technique recognizes that the value of an income property depends on net rather than gross income, as discussed above. In this technique, net income is converted into a present value estimate using a **capitalization rate** rather than a multiplier. The relationship between value and net income is measured as shown below:

$$\text{Capitalization rate} = \frac{\text{Net income}}{\text{Value}}$$

For example, consider a property that recently sold in an arm's-length transaction for $1 million. If this property is expected to generate net income of $100,000 annually, its implied capitalization rate is 10 percent. To estimate the value of a similar property expected to generate $105,000 in net income (gross income minus expenses), we can rearrange the capitalization rate formula as follows:

$$\text{Value} = \frac{\text{Net income}}{\text{Capitalization rate}}$$

$$\text{Value} = \frac{\$105,000}{.10}$$

$$\text{Value} = \$1,050,000$$

Dividing net income by 10 percent provides a market value estimate of $1,050,000 for this property. By observing market transactions, appraisers can determine the capitalization rate that best represents the relationship between net income and value, then use this measure to estimate the value of a subject property based on its net income. The accuracy of this technique, of course, depends on accurate estimates of the subject property's net income and the capitalization rate.

Discounted Cash-Flow Analysis

A third technique appraisers use in the income approach is discounted cash flow analysis. Unlike the previous two methods, which focus on a single year's income estimate to arrive at a value estimate, this technique involves forecasting the future benefits the property is expected to generate in each year of the expected

| Table 10.3 | Applying the Discounted Cash-Flow Technique |

	Year 1	Year 2	Year 3	Year 4	Year 5	Year 6	Year 7	Year 8	Year 9	Year 10	Year 11
Potential gross income	$625,000	$643,750	$663,063	$682,954	$703,443	$724,546	$746,283	$768,671	$791,731	$815,483	$839,948
- Vacancy losses	156,250	32,188	33,153	34,148	35,172	36,227	37,314	38,434	39,587	40,774	41,997
Effective gross income	$468,750	$611,563	$629,909	$648,807	$668,271	$688,319	$708,969	$730,238	$752,145	$774,709	$797,950
- Operating expenses	93,750	122,313	125,982	129,761	133,654	137,664	141,794	146,048	150,429	154,942	159,590
Net operating income	$375,000	$489,250	$503,928	$519,045	$534,617	$550,655	$567,175	$584,190	$601,716	$619,767	$638,360
- Debt service	224,000	224,000	224,000	224,000	224,000	224,000	224,000	224,000	224,000	224,000	N.A.
Before-tax cash flow	$151,000	$265,250	$279,928	$295,045	$310,617	$326,655	$343,175	$360,190	$377,716	$395,767	N.A.

Year 11 net operating income	$ 638,360
Overall capitalization rate	.10
Gross sale prices (NOI/R)	$6,383,600
- Selling expenses	319,180
Net sales price	$6,064,420
- Mortgage balance	1,503,000
Before-tax equity reversion	$4,561,420

Present value of before-tax cash flows and before-tax equity reversion at 13 percent: $2,909,233.

Real Estate Today
Close-Up

Applying the Appraisal Process in a Single-Family Home Appraisal

R ecall from earlier chapters the single-family home owned by Harold and Gladys Stewart. Suppose that an agreement has been reached between the Stewarts and Frank and Elizabeth Barr. The Barrs have agreed to purchase the property for $120,000. (Real estate sales contracts are discussed in Chapter 11.) The Barrs plan on borrowing 90 percent of the purchase price, using a mortgage loan from a local lender. As part of the loan approval process, the lender requires that an appraisal be performed by a qualified real estate appraiser to verify that the property value supports the requested loan amount. The following discussion describes the steps the appraiser will take to apply the appraisal process to this property.

Defining the Problem

The appraiser selected to perform the assignment for the Barrs' lender is Michelle Tipton, a state-certified appraiser. Tipton has ten years' experience in the appraisal industry and is qualified to perform appraisals on all types of properties. Her fee for this appraisal assignment is $250. The cost of hiring the appraiser will be paid by the Barrs, even though the appraiser performs the appraisal on behalf of the lender.

The Barrs and their lender provide Tipton with the basic information she needs to begin the appraisal process. To define the appraisal problem at hand, the appraiser must know what type of value she is trying to estimate, the property rights being appraised and the legal description of the property that is the subject of the appraisal. In this case, the purpose of the appraisal is to estimate the current market value of the property described as

All that tract or parcel of land, situated in St. Joseph, Buchanan County, Missouri, together with

all improvements thereon, known as 1097 Timbers Crossing. Such property is more accurately described as Lot 3, Block G, of the Harris Billups Estate, as recorded in Plat Book 8, page 37, in the Office of the Clerk of the Circuit Court of Buchanan County, Missouri.

The property rights being appraised are those that compose a fee simple absolute ownership interest in the subject property. All of this information is entered in the "Subject" section of the URAR, as shown in Figure 10.1.

Selecting and Collecting the Data

After defining the appraisal problem, the appraiser begins selecting and collecting the data she will need to estimate the value of the subject property. She begins by personally inspecting the property to familiarize herself with its neighborhood, as well as the physical characteristics of the site and improvements.

As indicated in the "Neighborhood" section of Figure 10.1, the property is located in an urban area that is more than 75 percent developed, has a stable growth rate and stable property values and where supply and demand conditions appear to be in balance. In addition, Tipton notes that the ages of homes in this neighborhood range from new to 50 years old and that prices range from $70,000 to $155,000. Single-family homes compose approximately 85 percent of all properties in this area, with two-family to four-family structures, four-or-more-family structures and commercial uses comprising 5 percent each. Tipton believes that a change in land use in this neighborhood is not likely in the near future. She also defines the boundaries of the neighborhood and its characteristics and provides additional comments about the market conditions in the subject neighborhood, as shown on the report.

Figure 10.1 Uniform Residential Appraisal Report

File No. 96-100 Page # 1

Summary Appraisal Report
Property Description

UNIFORM RESIDENTIAL APPRAISAL REPORT

File No. 96-100

SUBJECT

Property Address 1097 Timbers Crossing City St. Joseph State MO Zip Code 94334
Legal Description Lot 3, Block G, Harris Billups Estate, Plat Book 8, P. 37 County Buchanan
Assessor's Parcel No. 9223-03-0471 Tax Year 1994 R.E. Taxes $ 1,207.10 Special Assessments $ N/A
Borrower Barr, Frank & Elizabeth Current Owner Stewart Occupant: [X] Owner [ ] Tenant [ ] Vacant
Property rights appraised [X] Fee Simple [ ] Leasehold Project Type [ ] PUD [ ] Condominium (HUD/VA only) HOA $ N/A /Mo.
Neighborhood or Project Name Harris Billups Estate Map Reference Census Tract
Sale Price $ 120,000 Date of Sale Description and $ amount of loan charges/concessions to be paid by seller None
Lender/Client Barber Savings Association Address 4390 N. Main St., St. Joseph MO 94330
Appraiser Michelle Tipton Address 2125 S. Main St., St. Joseph MO 94330

NEIGHBORHOOD

Location	[X] Urban	[ ] Suburban	[ ] Rural
Built up	[X] Over 75%	[ ] 25-75%	[ ] Under 25%
Growth rate	[ ] Rapid	[X] Stable	[ ] Slow
Property values	[ ] Increasing	[X] Stable	[ ] Declining
Demand/supply	[ ] Shortage	[X] In balance	[ ] Over supply
Marketing time	[ ] Under 3 mos.	[X] 3-6 mos.	[ ] Over 6 mos.

Predominant occupancy: [X] Owner [ ] Tenant [X] Vacant (0-5%) [ ] Vac.(over 5%)

Single family housing
PRICE $(000): Low 70 / High 155 / Predominant 120
AGE (yrs): Low 00 / High 50 / Predominant 20

Present land use %
One family 85
2-4 family 5
Multi-family 5
Commercial 5

Land use change [X] Not likely [ ] Likely [ ] In process To:

Note: Race and the racial composition of the neighborhood are not appraisal factors.
Neighborhood boundaries and characteristics: Area of mostly single family homes located north of Oak Park Blvd., west of Highway 60, South of Floral Road and east of Dixie Drive.
Factors that affect the marketability of the properties in the neighborhood (proximity to employment and amenities, employment stability, appeal to market, etc.): The subject is located close to neighborhood shopping, parks, public schools and employment centers. The subject's neighborhood exhibits the typical appeal and condition for the area. The presence of 5% commercial utilization is limited to the main thoroughfares and does not adversely affect the subject's value or marketability.

Market conditions in the subject neighborhood (including support for the above conclusions related to the trend of property values, demand/supply, and marketing time -- such as data on competitive properties for sale in the neighborhood, description of the prevalence of sales and financing concessions, etc.): Mortgage money is readily available in the St. Joseph market. Any loan discounts, interest buydowns or concessions do not adversely affect the subject. The subject is located in a family oriented neighborhood whose supply and demand appear to be in balance.

PUD

Project Information for PUDs (If applicable) - - Is the developer/builder in control of the Home Owners' Association (HOA)? [ ] Yes [ ] No
Approximate total number of units in the subject project _____ Approximate total number of units for sale in the subject project _____
Describe common elements and recreational facilities: N/A

SITE

Dimensions 80 x 120 (Subject to survey) Topography Typical Level
Site area 9600 Corner Lot [ ] Yes [X] No Size Typical
Specific zoning classification and description Residential (RM-25) Shape Rectangular
Zoning compliance [X] Legal [ ] Legal nonconforming (Grandfathered use) [ ] Illegal [ ] No zoning Drainage Apparently Adequate
Highest & best use as improved: [X] Present use [ ] Other use (explain) View Residential

Utilities	Public	Other	Off-site Improvements	Type	Public	Private
Electricity	[X]		Street	Asphalt	[X]	[ ]
Gas			Curb/gutter	None	[ ]	[ ]
Water	[X]		Sidewalk	None	[ ]	[ ]
Sanitary sewer	[X]		Street lights		[X]	[ ]
Storm sewer	[X]		Alley	None		

Landscaping Adequate/ Typical
Driveway Surface Asphalt
Apparent easements None observed
FEMA Special Flood Hazard Area [ ] Yes [X] No
FEMA Zone Map Date
FEMA Map No.

Comments (apparent adverse easements, encroachments, special assessments, slide areas, illegal or legal nonconforming zoning use, etc.): No apparent adverse easements, encroachments or conditions observed.

DESCRIPTION OF IMPROVEMENTS

GENERAL DESCRIPTION		EXTERIOR DESCRIPTION		FOUNDATION		BASEMENT		INSULATION	
No. of Units	1	Foundation	Concrete	Slab	Yes	Area Sq. Ft. N/A		Roof	[ ]
No. of Stories	1	Exterior Walls	CBS	Crawl Space	No	% Finished		Ceiling	[ ]
Type (Det./Att.)	Detached	Roof Surface	Shingle	Basement	No	Ceiling		Walls	[ ]
Design (Style)	Ranch	Gutters & Dwnspts.	Typical	Sump Pump	N/A	Walls		Floor	[ ]
Existing/Proposed	Yes/No	Window Type	Awning	Dampness	N/A	Floor		None	[ ]
Age (Yrs.)	15	Storm/Screens	No/Yes	Settlement	N/A	Outside Entry		Unknown	[X]
Effective Age (Yrs.)	14 - 17	Manufactured House	No	Infestation	N/A				

ROOMS	Foyer	Living	Dining	Kitchen	Den	Family Rm.	Rec. Rm.	Bedrooms	# Baths	Laundry	Other	Area Sq. Ft.
Basement												N/A
Level 1		X	X	X		X		3	2	X		1950
Level 2												

Finished area above grade contains: 7 Rooms; 3 Bedroom(s); 2 Bath(s); 1,950 Square Feet of Gross Living Area

INTERIOR	Materials/Condition	HEATING		KITCHEN EQUIP.		ATTIC		AMENITIES		CAR STORAGE: 2	
Floors	Carpet/Vinyl/*	Type	Centrl	Refrigerator	[X]	None	[X]	Fireplace(s) #		None	[ ]
Walls	Plaster/Avg	Fuel	Electr	Range/Oven	[X]	Stairs		Patio Concrete	[X]	Garage	# of cars
Trim/Finish	Wood/Average	Condition	Avg	Disposal	[ ]	Drop Stair		Deck	[ ]	Attached	
Bath Floor	Vinyl/Average	COOLING		Dishwasher	[ ]	Scuttle	[X]	Porch Open	[X]	Detached	
Bath Wainscot	Ceramic/Avg	Central	X	Fan/Hood	[ ]	Floor		Fence	[ ]	Built-In	
Doors	Wood/Average	Other		Microwave	[ ]	Heated		Pool	[ ]	Carport	2
* Average		Condition	Avg	Washer/Dryer	[X]	Finished				Driveway	Single

Additional features (special energy efficient items, etc.): Typical, ceiling fans (4).

COMMENTS

Condition of the improvements, depreciation (physical, functional, and external), repairs needed, quality of construction, remodeling/additions, etc.: The subject shows average condition on the interior and exterior and exhibits the typical appeal for the area. No functional or external obsolescence observed.

Adverse environmental conditions (such as, but not limited to, hazardous wastes, toxic substances, etc.) present in the improvements, on the site, or in the immediate vicinity of the subject property.: No apparent adverse environmental conditions were observed.

Freddie Mac Form 70 6/93 PAGE 1 OF 2 Fannie Mae Form 1004 6/93

Uniform Residential Appraisal Report *(Continued)*

Figure 10.1

UNIFORM RESIDENTIAL APPRAISAL REPORT

File No. 96-100 Page # 2

Valuation Section

File No. 96-100

COST APPROACH

ESTIMATED SITE VALUE 32,000 = $ 32,000

ESTIMATED REPRODUCTION COST-NEW-OF IMPROVEMENTS:

Dwelling 1,950 Sq. Ft. @$ 58.00 = $ 113,100

N/A Sq. Ft. @$ =

Appliances/Patio/Porch = 2,500

Garage/Carport 430 Sq. Ft. @$ 11.00 = 4,730

Total Estimated Cost New = $ 120,330

Less Physical Functional External

Depreciation 30,083 = $ 30,083

Depreciated Value of Improvements = $ 90,247

As-Is Value of Site Improvements drive, landscp. = $ 2,200

INDICATED VALUE BY COST APPROACH = $ 124,447

Comments on Cost Approach (such as, source of cost estimate, site value, square foot calculation and for HUD, VA and FmHA, the estimated remaining economic life of the property): Cost estimates derived from Marshall Valuation Services publications.

The subject's land to building ratio is typical for the area and does not adversely affect the subject value or marketability.

Est. remaining economic life: 40-45 years

SALES COMPARISON ANALYSIS

ITEM	SUBJECT	COMPARABLE NO. 1		COMPARABLE NO. 2		COMPARABLE NO. 3	
Address	1097 Timbers Crossin St. Joseph	1255 NE 34 Street		1297 NE 34 Street		1539 NE 38 Street	
Proximity to Subject		1 Block Southwest		1 Block South		5 Blocks Northeast	
Sales Price	$ 120,000	$ 119,000		$ 126,500		$ 121,000	
Price/Gross Living Area	$ 61.54	$ 63.47		$ 65.89		$ 61.58	
Data and/or Verification Source	Inspection	MLS		MLS		MLS	
VALUE ADJUSTMENTS	DESCRIPTION	DESCRIPTION	+(−)$ Adjust.	DESCRIPTION	+(−)$ Adjust.	DESCRIPTION	+(−)$ Adjust.
Sales or Financing Concessions		VA	−1,000	Conventional		Conventional	
Date of Sale/Time		8/96		9/96		7/96	
Location	Average	Average		Average		Average	
Leasehold/Fee Simple	Fee Simple	Fee Simple		Fee Simple		Fee Simple	
Site	9600	Corner/Avg		Corner/Avg		Inside/Avg	
View	Residential	Commercial	+2,000	Residential		Residential	
Design and Appeal	Ranch	Ranch/Avg		Ranch/Avg		Ranch/Avg	
Quality of Construction	CBS	CBS		CBS		CBS	
Age	15	16		14		16	
Condition	Average	Average		Average		Average	
Above Grade Room Count	Total 7 Bdrms 3 Baths 2	Total 7 Bdrms 3 Baths 2		Total 7 Bdrms 3 Baths 2		Total 7 Bdrms 3 Baths 2	
Gross Living Area	1,950 Sq. Ft.	1,875 Sq. Ft.	+1,125	1,920 Sq. Ft.		1,965 Sq. Ft.	
Basement & Finished Rooms Below Grade	N/A	None		None		None	
Functional Utility	Average	Average		Average		Average	
Heating/Cooling	Central	Central		Central		Central	
Energy Efficient Items	Typical	Typical		Typical		Typical	
Garage/Carport		Carport (2)		Garage (2)	−5,000	Carport (2)	
Porch, Patio, Deck, Fireplace(s), etc.	Porch Patio	Porch Patio		Porch Patio		Porch Patio	
Fence, Pool, etc.	Average	Average		Fence	−1,000	Average	
Net Adj. (total)		[X] + [ ] − $	2,125	[ ] + [X] − $	6,000	[X] + [ ] − $	0
Adjusted Sales Price of Comparable		$ 121,125		$ 120,500		$ 121,000	

Comments on Sales Comparison (including the subject property's compatibility to the neighborhood, etc.): All comparables utilized are of similar single family homes located in the same neighborhood as the subject with a range from $120,500 to $121,125. A time adjustment could not be supported by the market.

ITEM	SUBJECT	COMPARABLE NO. 1	COMPARABLE NO. 2	COMPARABLE NO. 3
Date, Price and Data Source, for prior sales within year of appraisal	N/A	N/A	N/A	N/A

Analysis of any current agreement of sale, option, or listing of subject property and analysis of any prior sales of subject and comparables within one year of the date of appraisal: The subject was not listed for sale on the open market.

INDICATED VALUE BY SALES COMPARISON APPROACH $ 121,000

INDICATED VALUE BY INCOME APPROACH (If Applicable) Estimated Market Rent $ 1275 /Mo. x Gross Rent Multiplier 95 = $ 121,125

This appraisal is made [X] *as is* [ ] subject to the repairs, alterations, inspections or conditions listed below [ ] subject to completion per plans & specifications.

Conditions of Appraisal: No personal property was included in the estimate of value.

Final Reconciliation: Weight was given to all three approaches, with the most weight given to the market data approach as it best reflects the action of the buyers and sellers.

RECONCILIATION

The purpose of this appraisal is to estimate the market value of the real property that is the subject of this report, based on the above conditions and the certification, contingent and limiting conditions, and market value definition that are stated in the attached Freddie Mac Form 439/FNMA form 1004B (Revised 6/93).

I (WE) ESTIMATE THE MARKET VALUE, AS DEFINED, OF THE REAL PROPERTY THAT IS THE SUBJECT OF THIS REPORT, AS OF (WHICH IS THE DATE OF INSPECTION AND THE EFFECTIVE DATE OF THIS REPORT) TO BE September 4, 1996 $ 121,000

APPRAISER Michelle Tipton

Signature

Name Michelle Tipton

Date Report Signed September 4, 1996

State Certification # St.Cert.Res.REA RD 010092 State MO

Or State License # State MO

SUPERVISORY APPRAISER (ONLY IF REQUIRED):

Signature

Name

Date Report Signed

State Certification #

Or State License #

[ ] Did [ ] Did Not Inspect Property

State

State

In the "Site" section of the URAR, the appraiser reports the site dimensions, the size of the site, whether the property is a corner lot, the zoning classification, zoning compliance, the utilities available to the site, off-site improvements and other site-related information. Notice that this section requires the appraiser to identify the highest and best use of the site. Of course, if the appraiser determines that the highest and best use of the site is not single-family residential, the URAR form should not be used to report the value estimate.

The site in this example is rectangular (80 feet by 120 feet), is zoned for residential use and has access to public electricity, water and sewer. The property is not on a corner, and the street is asphalt. The site appears to be well drained, has adequate landscaping and has an asphalt driveway. The property is not located in a flood zone as defined by the Federal Emergency Management Agency (FEMA).

The appraiser also notes the major characteristics of the improvements on the site, as shown in the "Description of Improvements" section of Figure 10.1. The single-family detached house located on this site is a one-story, ranch-style home built with concrete block and stucco (CBS) on a concrete slab foundation. The roof is asphalt shingles, with typical gutters and downspouts. The windows are awning type with screens. The house consists of a living room, a dining room, a kitchen, a family room, three bedrooms, two bathrooms and a laundry room. The size of the home is 1,950 square feet. The interior walls are plaster with wooden doors and trim. The floors are covered in carpet and vinyl tile. The house is served by a central heating and cooling unit that operates on electricity. The house has no attic storage, but it does have a small concrete patio and an open porch. As is typical in this market, kitchen equipment included with the property includes a refrigerator, range and washer/dryer. The house has a two-car carport of 430 square feet.

The URAR also has a designated section for the appraiser to comment on any additional features of the property, the overall condition of the improvements and any adverse environmental conditions that might affect property value. In this example, the appraiser notes no unusual factors that should be noted.

Now that the appraiser is familiar with the property, she must collect the specific information she will need to apply the three approaches to value. For the cost approach, the information required includes construction cost data and a site value estimate. For the sales comparison approach, she must identify comparable properties that have sold recently in the subject property's neighborhood. For the income approach, she must obtain information about the income-earning ability of the subject property and the relationship between income and value that prevails in the market. We will consider each of these approaches in detail.

Applying the Cost Approach

To complete the first step in the cost approach, Tipton uses the sales comparison approach to estimate the value of the site as if it were vacant. Her estimate of the site value is $32,000. Second, Tipton consults a residential construction cost estimating guide and finds that this type of dwelling costs approximately $58 per square foot to produce. The appliances, porch and patio cost approximately $2,500, and the carport costs $11 per square foot. Because the house is 15 years old, Tipton determines that depreciation from all sources is approximately 25 percent of the total production cost. Finally, she estimates the value of site improvements (asphalt driveway and average landscaping) at approximately $2,200. All of this information is summarized in the "Cost Approach" section of the URAR.

Applying the Sales Comparison Approach

The approach that receives the most emphasis in the URAR is the sales comparison approach. In this case, Tipton has identified three comparable properties that have sold recently in the subject property's market area. The address of each comparable, its proximity to the subject and its recent sales price is entered into the "Sales Comparison Analysis" section of the URAR. Tipton then considers each of the elements of comparison discussed in this chapter to determine whether adjustments are necessary to account for differences between the subject property transaction and the comparables.

For example, the buyer of comparable 1 used a VA-guaranteed mortgage loan, which represents favorable financing terms in this market. To eliminate the impact of financing terms on the sales price, Tipton deducts $1,000 from the sale prices of comparable 1. Comparable 2 requires several adjustments for differences in its size, its view, its garage (instead of carport) and the presence of a privacy fence around the property. As indicated on the form, Tipton adds $1,125 to the price of the comparable because it is smaller than the subject. She also adds $2,000 to the sales price of comparable 2 because it is near commercial land uses, but subtracts $5,000 because of the enclosed garage and $1,000 because of the privacy fence. Comparable 3 requires no adjustments. Notice that positive adjustments are made when the comparable is inferior to the subject and that negative adjustments are made when the comparable is superior to the subject. Adjustments are never made to the subject property.

The adjusted sales prices of the three comparables suggest that the market value of the subject property by this approach is between $120,500 and $121,125. Michelle concludes that the value indicated by this approach is $121,000.

Applying the Income Approach

The income approach usually receives little emphasis in appraisal assignments involving owner-occupied, single-family homes because single-family homes are bought for consumption, rather than purely investment, purposes. The income approach is designed for estimating the value of income-producing investment properties, not owner-occupied homes. When applying the income approach, a variation of the GIM technique is used to arrive at a value estimate. Known as the **gross rent multiplier** (GRM) technique, the appraiser collects information about the monthly rents and sales prices of homes in the area, then arrives at an estimate of the monthly gross rent multiplier for the market. In this case, the appraiser finds two homes in the market that were operated as rental properties and have recently sold. From these transactions, she finds that the monthly market rent for the subject property is approximately $1,275 and the gross rent multiplier is 95. She uses this information to calculate a value estimate using the income approach of $121,125 (1,275 × 95).

Reconciliation

Now that she has used each of the three approaches, Tipton must reconcile the three value indications into a final estimate of value. Tipton believes that all three approaches to value deserve some consideration, but gives most weight in the reconciliation step to the sales comparison approach. In the appraiser's professional judgement, the estimated market value of the property is $121,000. ■

---

holding period. The benefits are classified in two categories: cash flow from operations and cash flow from reversion. Once they are estimated, the appraiser converts these cash flows into a present value estimate by capitalizing them at the appropriate discount rate.

Consider an appraisal assignment involving a new warehouse with 50,000 square feet of rentable area. After evaluating competing warehouses in this market, the appraiser estimates market rent for this space at $12.50 per square foot in the first year, with annual increases of 3 percent. The vacancy rate for this property is expected to be 25 percent in the first year and 5 percent thereafter. The appraiser estimates operating expenses (utilities, management fees, property taxes, maintenance, etc.) at 20 percent of effective gross income. An outstanding mortgage on this property has with a balance of $2.2 million. The loan requires annual payments of $224,000 for the next 20 years. Discussions with local real estate investors suggest that the typical buyer for this property would have an expected holding period of ten years. The appraiser believes that the selling price at the end of year 10 can be forecast by applying an overall capitalization rate of 10 percent to year 11's net operating income. Selling expenses are forecast at 5 percent. The appraiser uses this information to calculate the annual before-tax cash flows from operations and the before-tax equity reversion as shown in Table 10.3.

The appraiser also evaluates recent transactions of similar properties to determine the appropriate discount rate for converting the forecasted cash flows into a present value estimate. From these transactions, the appraiser determines that the appropriate discount rate is 13 percent. Discounting the cash flows at this rate yields a present value estimate of $2,909,233, which is then rounded to $2.9 million. (The process of discounting future values into present values is described in detail in Chapter 14.)

Chapter Review

1. Real estate appraisers are specialists who possess the skills and knowledge necessary to estimate property value. The appraisal industry is subject to state regulation as a result of the Financial Institutions Reform, Recovery and Enforcement Act of 1989, which requires that appraisals for properties involved in federally related transactions be performed by state-licensed or state-certified appraisers.

2. The type of value that appraisers most often estimate is market value, or a property's most probable selling price in a well-defined situation.

3. Some of the key principles underlying appraisal practice are (1) anticipation, (2) change, (3) substitution and (4) contribution.

4. The steps in the appraisal process include (1) definition of the problem, (2) data selection and collection, (3) highest and best use analysis, (4) application of the three approaches to value, (5) reconciliation and (6) report of the defined value.

5. In the sales comparison approach to value, appraisers compare the subject property to similar properties that have sold recently. After adjusting for differences in the appropriate elements of comparison, the prices of these comparables provide an indication of the value of the subject property.

6. In the cost approach, appraisers assess value by estimating a property's cost of production. The steps in the cost approach are (1) estimate the value of the site, (2) estimate the cost to produce the improvements, (3) estimate accrued depreciation, (4) subtract depreciation from production cost and (5) add site value.

7. In the income approach, appraisers estimate value by forecasting the future income expected to be generated by the property, then converting that forecast into a present value. Techniques include gross income multiplier analysis, net income capitalization and discounted cash-flow analysis.

Key Terms

---

accrued depreciation   loss in value from any cause.

anticipation   the idea that the current value of a property depends on the anticipated utility or income that will accrue to the property owner in the future.

appraisal process   a systematic procedure employed to arrive at an estimate of value and convey that estimate to the appraisal user.

assessed value   the estimated value of a property for tax purposes.

capitalization rate   the relationship between income and value, where the capitalization rate equals net operating income divided by property value.

certified general appraiser   an appraiser who is certified by the state to perform appraisals on all property types.

certified residential appraiser   an appraiser who is certified by the state to perform residential appraisals regardless of complexity.

change   the idea that economic, social, political and environmental forces are constantly causing changes that affect the value of real estate.

contribution   the idea that the value of a component part of a property depends on the amount it contributes to the value of the whole.

cost approach   a method used to estimate value by implementing the following steps: (1) estimate the value of the site as though it were vacant, (2) estimate the cost to produce the improvements, (3) subtract accrued depreciation and (4) add site value to the estimated depreciated cost of the improvements.

economic obsolescence   loss in value resulting from factors outside the property that affect its income-producing ability or degree of use.

functional obsolescence   loss in value that occurs because a property has less utility or ability to generate income than a new property designed for the same use.

gross income multiplier   the relationship between income and value, where the gross income multiplier equals value divided by gross income.

gross rent multiplier   the relationship between rent and value, where the gross rent multiplier equals value divided by gross rent.

highest and best use   that use, found to be legally permissible, physically possible and financially feasible, that results in the highest land value; that use of land most likely to result in the greatest long-term economic return to the owner.

income approach   a method used to estimate value by discounting or capitalizing the expected future income that is expected to accrue to the property owner.

insurable value   an estimate of value for insurance purposes.

investment value   the worth of a property to a particular investor, based on that investor's personal standards of investment acceptability.

licensed appraiser   a person licensed by the state to perform noncomplex residential appraisals.

market value   the most probable price that a property should bring in a competitive and open market under all conditions requisite to a fair sale, the buyer and seller each acting prudently and knowledgeably, and assuming the price is not affected by undue stimulus. Implicit in this definition is the consummation of a sale as of a specified date and the passing of title from seller to buyer under conditions whereby:

1. buyer and seller are typically motivated;
2. both parties are well informed or well advised and acting in what they consider their best interests;
3. a reasonable time is allowed for exposure in the open market;
4. payment is made in terms of cash in U.S. dollars or in terms of financial arrangements comparable thereto; and
5. the price represents the normal consideration for the property sold unaffected by special or creative financing or sales concessions by anyone associated with the sale.

neighborhood   an area containing properties of similar type. It also can be defined by reference to geographical area; to social, religious or ethnic ties; or to income group.

physical deterioration   loss in value that occurs from ordinary wear and tear, weather, vandalism or neglect.

price   actual amount paid for a property in a particular transaction.

replacement cost   the estimated cost of replacing the property being appraised with a property built at today's prices, by current construction methods and with the same usefulness as the one being appraised.

reproduction cost   the cost of constructing an exact replacement of the property being appraised with the same or similar materials, at today's prices.

sales comparison approach   a method used to estimate value by comparing the property to other properties that have recently sold for known prices.

substitution   the idea that a prudent buyer will pay no more for a property than the cost of acquiring an equally desirable substitute in the open market.

Study Exercises

1. Based on the most widely accepted definition, what is market value?

2. Define the following concepts: value in exchange, value in use, investment value.

3. Does the concept of market value reflect the perceptions of the typical buyer in a market or of a specific buyer? What is the difference?

4. Under what conditions is price equivalent to market value?

5. In what circumstances is it possible for the production cost of a property to exceed its market value?

6. Define the following: assessed value, insurable value.

7. List and define the four key appraisal principles discussed in the chapter.

8. Outline the steps in the appraisal process.

9. What issues must be considered in step one of the appraisal process?

10. Define the concept of highest and best use. Why is this an important step in the appraisal process?

11. Consider a property worth $45,000 as a vacant commercial site. The property is improved with a single-family residence. As such, the property is worth $35,000. If it costs $5,000 to demolish the structure, what is the value of the site? What is the value of the structure? What is the highest and best use of this property?

12. List the steps involved in each of the three approaches to value.

13. Why is reconciliation a necessary step in the appraisal process?

14. List the six elements of comparison in the sales comparison approach.

15. Consider a vacant, lakefront lot measuring 90 feet by 120 feet in a residential subdivision. Three similar vacant lots have sold recently. Comparable 1 measures 85 feet by 120 feet and is also located on the lake. It sold for $35,000 one week ago. Comparable 2 is also on the lake, and it measures 85 feet by 120 feet. It sold one year ago for $30,000. Comparable 3 sold six months ago for $31,000. It is a hillside lot that offers an exceptional view. The lot measures 80 feet by 120 feet. Complete the market data grid provided below to estimate the value of the subject property.

Sales Comparison Market Data Grid

		Comparables		
	Subject	*# 1*	*# 2*	*# 3*
Sales price	—	$35,000	$30,000	$31,000
Size in square feet	10,800	10,200	10,200	9,600
Price per square foot	—			
Date of sale	Current	– 1 week	– 1 year	– 6 months
Adjustment for changing market conditions	—			
Adjusted price per square foot	—			
Location	Lake	Lake	Lake	Hillside
Adjustment for location	—			
Adjusted price per square foot	—			
Indicated value of subject property:				

16. Define the following: accrued depreciation, physical deterioration, functional obsolescence, economic obsolescence.

17. Consider the example discussed in Table 10.2. If the actual market value of the land were $190,000, and the cost to reproduce the structures were $610,000, what market value would be indicated by the cost approach?

18. Define the following concepts: gross income multiplier, capitalization rate.

19. An investor considers the purchase of an 11,000-square-foot warehouse expected to command $8.40 per square foot in annual rents. Two comparable warehouses have recently sold in the market. Comparable 1 measures 12,000 square feet and sold recently for $450,000. Comparable 2 measures 8,600 square feet and sold recently for $322,500. Compute the gross income multiplier that is implied by these transactions, and estimate the value of the subject property.

20. Suppose the investor in the above question is concerned that the subject property may be more expensive to operate than the comparable properties. Analysis of the operating expenses for each of the properties reveals the following net income estimates:

> Subject property $52,400
> Comparable 1 $65,600
> Comparable 2 $47,000

Compute the capitalization rate implied by these transactions to estimate the value of the subject property by the net income capitalization technique.

For Further Reading

The Appraisal of Real Estate, 10th ed. (Chicago: The Appraisal Institute, 1992).

Boykin, J. H., and A. A. Ring. *The Valuation of Real Estate,* 4th ed. (Englewood Cliffs, N.J.: Prentice Hall, 1993).

PART FOUR

Real Estate
Transactions

CHAPTER 11

Contracts in Real Estate Transactions

The real estate sales contract is a detailed and complex document that establishes the terms under which ownership of a property will be transferred.

Chapter Preview

A CONTRACT IS the legal device used by two or more persons (called *parties*) to indicate they have reached an agreement. In essence, a contract is an exchange of promises by two or more persons, conditioned on certain events and enforceable by law. Thus far in this text, we have examined a variety of topics in which contracts play an important role. For example, we discussed listing agreements and buyer representation agreements when describing the real estate brokerage process, and we discussed property management agreements and leases in a previous chapter. Other contracts that are common in real estate transactions are those that represent the agreement to transfer ownership.

As we discussed in Chapter 7, the legal document used to transfer real estate ownership from one party to another is known as a *deed.* This chapter concentrates on the real estate sales contract, which defines the agreement between a buyer and seller to eventually transfer ownership in real property. In general, the sales contract provides the rules governing the parties' rights and duties during the time between the agreement to transfer real property and the actual transfer of title using a deed. In addition to sales contracts, we will consider the use of option-to-buy contracts and escrow arrangements in the real estate transaction process.

Specifically, we will examine

- the necessary elements of a contract;
- the purpose and structure of the real estate sales contract;
- option-to-buy contracts;
- escrow arrangements; and
- performance and breach of contract.

225

NECESSARY ELEMENTS OF A CONTRACT

The required elements of any valid contract consist of (1) an offer, (2) an acceptance, (3) consideration, (4) parties with capacity and (5) a lawful purpose. Contracts involving real estate have a sixth element—that the agreements be in writing (one exception is a lease for one year or less).

Offer and Acceptance

Before any contract can be created, one person must make an offer to another. In essence, an **offer** is a statement that specifies the position of the offer's maker (who is called an *offeror*). The offeror states implicitly in an offer that he or she is willing to be bound by the stated position. An offer becomes an enforceable contract when it is accepted by the party who receives it. The receiving party is called an *offeree,* and his or her acceptance should create a contract.

Generally, an **acceptance,** which expresses satisfaction with an offer, must reflect the precise terms and conditions stated in the offer. If the terms in the purported acceptance differ materially from those of the offer, no contract is formed. Indeed, such an attempted acceptance becomes a **counteroffer.** With a counteroffer, the original offeror and offeree switch legal positions, and a contract may result when a counteroffer is accepted.

Consideration

The law requires that an exchange of consideration occur before a contract is enforceable. **Consideration** often is described as anything that incurs a legal detriment or the forgoing of a legal benefit. What that means, in simple terms, is that each party to a contract must give up something. In a typical real estate contract, the seller gives up title to the land in return for money; the buyer gives up the right to the money in return for title to the land.

Capacity of Parties

To have a valid contract, all parties involved must have contractual **capacity.** The law insists that all parties have the mental capability to know what the contract represents and to understand its terms. Most commonly, two categories of people are said to lack capacity to contract. First, those who have been declared mentally incompetent are protected from people who attempt to take advantage of their mental conditions. Because the law cannot distinguish people with unjust intent from those with good intentions, insane persons can void all of their contractual obligations. Therefore, such a contract, although binding on the competent party, is **voidable,** or can be rescinded, at the election of the incompetent party's guardian.

The second category of people who lack contractual capacity consists of minors; that is, those who have not reached the age of majority. Although some minors (typically defined as people younger than 18 years of age) have the intelligence to comprehend even the most complex transactions, the law provides them with protection.

Any time before a person reaches the age of majority and within a reasonable period thereafter, nearly all contracts that the minor has entered into may be voided by the minor. Certain types of contracts involving a minor's purchase of necessities—such items as food, clothing and medical care, essential for the preservation and reasonable enjoyment of life—cannot be voided. Because real estate seldom is considered a necessity, however, minors generally lack the capacity to purchase or sell it. Therefore, when one party to a contract involving the transfer of real estate is a minor, that contract is voidable.

If a contract is voided, the minor and adult parties must return any consideration that was exchanged. Therefore, an adult must beware of buying real estate from or selling it to a minor, as such a transaction subsequently may be undone.

Lawful Purpose

A valid contract must have as its ultimate purpose some legal act or function. For example, a contract for the delivery of illegal drugs is not enforceable—at least not in the courts. Although people sometimes subsequently put real estate to an illegal use, the sale or lease of real estate seldom directly involves illegal intentions; therefore, this element of a valid contract generally is less crucial than the other elements.

Even so, both buyers and sellers should be aware that any illegal purpose in a contract may make it void. For example, suppose a sales contract specifies the buyer's intent to utilize the property in violation of current zoning provisions. This clause may give the buyer an "out" that the seller may not recognize.

Writing Requirement

Contracts may be either implied or expressed, and expressed contracts may be oral or written. All contracts involving land or items attached to it, however, must be in writing before a court will enforce them. Contracts involving the sale of timber and crops may be oral and remain binding. The rules governing these types of contracts are found in the Uniform Commercial Code. Each state's law should be consulted regarding the requisites of such contracts.

The writing requirement is found in each state's **statute of frauds,** a law designed to prevent fraudulent practices by requiring that certain contracts, including those involving real property, be in writing and signed. Real estate contracts must be written to reduce the possibility that a court may be defrauded or tricked into ruling improperly when the subject matter is valuable real estate. The required writing does not have to be a formally drafted document. Indeed, any written words that indicate the parties' positions and that are signed by the parties involved satisfy the statute of frauds. For example, the words "I agree to sell my farm to Robert Harris for $50,000," written on a paper napkin, are enforceable by Robert if they are signed by the farm owner. Of course, it is assumed that the owner has only one farm; otherwise, the property designated as "my farm" is not adequately described. An adequate written description of the real property being sold is essential. Methods of legal description are discussed in Chapter 7.

Although the statute of frauds requires that contracts involving real estate be in writing, there are exceptions to this rule. Courts may, for instance, enforce an oral contract if the parties have partially performed their agreement. **Partial performance** is the fulfillment of the terms of an agreement to such an extent that the existence of the agreement may be reasonably inferred, even though no written contract exists. If a court can determine from the parties' actions what their intentions were, it may hold that a contract exists despite the lack of a written document. Generally, mere payment of some money by the buyer is not sufficient to replace a written contract.

Payment plus possession by the buyer and physical improvements made to the property, however, point to the existence of some kind of contractual understanding, and the courts often rule in favor of such a buyer—but not always, as the buyers learned in the Legal Highlight on page 229.

REAL ESTATE SALES CONTRACTS

Contracts in real estate transactions can take many forms, including leases, listing agreements buyer representation agreements and property management agreements. Perhaps the most common contract in a real estate transaction is the real estate sales contract. Sales contracts provide for the eventual transfer of title to real property. **Title,** or the legal right to ownership of land, is passed by use of a **deed** and does not change hands until the transaction actually is closed, or brought to a successful conclusion. (Title closings are discussed in Chapter 15). The sales contract's purpose is to provide the rules governing the parties' rights and duties during the time between the agreement to transfer real property and the actual transfer of title. A time period of 10 to 90 days generally is necessary to allow the buyer to secure financing, check the seller's title and obtain property insurance.

Groundwork for Negotiating a Sales Contract

In the example in Chapter 8, Harold and Gladys Stewart (the sellers) of St. Joseph, Missouri, hired Smith & Smyth Realty Company to locate a buyer for their house. Assume that Frank and Elizabeth Barr (the buyers) are interested in buying a home in St. Joseph. As an agent of the sellers, Tom Smith shows the Stewart house to the Barrs, and they fall in love with it. Remember that the Stewarts' asking price is $125,000; however, even though the Barrs really like the house, they feel they should not pay more than $120,000 for it.

Now the negotiation stage begins. In a sale of personal property, a buyer and seller usually discuss orally what they will pay and accept. Once a price is reached, a handshake may seal the deal. A sale of real estate, however, is not so simple. Owing to the required formalities of a written contract, parties to a real estate sale are more likely to have carefully thought out the sale or purchase and their obligations under such a transaction. Although negotiations in a real estate deal may be oral, the parties traditionally conduct their give-and-take sessions by exchanging written offers and counteroffers. Written offers are used in the negotiating stage so that a binding written agreement will exist if either party decides to accept the other's offer. Most states allow real estate brokers

Real Estate Today *Legal Highlight*

Validity of an Oral Contract

The statute of frauds requires that contracts for the sale of real estate be written to be enforceable. Richard and Mary Kelly learned this to their sorrow. The Kellys reached an oral agreement with William Ryan to purchase his residential waterfront property in Greenwich, Connecticut, for $2,125,000 in cash. The sale was subject to securing approval from the Coastal Area Management Commission for construction on the property that would double the size of the existing house and add a tennis court. The Kellys had a wetlands survey made and site plans prepared for submission of the application. A few days later, their attorney submitted a contract to Ryan's attorney, which essentially put the oral agreement into writing. Ryan refused to sign, and the next day, he contracted to sell the property to a third party. The Kellys sued, seeking specific performance by Ryan of the oral contract. They lost. The court ruled that

> however plain and complete the terms of an oral contract for the sale and purchase of real estate, it cannot be enforced against a party thereto

unless he, or his agent, has signed a written memorandum which recited the essential elements of the contract with reasonable certainty.

Even though the Kellys had a definite oral agreement with Ryan, as the Hollywood producer Sam Goldwyn used to say, "An oral agreement isn't worth the paper it's written on." The Kellys also argued that they had made "substantial improvements" to the property on the basis of the oral agreement, thus defeating the written requirement in the statute of frauds. The court did not agree, holding that the survey and site plans, at a cost of less than $5,000, were not "substantial" to a property with a value of more than $2 million. The lesson is clear: *Never, never, never* rely on an oral contract in the sale or purchase of anything of value, particularly not in the sale or purchase of real estate. ■

Source:
Kelly v. Ryan, Nos. CV 91 011 53 81, CV 91 011 54 38 S. (Connecticut Superior Court, 1991).

---

to fill in the blanks on standard sales contracts that have been approved by the state bar association or by a qualified attorney.

Smith, the Stewart's real estate broker, could, for example, have the Barrs make their offer by signing a sales contract form that has been filled in with the terms of their offer. If the Stewarts agree to the offer made, their signatures on the contract would represent their acceptance and, at the same time, would create an enforceable contract. However, if the sale involves more than just filling in the blanks, or if a number of special provisions to the contract exist, the broker should advise the buyers and sellers to seek legal counsel.

The Sales Contract

Whether the real estate sales contract is drafted by an attorney or completed by a broker, it should contain several key elements to ensure that the transaction does not terminate before the transfer of title. A well-drafted contract provides the answers to all questions that arise during the time between the signing of the agreement and the closing, as well as the obligations of both buyer and seller.

To study in detail the functions of the sales contract, let's return to the Stewarts and the Barrs. After several offers are exchanged, the Barrs agree to buy the Stewarts' house for $120,000. The price is the major concern of the parties, but there are many other areas of importance. A typical contract, shown in Figure 11.1, demonstrates these areas. The document shown is intended for instructional use only and should not be used in practice, as it may not meet all particular circumstances. The portions printed in italics are left blank in the printed form, to be filled in by the attorney or broker.

Description of Property and Fixtures   The sales contract begins by identifying the parties to the agreement. Section I in Figure 11.1 specifies the parties to the agreement and the property being sold. This description must be sufficiently accurate so that all concerned may know what property is involved. A precise legal description, as required in a deed, is not absolutely necessary to make the contract binding, but a careful and accurate description is desirable to eliminate the possibility of dispute over the property.

Items of property that were once movable but have become attached to land are fixtures and therefore are considered part of the real estate. Section I of Figure 11.1 provides that fixtures will remain on the property and that title to them will pass to the buyer. Fixtures typically include built-in lighting fixtures and appliances, heating and air-conditioning units (especially those that heat and cool an entire house), water heaters and plumbing equipment. Other items that may be specified include carpets, curtains, curtain rods and anything else the parties may stipulate. If the seller wishes to keep any fixture, such as an antique chandelier, his or her right to remove it must be stated in the contract. The buyer in such a case then may wish to stipulate that the removed item be replaced by one acceptable to the buyer.

Purchase Price   Section II of this sample contract states the purchase price and the way it is to be paid. As noted earlier, the buyer usually must give some monetary deposit to demonstrate good faith, and what is to be done with this earnest money must be stated in the sales contract. Normally, the earnest money is applied to the purchase price.

To protect the buyer, it is vital that the contract be conditional on the buyer's ability to obtain adequate financing. For example, if the Barrs are unable to borrow 90 percent of $120,000 ($108,000) and yet are held responsible for the purchase, their financial position could become disastrous.

Title   Section III concerns the type of deed to be given by the seller. A general warranty deed, as used in this sample contract, is the most common. A general warranty deed requires the seller to provide title to the property that is free of all restrictions except those specified. Such restrictions may include zoning ordinances affecting the property, general utility easements, subdivision covenants and any other ownership limitations that are recorded. Section III also requires

---

Sales Contract   **Figure 11.1**

This contract is for the purchase and sale of certain real estate between *Frank L. and Elizabeth M. Barr of St. Joseph, Missouri,* hereinafter referred to jointly as "Buyer," and *Harold J. and Gladys A. Stewart of St. Joseph, Missouri,* hereinafter referred to jointly as "Seller."

I   Buyer agrees to buy and Seller agrees to sell in fee simple the following described property: *All that tract or parcel of land, situated in St. Joseph, Buchanan County, Missouri, together with all improvements thereon, known as 1097 Timbers Crossing. Such property is more accurately described as Lot 3, Block G, of the Harris Billups Estate, as recorded in Plat Book 8, page 37, in the Office of the Clerk of the Circuit Court of Buchanan County, Missouri.*

Included as part of such property are all fixtures unless otherwise stated. Such fixtures include but are not limited to all lighting fixtures and satellite TV antennae attached thereto; all water heating and plumbing equipment therein; and all plants, trees and shrubbery now on the property.

II   The purchase price of this property shall be *One Hundred Twenty Thousand Dollars ($120,000),* to be paid as follows:

(a)   Buyer has paid in escrow *Four Thousand Dollars ($4,000)* as earnest money, to be applied as part of the purchase of this property at the close of the transaction. If this sale, due to Buyer's default, is not consummated, this earnest money shall be forfeited to Seller unless provided otherwise. In the event the sale is not consummated for reasons other than the default of Buyer, this earnest money shall be refunded to Buyer. The forfeiture to Seller or return to Buyer of this earnest money shall not affect in any way either party's claims for damages or other remedies as a result of the failure to consummate this sale.

(b)   The balance of the purchase price shall be paid from the proceeds of a conventional loan for the maximum number of years allowable at the prevailing rate of interest at the time of closing. This loan shall be *90%* of purchase price.

(c)   Buyer agrees to pay all closing costs related to this loan.

(d)   The balance shall be paid in cash at closing.

(e)   If Buyer is unable, after making a good-faith effort, to secure adequate financing as provided herein, this contract may be canceled at Buyer's option.

III   Seller agrees to furnish good and marketable fee simple title to this property, as evidenced by a general warranty deed. This deed shall be executed and delivered to the escrow agent within *five (5) days* of the execution by Seller of this contract. Buyer shall have a reasonable time to examine title to this property. If Buyer finds any legal defects to the title, Seller shall be furnished with a written statement thereof and given a reasonable time to correct any defects. If Seller fails to satisfy any valid objections to the title, then at the option of Buyer, upon written notice to Seller, this contract may be canceled and shall be null and void. Seller's warranty deed shall be subject to all easements and restrictions of record. It is agreed that "a reasonable time" means such a time period that would permit this transaction to close on or before the date provided in this contract.

IV   (a)   Escrow shall be opened with *St. Joseph Bank,* which shall hold the earnest money paid by Buyer and Seller's warranty deed until such time when the escrow agent is in a position to record all documents required hereunder and make all disbursements provided under this contract. This transaction shall close as soon as practical after the parties have complied with all the conditions of this contract, but the closing shall occur not later than *sixty (60) days* after the execution of this contract.

Figure 11.1 Sales Contract *(Continued)*

(b) The following items shall be prorated as of the close of this transaction: *real estate taxes due but not delinquent, special assessments and prepaid insurance premiums.*

(c) Possession of the property shall be given at closing.

V Seller warrants that when the sale is completed, the improvements on the property will be in the same condition as they are on the date of this contract, natural wear and tear excepted. However, should the premises be destroyed or substantially damaged before this sale is consummated, then at the election of the purchaser

(a) this contract may be canceled, or

(b) Buyer may consummate the purchase and receive the benefit of such insurance as accrues to Seller on account of such loss or damage. This election is to be exercised within *ten (10) days* after the amount of Seller's insurance coverage is determined.

VI Seller agrees to furnish certification from a bonded pest control company that property is free and clear from any wood-destroying organisms.

VII Seller warrants that all appliances and utilities will be in good working order at the time of closing.

VIII In negotiating this contract, *Smith & Smyth Realty Company* has rendered a valuable service and is to be paid a commission which shall be *seven (7) percent of the purchase price.* This commission shall be payable to Broker from Seller's proceeds. Seller agrees that if he defaults and fails to consummate this sale, except for the exercise of some elective or optional right of cancellation hereunder or for Seller's inability to cure any title defects, Seller shall pay Broker the full commission, and the earnest money shall be returned to Buyer. Buyer agrees that if he defaults or fails to consummate this sale, except for the exercise of some elective or optional right of cancellation hereunder or for Seller's inability to cure any title defects, Buyer shall pay Broker the full commission. In the event that Buyer becomes liable for the commission, Buyer and Seller agree that Broker may apply the earnest money deposited by Buyer toward payment of that commission.

IX This contract constitutes the sole and entire agreement between the parties hereto, and no modification of this contract shall be binding unless attached hereto and signed by all parties to this agreement.

IN WITNESS WHEREOF, Buyer and Seller set their signatures on the respective dates opposite their signatures. The date of this contract shall be the date it is signed by Seller.

Date of _____   _____ (Buyer) (seal)

Date of _____   _____ (Seller) (seal)

Escrow arrangement accepted by

_____   By_____

St. Joseph Bank and Trust Co., Escrowee   *Paul K. Preston, Vice President* the buyer to search the public records for any title defects. The method and responsibilities of searching for a legal title to real property and the ways of protecting that title (with title insurance, for example) are discussed in Chapter 15. The purposes of the warranty deed and of other types of deeds are described in Chapter 7. Essentially, the buyer must take steps to discover any problems associated with the seller's title and give the seller written notice of such defects. The seller then must resolve the defects in the title, or the contract no longer is binding.

Escrow   An escrow arrangement is established in section IV. The buyer's earnest money and the seller's warranty deed are to be held by a third party until the sale is completed. Often, the sales contract omits the requirement that the deed be delivered to an escrow agent. In that situation, the real estate broker holds the buyer's earnest money in an escrow account. The advantages of using an escrow agent other than the broker are discussed below.

The size of the earnest money deposit is a matter for negotiation. From the seller's point of view, it should be large enough to deter the buyer from not consummating the transaction and to provide some compensation for the seller and broker if the buyer backs away from the sale. Even though the owner remains in possession, he or she may suffer a loss in profit because the property has been taken off the market in anticipation of the contracted sale, and the listing agreement may specify that all or part of the earnest money will go toward the broker's commission in case of default by the buyer.

Property Destruction   Section V is crucial in protecting the parties' interests. What happens if the improvements on the property (that is, the house and landscaping) are destroyed or damaged by fire, wind or some other hazard during the time between execution of the contract and the closing? Does the seller or buyer suffer the risk of loss during this time period? The sales contract should specify the answers to these questions. As in our sample contract, the buyer usually is given the option of canceling the contract or completing the sale and collecting any insurance payable to the seller. A time limit should be placed on the buyer's election under this section.

Miscellaneous Provisions   The sixth and seventh sections in Figure 11.1 are self-explanatory. They are placed in a sales contract to provide some protection to the buyer concerning pest infestation and the appliances and utilities, such as the electrical and plumbing systems. It should be understood that the seller's compliance with these provisions does not ensure that the buyer has absolute protection. The seller generally is not liable if pests invade the house or if the appliances break down after title is transferred to the buyer. Hence, the buyer may wish to have a building inspector go over the house, appliances and utilities before the transaction is closed. This type of inspection, of course, is done at the buyer's expense.

Broker's Commission   Section VIII is used only when a real estate broker is involved in the sales transaction. The broker's commission generally comes from the seller, and a seller who breaches this contract without justification still must pay the commission. If the buyer unreasonably refuses to perform the required duties under the contract, the buyer becomes liable for the entire commission.

The contractual provision in the sample contract states that the buyer's earnest money shall apply to the commission if the buyer breaches the contract.

The provision in the example directing that all earnest money go to paying the broker's commission in case of default by the buyer is quite favorable to the broker. When negotiating a listing contract, the seller probably would want to modify this provision to at least provide for sharing the earnest money in case of default (a common provision).

The buyer still is legally liable for damages exceeding the amount of the earnest money if he or she defaults on the contract. This liability includes the remainder of the commission owed and damages to the seller. As a practical matter, however, it is difficult to obtain money from a buyer after default.

The harsh monetary penalty imposed on the buyer who refuses to complete a transaction generally makes any buyer think twice before doing so. This is a primary reason for requiring a substantial earnest money deposit. It should be noted, however, that the buyer also is protected by this provision, as the seller becomes liable for the entire commission if he or she backs out of the transaction.

Conclusion to the Contract   The sample contract concludes with a statement that any changes in the agreement must be made in writing with the consent of all parties. The contract then is signed by the seller, buyer and escrow agent. The date of the sample contract in Figure 11.1 is the date opposite the seller's signature. This date governs the date on which the parties' performance is due under the contract.

Escrow Arrangements

Before title to real property can be transferred, a deed must be delivered by the seller and accepted by the buyer. In the absence of effective delivery, title is not transferred. The escrow is a legal device that assists in the delivery of a deed. An escrow arrangement can be created by a separate contractual agreement or within the contract covering the sale. (See section IV of Figure 11.1.)

What would happen if the seller died or became incapacitated before the closing under a sales contract or before the buyer completed his or her payments under a contract for a deed? The seller could not sign the deed and deliver it to the buyer. Indeed, if the seller died, title to his or her property would pass to those designated in the will or to the nearest relatives. Thereafter, the contract to sell the property could not be performed, or fulfilled. To prevent this potential obstacle, a simple escrow arrangement could be created. Once a seller has delivered the required deed to an escrow agent (some neutral third party named by the seller and buyer), courts have held that a buyer who has fulfilled all of the terms of the contract can obtain the deed from the escrow agent. The escrow agent must, of course, follow the instructions given by the parties to the contract so long as such instructions are reasonable and within the agent's powers.

The escrow arrangement also protects the buyer's interests in that once the deed is delivered to the escrow agent and all other escrow conditions are satisfied, generally, the seller's creditors can no longer seize that property for payment of the seller's debts.

OPTION-TO-BUY CONTRACTS

Another type of contract that is often useful in real estate transactions is the option-to-buy contract. Sometimes a party is interested in buying a specific property, but is not yet ready to sign a sales contract. The option-to-buy contract is one way to ensure that the property will not be sold to another party before the person who holds the option to buy has made a final decision.

The **option-to-buy contract** is an agreement between a property owner and a potential buyer that states that the seller agrees to keep an offer open for acceptance during a stated period of time. If the buyer decides to exercise the option before it expires, the seller must sell the property at the specified price. For example, a seller may state that he or she will sell the property to the option holder for $75,000 and will allow the holder to accept this offer at any time within the next six months. To ensure that the option is binding, it must be in writing and contain all of the necessary elements of a valid contract: offer, acceptance, consideration, parties with capacity and lawful purpose.

The amount of consideration for the option depends on the circumstances. Suppose, for example, that broker Judy Michaud is trying to assemble six properties as a tract for a shopping center. She offers Blanche, the owner of one of the six properties, an option-to-buy contract to purchase her house for $110,000, even though the property is worth only $90,000 as a residence. Blanche's property is worth the larger amount only if it can be used for the shopping center, and to achieve this, Judy must both obtain contracts from the other property owners and secure rezoning of the entire tract.

Thus, Judy offers Blanche an option contract that gives Judy the right to purchase the property for $110,000 any time in the next six months. Blanche might be happy to accept consideration of $1,000 or even less for agreeing to this arrangement because she will receive a very good price for her house if Judy is successful in putting the deal together. The consideration received by Blanche for the option granted to Judy is hers to keep regardless of whether Judy exercises her option to buy. Thus, the consideration received by Blanche is her compensation for giving up the right to sell the property to anyone other than Judy for the next six months.

PERFORMANCE AND BREACH OF CONTRACT

Failure to perform a required contractual obligation is called a *breach* of contract. If a party to an agreement breaches its terms, the other party has a choice of remedies. Let's assume the seller, who has signed a valid real estate sales contract, refuses to transfer title to the buyer. The buyer may then sue for **specific performance**—that is, ask the court to order the breaching party to perform the terms of the contract. Alternatively, the buyer may sue for monetary damages or seek return of the earnest money and forget about the transaction.

A suit for specific performance is possible only if the contract concerns a unique item. Because land and improvements on land are considered one-of-a-kind items, a buyer probably will be successful in obtaining an order of specific performance. As an alternative, a buyer may seek payment for any damages that result from the seller's breach. Such damages could include compensation for the buyer's loss of time and the buyer's expenses related to the sale, such as fees for a title search, a land survey and a building inspection. As the sales contract should provide, the buyer may have the earnest money refunded and the obligations discharged. (See section II of Figure 11.1.)

If a buyer refuses to perform his or her duties under a valid contract, the seller also has the right to sue. In many states, the seller's rights are limited, however, to recovering monetary damages—which may include the earnest money—as provided in the contract. Usually, a seller cannot seek specific performance because courts do not feel that a ready, willing and able buyer is a unique commodity. Eventually, some other purchaser will be found.

This discussion of remedies for a breached contract is based on the presumption that the party's nonperformance is not excused. A well-drafted contract provides that the parties will be discharged from performance in the event of certain conditions. For example, if the Barrs, after exercising good faith, fail to obtain adequate financing, the contract may be canceled without obligation. (See section II of Figure 11.1.) In such an event, the Barrs' earnest money would be returned to them in full. The Stewarts' failure to correct any defects in their title also would release the Barrs from going forward with the purchase. (See section III of Figure 11.1.)

Chapter Review

1. A contract is a legal document that represents an agreement between two or more parties. The essential elements required before any contract is binding include (1) an offer, (2) an acceptance, (3) consideration, (4) parties with legal capacity and (5) a lawful purpose. In addition, all states require that a contract involving any interest in land must be in writing and signed by the party against whom enforcement is sought.

2. Real estate sales contracts are, in essence, gap fillers. Such a contract must govern the parties' rights between the time an agreement is reached and the time the transaction is formally completed, or closed.

3. Several kinds of contracts may be used in a real estate transaction. Among the common types are the traditional sales contract and the option-to-buy contract.

4. The traditional real estate sales contract should consist of provisions specifying (1) the property description, (2) the purchase price and the way it is to be paid, (3) the escrow arrangement, (4) the effect on the contract of the destruction of improvements, (5) the pest-free warranty and (6) the broker's commission, if any.

5. Failure to perform contractual duties is a breach of contract. Remedies available to a buyer for the seller's breach include an order for specific performance, monetary damages or the return of the earnest money. A

seller generally cannot seek the specific performance of a buyer who has breached the contract.

--- Key Terms ---

acceptance   an expression of satisfaction with an offer.

capacity   legal ability to understand and accept the terms of a contract.

consideration   anything that incurs legal detriment or the forgoing of a legal benefit.

contract   a legal device used by two or more persons to indicate they have reached an agreement.

counteroffer   a response to an offer that represents a new offer.

deed   a written document that evidences ownership.

offer   a statement that specifies the position of its maker (offeror) and indicates that the offeror is willing to be bound by the conditions stated.

option-to-buy contract   a contract that gives one party the right, but not an obligation, to purchase a property within a specified time horizon at a specified price.

partial performance   fulfillment of the terms of an agreement to such an extent that the existence of the agreement may be reasonably inferred.

specific performance   a requirement that the terms of a contract be exactly complied with.

statute of frauds   a law designed to prevent fraudulent practices involving contracts.

title   the legal right to ownership.

voidable   capable of being rescinded, as a contract entered into by a minor or by a person who has been declared insane.

--- Study Exercises ---

1.   List and explain the six essential elements of a valid real estate sales contract.

2.   In a contract, what is meant by capacity? By consideration?

3.   Mark offered to buy Charlie's four-acre tract for $20,000, and they shook hands on the deal. Both men went to an attorney to draft the formal contract. The next day, Mark signed the written contract, but Charlie refused to do so because he had received a higher offer. What recourse,

if any, does Mark have against Charlie for failing to abide by their oral agreement?

4. Suppose instead that Mark and Charlie (see question 3) had agreed on the deal and Mark wrote the terms of the sale on the back of an envelope, which both signed. They knew they needed an attorney to flesh out the agreement and draft a formal contract. Charlie refused to sign the formal contract, having received a higher offer. Could Mark force Charlie to carry out the contract?

5. Nell and Edward agreed that Nell would purchase Edward's house and lot. Because both parties wanted to avoid the expense of having a formal contract drafted, they signed their names below the following handwritten statement: "Nell hereby agrees to buy from Edward the house at 1023 Washington Avenue for $65,000. Closing to be within 60 days. September 13, 1992." Nell had planned to borrow 90 percent of the purchase price, but failed to qualify for this loan. Does Nell's inability to obtain a loan excuse her from performance of the agreement as written?

6. After Kristy finished college and started working, she found a small house that she wanted to buy, but could not afford. As an alternative, she agreed to lease the house with an option to buy it. To be valid, what must the option agreement include?

For Further Reading

Gibson, F., J. Karp, and E. Klayman. *Real Estate Law,* 3d ed. (Chicago: Real Estate Education Company, 1992).

de Heer, R. *Realty Bluebook,* 31st ed. (Chicago: Real Estate Education Company, 1996).

CHAPTER 12
Principles of Real Property Insurance

Farmers often add special provisions for flood coverage to their property insurance policies to protect themselves from weather-related crop failures.

Chapter Preview

THERE ARE THREE primary reasons for the inclusion of an overview of real property insurance in this book. First, and of greatest importance, every property owner needs to understand the broad principles of property and liability risk and insurance to purchase coverage wisely to protect against these perils. Second, property insurance coverage is required by mortgage lenders. Unless adequate protection against loss is in place, a lender will not advance the funds needed to purchase a property. Third, real estate property insurance is an important part of the business of many real estate brokerage firms because this activity complements their other activities and adds to the firms' profits.

In addition to discussing various aspects of property ownership, this chapter will examine the homeowner's policy, including

- risks covered;
- replacement cost coverage;
- personal articles floater policies;
- coinsurance;
- renter's and condominium owner's insurance; and
- liability insurance.

We also will look at two special types of insurance of interest to homeowners:

- Flood insurance
- Mortgage life insurance

Finally, we will examine property insurance for commercial property, particularly the businessowner's policy for small and medium-sized businesses.

RISKS OF PROPERTY OWNERSHIP

The ownership and use of real property involve several types of insurable **risk**—the chance of loss. These risks fall into four broad categories:

1. Loss of property because of fire, wind, water, vandalism or other hazards
2. Loss of the use of property
3. Additional expenses resulting from the loss of use of property
4. Liability losses resulting from negligence in the use of property resulting in bodily injury, property damage, medical expenses or related costs

In addition to the risk of real property loss, a family may suffer financial loss, particularly the inability to make mortgage payments, because of the death or disability of a wage earner.

All these hazards involve risk to the individual, family or business. An individual may suffer a catastrophic fire that completely destroys his or her home and its furnishings. A family may lose its home through inability to meet mortgage payments after the head of the household dies. A business may face a large liability payment because a customer is injured in a fall on the premises. The financial consequences of each of these risks can be eliminated or lessened through insurance.

Insurance against risk is possible because of the law of large numbers: what is unpredictable for an individual becomes predictable for a large number of individuals. For example, most families never lose their homes to fire, and the probability that a single family will do so in any particular year is so small as to be unpredictable. But an insurer can predict potential losses from fires among a large group of insured properties with considerable accuracy. Such predictability makes it possible for a company to assume risk for an insured party through a **policy** (contract) upon payment of a **premium** (fee).

Unless the company concentrates its coverage too heavily in one area, so that it might be affected very adversely by a natural disaster such as a hurricane or a massive forest fire, it should be able to pay the losses suffered by individual policyholders from policy income.

INSURANCE AGAINST PROPERTY LOSSES

Property insurance protects the policyholder against direct and indirect losses on insured risks. **Direct losses** are the costs of replacing or repairing property destroyed or damaged. **Indirect losses** are the additional living expenses or losses of business income suffered before the property can be restored. **Liability insurance** protects the insured against lawsuits brought in response to supposed acts of negligence that result in injury or loss of property to the public.

The Homeowner's Policy

The **homeowner's policy** is designed as a single package to provide coverage of losses from fire and other perils, personal liability, medical payments and theft. It is required by mortgage lenders and prudent homeowners. Under

Coverage under the HO-3 Homeowner's Policy | **Table 12.1**

Coverage	Loss Covered	Amount
A	Dwelling	Minimum of $20,000
B	Other structures	10% of coverage A
C	Personal property	50% of coverage A
D	Loss of use	20% of coverage A
E	Personal liability	$100,000
F	Medical payments to others	$1,000 per person, $25,000 per accident

the most widely used form, HO-3, the homeowner must purchase at least $20,000 coverage on the dwelling, with other coverages as shown in Table 12.1.

These amounts can be modified to meet most needs. For example, a property owner might purchase $100,000 coverage on his or her dwelling (coverage A). In this case, other structures on the residential premises, such as garages or pool houses, are covered for $10,000 (coverage B) and personal property for $50,000 (coverage C). Special limits of liability exist for certain items—for example, $200 for money, bank notes and precious metals; $2,000 for guns; $2,500 for silverware, goldware and pewterware; $2,500 for business property on the premises; and only $250 for business property away from the premises. Thus, if you have a $5,000 computer, you should increase coverage on this item. These special limits and the total amount of insurance may be increased by payment of a larger premium.

Some items of personal property are not covered. These include

- animals, birds and fish;
- motorized vehicles, except nonlicensed vehicles such as mowers used in the maintenance of the premises or electric wheelchairs (Motorized vehicles are insured under automobile policies.);
- aircraft;
- property of unrelated roomers;
- business property;
- tape players and tapes used in motor vehicles; and
- separately described property specifically insured (This exclusion prevents the insured from collecting twice for a loss on the same item.).

Coverage D provides payment for additional living expenses if the residence is made uninhabitable by one of the covered perils. If the home in our example were damaged by a runaway truck or a fire and could not be occupied for two months while repairs were being made, the insurer would pay the necessary increased living expenses for the family up to $10,000.

Personal liability (coverage E) and medical payments to others (coverage F) will be discussed later in this chapter, when we consider liability insurance.

Replacement Cost Coverage   In the homeowner's policy, payment for loss or damage to personal property normally is limited to **actual cash value,** generally interpreted to mean the cost of replacing the destroyed or damaged property minus the amount by which the property had fallen in value as a result of normal wear and tear since it was new. Thus, a six-year-old television set originally costing $450 that would cost $500 to replace today might have an actual cash value of only $200. In other words, it would have a market value of $200. Unless the household furnishings, clothing and other personal property in a home are virtually new, the difference between replacement cost and actual cash value could be financially devastating, even if the peril were covered by insurance.

Fortunately, the homeowner can purchase a **personal property replacement cost endorsement,** which allows the policyholder to recoup the full replacement cost of stolen or damaged goods. Replacement cost is limited to 400 percent of the actual cash value at the time of loss and excludes art, antiques, stamps, coins and other collectibles, as these items often are difficult or impossible to replace. Coverage of such special items requires a separate floater rider.

Personal Articles Floater Policies   Suppose a family collects antique porcelains, guns or coins; or perhaps Great-Aunt Mabel left the family several pieces of valuable heirloom jewelry. Because of the limitations in the homeowner's policy, these items probably are not fully covered. For this protection, a **personal articles floater policy** can be obtained. This insures specific scheduled (listed) property for specific amounts. It usually is necessary to be able to establish the value of articles that are insured, sometimes through a qualified appraisal.

Credit Card Forgery and Counterfeit Money Losses   The personal property portion of the homeowner's policy also covers losses of up to $1,000 from the unauthorized use of a policyholder's credit card. In addition, it covers losses that might occur when the policyholder accepts counterfeit money or when someone forges the policyholder's name on a check.

Factors Influencing Rates   Homeowner's insurance rates are influenced by a number of factors, including location, type of construction and amount of deductibles. A house located in a community that has a highly rated fire department and an adequate water supply is much less likely to suffer a severe fire loss than a house located in a rural area with no fire department. Thus, the owner of the house in the urban area will pay a lower insurance rate per $1,000 of coverage than the owner of the house in the unprotected rural area. Other rate classifications fall in between these extremes. A suburban house located more than five miles from a fire station will pay a higher rate than one located near a fire station, as will the house located more than 1,000 feet from a fire hydrant.

Type of construction also affects insurance rates. Whatever its other virtues, a wooden house is more susceptible to fire than a masonry house; a wooden roof catches fire more easily than one covered with fiberglass shingles. In general, the more fire-resistant the construction of a home, the lower its insurance rates.

Whatever the type of construction, it is possible to reduce insurance rates by reducing the chance of loss. For example, many companies offer discounts for the installation of burglar and fire alarm systems, sprinkler systems or smoke alarms.

Another way to reduce premiums is to increase the amount of deductibles. The homeowner's policy is written with a deductible, usually $250, for any one occurrence. If lightning strikes the house and destroys a new $700 television, for example, the insurance company would pay $450 ($700 minus the $250 deductible). Increasing the deductible will reduce the premium, but the homeowner then becomes a self-insurer for the deductible and must be prepared to cover this additional loss.

Coinsurance   Actual cash value (replacement cost less depreciation) is paid for losses to personal property under the homeowner's policy. Replacement cost without deduction for depreciation up to the face value of the policy is paid for losses to the building under coverages A and B, however.

Full payment of partial losses to buildings under the homeowner's policy is made only if insurance equal to 80 percent of the replacement cost of the building was carried at the time of loss. If not, the policyholder becomes a coinsurer with the company. **Coinsurance** is the joint assumption of risk by two or more parties. In that case, the policy pays only (1) the actual cash value of the loss or (2) "that proportion of the cost to repair or replace, without deduction for depreciation, of that part of the building damaged, which the total amount of insurance in [the] policy on the damaged building bears to 80% of the replacement cost of the building."

Let us illustrate with a simple example. Suppose that Roger and Laura Whitaker's house has a replacement cost of $100,000, and they carry $80,000 in insurance. The Whitakers suffer $20,000 in damages to the home when a portion of the roof collapses after a record snow and sleet storm. How much would they recover from the insurance company? The percentage of recovery is determined by the following formula:

$$\frac{\text{Amount of insurance coverage}}{80\% \text{ of the replacement cost of the building}} = \text{Percentage recovery}$$

In this case, all of the loss will be paid by the company:

$$\frac{\$80,000}{\$80,000} = 1, \text{ or } 100 \text{ percent}$$

Suppose, however, that the Whitakers carried only $60,000 worth of insurance on the building. In that case, the Whitakers would recover only 75 percent ($7,500) of the loss:

$$\frac{\$60,000}{\$80,000} = .75 \text{ or } 75 \text{ percent}$$

Why do companies include a coinsurance clause? Most insurance claims do not involve a total loss. Consequently, in the absence of the coinsurance clause, the policyholder who carried insurance covering only partial value would receive greater relative benefits than one who carried full coverage. Suppose, for example, that the Springers and the Michauds each live in a ten-year-old house having a $100,000 replacement value. The Springers carry $100,000 worth of insurance on their home, while the Michauds carry only $60,000. In case of total loss, the Springers' insurance proceeds would be adequate to replace their house, while the Michauds would receive only $60,000. Suppose, however, that each suffered a $20,000 loss. Again, the Springers would be fully compensated, but if the Michauds also were paid $20,000, they obviously would be receiving much more for their insurance dollar. Under the coinsurance clause, however, the Michauds would recover only 75 percent of their loss:

$$\frac{\$60,000}{\$80,000} = .75 \text{ or } 75 \text{ percent}$$

As inflation boosts replacement costs, it becomes increasingly important to evaluate the amount of coverage on one's home, as the subjects of the Case Study on page 247 discovered. An alternative is to include a replacement cost endorsement, a common feature in homeowner's policies.

Renter's and Condominium Owner's Insurance   Renters and condominium or cooperative owners do not need insurance on their dwelling units because this coverage is provided by the landlord or the condominium or cooperative association. However, they do need coverage for their personal property and personal liability. Consequently, special versions of the homeowner's policy are designed for renters and condominium owners.

Form HO-4 covers a tenant's personal property against loss or damage and also provides personal liability insurance. If the insured makes any alterations or additions to the dwelling, losses of this property are covered for up to 10 percent of the amount of personal property coverage.

Form HO-6 is designed for the owners of condominium units and cooperative apartments. In addition to coverage for personal property and personal liability, the policy provides a minimum of $1,000 of insurance for alterations, appliances, fixtures and other improvements that are not covered by the condominium or cooperative association's insurance on the dwelling.

The Modified Coverage Form HO-8   Owners of older homes (usually those located in urban neighborhoods) often have a problem because the replacement cost of their properties is considerably greater than the market value. For example, a house may have a replacement cost of $100,000, but a market value of only $60,000. So that he or she does not become a coinsurer under a standard homeowner's policy, the owner would have to carry at least $80,000 in coverage on the dwelling. The owner may be quite reluctant to do this on a house worth only $60,000, and the insurer may also be reluctant to insure the house for that amount. Thus, to provide homeowner's insurance for these properties, the HO-8 form was developed.

Under the HO-8 form, losses are paid based on the amount required to repair or replace a property using common construction materials and methods, not on replacement cost. In addition, theft coverage is limited to $1,000 per occurrence and applies only to losses that occur on the premises or in a bank or public warehouse.

Real Estate Today   *Case Study*

The Impact of Inflation on Adequacy of Insurance Coverage

Jim and Joan Foil insured their home in suburban Birmingham, Alabama, for $70,000 when they bought it about nine years ago. Even though they paid $90,000 for the property, Jim considered the amount of insurance adequate because the lot represented $15,000 of the total cost. Furthermore, even a disastrous fire would not destroy the driveway, foundation and water and sewer lines.

One night, Jim poured vegetable oil in his popcorn popper, plugged it in and then forgot it. When he remembered and removed the lid, the hot oil blazed up fiercely. By the time the firefighters left four hours later, the house and furnishings had suffered $35,000 in fire, smoke and water damage.

The next day, the Foils got another shock. Because they had ignored their insurance agent's advice to add coverage as inflation increased building costs, the loss was not fully covered. The Foils were considered coinsurers.

For the loss to be fully covered, the Foils would have needed to carry approximately $98,000 in insurance, 80 percent of the estimated replacement cost of $122,500. Because they had only $70,000 in coverage, the insurance company would pay only 71 percent of

the loss ($70,000 ÷ $98,000). The family had to dig into its savings for $10,150 to complete the repairs. Previous plans for a European vacation and new furniture had to be forgotten.

Suppose that events had taken another turn. When the oil blazed up, Jim had the presence of mind to put the top back on the popper and smother the fire. The kitchen suffered only minor smoke damage. But Jim did some hard thinking about what might have happened, and the next day, he phoned his insurance agent, Judy Akers, and asked about increasing the coverage. Judy estimated replacement cost for the Foils' home at approximately $126,566 using the simplified cost guide shown on the following pages.

The Foils raised the amount of their insurance to $115,000, considerably above the 80 percent required but still less than full coverage. They again reasoned that the chances of a total loss were small and that, in any case, the foundation and other such improvements would not be destroyed. They resolved, however, to carefully check their coverage each year to make sure they were keeping up with the inflation in replacement costs. ■

Home Cost Estimator

61 74091-20 S

You need 80% of replacement cost to cover partial dwelling losses without depreciation. You should have 100% of replacement cost to cover a TOTAL loss (if eligible, a special endorsement can be added to maintain 100% replacement). The intent of this ESTIMATOR is to furnish an easy method for <u>approximating</u> the cost to rebuild under AVERAGE circumstances. Higher valued homes or unique construction might require a different approach. In either case, get in touch with us. WE CAN HELP.

NAME *Jim and Joan Foil*   POLICY # *AX53B2*

ADDRESS *1653 Wiltshire Rd, Birmingham Alabama*   ZIP *35263*
STREET   CITY   STATE

STEP 1   CONSTRUCTION YEAR CLASSES

Read the following class descriptions and select the one that **most nearly** applies to your home.

1980 TO PRESENT/PRE-1980 CLASSES

Class A/AA
- simple rectangular shape
- one-foot roof overhang
- inexpensive floor coverings
- painted or simulated wood-grain softwood cabinets

CLASS A

Class B/BB
- rectangular or L-shaped
- one-and-one-half-foot roof overhang
- basic grade floor coverings
- moderate hardwood kitchen cabinetry
- average materials and quality

CLASS B

Class C/CC
- larger L-shape or rectangle
- one-and-one-half-foot roof overhang
- above-average hardwood cabinets
- carpeting, vinyl, hardwood, and ceramic tile floors
- average to above-average materials and quality

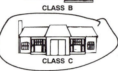
CLASS C

Class D/DD
- two-foot roof overhang
- carpeting, hardwood, slate and ceramic tile floors
- extra baths are common and adjoin bedrooms
- large rooms and special purpose rooms
- usually custom designed by architect for owner
- above-average materials and quality

CLASS D

PRE-1940 CLASSES

Class X
- similar to Basic Class A
- plain box-shaped design
- one-foot roof overhang
- minimal softwood cabinetry
- hardwood and linoleum floors

CLASS X

Class Y
- similar to Basic Class B
- one-and-one-half-foot roof overhang
- adequate hardwood cabinetry and trim
- dining room and porches common
- plaster walls and ceilings
- hardwood, linoleum and ceramic tile floors
- average materials and quality

CLASS Y

Class Z
- similar to Basic Class C
- large rectangular shaped design
- one-and-one-half-foot roof overhang
- ample hardwood cabinetry
- large dining room, foyer and porch common
- plaster walls and ceilings
- hardwood, vinyl and ceramic tile, and slate floors
- average to above-average materials and quality

CLASS Z

STEP 2   UNIT COUNT

Enter number of units

1	Living Room
3	Bedrooms
2	Bathrooms (3 or more fixtures)
1	Kitchen
1	Dining Room
1	Family and/or Recreation Room
	Den, Study, or Office
	Unfinished Attic (not crawl space)
	Unfinished Basement
	Stone Exterior Walls
	Clay Tile or Slate Roof
1	Two-Car Attached Garage
	Two-Car Built-in Garage
	Three-Car Carport
	Double-Size Rooms (over 300 sq. ft.)
10	Total multiplied by 3 = *30* (a)
	Dinette or Breakfast Nook
1	Half Baths (2 or less fixtures)
1	Laundry Room with Adjacent Half Bath
	Brick Exterior Walls
1	Central Air Conditioning
	Enclosed Porch
	One-Car Attached Garage
	One-Car Built-in Garage
	One or Two-Car Carport
	Large Rooms (200 to 300 sq. ft.)
3	Total multiplied by 2 = *6* (b)
	Foyer or Entrance Hall
	Walk-in Closet or Dressing room
1	Work, Storage, or Laundry Room
	Open Porch, Breezeway, or Large Deck
1	Fireplace
2	Total — Repeat here = *2* (c)

ADD a + b + c for UNIT COUNT *38*

STEP 3 BASE COSTS

Locate the construction year class column below (from Step 1). In the class columns find the Base Cost opposite the unit count (from Step 2).

UNIT COUNT	1980 TO PRESENT CLASSES				PRE-1980 CLASSES				PRE-1940 CLASSES		
	A	B	C	D	AA	BB	CC	DD	X	Y	Z
25	$ 37,400	$ 49,200	$ 64,500	$ 79,700	$ 42,800	$ 55,100	$ 68,900	$ 84,600	$ 53,100	$ 64,000	$ 74,800
26	38,800	51,100	66,900	82,800	44,500	57,200	71,500	87,900	55,200	66,400	77,700
27	40,400	53,100	69,600	86,000	46,200	59,500	74,300	91,300	57,300	69,000	80,700
28	41,900	55,100	72,200	89,300	47,900	61,700	77,100	94,800	59,500	71,600	83,800
29	43,300	57,000	74,700	92,300	49,600	63,800	79,800	98,000	61,600	74,100	86,600
30	44,800	59,000	77,300	95,600	51,300	66,100	82,600	101,500	63,700	76,700	89,700
31	46,400	61,000	79,900	98,800	53,100	68,300	85,400	104,900	65,900	79,300	92,700
32	47,800	62,900	82,400	101,900	54,700	70,400	88,100	108,200	67,900	81,800	95,600
33	49,300	64,900	85,000	105,100	56,500	72,700	90,900	111,600	70,100	84,400	98,600
34	50,800	66,900	87,600	108,400	58,200	74,900	93,700	115,100	72,300	87,000	101,700
35	52,300	68,800	90,100	111,500	59,900	77,100	96,300	118,300	74,300	89,400	104,600
36	53,800	70,800	92,700	114,700	61,600	79,300	99,100	121,800	76,500	92,000	107,600
37	55,300	72,800	95,400	117,900	63,300	81,500	101,900	125,200	78,600	94,600	110,700
(38)	56,800	74,700	97,900	121,000	65,000	83,700	(104,600)	128,500	80,700	97,100	113,500
39	58,300	76,700	100,500	124,300	66,700	85,900	107,400	131,900	82,800	99,700	116,600
40	59,800	78,700	103,100	127,500	68,500	88,100	110,200	135,400	85,000	102,300	119,600
41	61,300	80,600	105,600	130,600	70,100	90,300	112,800	138,600	87,000	104,800	122,500
42	62,800	82,600	108,200	133,800	71,900	92,500	115,600	142,100	89,200	107,400	125,600
43	64,300	84,600	110,800	137,100	73,600	94,800	118,400	145,500	91,400	110,000	128,600
44	65,700	86,500	113,300	140,100	75,300	96,900	121,100	148,800	93,400	112,500	131,500
45	67,300	88,500	115,900	143,400	77,000	99,100	123,900	152,200	95,600	115,100	134,500
46	68,800	90,500	118,600	146,600	78,700	101,400	126,700	155,700	97,700	117,700	137,600
47	70,200	92,400	121,000	149,700	80,400	103,500	129,400	158,900	99,800	120,100	140,400
48	71,700	94,400	123,700	152,900	82,100	105,700	132,200	162,400	102,000	122,700	143,500
49	73,300	96,400	126,300	156,200	83,900	108,000	135,000	165,800	104,100	125,300	146,500
50	74,800	98,400	128,900	159,400	85,600	110,200	137,800	169,200	106,300	127,900	149,600
51	76,200	100,300	131,400	162,500	87,300	112,300	140,400	172,500	108,300	130,400	152,500
52	77,700	102,300	134,000	165,700	89,000	114,600	143,200	176,000	110,500	133,000	155,500
53	79,300	104,300	136,600	169,000	90,700	116,800	146,000	179,400	112,600	135,600	158,500
54	80,700	106,200	139,100	172,000	92,400	118,900	148,700	182,700	114,700	138,100	161,400
55	82,200	108,200	141,700	175,300	94,100	121,200	151,500	186,100	116,900	140,700	164,500
56	83,800	110,200	144,400	178,500	95,900	123,400	154,300	189,500	119,000	143,300	167,500
57	85,200	112,100	146,900	181,600	97,500	125,600	156,900	192,800	121,100	145,700	170,400
58	86,700	114,100	149,500	184,800	99,300	127,800	159,700	196,300	123,200	148,300	173,400
59	88,200	116,100	152,100	188,100	101,000	130,000	162,500	199,700	125,400	150,900	176,500
60	89,700	118,000	154,600	191,200	102,700	132,200	165,200	203,000	127,400	153,400	179,400
add for each additional unit over 60	+1,500	+2,000	+2,600	+3,200	+1,700	+2,200	+2,800	+3,400	+2,100	+2,600	+3,000

STEP 4 LOCATION MULTIPLIERS

Use your zip code to select a multiplier.

ALABAMA
350-351 . . . . 1.20
352 . . . . (1.21)
354 . . . . 1.20
355 . . . . 1.19
356-358 . . . . 1.15
359 . . . . 1.16
360 . . . . 1.15
361, 369 . . . . 1.16
362 . . . . 1.16
363 . . . . 1.13
364-365 . . . . 1.20
366 . . . . 1.22
367 . . . . 1.15
368 . . . . 1.13

FLORIDA
320, 322 . . . . 1.19
321 . . . . 1.20
323 . . . . 1.13
324 . . . . 1.21
325 . . . . 1.22
326 . . . . 1.18
327 . . . . 1.31
328, 347 . . . . 1.31
329 . . . . 1.25
330-331, 333 . . . . 1.41
334 . . . . 1.44
335-337, 346 . . . . 1.27
338 . . . . 1.25
339 . . . . 1.43
342 . . . . 1.29
344 . . . . 1.18
349 . . . . 1.32

GEORGIA
300, 303 . . . . 1.26
301-302 . . . . 1.25
304, 313-314 . . . . 1.16
305-306 . . . . 1.19
307 . . . . 1.18
308-309 . . . . 1.15
310 . . . . 1.13
312 . . . . 1.14
315 . . . . 1.14
316 . . . . 1.13
317 . . . . 1.13
318 . . . . 1.13
319 . . . . 1.12

KENTUCKY
400-402 . . . . 1.27
403-404, 406-409 . . . . 1.22
405 . . . . 1.23
410 . . . . 1.36
411-412 . . . . 1.29
413-414, 417-418 . . . . 1.24
415-416 . . . . 1.27
420 . . . . 1.28
421, 427 . . . . 1.26
422-424 . . . . 1.28
425-426 . . . . 1.26

MICHIGAN
480, 482-483 . . . . 1.57
481 . . . . 1.56
484-485 . . . . 1.43
486-487 . . . . 1.38
488 . . . . 1.40
489, 492 . . . . 1.42

MICHIGAN cont.
490-491 . . . . 1.36
493-495 . . . . 1.32
496-497 . . . . 1.29
498 . . . . 1.39
499 . . . . 1.33

NORTH CAROLINA
270 . . . . 1.36
271 . . . . 1.38
272-273 . . . . 1.38
274 . . . . 1.38
275 . . . . 1.46
276-277 . . . . 1.49
278 . . . . 1.26
279 . . . . 1.26
280-281 . . . . 1.38
282 . . . . 1.42
283 . . . . 1.28
284 . . . . 1.26
285 . . . . 1.20
286 . . . . 1.19
287-289 . . . . 1.19

OHIO
430-431 . . . . 1.34
432 . . . . 1.36
433 . . . . 1.35
434, 436 . . . . 1.43
435 . . . . 1.38
437-438 . . . . 1.34
439 . . . . 1.38
440 . . . . 1.47
441 . . . . 1.51
442-443 . . . . 1.46

OHIO cont.
444-445 . . . . 1.39
446-447 . . . . 1.39
448 . . . . 1.37
449 . . . . 1.36
450 . . . . 1.34
451 . . . . 1.34
452 . . . . 1.34
453-455 . . . . 1.37
456 . . . . 1.34
457 . . . . 1.34
458 . . . . 1.36

SOUTH CAROLINA
290-291 . . . . 1.18
292 . . . . 1.20
293, 296 . . . . 1.17
294 . . . . 1.23
295 . . . . 1.15
297-298 . . . . 1.12
299 . . . . 1.22

TENNESSEE
370-371, 384 . . . . 1.19
372 . . . . 1.20
373 . . . . 1.17
374 . . . . 1.18
376-378 . . . . 1.18
379 . . . . 1.19
380 . . . . 1.18
381 . . . . 1.19
382 . . . . 1.16
383 . . . . 1.18
385 . . . . 1.18

STEP 5 REPLACEMENT COST ESTIMATE

a. Enter the BASE COST from Step 3.

b. Enter the MULTIPLIER from Step 4 and multiply it by the base cost.

c. The result is the estimated replacement cost of your home.

$ *104,600*	Base Cost
× *1.21*	Location Multiplier
= $ *126,566*	Estimated Replacement Cost

©1996, E. H. BOECKH

Real Estate Today

Close-Up

Taking Inventory before *the Disaster Occurs*

Suppose you come home to find your home's back door forced open and the house ransacked. Or you are awakened by smoke and must flee for your life while fire destroys your home and its furnishings. As horrifying as these events are, they will soon be followed by a new ordeal—proving to the insurance adjuster what items of personal property you lost and their value.

To get a feel for how difficult this might be, try making from memory a complete inventory of all your clothes and kitchen utensils. Even though these items can add up to hundreds and even thousands of dollars, most homeowners would find this to be an extremely difficult task. They also would have a difficult time proving their loss to an insurance adjuster unless they previously had made an inventory, preferably backed up by a photographic record.

Suppose the burglars took your complete set of silverware for twelve. Could you prove to the adjuster you actually had a set of silverware for twelve? You could if you had a photograph in your bank safe-deposit box showing the silverware laid out on your dining room table. Or suppose the fire destroyed the valuable antique dining table and chairs left to you by Great-Aunt Matilda. When you put in a claim for these items to the insurance company for $10,000, the adjuster might regard you with some skepticism and ask you to prove this high value. Could you? You could if you had in your safe-deposit box an appraisal of your valuable items made by a professional appraiser, preferably backed by photographs, movies or videotapes and bills of sale for other expensive items you purchased.

Making an Inventory and a Photographic Record

Making your own home inventory takes time and is somewhat tedious, but it is time well spent. Personal property inventory booklets are usually available from an insurance agent or a bookstore. These booklets often list items owned by most families and have spaces to list the year bought, the original cost and the estimated current value.

Photographs are an excellent, and even essential, backup to the written inventory. Each room should be photographed from several angles to include all the furnishings, and separate photos should be taken of closets, cabinets and drawers. It is also desirable to take individual photos of valuable items, including close-ups of details. These photographs can be taken as slides (which take up little space and can be projected to help pick out details), as color prints (which can be included along with the written inventory in some inventory albums), as movies or on videotape.

In addition to the inventory list and photographs, it is wise to include detailed descriptions of expensive items, along with sales receipts. For things such as stereos, televisions and cameras, list the manufacturer, serial number, model, year of purchase and original cost of each. For antiques or other collectibles, give descriptions and list such items as size, material, style, country of origin, inscriptions, where and when bought and price paid. It may also be desirable to obtain professional appraisals of valuable items of this type.

Once the inventory has been completed, it serves two important functions. First, it can be used to check the adequacy of personal property insurance protection. Most people are quite surprised at the total value of their personal possessions, and many need to increase their personal property insurance coverage. Others find they have items such as valuable collections of silver, pewter or fine art that are not fully covered under their homeowner's policies and require additional coverage.

The second use of the inventory is to substantiate claims in the event of loss. The inventory should be stored in a safe place outside the home, preferably in a bank box. A copy might also be kept in an office, with the family lawyer or with the insurance agent. The place the inventory should not be kept is in the home; not only might the inventory be destroyed by fire, but providing this information to burglars would really help make their day.

An inventory of your possessions involves some cost and time, but it will be invaluable in proving loss to your insurance company. It can also help you check the adequacy of insurance coverage and aid the police in recovering any stolen property. ■

EARTHQUAKE INSURANCE

Losses from earthquakes are not covered under the standard homeowner's policy. Fortunately, the chance of losses from earthquakes is very rare; however, when they occur, losses can be catastrophic. It is possible to purchase an earthquake endorsement to the homeowner's policy to cover this risk, but the cost is relatively high, and a deductible of up to 10 percent applies separately to coverages A, B and C. For these reasons and the low probability of loss, few homeowners purchase this coverage. For example, total property losses caused by the 1989 San Francisco earthquake were estimated at more than $10 billion, but only $1 billion was covered by insurance.

LIABILITY INSURANCE

Liability insurance protects the insured against lawsuits brought in response to supposed acts of negligence that result in injury or loss of property to the public. For example, someone might be injured in a fall on ice-covered steps and sue for damages, claiming that the owner's failure to remove the ice promptly constituted negligence.

As shown in Table 12.1, coverage E of the homeowner's policy, personal liability, protects the property owner up to the limits of liability from damages for which the insured is legally liable to pay and also pays the cost of legal defense against such claims. Even though the standard homeowner's policy now provides $100,000 in liability protection, this does not provide enough protection for most homeowners, and it is wise to purchase additional coverage, perhaps including an umbrella liability policy (discussed in the following section).

Coverage F, medical payments, pays the necessary medical expenses of people injured on the premises except for residents and residence employees. For example, when Aunt Maude breaks her arm falling over the loose porch boards, she need not sue you to collect the money to pay her doctor's bill; this coverage will provide the money for the medical expenses.

The Personal Excess Liability Policy

A **personal excess liability policy,** or umbrella liability policy, protects you from disastrous liability claims involving a home, an automobile or a boat. It is combined with liability coverage included under homeowner's and automobile insurance policies and provides no coverage until the maximum limits in these policies have been exceeded. Relatively high limits for these other policies are required, usually $300,000 for the homeowner's and $500,000 for the automobile insurance. Generally, the personal excess liability policy is subject to a $500 deductible for liability exposures not covered by homeowner's and automobile policies, such as lawsuits for libel, slander and defamation of character. It excludes malpractice, professional liability and business liability, as well as aircraft liability.

Given the high amounts of coverage, the cost of these policies is surprisingly low. This exact cost depends on a number of factors, but for a qualified person, generally, it is possible to acquire $2 million in coverage for less than $200 annually.

The umbrella policy should be considered essential, particularly in light of its low cost. Not only does the policy protect against large damage claims, it provides for the costs of legal fees in defending against such claims. These are often quite substantial.

FLOOD INSURANCE

People have shown their ignorance of nature throughout history by building on floodplains. Periodically, Mother Nature shows her displeasure with this practice by using the floodplains as they were intended to be used—as places to dump excess water. As a result, flood losses in the United States exceed $1 billion annually.

Private insurance companies have been unwilling to insure against flood damage because a major storm could result in financially disastrous losses. The National Flood Insurance Act of 1968 made federally subsidized flood insurance available to property owners in flood-prone areas, and in 1973, such insurance was ruled mandatory on all loans made by federally regulated banks and savings and loan associations in such areas.

The affected communities must enact certain land-use controls to minimize building on the floodplains and require that existing structures be floodproofed by raising them (or through other measures). These controls are designed to reduce the likelihood of flood losses, although critics charge that the subsidized insurance program actually has increased building on environmentally sensitive floodplains by reducing the financial risk of the practice. Whatever the merits of this argument, the homeowner who lives in a flood-prone area is well advised to carry this type of insurance.

MORTGAGE LIFE INSURANCE

Almost all younger families require a mortgage to purchase a house. Even in two-income families, the death of either wage earner may make it difficult or impossible for the family to continue to meet the mortgage payments, and thus, the home may be lost.

This risk can be eliminated through **mortgage life insurance,** a diminishing term life insurance policy whose amount is keyed to the outstanding mortgage balance. In case of the death of the insured, the policy proceeds will be available to pay off the mortgage, leaving the family home free of debt. Alternatively, of course, this risk can be covered by adding additional coverage under another life insurance policy. A lender cannot require that a borrower obtain mortgage life insurance as a condition of approving the loan. Note that mortgage *life* insurance and mortgage insurance are different concepts. Mortgage insurance, as discussed in Chapter 13, protects the lender rather than the borrower.

BUSINESSOWNER'S POLICY

Commercial property insurance is quite complex and generally beyond the scope of this chapter. However, we will examine the **businessowner's policy** (BOP), a package policy for small and medium-sized retail stores, office buildings, apartment buildings and similar businesses that is very similar to the homeowner's policy for residences.

The businessowner's policy covers the following:

- Buildings on a replacement cost basis. The amount of coverage is increased by a stated inflationary percentage each quarter.
- Business personal property on a replacement cost basis
- Additional coverages, including debris removal, fire department service charges, business income losses, extra expenses and pollutant cleanup and removal
- Optional coverages, which can cover outdoor signs, the building exterior, grade floor glass, burglary, robbery and employee dishonesty
- Business liability insurance

The standard deductible is $250 per occurrence for all property coverages, as well as for burglary, robbery and employee dishonesty. The deductible does not apply to business income losses, extra expenses and fire department service charges.

Chapter Review

1. The three categories of risk associated with the ownership and use of real property are (1) loss of property because of some peril, (2) liability losses resulting from negligence in the use of property and (3) financial losses because of the death or disability of the owner.

2. Insurance of risk is possible because of the law of large numbers: what is unpredictable for an individual becomes predictable for a large number of individuals.

3. Two types of property insurance losses exist: (1) direct losses—the costs of replacing or repairing the property destroyed or damaged; and (2) indirect losses—the additional living expenses or losses of business income suffered before the property can be restored.

4. The homeowner's policy is designed as a single packet to provide coverage of losses from fire and other perils, personal liability, medical payments and theft.

5. Full payment for repair or replacement of buildings damaged under a homeowner's policy is made only if insurance equal to 80 percent of the replacement cost of the building was carried at the time of loss. If not, the policyholder becomes a coinsurer with the company.

6. Federally subsidized flood insurance is available to property owners in flood-prone areas, provided that their communities enact certain land-use controls to minimize potential losses.

7. The risk that a family will lose its home because its members are unable to continue making mortgage payments following the death of a wage earner can be eliminated through mortgage life insurance.

8. The businessowner's policy is a package policy for small businesses that covers real and personal property, business liability and other business property risks.

Key Terms

actual cash value   the cost of replacing an insured item minus the amount by which the item has depreciated in value since it was new.

businessowner's policy   an insurance policy for small and medium-sized businesses.

coinsurance   the joint assumption of risk by two or more parties.

direct losses   costs of replacing or repairing property destroyed or damaged.

homeowner's policy   an insurance policy that provides coverage of losses from fire and other perils, personal liability, medical payments and theft.

indirect losses   additional living expenses or loss of business income suffered before a damaged property is restored.

liability insurance   insurance that protects the insured against lawsuits brought in response to supposed acts of negligence that result in injury or loss of property to the public.

mortgage life insurance   a diminishing term life insurance policy whose amount is keyed to the outstanding mortgage balance.

personal articles floater policy   an insurance policy that insures specific personal property items for specific amounts.

personal excess liability policy   an insurance policy that insures against disastrous liability claims involving a home, automobile or boat.

personal property replacement cost endorsement   an insurance policy that allows the holder to recoup the full replacement cost of stolen or damaged goods rather than the actual cash value of the goods.

policy   a contract providing insurance coverage.

premium   the consideration paid for an insurance policy.

risk   the chance of loss; also, the uncertainty about the actual rate of return an investment will provide over the holding period.

Study Exercises

1. What are the three categories of risk associated with the ownership and use of real property?

2. What is the law of large numbers, and why does it make the insurance of risk possible?

3. What is the difference between direct and indirect property losses?

4. In Table 12.1, which items are direct losses? Which are indirect losses?

5. Use the home cost estimator in this chapter to find the estimated replacement cost for a brick exterior, three-bedroom, two-and-a-half-bath home with living room, kitchen, separate dining room, family room and laundry. The house also has an attached two-car garage, two fireplaces and central air-conditioning. The style of this house is Class B, and it is located in the 303 zip code in Georgia.

6. For an identical home (see question 5) located in the 440 zip code in Ohio, how much difference would there be in estimated replacement cost?

7. If the house from question 5 is remodeled by adding another bedroom and enclosing the porch, how much additional replacement value would result?

8. What is replacement cost coverage, and why is it important for both personal property and the dwelling?

9. Define and describe the principle of coinsurance.

10. Joe and Ann Homeowner carry a $70,000 homeowner's policy on their house, which is valued at $100,000. If they suffered a $20,000 fire loss, what percentage of the loss would the insurance company pay?

11. The Owensbys paid $80,000 for their house in 1985 and insured it for that amount. The replacement cost of the house had escalated to $120,000 by 1996, when it was destroyed by fire. How much will the insurance company pay for the total loss?

12. Suppose the Owensbys (see question 11) had damage only to the kitchen that would cost $12,000 to repair. What amount would they be paid by the insurance company for the loss? How much insurance would they have needed to be reimbursed in full for the loss?

13. What is the purpose of liability insurance?

14. Why is it important for the owner of a condominium to carry condominium owner's insurance even though the condominium association carries insurance on the structure?

For Further Reading

Baldwin, B. G. *The Complete Book of Insurance: The Consumer's Guide to Insuring Your Life, Health, Property, and Income* (Chicago: Irwin Professional Publishing, 1996).

Sloane, Leonard. *The New York Times Personal Finance Handbook* (New York: Random House, 1995).

CHAPTER 13
Financing Residential Property

It is illegal for lenders to engage in the practice known as "redlining"—that is, refusing to grant a mortgage loan for properties located in certain areas of a community. Redlining fuels urban blight and discourages development.

Chapter Preview

THE ECONOMIC CHARACTERISTICS of real estate make mortgage credit both necessary for most homebuyers and attractive to many lenders. The relatively large amounts of money required and the length of time funds must be committed often make it necessary for homebuyers to borrow the major portion of the purchase price of their homes. Because of the durability of land and improvements, many lenders are willing to provide debt capital for real estate purchases as long as the assets serve as adequate collateral for the loans. As we saw in Chapter 5, a specialized legal framework for real estate financing exists whereby real estate assets can be pledged as security for a debt, and if the borrower should default on the loan, the value of the property can be used to satisfy the debt. Mortgage credit is widely used in the financing of all types of real estate, but the focus of this chapter is on acquiring financing for owner-occupied residential real estate.

The objective of this chapter is to describe the process of obtaining financing for residential property. Specifically, we will

- discuss the mortgage concept and U.S. mortgage practice;
- review the structure of the U.S. housing finance system and its most prominent participants;
- examine the loan origination process by considering the loan application procedure;
- discuss several federal regulations designed to protect mortgage consumers; and
- outline the underwriting guidelines used by lenders to evaluate loan applications.

UNDERSTANDING THE MORTGAGE CONCEPT

The basic factor that differentiates real estate credit from most other loans is the concept of secured debt. A borrower's promise to repay an **unsecured loan** is not backed by a lien or an encumbrance on a specific property, and if a borrower defaults, the lender's only recourse is to make a claim against the borrower's general assets. The lender's ability to collect depends on the amount and quality of those assets and the debtor's income-earning ability. It is hard to imagine financial institutions making many real estate loans on such a basis because the size of such loans is relatively large, and their duration is so long that the borrower's financial condition could change drastically before the loan is repaid.

In most cases, therefore, borrowers acquire financing for real estate purchases using **secured loans.** In this type of loan, the property being purchased is pledged as security for the debt, and a lien or another encumbrance is created on the title to the property. If the borrower is unable or unwilling to repay the debt as scheduled, the lender can take legal action to sell the specified property to recover the loan funds. This type of credit instrument makes it feasible for lenders to make relatively large, long-term loans for the purchase of real estate.

History of the Mortgage Concept

A **mortgage** is a pledge of property to secure a debt. The concept dates back to early Egyptian, Greek and Roman times. Under early Roman law, nonpayment of a mortgage loan entitled the lender to make the borrower the lender's slave. Eventually, Roman law was changed to permit the unpaid debt to be satisfied by the sale of the mortgaged property.

Although the concept of pledging property to secure a debt was widespread in England by the eleventh century, the Christian strictures against usury prohibited the charging of interest on loans. Instead, Christian lenders simply took over a debtor's property and collected rents until the debt was paid. Jewish lenders, not being bound by Christian precepts, charged interest and left borrowers in possession of their property. By the fourteenth century, however, the charging of interest to borrowers left in possession of their property, known as **hypothecation,** became universal.

These early mortgages provided that if the borrower met all the terms of the loan and completely repaid the debt, the mortgage was then terminated, and the title was returned to the borrower. If any condition was not met, however, the borrower lost all rights to the property, including all money previously paid, and the property was sold to repay the debt. Gradually, a system was developed to more equitably protect the rights of the parties to a loan secured by real estate, and many of these concepts serve as the basis for modern mortgage laws in the United States.

Modern Mortgage Concepts

U.S. courts typically consider a mortgage as a voluntary lien on real estate, given to secure the payment of a debt. The borrower remains in possession of the property, but some states recognize the lender as the owner of the mortgaged property, while others interpret a mortgage purely as a lien on the property. States that have adopted the concept of **title theory** recognize that the mortgagee (lender) has the right to possession of the mortgaged property immediately upon default by the mortgagor (borrower). The property can be sold at this point, with the sale proceeds used to satisfy the debt. In **lien theory** states, however, if the mortgagor defaults, the lender must foreclose on the lien through a court action to acquire possession, then offer the property for sale and apply the funds received from the sale to extinguish the debt. In both title and lien theory states, any proceeds from a foreclosure sale in excess of the loan amount and any costs of sale must be returned to the borrower. In the normal course of a mortgage, the question of title versus lien theory is irrelevant. Only if the borrower defaults will the property be sold to satisfy the debt.

U.S. MORTGAGE PRACTICE

Although practice varies somewhat from state to state, the obligation secured by a mortgage generally is acknowledged by a **promissory note**—that is, a written promise to pay money owed. The promissory note document contains the names of the borrower and lender, the amount of the debt, the interest rate and repayment terms, reference to the security instrument and other details of the loan agreement. The promissory note makes the borrower personally liable for the debt. If the borrower violates the terms of the promissory note, the lender can take steps to foreclose on the debt. Figure 13.1 contains an example of a promissory note.

Typical Provisions of a Promissory Note

While much of the language in this sample promissory note is self-explanatory, a few items deserve special emphasis. Section IV of the note is a **prepayment clause.** The borrower in this note has the right to prepay any or all of the principal any time before it is due without penalty. Section V specifies a late charge for overdue payments, classifies any late payment as a default on the terms of the agreement and, in the event of default, permits the lender to accelerate the full amount of principle that has not been paid and any interest owed on that amount. This last item is known as an **acceleration clause.** Section VI makes all those who sign this note jointly and severally liable for the debt. Thus, the lender can demand payment from one or all of the borrowers at its option. Section VII of this note contains a **due-on-sale clause.** In the event the borrower sells or transfers all or any part of the property secured by the mortgage associated with this note, the lender may, at its option, require immediate payment of all amounts owed.

The promise to repay the debt is secured by a pledge of property as specified in the mortgage document or another security instrument, which typically contains the names of the mortgagor and mortgagee, a description of the property involved, reference to the promissory note and various provisions common to the mortgage arrangement. Figure 13.2 contains an example of a mortgage document.

| **Figure 13.1** | Promissory Note |

February 5, 19 96   St. Joseph , Missouri
                             (City)   State

1097 Timbers Crossing
(Property Address)

I. Borrower's Promise to Pay
In return for a loan that I have received, I promise to pay U.S. $108,000 (this amount is called "principal"), plus interest, to the order of the Lender. The Lender is First Savings Bank. I understand that the Lender may transfer this Note. The Lender or anyone who takes this Note by transfer and who is entitle to receive payments under this Note is called the "Note Holder."

II. Interest
Interest will be charged on unpaid principal until the full amount of principal has been paid. I will pay interest at a yearly rate of 8.00%.

III. Payments

(a) Time and Place of Payments
I will pay principal and interest by making payments every month.
I will make my monthly payments on the 1st day of each month beginning on April 1, 1996. I will make these payments every month until I have paid all of the principal and interest and any other charges described below that I may owe under this Note. My monthly payments will be applied to interest before principal. If, on April 1, 2026, I still owe amounts under this Note, I will pay those amounts in full on that date, which is called the "maturity date."

(b) Amount of Monthly Payments
My monthly payment will be in the amount of U.S. $792.47.

IV. Borrower's Right to Prepay
I have the right to make payments of principal at any time before they are due. A payment of principal only is known as a "prepayment." When I make a prepayment, I will tell the Note Holder in writing that I am doing so. I may make a full prepayment or partial prepayments without paying any prepayment charge. The Note Holder will use all of my prepayment to reduce the amount of principal that I owe under this Note. If I make a partial prepayment, there will be no changes in the due date or in the amount of my monthly payment unless the Note Holder agrees in writing to those changes.

V. Borrower's Failure to Pay as Required

(a) Late Charge for Overdue Payments
If the Note Holder has not received the full amount of any monthly payment by the end of five calendar days after the date it is due, I will pay a late charge to the Note Holder. The amount of the charge will be 10% of my overdue payment of principal and interest. I will pay this late charge promptly, but only once on each late payment.

(b) Default
If I do not pay the full amount of each monthly payment on the date it is due, I will be in default.

Promissory Note *(Continued)* **Figure 13.1**

(c)   Notice of Default

If I am in default, the Note Holder may send me a written notice telling me that if I do not pay the overdue amount by a certain date, the Note Holder may require me to pay immediately the full amount of principal that has not been paid and all the interest that I owe on that amount. That date must be at least 30 days after the date on which the notice is delivered or mailed to me.

(d)   No Waiver by Note Holder

Even if, at a time when I am in default, the Note Holder does not require me to pay immediately in full as described above, the Note Holder will still have the right to do so if I am in default at a later time.

(e)   Payment of Note Holder's Costs and Expenses

If the Note Holder has required me to pay immediately in full as described above, the Note Holder will have the right to be paid back by me for all of its costs and expenses in enforcing this Note to the extent not prohibited by applicable law. Those expenses include, for example, reasonable attorney's fees.

VI.   Obligations of Persons under this Note

If more than one person sign this Note, each person is fully and personally obligated to keep all of the promises made in this note, including the promise to pay the full amount owed. The Note Holder may enforce its rights under this Note against each person individually or against all of us together. This means that any one of us may be required to pay all of the amounts owed under this note.

VII.   Uniform Secured Note

This Note is a uniform instrument with limited variations in some jurisdictions. In addition to the protections given to the Note Holder under this Note, a Mortgage, Deed of Trust or Security Deed (the "Security Instrument"), dated the same date as this Note, protects the Note Holder from possible losses that might result if I do not keep the promises I make in this Note. That Security Instrument describes how and under what conditions I may be required to make immediate payment in full of all amounts I owe under this Note. Some of those conditions are described as follows:

Transfer of the Property. If all or any part of the Property or any interest in it is sold or transferred without the Lender's prior written consent, the Lender may, at its option, require immediate payment in full of all sums secured by the Security Instrument. If the Lender exercises this option, the Lender shall give the Borrower notice of acceleration. The notice shall provide a period of not less than 30 days from the date the notice is delivered or mailed within which the Borrower must pay all sums secured by the Security Instrument. If the Borrower fails to pay these sums prior to the expiration of the period, the Lender may invoke remedies permitted by the Security Instrument.

Witness the Hand(s) and Seal(s) of the Undersigned

_____ (Seal)—Borrower
_____ (Seal)—Borrower

Figure 13.2   Mortgage

This Mortgage ("Security Instrument") is given on ___February 5___ , ___1996___ . The mortgagor is ___Frank L. and Elizabeth M. Barr___ ("Borrower"). This Security Instrument is given to ___First Savings Bank___ ("Lender"), which is organized and existing under the laws of the State of ___Missouri___ , and whose address is ___220 Las Olas Boulevard, St. Joseph, Missouri___ . Borrower owes Lender the principal sum of U.S. $ ___108,000___ . This debt is evidenced by Borrower's Note dated the same date as this Security Instrument, which provides for monthly payments, with the full debt, if not paid earlier, due and payable on ___April 1, 2026___ . This Security Instrument secures to Lender (a) the repayment of the debt, with interest, evidenced by the Note, (b) the payment of all other sums necessary to protect the security of this Security Instrument and (c) Borrower's covenants and agreements under this Security Instrument and the Note. For this purpose, Borrower does hereby mortgage, grant and convey to Lender the following described property located in ___Buchanan___ County, in the State of ___Missouri___ :

___Lot 3, Block G, of the Harris Billups Estate, as recorded in Plat Book 8, page 37, in the Office of the Clerk of the Circuit Court of Buchanan County, Missouri___ , which has the address of ___1097 Timbers Crossing___ , together with all improvements now or hereafter erected on the Property, and all easements, appurtenances and fixtures now or hereafter a part of the Property. All replacements and additions shall also be covered by this Security Instrument.

Borrower covenants that Borrower is lawfully seised of the estate hereby conveyed and has the right to mortgage, grant and convey the Property and that the Property is unencumbered, except for encumbrances of record. Borrower warrants and will defend generally the title to the Property against all claims and demands, subject to any encumbrances of record.

This Security Instrument implicitly contains all uniform covenants permitted by laws of the applicable jurisdictions to constitute a uniform security interest covering real property.

By signing below, Borrower accepts and agrees to the terms and covenants contained in this Security Instrument and in any rider(s) executed by Borrower and recorded with it.

_____ (Seal)—Borrower

_____ (Seal)—Borrower

Typical Provisions of a Security Instrument

The language of the security instrument—in this case, a mortgage—is intended to provide the mortgagee with protection against financial losses resulting from default on the promissory note. The uniform covenants referred to in the security instrument represent promises between the borrower and lender regarding the repayment of the debt, provisions for maintaining the property and keeping insurance premiums and property taxes current, the lender's right to inspect the property and numerous other issues. If the borrower fails to meet the terms of either the promissory note or the security instrument, the lender may foreclose on the debt as described below.

UNDERSTANDING THE FORECLOSURE PROCESS

When a borrower fails to make payments or defaults on other terms of the mortgage agreement, the mortgagee can begin foreclosure proceedings to enforce its rights. **Foreclosure** refers to the process of seizing control of the collateral for a loan and using the proceeds from its sale to satisfy a defaulted debt. Usually, however, the mortgage holder will attempt to work out some type of alternative payment program to avoid the sale of the collateral. Not only is this practice much better for the lender's community relations efforts, it also avoids the time-consuming, expensive and generally unprofitable foreclosure process. Foreclosure is, for the most part, an avenue of last resort.

Types of Foreclosure

Specific foreclosure laws vary from state to state, though three general types of foreclosure proceedings exist. In states that recognize **judicial foreclosure,** the mortgagee must request a court-ordered sale of the property after proving that the borrower has defaulted on the terms of the agreement. Some states allow **nonjudicial foreclosure.** In this situation, the security instrument (either a mortgage or deed of trust) grants the power of sale to the lender should the borrower default. Finally, a few states recognize **strict foreclosure,** whereby the lender receives title to the property immediately upon default by the borrower. The lender can then dispose of the property by sale or keep it as satisfaction of the debt.

Regardless of the specific type of foreclosure recognized, most states require the lender to return to the borrower any proceeds from a foreclosure sale in excess of the loan amount, as well as certain fees. On the other hand, some states permit the mortgagee to pursue a **deficiency judgment** against the mortgagor if the proceeds are insufficient to satisfy the debt. If the courts grant the judgment, the borrower is held responsible for the remaining amount of debt after the foreclosure sale. Other states do not allow deficiency judgments, and lenders must accept the proceeds of a sale as satisfaction of the debt.

Alternative Security Instruments

The cumbersome foreclosure process is simplified in many states through the use of a security instrument similar to a mortgage called a **deed of trust** or trust deed. The deed of trust is executed at the time the loan is originated to convey title to a third party, called the *trustee*. The trustee's title to the property lies dormant as long as the borrower, or trustor, meets the terms of the debt. In the event of default, however, the trustee sells the property to pay off the debt to the lender, which is the beneficiary of the trust.

Another financing device that simplifies the foreclosure process is the **land contract,** or contract for a deed. While not a mortgage in the technical sense, the land contract establishes an obligation to transfer title from a seller to a buyer at some future date based on an agreed-upon payment schedule. The seller retains ownership of the property until the buyer has paid a certain percentage of the purchase price, sometimes 100 percent. The contract gives the buyer equitable ownership—that is, the right to use the property while making payments—but legal ownership is retained by the seller. If the buyer defaults on the contract, the seller already has ownership of the property, and no foreclosure is necessary.

Because the buyer has fewer rights under a land contract than under a mortgage or deed of trust, the land contract is used almost exclusively when financing cannot be easily obtained in other ways. For example, individual subdivision lots often can be financed through the use of a land contract with a very small down payment paid to the seller. Such loans usually are unobtainable from traditional mortgage lenders. Because the seller is the legal owner until the land contract is satisfied, the buyer who uses a land contract should make certain that the contract is carefully written to prevent the seller from encumbering the property before legal ownership is transferred.

Some Final Thoughts Related to Foreclosure

If a borrower is unable or unwilling to continue making payments on a mortgage debt and foreclosure is imminent, it may be possible to sell the mortgaged property rather than default. If the loan contains a due-on-sale clause, the mortgagor must repay the debt before the property can be sold. In many cases, the satisfaction of the debt and the sale of the property occur simultaneously, with the proceeds of any sale being applied first to the debt. If no due-on-sale clause is imposed, however, the borrower may sell the property "subject to" the existing mortgage, whereby the buyer begins making the required payments to the lender. In this type of transfer, the original borrower remains personally liable for the debt should the buyer subsequently default on the loan.

Another method of transferring mortgaged property if no due-on-sale clause is imposed is known as *assumption*. In this situation, the original borrower sells the property, and the buyer assumes responsibility for the debt. Whether the original borrower remains personally liable for the debt should the buyer default depends on the terms of the loan.

Finally, if foreclosure is imminent and a buyer cannot be found, a borrower who can no longer meet the obligations of a loan may attempt to transfer title to the property to the lender. Lenders may willingly accept a **deed in lieu of foreclosure** to avoid the expenses of a lengthy foreclosure process.

STRUCTURE OF THE U.S. HOUSING FINANCE SYSTEM

The residential lending process begins when a potential borrower contacts a mortgage lender in the hopes of acquiring a loan, either to finance the purchase of a property or to refinance property currently owned. The process of creating a new loan agreement between borrower and lender is known as **loan origination.** In essence, the borrower purchases the use of the lender's funds over time by paying interest to the lender. Therefore, loan origination refers to the transactions that occur between borrowers and lenders in the **primary mortgage market.** When existing loans are sold by originators to investors or from one investor to another, these transactions are said to occur in the **secondary mortgage market.** This market greatly facilitates the flow of mortgage funds between regions of the country. In the primary mortgage market, demand for loans depends on potential borrowers' desires and abilities to qualify for loans, while the supply of loans depends on mortgage lenders' willingness to provide debt capital to the borrowers. As with all markets, the price of mortgage capital (the interest rate) depends on the relative supply and demand for the product at any given point in time. Obviously, these two markets are interdependent and together serve as the foundation of the U.S. **housing finance system.**

The U.S. housing finance system is defined as the arrangements and institutions that facilitate the financing of residential buildings using the mortgage concepts discussed above. The many facets of our current system evolved over many years, but its roots lie in New Deal legislative actions taken by the federal government in the wake of massive defaults on owner-occupied housing during the Great Depression of the 1930s. During this time period, the stock market and banking industry were in virtual collapse, new construction was at a standstill and unemployment was rampant.

The housing market was particularly hardhit during the Depression era due to the reduction in available mortgage credit. As a matter of national policy, the federal government took steps to provide a steady flow of funds to the housing sector and to shield it from future depressions. The results of these and subsequent actions by the federal government have had a tremendous impact on the current status of our nation's housing finance system. To understand this system requires a review of the history of the government's role in the mortgage market. We begin with a discussion of the Federal Housing Administration.

Federal Housing Administration

Prior to 1929, most residential mortgages were short-term, interest-only loans: although a loan's interest rate was fixed, regular payments covered interest only for the term of the loan, and the entire principal was due at the end of the term. During the Depression, many borrowers could not repay their debts when the loans came due, and if lenders refused to refinance the loans, default was almost unavoidable. Without intervention from the federal government, the future of the housing market looked dismal at best. New construction had virtually ceased, and many existing, short-term, interest-only mortgages were already in default.

In response to the economic crisis, the Federal Housing Administration (FHA) was created in 1934 to, among other things, restore confidence in the mortgage market. As a federal agency, the FHA had a dramatic impact on the housing finance system. The FHA helped establish rigorous borrowing and lending standards that reduced lenders' risk and promoted the use of long-term, fully amortizing loans that were more consistent with household budgets than the interest-only loans prevalent at the time. (The distinction between these loan types is fully explored in Chapter 14.) In addition, the FHA established a mortgage insurance program to cover losses to lenders that originated these loans using the approved borrowing and lending standards.

Instead of lending money directly to borrowers, the primary role of the FHA in the housing finance system is to act as an insurance company for private lenders that originate loans for home purchases, repairs and improvements. To participate in its most popular program today, the 203(b) program, a borrower purchases mortgage insurance from the FHA on behalf of the lender by paying an initial fee of 2.25 percent of the loan amount at the time of origination, followed by an annual fee of ½ of 1 percent of the original loan amount for the full term of the loan, up to 30 years. (Notice that the annual cost of FHA mortgage insurance is not reduced until the loan is completely repaid.) If a borrower defaults on an **FHA-insured loan,** the insurance premiums collected from all borrowers in the program are used to protect the lender against losses resulting from foreclosure. In return for reducing the lender's risk in this manner, the borrower can receive a loan for as much as 97 percent of the value of the property at an affordable interest rate. Although anyone is eligible to apply for an FHA-insured loan, the maximum loan amount available depends on the location of the property. In some high-cost areas, the loan limit is approximately $150,000. Loans for larger amounts are not eligible for FHA insurance.

The success of the FHA in the 1930s greatly standardized the mortgage lending process in the United States and reduced lenders' risk exposure from mortgage loans. Life insurance companies with policy reserves to invest were especially attracted to these standardized mortgages, which resulted in much needed capital flows into depressed areas of the country. Many mortgage bankers began actively originating FHA-insured loans in capital-deficit areas and selling them to investors, such as life insurance companies in search of high-yielding, relatively safe investments. With the help of other government and nongovernment initiatives in the mortgage industry, the secondary mortgage market expanded rapidly as many other types of investors were attracted to mortgage investments.

Private Mortgage Insurance

Insurance against mortgage default was not unheard of in the mortgage market even before 1934. In fact, numerous **private mortgage insurance** (PMI) companies existed in the U.S. prior to the collapse of the real estate market. The high number of loan defaults, however, caused a complete failure of the PMI industry during the Depression. Not until the establishment of the Mortgage Guaranty Insurance Corporation (MGIC) in 1957 would PMI reappear in the U.S. mortgage market. Since then, numerous PMI companies have been established, and PMI is once again an important aspect of the mortgage industry.

There are several reasons borrowers may choose to use PMI rather than FHA insurance. First, PMI is available for loan amounts much larger than the maximum FHA-insured loan. Second, the cost of PMI is generally less than the cost of FHA mortgage insurance because the annual premium is based on the current loan balance. Third, many lenders allow a borrower to cancel the PMI when the balance on the loan falls to below 80 percent of the value of the property. This is not an option for FHA borrowers.

Federal National Mortgage Association

To increase liquidity in mortgage investments and further stimulate the flow of funds between geographic areas with excess capital and areas with excess demand, Congress decided that a formal secondary market was needed in which mortgages originated in one area could easily be sold to investors in other areas. Only by attracting sufficient capital from the investment community would mortgage markets be able to meet the demand for mortgage funds at prices borrowers could afford. Congress created the Federal National Mortgage Association (FNMA) in 1938 to buy mortgages from lenders and to serve as a clearinghouse for the secondary mortgage market. **Fannie Mae,** as the agency became known, was originally established as a government agency to (1) operate a secondary market for FHA-insured loans and (2) to provide FHA-insured loans to low-income borrowers in remote areas who would not otherwise have access to the mortgage market.

Over time, Congress altered the role of Fannie Mae, and in 1968, the agency was converted into a private corporation, wholly owned by investors. Even though Fannie Mae is a private entity, the federal government continues to influence its operations. Today, one-third of the board of directors of the corporation are appointed by the President of the United States, and the U.S. Treasury is authorized to lend the corporation money if necessary to ensure its smooth operation in the secondary mortgage market. Fannie Mae serves as a clearinghouse for FHA-insured loans, as well as loans guaranteed by the Department of Veterans Affairs (VA) and private mortgage insurance companies.

VA Loan Guarantee Program

Another important government agency in the development of the housing finance system has been the Department of Veterans Affairs. Immediately after World War II, the VA began to guarantee mortgage loans on a large scale as part of the so-called GI Bill of Rights. Congress passed legislation at the end of the war that allowed veterans to obtain mortgage loans for home purchases with little or no down payment and low interest rates. The VA loan program guarantees the payment of a mortgage loan made by a private lender to a qualified veteran should the borrower default. Unlike FHA-insured loans, however, **VA-guaranteed loans** do not require borrowers to pay premiums for the insurance. Much of the housing boom that occurred during the postwar period is attributed to the tremendous number of VA-guaranteed loans originated to provide housing for returning veterans. Although the program has changed in many respects since it inception, the VA loan guarantee program continues to account for approximately 10 percent of new loans originated each year.

Government National Mortgage Association

The reorganization of Fannie Mae in 1968 led to the creation of a new federal agency, the Government National Mortgage Association (GNMA), or **Ginnie Mae.** When Fannie Mae became a privately owned corporation, it no longer provided special-assistance loans directly to borrowers. To fill this void, Ginnie Mae was organized as a vehicle for providing subsidized loans to borrowers through various FHA loan programs. For example, a lender can originate a home mortgage for a lower-income borrower at a below-market interest rate, then sell that loan to Ginnie Mae for full market value. After purchasing the loan, GNMA can either sell it at a loss or hold the loan in its own portfolio. Losses are paid for by funds appropriated by the Department of Housing and Urban Development (HUD), GNMA's primary agency.

In 1970, GNMA introduced a payment guarantee program aimed at expanding the supply of funds for the mortgage market. Under this program, which is backed by the full faith and credit of the U.S. government, Ginnie Mae guarantees the timely payment of principal and interest on mortgages insured by other federal agencies. That is, if an investor buys mortgages insured by the FHA, GNMA guarantees that payments from the borrowers will occur as scheduled. This guarantee, combined with the insurance against default provided by the FHA, made mortgages very attractive for investors who did not wish to be concerned with late payments from borrowers. Thanks to this program, many new types of financial instruments were developed that allow investors to invest in the mortgage market without directly holding mortgages. Referred to collectively as **mortgage-backed securities** (MBSs), these instruments have proven to be highly effective at attracting investment funds to the mortgage market.

Mortgage-backed securities are securities issued by mortgage holders to investors who wish to invest indirectly in the mortgage market. The mortgage holders combine loans made to many different borrowers into mortgage pools, then sell securities backed by the underlying mortgages. Proceeds from the sale of these securities allow mortgage holders to originate new mortgages to borrowers. Investors who wish to commit their funds to the mortgage market can do so by purchasing a variety of MBS, including such securities as pass-through certificates, mortgage-backed bonds, pay-through bonds and collateralized mortgage obligations. Although the specific details of these securities are beyond the scope of this text, it is important to note that the creation of MBS is often credited with the dramatic inflow of capital to the mortgage market that occurred in the 1970s.

Federal Home Loan Mortgage Corporation

Another important action taken by the federal government designed to increase the flow of funds to the mortgage market was the creation of the Federal Home Loan Mortgage Corporation (FHLMC) in 1970. At this time, the secondary market was well established for FHA-insured and VA-guaranteed loans, but no secondary market was in place for **conventional loans.** Conventional loans are those that are not insured by government agencies, either because their loan-to-value ratios are lower than 80 percent or because they carry private mortgage insurance. Congress authorized the FHLMC, or **Freddie Mac,** to operate a secondary market for conventional loans similar to the one provided by Fannie Mae and Ginnie Mae for FHA and VA mortgages. Freddie Mac is now a major player in the market for all types of mortgages, both conventional and FHA-VA.

Now that we understand the basic structure of the housing finance system of the United States, we can begin a closer look at the participants who operate within it and account for the tremendous volume of mortgage market activity.

MORTGAGE MARKET PARTICIPANTS

In the third quarter of 1995, mortgage debt outstanding in the United States totaled more than $4.6 trillion, with about 32 percent of that amount secured by one-family to four-family structures. The system by which this large amount of capital is committed to mortgage loans on the national level involves numerous government and quasi-government agencies. While these agencies serve as the backbone of the housing finance system, many other participants are required to put this capital in the hands of borrowers. These participants can be categorized into two groups: investors and originators. In practice, many participants in the system belong to both groups simultaneously. Table 13.1 shows one-family to four-family mortgage debt outstanding by holder type in the United States in the third quarter of 1995.

Mortgage Originators and Investors

Who are the mortgage originators? The most visible suppliers in the primary mortgage market include mortgage bankers, mortgage brokers, commercial banks, savings and loan institutions and credit unions. Mortgage bankers originate about half of all residential mortgage loans in the United States each year. Although we typically think of a banker as someone who accepts deposits from savers and then lends that money to borrowers, mortgage bankers do not accept deposits from savers. Instead, they borrow money from commercial banks, then use these funds to originate new loans to mortgage borrowers. Mortgage bankers then sell the loans they originate to investors in the secondary market, but may continue to service the loans (collect and process payments) for a fee on behalf of the investor. The revenues to mortgage bankers include origination fees charged to applicants, servicing fees paid by investors and the spread between the price of borrowed funds and loaned funds.

Closely related to mortgage bankers are mortgage brokers. Mortgage brokers typically do not lend funds directly to borrowers, but simply act as brokers between loan applicants and lenders. Unlike bankers, brokers typically do not continue to service the loans they sell. Mortgage brokers' revenues depend on the origination fees charged to borrowers. In general, neither mortgage bankers nor mortgage brokers intentionally hold mortgage loans in portfolios for their own benefit.

Table 13.1		Mortgage Debt Outstanding, 1995, by Holder and Property Types				
	Mortgage Debt (billions of dollars)	Percentage of Total	One-Family to Four-Family	Multifamily	Commercial	Farm
Savings institutions	604.6	13.0%	13.6%	22.4%	7.4%	0.3%
Life insurance companies	217.9	4.7%	0.2%	8.7%	25.0%	11.4%
Commercial banks	1,072.8	23.0%	18.5%	15.0%	48.8%	28.2%
Federal and related agencies (a)	314.4	6.8%	6.4%	13.2%	1.6%	44.8%
Mortgage pools and trusts (b)	1,797.2	38.6%	47.8%	15.4%	6.0%	N.A.
Individuals and others (c)	647.8	13.9%	13.5%	25.4%	11.2%	15.2%
All holders	4,654.6	100%	100%	100%	100%	100%

(a) Includes outstanding principal balances of mortgages backing securities insured or guaranteed by government agencies.
(b) Includes outstanding principal balances of mortgages backing securities insured or guaranteed by government agencies.
(c) Includes mortgage banks, real estate investment trusts, state and local credit agencies, retirement and pension funds and credit unions.

Source: *Federal Reserve Bulletin,* March 1996, Table A-38.

Commercial banks are private financial institutions organized to accept deposits from individuals and businesses and to loan these funds to all types of borrowers. Although residential mortgage lending is a small part of most commercial banks' business, commercial banks held approximately 23 percent of all outstanding mortgage debt in the United States as of the third quarter of 1995. Commercial banks use their own funds to originate mortgage loans in the primary market and to buy loans in the secondary mortgage market. They provide mortgages on residential and income-producing properties, as well as construction loans for developers and lines of credit for mortgage bankers.

Savings and loan institutions (S&Ls) have a long history of providing capital for housing purchases. The first S&L was founded in 1831 with the goal of accepting deposits from savers and loaning those funds to residential borrowers. Since that time, the original intent behind these institutions has remained largely unchanged, but the S&L industry has undergone dramatic cycles of growth and decline. Even after the collapse of many S&Ls during the 1980s, these institutions continue to play a major role in the housing finance system. S&Ls continue to originate many new loans, both for their own portfolios and for sale in the secondary market. In 1995, savings institutions held approximately 13.6 percent of all outstanding mortgage debt on one-family to four-family structures.

Credit unions are an important source of consumer loans and savings institutions for many Americans. Members of a specific industry or community can join a credit union and enjoy access to their deposits through checking or savings accounts. Because profits are returned to the members, the yield available to credit union members on their deposits is slightly higher than that of other thrift institutions. Most credit unions originate mortgages only for their own portfolios, though some do sell their loans in the secondary mortgage market.

Although the participants discussed above originate the bulk of all new mortgage loans, many of them do not hold all of the loans in their own portfolios, but instead sell them to other investors in secondary mortgage market transactions. As shown in Table 13.1, mortgage investors include financial institutions such as banks, S&Ls and life insurance companies, as well as nonfinancial institutions such as government agencies, mortgage pools and trusts, and individual investors. In 1995, government-related agencies held 6.8 percent of outstanding mortgage debt, mortgage pools and trusts held 38.6 percent and 13.9 percent was held by individuals and others.

UNDERSTANDING THE MORTGAGE LOAN ORIGINATION PROCESS

Now that we understand the legal and institutional characteristics of the mortgage market, we turn our attention to the mortgage loan origination process. We begin by reviewing the FNMA/FHLMC Uniform Residential Loan Application, then consider borrower and property qualification criteria, as well as various federal laws and rules that regulate the mortgage lending industry.

FNMA/FHLMC Uniform Residential Loan Application

Because most of the mortgage loan originators we discussed above want to have the option of selling their loans in the secondary market, the origination process is fairly standardized throughout the United States. In fact, the two principal secondary market participants, Fannie Mae and Freddie Mac, have jointly approved an application form to be used with any loan that may eventually wind up in their secondary markets. The information solicited from the applicant by this form is then evaluated by the lender to help it reach a decision regarding loan approval or denial. A sample Uniform Residential Loan Application form is shown in Figure 13.3.

Information Required from Borrower The information required to complete the Uniform Residential Loan Application is divided into various categories. Section I of the form allows the borrower to describe the type of mortgage requested, including the loan amount, interest rate and term. Section II requests property information and the purpose of the loan. Section III requests information on the borrower. Because most residential loans are made to married couples, both husband and wife must disclose their names, ages, Social Security numbers, present addresses and former addresses for the past two years. In Section IV, the applicant is required to disclose information regarding employment history, including employer names, addresses and telephone numbers. Proof of this information may be required in the form of check stubs, W-2 forms and other documents. The self-employed borrower must submit tax returns for at least two

Figure 13.3 Uniform Residential Loan Application

Uniform Residential Loan Application

This application is designed to be completed by the applicant(s) with the lender's assistance. Applicants should complete this form as ''Borrower'' or ''Co-Borrower'', as applicable. Co-Borrower information must also be provided (and the appropriate box checked) when ☐ the income or assets of a person other than the ''Borrower'' (including the Borrower's spouse) will be used as a basis for loan qualification or ☐ the income or assets of the Borrower's spouse will not be used as a basis for loan qualification, but his or her liabilities must be considered because the Borrower resides in a community property state, the security property is located in a community property state, or the Borrower is relying on other property located in a community property state as a basis for repayment of the loan.

I. TYPE OF MORTGAGE AND TERMS OF LOAN

Mortgage Applied for:	☐ V.A. ☐ FHA	☐ Conventional ☐ FmHA	☐ Other:	Agency Case Number		Lender Case Number
Amount $	Interest Rate %	No. of Months	Amortization Type:	☐ Fixed Rate ☐ GPM	☐ Other (explain): ☐ ARM (type):	

II. PROPERTY INFORMATION AND PURPOSE OF LOAN

Subject Property Address (street, city, state, ZIP) — No. of Units

Legal Description of Subject Property (attach description if necessary) — Year Built

| Purpose of Loan | ☐ Purchase ☐ Refinance | ☐ Construction ☐ Construction-Permanent | ☐ Other (explain): | Property will be: ☐ Primary Residence ☐ Secondary Residence ☐ Investment |

Complete this line if construction or construction-permanent loan.

| Year Lot Acquired | Original Cost $ | Amount Existing Liens $ | (a) Present Value of Lot $ | (b) Cost of Improvements $ | Total (a + b) $ |

Complete this line if this is a refinance loan.

| Year Acquired | Original Cost $ | Amount Existing Liens $ | Purpose of Refinance | Describe Improvements ☐ made ☐ to be made Cost: $ |

| Title will be held in what Name(s) | Manner in which Title will be held | Estate will be held in: ☐ Fee Simple ☐ Leasehold (show expiration date) |

Source of Down Payment, Settlement Charges and/or Subordinate Financing (explain)

III. BORROWER INFORMATION

Borrower	Co-Borrower
Borrower's Name (include Jr. or Sr. if applicable)	Co-Borrower's Name (include Jr. or Sr. if applicable)
Social Security Number / Home Phone (incl. area code) / Age / Yrs. School	Social Security Number / Home Phone (incl. area code) / Age / Yrs. School
☐ Married ☐ Unmarried (include single, divorced, widowed) ☐ Separated / Dependents (not listed by Co-Borrower) no. ages	☐ Married ☐ Unmarried (include single, divorced, widowed) ☐ Separated / Dependents (not listed by Borrower) no. ages
Present Address (street, city, state, ZIP) ☐ Own ☐ Rent No. Yrs.	Present Address (street, city, state, ZIP) ☐ Own ☐ Rent No. Yrs.

If residing at present address for less than two years, complete the following:

Former Address (street, city, state, ZIP) ☐ Own ☐ Rent No. Yrs.	Former Address (street, city, state, ZIP) ☐ Own ☐ Rent No. Yrs.
Former Address (street, city, state, ZIP) ☐ Own ☐ Rent No. Yrs.	Former Address (street, city, state, ZIP) ☐ Own ☐ Rent No. Yrs.

IV. EMPLOYMENT INFORMATION

Borrower	Co-Borrower
Name & Address of Employer ☐ Self Employed / Yrs. on this job / Yrs. employed in this line of work/profession	Name & Address of Employer ☐ Self Employed / Yrs. on this job / Yrs. employed in this line of work/profession
Position/Title/Type of Business / Business Phone (incl. area code)	Position/Title/Type of Business / Business Phone (incl. area code)

If employed in current position for less than two years or if currently employed in more than one position, complete the following:

Name & Address of Employer ☐ Self Employed / Dates (from - to) / Monthly Income $	Name & Address of Employer ☐ Self Employed / Dates (from - to) / Monthly Income $
Position/Title/Type of Business / Business Phone (incl. area code)	Position/Title/Type of Business / Business Phone (incl. area code)
Name & Address of Employer ☐ Self Employed / Dates (from - to) / Monthly Income $	Name & Address of Employer ☐ Self Employed / Dates (from - to) / Monthly Income $
Position/Title/Type of Business / Business Phone (incl. area code)	Position/Title/Type of Business / Business Phone (incl. area code)

Freddie Mac Form 65 10/92   Fannie Mae Form 1003 10/92

Uniform Residential Loan Application *(Continued)*

Figure 13.3

V. MONTHLY INCOME AND COMBINED HOUSING EXPENSE INFORMATION

Gross Monthly Income	Borrower	Co-Borrower	Total	Combined Monthly Housing Expense	Present	Proposed
Base Empl. Income *	$	$	$	Rent	$	
Overtime				First Mortgage (P&I)		$
Bonuses				Other Financing (P&I)		
Commissions				Hazard Insurance		
Dividends/Interest				Real Estate Taxes		
Net Rental Income				Mortgage Insurance		
Other (before completing, see the notice in "describe other income," below)				Homeowner Assn. Dues		
				Other:		
Total	$	$	$	Total	$	$

* Self Employed Borrower(s) may be required to provide additional documentation such as tax returns and financial statements.

B/C	**Describe Other Income** *Notice:* Alimony, child support, or separate maintenance income need not be revealed if the Borrower (B) or Co-Borrower (C) does not choose to have it considered for repaying this loan.	Monthly Amount
		$

VI. ASSETS AND LIABILITIES

This Statement and any applicable supporting schedules may be completed jointly by both married and unmarried Co-Borrowers if their assets and liabilities are sufficiently joined so that the Statement can be meaningfully and fairly presented on a combined basis; otherwise separate Statements and Schedules are required. If the Co-Borrower section was completed about a spouse, this Statement and supporting schedules must be completed about that spouse also.

Completed ☐ Jointly ☐ Not Jointly

ASSETS Description	Cash or Market Value
Cash deposit toward purchase held by:	$
List checking and savings accounts below	
Name and address of Bank, S&L, or Credit Union	
Acct. no.	$
Name and address of Bank, S&L, or Credit Union	
Acct. no.	$
Name and address of Bank, S&L, or Credit Union	
Acct. no.	$
Name and address of Bank, S&L, or Credit Union	
Acct. no.	$
Stocks & Bonds (Company name/number & description)	$
Life insurance net cash value	$
Face amount: $	
Subtotal Liquid Assets	$
Real estate owned (enter market value from schedule of real estate owned)	$
Vested interest in retirement fund	$
Net worth of business(es) owned (attach financial statement)	$
Automobiles owned (make and year)	$
Other Assets (itemize)	$
Total Assets a.	$

Liabilities and Pledged Assets. List the creditor's name, address and account number for all outstanding debts, including automobile loans, revolving charge accounts, real estate loans, alimony, child support, stock pledges, etc. Use continuation sheet, if necessary. Indicate by (*) those liabilities which will be satisfied upon sale of real estate owned or upon refinancing of the subject property.

LIABILITIES	Monthly Pmt. & Mos. Left to Pay	Unpaid Balance
Name and address of Company	$ Pmt./Mos.	$
Acct. no.		
Name and address of Company	$ Pmt./Mos.	$
Acct. no.		
Name and address of Company	$ Pmt./Mos.	$
Acct. no.		
Name and address of Company	$ Pmt./Mos.	$
Acct. no.		
Name and address of Company	$ Pmt./Mos.	$
Acct. no.		
Name and address of Company	$ Pmt./Mos.	$
Acct. no.		
Alimony/Child Support/Separate Maintenance Payments Owed to:	$	
Job Related Expense (child care, union dues, etc.)	$	
Total Monthly Payments	$	
Net Worth (a minus b) ▶	$	Total Liabilities b. $

Freddie Mac Form 65 10/92

Fannie Mae Form 1003 10/92

| **Figure 13.3** | Uniform Residential Loan Application *(Continued)* |

VI. ASSETS AND LIABILITIES (cont.)

Schedule of Real Estate Owned (If additional properties are owned, use continuation sheet.)

Property Address (enter S if sold, PS if pending sale or R if rental being held for income)	Type of Property	Present Market Value	Amount of Mortgages & Liens	Gross Rental Income	Mortgage Payments	Insurance, Maintenance, Taxes & Misc.	Net Rental Income
		$	$	$	$	$	$
Totals		$	$	$	$	$	$

List any additional names under which credit has previously been received and indicate appropriate creditor name(s) and account number(s):

Alternate Name	Creditor Name	Account Number

VII. DETAILS OF TRANSACTION

a. Purchase price	$
b. Alterations, improvements, repairs	
c. Land (if acquired separately)	
d. Refinance (incl. debts to be paid off)	
e. Estimated prepaid items	
f. Estimated closing costs	
g. PMI, MIP, Funding Fee	
h. Discount (if Borrower will pay)	
i. Total Costs (add items a through h)	
j. Subordinate financing	
k. Borrower's closing costs paid by Seller	
l. Other Credits (explain)	
m. Loan amount (exclude PMI, MIP, Funding Fee financed)	
n. PMI, MIP, Funding Fee financed	
o. Loan amount (add m & n)	
p. Cash from/to Borrower (subtract j, k, l & o from i)	

VIII. DECLARATIONS

If you answer "Yes" to any questions a through i, please use continuation sheet for explanation.

	Borrower Yes	No	Co-Borrower Yes	No
a. Are there any outstanding judgments against you?				
b. Have you been declared bankrupt within the past 7 years?				
c. Have you had property foreclosed upon or given title or deed in lieu thereof in the last 7 years?				
d. Are you a party to a lawsuit?				
e. Have you directly or indirectly been obligated on any loan which resulted in foreclosure, transfer of title in lieu of foreclosure, or judgment? (This would include such loans as home mortgage loans, SBA loans, home improvement loans, educational loans, manufactured (mobile) home loans, any mortgage, financial obligation, bond, or loan guarantee. If "Yes," provide details, including date, name and address of Lender, FHA or V.A. case number, if any, and reasons for the action.)				
f. Are you presently delinquent or in default on any Federal debt or any other loan, mortgage, financial obligation, bond, or loan guarantee? If "Yes," give details as described in the preceding question.				
g. Are you obligated to pay alimony, child support, or separate maintenance?				
h. Is any part of the down payment borrowed?				
i. Are you a co-maker or endorser on a note?				
j. Are you a U.S. citizen?				
k. Are you a permanent resident alien?				
l. Do you intend to occupy the property as your primary residence? If "Yes," complete question m below.				
m. Have you had an ownership interest in a property in the last three years?				
(1) What type of property did you own–principal residence (PR), second home (SH), or investment property (IP)?				
(2) How did you hold title to the home–solely by yourself (S), jointly with your spouse (SP), or jointly with another person (O)?				

IX. ACKNOWLEDGMENT AND AGREEMENT

The undersigned specifically acknowledge(s) and agree(s) that: (1) the loan requested by this application will be secured by a first mortgage or deed of trust on the property described herein; (2) the property will not be used for any illegal or prohibited purpose or use; (3) all statements made in this application are made for the purpose of obtaining the loan indicated herein; (4) occupation of the property will be as indicated above; (5) verification or reverification of any information contained in the application may be made at any time by the Lender, its agents, successors and assigns, either directly or through a credit reporting agency, from any source named in this application, and the original copy of this application will be retained by the Lender, even if the loan is not approved; (6) the Lender, its agents, successors and assigns will rely on the information contained in the application and I/we have a continuing obligation to amend and/or supplement the information provided in this application if any of the material facts which I/we have represented herein should change prior to closing; (7) in the event my/our payments on the loan indicated in this application become delinquent, the Lender, its agents, successors and assigns, may, in addition to all their other rights and remedies, report my/our name(s) and account information to a credit reporting agency; (8) ownership of the loan may be transferred to successor or assign of the Lender without notice to me and/or the administration of the loan account may be transferred to an agent, successor or assign of the Lender with prior notice to me; (9) the Lender, its agents, successors and assigns make no representations or warranties, express or implied, to the Borrower(s) regarding the property, the condition of the property, or the value of the property.

Certification: I/We certify that the information provided in this application is true and correct as of the date set forth opposite my/our signature(s) on this application and acknowledge my/our understanding that any intentional or negligent misrepresentation(s) of the information contained in this application may result in civil liability and/or criminal penalties including, but not limited to, fine or imprisonment or both under the provisions of Title 18, United States Code, Section 1001, et seq. and liability for monetary damages to the Lender, its agents, successors and assigns, insurers and any other person who may suffer any loss due to reliance upon any misrepresentation which I/we have made on this application.

Borrower's Signature	Date	Co-Borrower's Signature	Date
X		X	

X. INFORMATION FOR GOVERNMENT MONITORING PURPOSES

The following information is requested by the Federal Government for certain types of loans related to a dwelling, in order to monitor the Lender's compliance with equal credit opportunity, fair housing and home mortgage disclosure laws. You are not required to furnish this information, but are encouraged to do so. The law provides that a Lender may neither discriminate on the basis of this information, nor on whether you choose to furnish it. However, if you choose not to furnish it, under Federal regulations this Lender is required to note race and sex on the basis of visual observation or surname. If you do not wish to furnish the above information, please check the box below. (Lender must review the above material to assure that the disclosures satisfy all requirements to which the Lender is subject under applicable state law for the particular type of loan applied for.)

BORROWER

☐ I do not wish to furnish this information

Race/National Origin:
☐ American Indian or Alaskan Native
☐ Asian or Pacific Islander
☐ White, not of Hispanic Origin
☐ Black, not of Hispanic origin
☐ Hispanic
☐ Other (specify) _____

Sex: ☐ Female ☐ Male

CO-BORROWER

☐ I do not wish to furnish this information

Race/National Origin:
☐ American Indian or Alaskan Native
☐ Asian or Pacific Islander
☐ White, not of Hispanic Origin
☐ Black, not of Hispanic origin
☐ Hispanic
☐ Other (specify) _____

Sex: ☐ Female ☐ Male

To be Completed by Interviewer		
This application was taken by:	Interviewer's Name (print or type)	Name and Address of Interviewer's Employer
☐ face-to-face interview	Interviewer's Signature Date	
☐ by mail		
☐ by telephone	Interviewer's Phone Number (incl. area code)	

Freddie Mac Form 65 10/92

Fannie Mae Form 1003 10/92

years prior to the application, as well as profit and loss statements prepared by an accountant.

In Section V the applicant must disclose information regarding monthly income and present and and proposed monthly housing expenses. Section VI requires the borrower to fully disclose his or her assets and liabilities, including real estate owned, stocks, bonds, life insurance policies, checking and savings accounts, credit cards, other outstanding loans and alimony and child support obligations. In Section VII, the borrower must disclose the details of the real estate transaction for which the loan will be used, including the purchase price of the property. Section VIII contains various questions about facts that may affect the borrower's creditworthiness. By providing his or her signature on the application, the borrower acknowledges that the purpose of the application is to acquire a loan to be secured by the real estate described in the application. In addition, the borrower promises that the information provided in the application is true and authorizes the lender to verify its accuracy. The application also requests certain information used by the government to monitor lender activities and requires the lender's representative to sign the application.

Duties of the Originator

Upon receiving a completed Uniform Residential Loan Application, the lender has various duties to the borrower as determined by federal lending regulations. These regulations are intended to provide protection to mortgage consumers. Important federal legislation to participants in the mortgage lending industry includes the Equal Credit Opportunity Act (Regulation B), the Consumer Credit Protection Act (Regulation Z), the Real Estate Settlement Procedures Act, the Flood Disaster Protection Act and the Fair Credit Reporting Act.

Equal Credit Opportunity Act   The Equal Credit Opportunity Act has influenced the mortgage lending industry since 1974. Under this act, an applicant must be notified within 30 days of application that his or her loan request has been approved, denied or determined to be incomplete. In addition, the act prohibits lenders from discriminating against borrowers on ·the following bases: race, color, religion, national origin, sex, marital status and age, as well as whether all or part of an applicant's income is derived from public assistance programs or whether the applicant has exercised any right under the Consumer Credit Protection Act.

Consumer Credit Protection Act   Title I of the Consumer Credit Protection Act is frequently referred to as *Regulation Z,* or the *Truth-in-Lending Law.* Under this regulation, lenders are required to disclose the full details of a loan to the applicant within three business days of application, including exactly how much the loan will cost. The goal of the Truth-in-Lending requirement is to permit borrowers to shop for the best deals among competing lenders. Specifically, lenders are required to inform applicants of the total finance charges associated with a loan and the annual percentage rate (APR) of interest. In the event a loan is to be used to refinance a property already owned by the applicant, Regulation Z requires that the lender inform the borrower of the right to rescind the loan within three business days of origination. The APR is the effective annual interest rate that the borrower will pay after all fees and charges are taken into consideration. The APR is often quite different from the stated interest rate used to determine the payments on the loan. By comparing the APRs of various lenders, a consumer can determine which lender offers the best deal and thereby make an informed decision about the loan.

Real Estate Settlement Procedures Act   The Real Estate Settlement Procedures Act (RESPA) is another important source of regulation in the mortgage lending industry. This act applies to federally related mortgage loans and creates several different duties for mortgage lenders following a residential mortgage loan application. First, RESPA requires lenders to provide each borrower with a copy of a special information booklet prepared by the U.S. Department of Housing and Urban Development. The information contained in *Settlement Costs and You: A HUD Guide for Homebuyers* is designed to describe and explain the settlement costs a borrower is likely to incur when purchasing a home using mortgage financing.

Second, RESPA requires lenders to provide each borrower with a good-faith estimate of the settlement costs associated with the loan within three business days of the application. We examine these costs and the loan closing process in detail in Chapter 15. Third, the act prohibits kickbacks or referral fees paid to parties who refer a borrower to a lender. Fourth, the act gives each applicant the right to request and receive a copy of any appraisal used to evaluate the property pledged as security for the debt. Although the borrower is typically charged a fee for the appraisal, it technically belongs to the lender, not the borrower.

Fifth, RESPA requires the use of the HUD-1 Uniform Settlement Statement by a settlement agent at a loan closing. As we will see in Chapter 15, this settlement statement shows line-by-line costs that will be incurred as a result of the pending real estate transaction, and a copy of this completed form must be made available to both the buyer and seller. Furthermore, the act establishes the borrower's right to inspect this statement one day prior to the actual closing. At that time, the lender must accurately disclose all known closing costs and must provide a good-faith estimate of all uncertain closing costs that will be charged to the borrower. To enforce this right, the borrower must make a written request to the lender on or before the business day prior to settlement.

Sixth, RESPA requires that lenders disclose whether a loan is expected to be sold in the secondary market. If the loan is sold, the lender is required to disclose this information to the borrower within 15 days of transfer. While the borrower can do little to stop the transfer of the loan, it is important to know who the loan servicer is and how to contact the new servicer after a transfer.

Finally, RESPA limits the amount of money lenders can require a borrower to deposit to cover such recurring expenses as property taxes, hazard insurance premiums and other periodic assessments. In addition to the principal and interest payments due from a borrower each month, lenders may also require that the borrower's loan payment include reserve payments to be deposited into an escrow account. As the property tax bill or insurance premiums come due, the lender simply pays the bill from the funds in the escrow account. Having the money on deposit ensures that payment will be made promptly, thus protecting the lender's interest in the collateral for the loan. If these bills are not paid, the property could be destroyed without a current insurance policy, or a tax lien that has priority over the lender's lien or encumbrance could be placed on the property. Either of these events could significantly diminish the protection provided to the lender by the mortgage concept. RESPA limits the amount of reserves that the lender can collect at closing to one-sixth of the annual property taxes and insurance.

Other Federal Legislation Remaining federal legislation that regulates the mortgage lending industry includes the Flood Disaster Protection Act and the Fair Credit Reporting Act. The Flood Disaster Protection Act requires lenders to disclose to a borrower whether the property he or she purchases lies within a flood hazard area. If so, a lender must require the borrower to obtain flood insurance if it is available. Flood insurance is generally available only through the Federal Emergency Management Administration's (FEMA's) National Flood Insurance Program. This act puts the burden of notifying borrowers that their properties are subject to damage from flooding squarely on the shoulders of lenders.

The Fair Credit Reporting Act affects primarily credit reporting agencies, but it also affects the users of information obtained from these agencies. The act requires lenders to obtain permission before investigating an applicant's credit history and to handle the applicant's credit information with due care. If an applicant's loan request is denied based on information contained in a credit report, the lender must notify the applicant of this fact and provide the borrower with the name, address and telephone number of the credit agency that supplied the information.

Mortgage Underwriting

Once the application for a mortgage loan has been received from the applicant, the lender must evaluate the applicant's creditworthiness, as well as the suitability of the property as security for the debt. From the lender's perspective, lending money to a borrower is an investment in the borrower's willingness and ability to repay the debt under the terms of the agreement. As discussed earlier, the property can be used to satisfy the debt (through the foreclosure process) if the borrower is unable or unwilling to abide by the terms of the loan. The process of evaluating the risk of an applicant and a property to make a decision regarding a loan application is known as **underwriting.** We consider the underwriting process for borrowers and properties separately.

Qualifying an Applicant To evaluate an applicant's creditworthiness, lenders typically examine the applicant's sources of income, net worth and credit history, then perform a risk assessment. The sources of income that are considered relevant include wages or salary, self-employment, rent, interest, investment and commission, as well as child support, alimony, separate maintenance income, retirement, pension, disability and welfare benefits. Note that disclosure of information regarding child support, separate maintenance income and alimony is not required if the applicant does not wish these to be considered as income sources. The Uniform Residential Loan Application described above is used to provide information on these sources of income to the lender, and the lender must verify the accuracy of this information. Similarly, the application provides information regarding assets and liabilities that determine the applicant's net worth, which can be verified with permission of the applicant. Lenders also obtain permission to request an up-to-date **residential mortgage credit report.** This report, which is required if the lender intends to sell the loan in the secondary market, contains information about outstanding judgments, liens or divorce proceedings, a list of similar credit inquiries within the previous 90 days and all available credit information for the past seven years from at least one national credit reporting agency. If any of this information reasonably suggests that the borrower will not be able or willing to repay the proposed debt, the lender can deny the loan application subject to the regulations imposed by the Fair Credit Reporting Act.

Qualifying the Property   In addition to collecting and verifying information on the borrower's creditworthiness, the lender must also collect and verify information regarding the property being pledged as security for the debt. First, the person pledging the property must in fact be the legal owner of the property. As we will discuss in Chapter 15, verifying the ownership or title to real estate requires careful inspection of the public records. If there are defects or clouds on the title to the property involved, the lender will reject the loan application. To protect their interests in property, lenders typically require borrowers to purchase title insurance or obtain title opinions from an attorney. In general, loans originated without title insurance cannot be sold in the secondary mortgage market.

In addition to verifying the applicant's right to pledge the property as security, the lender has incentive to verify that the value of the property supports the requested loan amount. If the value of the property is less than the amount of the debt, the borrower may be unwilling to meet his or her obligation. If the lender is faced with foreclosing on the loan in this situation, the sale of the property will not likely result in sufficient proceeds to satisfy the debt. Therefore, the lender may require an appraisal of the property's value before granting final approval for the requested loan amount. After receiving the appraisal report from a qualified appraiser, the lender must review the appraisal report to verify its acceptability. If the loan involved will be sold in the secondary mortgage market, the appraiser's conclusions must be presented on the Uniform Residential Appraisal Report form that is accepted by FNMA and FHLMC. We examined the topic of real estate appraisal in Chapter 10.

Risk Assessment

In addition to evaluating the borrower's residential mortgage credit report and the title and value of the pledged property, the lender must consider other factors when making the underwriting decision. Although no absolute rules exist to determine whether a borrower will be able to meet the obligations of a requested loan, lenders use guidelines in the underwriting process. While each lender establishes its own guidelines, secondary market participants (primarily Fannie Mae and Freddie Mac) provide general guidelines for loans they are willing to buy from loan originators. Because most lenders want to be able to sell their loans in this market, these guidelines are well accepted in the lending industry.

FNMA/FHLMC guidelines fall into three categories: loan-to-value ratios, down payment sources and income ratios.

Loan-to-Value Ratio Guidelines The **loan-to-value ratio,** or LTV ratio, is determined by dividing the requested loan amount by the lesser of the sales price or the appraised value of the property. Generally expressed as percentage amounts, higher LTV ratios imply greater risk. For example, suppose a lender provides $95,000 to a borrower who purchases a $100,000 house (LTV ratio of 95 percent). Because the borrower has little equity in the property, default is more likely if the value of the property should fall below the loan amount. If default does occur and the property is sold through the foreclosure process, it is doubtful that the proceeds of sale will be sufficient to cover the loan balance, past-due interest and expenses of sale. If the LTV ratio were only 50 percent, however, much lower probability of default exists. If the borrower should default, the proceeds from sale should be sufficient to protect the lender. As a general guideline, any loan with an LTV ratio of 80 percent or higher must carry private mortgage insurance, FHA mortgage insurance, or a VA loan guarantee to be acceptable in the secondary mortgage markets. While most conventional loans have maximum LTV ratios of 95 percent even with private mortgage insurance, some FHA-insured loans may have LTV ratios of up to 98.75 percent, and VA-guaranteed loan LTV ratios may be as high as 100 percent.

Down Payment Source Guidelines The second category of guidelines refers to sources for the borrower's down payment or equity for a home purchase. In general, secondary market guidelines require that funds used for the down payment be provided primarily by the borrower rather than from outside sources. If the borrower uses his or her own personal funds for the down payment, the borrower is likely to be more diligent in meeting the obligations of the loan. In most conventional loans with LTV ratios of 80 percent or more, at least 5 percent of a purchase price must represent the borrower's personal investment in the property. The remaining 15 percent could be a gift from an outside source, such as a family member or an employer, but never a loan. If the LTV ratio is less than 80 percent, however, the entire down payment amount can be a gift from an outside source. A lender that intends to sell a loan in the secondary market must verify that the down payment meets or exceeds this requirement by documenting its sources.

The down payment source requirements are applied differently for FHA and VA loans. Some FHA loan programs permit the borrower to contribute only 3 percent of the purchase price from personal savings, with the other 2 percent in the form of a gift from an outside source. Other FHA loan programs allow the entire down payment amount to be a gift to the borrower from outside sources. Many VA-guaranteed loans do not require a down payment at all, but the borrower is required to pay a funding fee that decreases as the down payment increases.

Income Ratio Guidelines Income ratios compose the third category of underwriting guidelines. These ratios are designed to assess a borrower's ability to repay the mortgage as specified in the loan documents. Two income ratios that are considered by secondary market participants and the various guaranteeing and insuring entities are the **mortgage debt ratio** (front-end ratio) and the **total debt ratio** (back-end ratio).

The mortgage debt ratio (MDR) is defined as the percentage of a borrower's gross monthly income that is required to meet monthly housing expenses. Monthly housing expenses include principal and interest payments, hazard insurance, property taxes, mortgage insurance, homeowners' association fees and any payments on existing or proposed second mortgages on the property. In general, the MDR must not exceed 28 percent on a conventional loan. For example, consider a loan applicant whose gross monthly income is $5,000. The applicant applies for a loan with monthly payments of $965. Monthly payments for hazard insurance, property taxes and mortgage insurance total $210. No second mortgages exist, and the home is not part of a homeowners' association. The MDR for this applicant is 23.5 percent ($1,175 ÷ $5,000 × 100), which is well below the maximum ratio allowed.

The total debt ratio (TDR) is defined as the percentage of a borrower's gross monthly income that is required to meet monthly contractual expenses. Contractual expenses include housing expenses as defined above, any revolving credit payments, payments on any installment loans with more than ten remaining payments and any alimony or child support. Notice that while applicants are not required to provide information regarding alimony and child support as an *income sources,* they must disclose this information if they represent *expenses.* As a guideline for conventional loans, total payments for all of the items listed above must not exceed 36 percent of a borrower's gross income. Continuing the example discussed above, if the applicant has an outstanding car loan that requires monthly payments of $280 and child support payments of $500 per month, the TDR would be 39.1 percent ($1,995 ÷ $5,000 × 100). In this case, the applicant would not qualify for the loan under this guideline.

When assessing the risk of a mortgage loan application, lenders calculate both of these ratios to verify that the borrower is capable of repaying the debt and meeting other contractual obligations. Borrowers must qualify under both ratios simultaneously to receive approval. While these ratios have evolved from years of experience with millions of loans, possible mitigating circumstances allow a lender to deviate from these guidelines. Such circumstances include a demonstrated ability to allocate a higher percentage of income to housing expenses, a low LTV ratio, a spotless credit report, large net worth or other similar factors. In addition, the ratio limits specified above apply to conventional loans only. For FHA-insured loans, the ratio limits are 29 percent for the front-end ratio and 41 percent for the back-end ratio. VA-guaranteed loans use a more detailed income standard and sometimes allow back-end ratios as high as 45 percent.

The Underwriting Decision

The final step in the loan origination process is for the lender to render an underwriting decision. As mentioned above, the Equal Credit Opportunity Act requires lenders to reach their decisions for completed applications within 30 days. If the loan is approved, the lender notifies the borrower of acceptance and, in most cases, issues a letter of commitment. If the loan is for home purchase rather than refinancing, the real estate closing process can occur as planned. If the lender denies the credit application, the lender must notify the applicant, give the reason for credit denial and provide a statement of nondiscrimination that is consistent with the provisions of the Equal Credit Opportunity Act.

Chapter Review

1. A specialized legal framework has evolved for loans in which real estate is pledged as security for a debt, though the details of the mortgage concept vary slightly from state to state. Most real estate loans involve a promissory note that makes the borrower personally liable for the debt, as well as a security instrument such as a mortgage or deed of trust, which enables the lender to foreclose on the property if the borrower defaults on the loan.

2. Loans are originated to borrowers in primary mortgage markets, and many loans are subsequently sold to investors in secondary mortgage market transactions. The primary and secondary mortgage markets, and the participants in those markets, have evolved into an efficient system for providing housing financing in the United States.

3. Some of the more prominent participants in the housing finance system include the Federal Housing Administration, the Department of Veterans Affairs, the Government National Mortgage Association, the Federal National Mortgage Association, the Federal Home Loan Mortgage Corporation, private mortgage insurers, mortgage bankers, mortgage brokers, commercial banks, savings and loan institutions and credit unions.

4. To ensure that investors are willing to accept such loans, lenders employ a standardized loan application process and rigorous underwriting criteria. Fannie Mae and Freddie Mac have jointly approved an application to be used with any loan that may eventually wind up in their secondary markets. This form solicits information about the borrower, the property and the details of the transaction.

5. The underwriting decision involves careful consideration of the borrower's ability and willingness to repay the debt, as well as the suitability of the property as collateral. Lenders evaluate each applicant's employment history, income sources, net worth and previous credit history to assess the risk of the loan application.

6. Using the general guidelines for risk assessment proposed by FNMA and FHLMC, lenders can screen out high-risk applicants and feel confident that their lending decisions are made on a sound basis. These guidelines fall into three categories: loan-to-value ratios, down payment sources and income ratios.

7. Mortgage market consumers are protected against discrimination, fraud and misrepresentation by various federal regulations that govern lender activity, including the Equal Credit Opportunity Act (Regulation B), the Consumer Credit Protection Act (Regulation Z), the Real Estate

Settlement Procedures Act, the Flood Disaster Protection Act and the Fair Credit Reporting Act.

Key Terms
---

acceleration clause   clause in a promissory note that permits the lender to demand payment in full of any unpaid principal and any interest due in the event of default.

conventional loan   mortgage loans not insured or guaranteed by a government agency but may carry private mortgage insurance.

deed in lieu of foreclosure   a process by which a borrower transfers ownership of a mortgaged property to the lender rather than face foreclosure.

deed of trust   a security instrument that conveys title to the property pledged as collateral to a trustee until the loan is repaid.

deficiency judgment   a judgment against a borrower following a foreclosure that permits the lender to recover any shortfall between the sale price and the balance of the loan.

due-on-sale clause   a clause in a promissory note that requires the borrower to repay all amounts due immediately upon transferring the property to a new owner.

Fannie Mae   Federal National Mortgage Association.

FHA-insured loan   a loan insured against default by the Federal Housing Administration.

foreclosure   the process of seizing control of the collateral for a loan and using the proceeds from its sale to satisfy a defaulted debt.

Freddie Mac   Federal Home Loan Mortgage Corporation.

Ginnie Mae   Government National Mortgage Association.

housing finance system   the arrangements and institutions that facilitate the financing of residential buildings.

hypothecation   the practice of leaving borrowers in possession of their property while repaying a loan with interest.

judicial foreclosure   a court ordered sale of the property following default by the mortgagor.

land contract   a contract that establishes an obligation to transfer title from a seller to a buyer at some future date based on an agreed upon payment schedule.

lien theory   a concept adopted by some states that recognizes that the mortgagee must foreclose on the property through a court action to acquire possession in the event of default.

loan origination the process of creating a new loan agreement between a borrower and a lender.

loan-to-value ratio the ratio obtained by dividing the loan amount by an estimate of property value.

mortgage a contract by which real property is pledged as security for a loan.

mortgage-backed securities securities issued by mortgage holders to investors who wish to invest indirectly in the mortgage market.

mortgage debt ratio the percentage of a borrower's gross monthly income that is required to meet housing expenses.

mortgagee the lender in a mortgage loan transaction.

mortgagor the borrower in a mortgage loan transaction.

nonjudicial foreclosure a situation in which the security instrument grants the lender power of sale should the borrower default.

prepayment clause a clause in a promissory note that determines the borrower's right to prepay any or all of the principal before it is due.

primary mortgage market transactions that occur between a borrower and a lender.

private mortgage insurance nongovernment insurance that provides protection for the lender against the borrower's default.

promissory note a written promise to pay money owed.

residential mortgage credit report a standardized credit report used in the underwriting process for residential loans.

secondary mortgage market transactions involving mortgages that occur between investors.

secured loan a loan for which a specific item has been pledged as collateral.

strict foreclosure a situation in which the lender is entitled to immediate ownership of the property should the borrower default.

title theory a concept adopted by some states that recognizes that the mortgagee has the right to immediate possession of mortgaged property in the event of default.

total debt ratio the percentage of a borrower's gross monthly income that is required to meet monthly contractual expenses.

underwriting process of evaluating the risk of a loan applicant and the property being pledged in order to make a decision regarding the loan application.

unsecured loan a loan for which no specific item has been pledged as collateral.

VA-guaranteed loan loans in which the lender is protected from a borrower's default by a guarantee of repayment from the Department of Veterans Affairs.

Study Exercises

1. Define the following: secured loan, unsecured loan, mortgage, hypothecation, promissory note, due-on-sale clause, prepayment clause, acceleration clause.

2. In what manner can a land contract simplify the foreclosure process?

3. Identify the parties involved in a deed of trust.

4. In states that permit its use, when would a deficiency judgment be in order?

5. Why is PMI generally less expensive than FHA insurance?

6. How does FHA mortgage insurance differ from VA loan guarantees?

7. What is meant by the term *conventional loan*?

8. List the five major types of mortgage originators.

9. List the nine factors that mortgage lenders may *not* use to discriminate against loan applicants as defined by the Equal Credit Opportunity Act.

10. Under the Equal Credit Opportunity Act, how long does a lender have to either accept or reject a completed loan application?

11. What is the general intention behind the Truth-in-Lending Law? List three requirements under this regulation.

12. Why does the APR not equal the stated interest rate on a loan? Which rate is usually higher?

13. List seven requirements lenders must observe in conjunction with RESPA.

14. What requirement is imposed on mortgage lenders by the Flood Distaster Protection Act?

15. List three requirements imposed on mortgage lenders by the Fair Credit Reporting Act.

16. What is contained in a residential mortgage credit report?

17. List the three categories of risk assessment guidelines used by mortgage lenders.

18. Consider a borrower who has gross annual income of $48,000 and applies for a mortgage that requires monthly payments of $1,040. Taxes and insurance premiums for the pledged property total $1,200 per year. The borrower has no other outstanding loans on the property, but she has 24 monthly payments of $260 on her car loan. Based on the MDR and TDR limits for a conventional loan, does she qualify for the loan? Could she qualify for an FHA-insured loan based on the appropriate MDR and TDR guidelines?

19. What is the maximum LTV ratio permitted by secondary mortgage markets on conventional mortgages that do not carry PMI?

For Further Reading

Brueggeman, William B., and Jeffrey D. Fisher. *Real Estate Finance and Investments,* 10th ed. (Homewood, Ill.: Irwin, 1996).

Dennis, Marshall W., and Michael J. Robertson. *Residential Mortgage Lending,* 4th ed. (Englewood Cliffs, N.J.: Prentice-Hall, 1995).

Greer, G. E. *Investment Analysis for Real Estate Decisions,* 4th ed. (Chicago: Dearborn Financial Publishing, Inc., 1997).

CHAPTER 14

Basic Financial Concepts and Mortgage Mechanics

Before potential homebuyers begin looking at specific properties, they need to have thoroughly analyzed their financial position to determine how much money they can afford to spend.

Chapter Preview

AN UNDERSTANDING OF basic financial concepts is essential for all real estate market participants. Real estate lending and borrowing decisions, value estimation and investment analysis all require knowledge of the relationship between risk and return, time value of money principles, financial decision rules and the mechanics of mortgage loans. The purpose of this chapter is to consider each of these concepts and demonstrate its role in the financial framework of real estate. Some readers are already familiar with these concepts, but for others, they represent an unexplored frontier. For the first group, many topics considered in this chapter will serve as a review. The second group will want to study the material quite carefully and make certain they master the concepts before moving on to subsequent topics. In all cases, it is helpful to think of the topics discussed in this chapter as tools that market participants should have at their disposal as they engage in real estate decision-making situations.

The topics considered in this chapter include the

- relationship between risk and return;
- six time value of money formulas;
- net present value and internal rate of return financial decision rules; and
- basic mechanics of fixed-rate mortgages, two-step mortgages and adjustable-rate mortgages.

THE RELATIONSHIP BETWEEN RISK AND RETURN

Financial decision making is defined as the process of comparing the expected benefits from a proposed course of action with the expected costs arising from that course of action. In the case of real estate investment decisions, for example, investors must compare the purchase price of property with profits (total revenues minus total costs) they expect to receive over the holding period.

Rather than dollar amounts, investment returns are frequently expressed as percentage rates of return. That is, $100 profit on an investment of $1,000 represents a 10 percent rate of return. Because the returns from an investment opportunity are expected to be realized in future time periods, and because the future is uncertain, it would be imprudent for an investor to make decisions without recognizing that the actual rate of return from a particular investment may vary significantly from initial expectations. Uncertainty about the actual rate of return an investment will provide over the holding period is known as **risk.** Because most of us are risk averse rather than risk seeking (we view higher levels of risk negatively), risk is an additional cost that must be considered when evaluating an investment opportunity.

For financial decision makers to accept an investment, they must expect to receive a sufficient return to justify its cost. Thus, in addition to considering the revenues and operating expenses resulting from a property investment, real estate investors must consider the risk that the expected rate of return from pursuing that investment may deviate from initial expectations. A riskier investment must promise a higher rate of return than less risky investment opportunities. If not, prudent decision makers prefer a less risky investment that earns the same level of return. Therefore, a positive relationship exists between risk and investors' required rates of return. This general relationship is depicted graphically in Figure 14.1.

The upward sloping line in the figure illustrates the required rate of return demanded by investors at various levels of risk. As the level of risk increases, so does the required rate of return. The point at which the risk/return line intersects the vertical axis is known as the *risk-free rate*. This point indicates the rate of return investors are willing to accept for an investment that poses no risk. Although one can argue that there is no such thing as a perfectly risk-free investment, the return available from investing in U.S. government securities, such as Treasury bills, is generally considered to be a risk-free rate because there is virtually no danger that the federal government will default on its obligation to pay to its debts. Even though an investment is risk-free, investors require a return that compensates them for giving up use of their funds over time. As we proceed to the right along the risk/return line, it is immediately apparent that higher risk implies higher required rates of return.

Types of Risk

Uncertainty about future returns from an investment opportunity arises from a variety of factors, but most risk can be characterized as business risk, financial risk, purchasing power risk or liquidity risk. **Business risk** is the uncertainty arising from changing economic conditions that affect an investment's ability to generate returns. **Financial risk** is the uncertainty associated with the

Relationship Between Risk and Return **Figure 14.1**

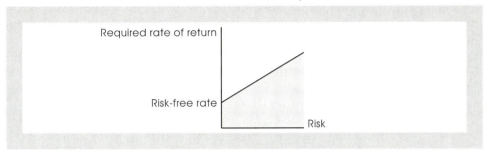

possibility of defaulting on borrowed funds used to finance an investment. **Purchasing power risk** (inflation risk) arises from the possibility that the goods and services that can be acquired with a given amount of money will decline. Thus, returns from an investment may be less valuable in real terms when they are received. **Liquidity risk** is the possibility of loss resulting from not being able to convert an asset into cash quickly should the need arise. Real estate is often considered to be less liquid than other investment assets, such as stocks or bonds, which can be traded almost immediately at the current market price. In general, investors' required rates of return are combinations of the returns required for each of these risk types *and* the risk-free rate of return.

The Time Value of Money

Another important consideration in financial decision making is the timing of the expected benefits and costs associated with investment opportunities. Even if risk is minimal, decision makers must recognize that delaying returns until some future time represents an added cost of an investment. As we saw above, investors require a rate of return for any investment whose benefits are expected to occur in the future, even if there is no risk. In other words, a dollar in hand today is worth more than a dollar to be received in the future because it can be either consumed immediately or put to work earning a return in another investment opportunity. This principle is known as the **time value of money.** To use this principle effectively in decision-making situations, investors must be able to convert future values into present values and present values into future values. The next section of this chapter presents six techniques for accomplishing these conversions while simultaneously accounting for the risk associated with an investment choice.

TIME VALUE OF MONEY FORMULAS

There is an old saying that "one bird in hand is worth two in the bush," and a dollar in hand is certainly worth more than one to be received sometime in the future. Thus, if given a choice between receiving $5 immediately or $5 one year from now, most of us would choose the first option. If the choice is between $5 immediately or $15 one year from now, however, the decision becomes more complicated. Which of these options is the better one *right now?* The answer depends on two issues: risk and the time value of money. As we discussed above, both of these issues are incorporated into the decision-making process by specifying an appropriate required rate of return. A variety of time value of money formulas exist that allow us to address the choices described above, as well as more involved investment decisions. After we consider the intuition behind the first two formulas, we will describe how two popular models of financial calculators (Hewlett-Packard 10B and Texas Instruments BAII PLUS) can be used to conduct time value of money analysis.

The first formula we will consider is used to find the future value of a lump sum. This formula allows decision makers to determine what an amount of money in hand today will be worth some time in the future if it increases at a constant rate each period.

Future Value of a Lump Sum

Suppose an investor buys ten acres of vacant land today for $70,000. If land values are expected to increase at the rate of 10 percent per year, what will the land be worth at the end of three years? In one year, the land is worth $70,000 plus 10 percent of $70,000. Written algebraically, the value of the land in one year is

$$\$70,000 + (.10 \times \$70,000) = \$77,000$$

This equation can also be written as

$$\$77,000(1+.10) = \$77,000$$

In two years, the land is worth $77,000 plus 10 percent of $77,000, or

$$\$77,000(1+.10) = \$84,700$$

At the end of three years, the original investment of $70,000 is worth

$$\$84,700(1+.10) = \$93,170$$

As shown here and in Table 14.1, the investment grows from $70,000 to $93,170, for a total increase of $23,170 over three years. The rate of growth is 10 percent annually, but the total growth is 33.1 percent ($23,170 ÷ $70,000 = .331). This example demonstrates the concept of **compound interest,** which means that during any given period, interest is earned not only on the original investment, but also on the interest previously earned. Thus, as in this example, after the first year, the value of the land increases by 10 percent of the previous year's value, where this value includes the initial investment plus increases during prior years. Note that multiplying the growth rate by the number of periods (10 percent × 3 = 30 percent) does not provide the total percentage change in value because such a calculation ignores interest earned on previously earned interest.

If the investor is concerned only with the value of the land at the end of three years, as opposed to each year's value, we can simplify this problem greatly. The value of $70,000 invested today at 10 percent interest for three years is $93,170:

$$70,000(1+.10)(1+.10) = \$93,170$$

Future Value of a Lump Sum   **Table 14.1**

Year	Present Amount	×	(1+*i*)	=	Future Amount
0	$70,000		(1.10)		$77,000
1	$77,000		(1.10)		$84,700
2	$84,700		(1.10)		$93,170
3	$93,170				

Equivalently, we can write the future value of $70,000 invested at 10 percent for three years as follows:

$$70,000 \ (1+.10)^3 = \$93,170$$

Writing the calculation in this manner leads to the formal specification of the concept of the **future value of a lump sum.** Equation (1) below is used to find the future value of a known present value when the future amount is to be received in a lump sum at a particular time (*n*):

$$FV = PV \ (1 + i)^n \qquad \qquad \textbf{(1)}$$

(where *FV* is the future value we seek to determine, *PV* is the present value, *i* is the rate of return and *n* is the number of periods).

Present Value of Lump Sums

The converse of the above problem requires a present value calculation; that is, what is the value today of a sum to be received some time in the future? Suppose an investor believes a parcel of land will be worth $93,170 in three years. If the investor requires a 10 percent annual rate of return on investments with comparable risk, how much would he or she be willing to pay for the land today? The **present value of a lump sum** is given by solving equation (1) to move *PV* to the left side of the equality sign as shown in equation (2).

$$PV \ = \ FV \ \left[\frac{1}{(1 + i)^n} \right] \qquad \qquad \textbf{(2)}$$

(where *PV* is the present value we seek to determine, *FV* is the known future value, *i* is the required rate of return, or discount rate, and *n* is the number of periods).

Applying the present value of a lump sum formula to this investment problem reveals that the present value of $93,170 to be received three years in the future is $70,000.

$$PV \ = \ \$93,170 \ \left[\frac{1}{(1 + .10)^3} \right] = \ \$70,000$$

Note that the equations for present value and future value are mathematically reverse operations, the key difference being the variable we try to find. If we know the present amount, we can find the future amount using the future value formula. Conversely, if we know the future amount, we can find the present amount using the present value formula. In solving time value of money problems, it is often helpful to recognize that when we calculate present values, we look "backward" in time, and when we calculate future values, we look "forward" in time. The process of finding present values is known as **discounting,** and the process of finding future values is known as **compounding.**

Both time and rate of return enter into present value calculations. The further into the future the money will be received, the lower the present value. Also, the greater the rate of discount, the lower the present value. The opposite is true for future value calculations. The longer a present amount is allowed to grow, the greater the future value. The greater the rate of growth, the greater the future value.

Using Financial Calculators To Solve for Present and Future Values

While the formulas presented above are relatively simple, we will consider four other formulas below that can become quite cumbersome to work with. We believe that students should work through these formulas to establish an understanding of how to use basic financial concepts in real estate decision making, but we also know that more efficient methods exist for working with time value of money factors once a base level of knowledge is established.

For many years, financial analysts used cumbersome tables that listed time value of money factors for various values of i and n. These tables were a grand improvement over pencil and paper, but today such tables have been replaced by relatively inexpensive financial calculators. Instead of laboriously working through these formulas or selecting the appropriate factor from a table and multiplying it by the appropriate present or future amount, we need only understand how to press a few keys on these wonderful devices. Spending time memorizing the formulas is not necessary for most readers of this text, but learning how to use a financial calculator is a worthwhile endeavor.

We encourage you to learn how your calculator works by first solving the problems using the formulas presented here, then by referencing the manual that came with your calculator to plug in the numbers and arrive at the answers. Doing so will ultimately give you confidence in your ability to use the calculator in more complex decision-making situations.

Each calculator manufacturer uses slightly different keys to solve time value of money problems, but some degree of uniformity exists. Almost all financial calculators have keys labeled PV, FV, I/Y or I/YR, and n or N. These buttons correspond to the notations used in equations (1) and (2) above. All of the problems considered in this chapter require that your calculator be set in "END" mode. If the screen displays the word "BEGIN" or "BGN," you will not be able to calculate the correct answer. To solve the two examples above using the Hewlett-Packard Model 10B and the Texas Instruments BAII PLUS, two of the most popular financial calculators, follow the steps listed below for each calculator. Refer to your calculator's manual if you have another brand or model. (Note that all of the keystroke examples in this chapter assume that you clear your calculator's memory before you begin the steps described.)

HP-10B Keystrokes: Future Value of a Lump Sum

(Be sure that your calculator is set in "END MODE." If the screen displays the word "BEGIN," press the gold key, then press the key labeled *BEG/END*.)

1. Set the number of compounding periods per year at 1	1, *goldkey, P/YR*
2. Enter the present value	70000, *PV*
3. Enter the number of periods	3, *N*
4. Enter the growth rate (interest)	10, *I/YR*
5. Solve for the future value	*FV* (calculator displays –93,170.00)

HP-10B Keystrokes: Present Value of a Lump Sum

1. Set the number of discounting periods per year at 1	1, *goldkey, P/YR*
2. Enter the future value	93170, *FV*
3. Enter the number of periods	3, *N*
4. Enter the growth rate (interest)	10, *I/YR*
5. Solve for the present value	*PV* (calculator displays –70,000.00)

BAII PLUS Keystrokes: Future Value of a Lump Sum

(Be sure that your calculator is set in "END MODE." If the screen displays the letters "BGN" in the top right corner, press the *2nd* key, followed by the key labeled *BGN*. Press the *2nd* key again, then press the key labeled *SET*. Finally, press the *2nd* key once more and then press *QUIT*.)

1. Set the number of compounding periods per year at 1	*2nd, P/Y,* 1, *ENTER, 2nd, QUIT*
2. Enter the present value	70000, *PV*
3. Enter the number of periods	3, *N*
4. Enter the growth rate (interest)	10, *I/Y*
5. Solve for the future value	*CPT, FV* (calculator displays –93,170.00)

BAII PLUS Keystrokes: Present Value of a Lump Sum

1. Set the number of discounting periods per year at 1	*2nd, P/Y,* 1, *ENTER, 2nd, QUIT*
2. Enter the future value	93170, *FV*
3. Enter the number of periods	3, *N*
4. Enter the growth rate (interest)	10, *I/Y*
5. Solve for the present value	*CPT, PV* (calculator displays –70,000.00)

Notice that when you follow the keystrokes described here, your calculator displays a negative sign in front of the final answer. The negative sign is a result of the algorithm used by the calculator to solve the time value of money formulas and should not be a great cause for concern. Just remember that if you enter a positive value in your calculator for a present value, then calculate future value, your calculator will always give you a negative future value. Similarly, if you enter a negative present value, the calculator will always give you a positive future value. The same is true for other time value of money calculations we will consider below. The negative sign indicates an outflow of money, while the positive sign indicates an inflow.

Applying the Present Value Formula to Cash Flow Streams

Up to this point, we have focused our attention on finding the value of present and future lump sums. In many real estate investments, however, a project generates flows of cash to the investor throughout the life of the investment. Consider an investment that promises to pay $500 in one year, $1,000 in two years and $1,500 in three years. If your required rate of return is 10 percent, how much would you be willing to pay for this investment? To solve this problem, first recognize that we know three future amounts. Applying the present value formula to each of these amounts with the proper values for the exponent n, then adding the three results, yields the total present value of this stream of cash flows. The present value of this stream at a discount rate of 10 percent is

$$PV = \$500 \left[\frac{1}{(1.1)^1} \right] + \$1,000 \left[\frac{1}{(1.1)^2} \right] + \$1,500 \left[\frac{1}{(1.1)^3} \right] = \$2,407.96$$

Thus, if we invested $2,407.96 in this project, we would earn exactly our required 10 percent rate of return.

In the event the stream of cash flows extends over many years, calculating the present value by repetition of the present value of a lump sum formula can be time-consuming. (We will describe how to use the cash flow features of financial calculators to solve this type of problem later in this chapter.) If the periodic cash flows are a series of equal amounts, however, the problem is greatly simplified. Such a series of equal cash flows is called an **annuity.**

Present Value of an Annuity

Consider an investment that promises to pay $1,000 at the end of each year for three years. The required rate of return is 10 percent. What is the present value of this stream of payments? Applying the present value of a lump sum formula three times and then adding the results yields

$$PV = \$1,000 \left[\frac{1}{(1.1)^1} \right] + \$1,000 \left[\frac{1}{(1.1)^2} \right] + \$1,000 \left[\frac{1}{(1.1)^3} \right] = \$2,486.85$$

While this calculation is certainly valid, it can be cumbersome when a large number of future cash flows are involved. Fortunately, there is a simpler method. Because the amounts in each period are equal, we can use the **present value of an annuity** formula shown in equation (3).

$$PVA = A \left[\frac{1 - \dfrac{1}{(1 + i)^n}}{i} \right] \qquad \textbf{(3)}$$

(where A is the amount each period [the annuity], i is the discount rate and n is the number of periods).

Applying this equation to the present problem yields

$$PVA = \$1,000 \left[\frac{1 - \dfrac{1}{(1.1)^3}}{.1} \right] = \$1,000 \, (2.48685) = \$2,486.85$$

Using a financial calculator to solve this problem is quite simple. Rather than entering a value using the *FV* key, we use the annuity payment key, which is usually labeled *PMT*. The following keystrokes demonstrate the steps required to solve this problem using the HP-10B and BAII PLUS calculators.

HP-10B Keystrokes: Present Value of an Annuity

1. Set the number of discounting periods per year at 1	1, *goldkey, P/YR*
2. Enter the annuity amount	1000, *PMT*
3. Enter the number of periods	3, *N*
4. Enter the discount rate (interest)	10, *I/YR*
5. Solve for the present value of the annuity	*PV* (calculator displays –2,486.85)

BAII PLUS Keystrokes: Present Value of an Annuity

1. Set the number of discounting periods per year at 1	*2nd, P/Y,* 1, *ENTER, 2nd, QUIT*
2. Enter the annuity amount	1000, *PMT*
3. Enter the number of periods	3, *N*
4. Enter the discount rate (interest)	10, *I/Y*
5. Solve for the present value of the annuity	*CPT, PV* (calculator displays –2,486.85)

The following example demonstrates the importance of the present value of annuity formula in a real estate context: calculating the outstanding balance on a mortgage loan. Suppose you have a mortgage that requires an annual payment of $16,274.54. The interest rate on the loan is 10 percent annually, and seven annual payments remain. What is the outstanding balance of the loan? In other words, what is the stream of payments (an annuity) worth to the lender today at a required rate of return of 10 percent? To find the answer, apply the formula to the annuity amount.

$$\text{PVA} = \$16,274.54 \left[\frac{1 - \dfrac{1}{(1.1)^7}}{.10} \right] = \$79,231.28$$

Using the HP-10B financial calculator, the entries are: $PMT = 16274.54$, $I/YR = 10$, $N = 7$. Pressing the *PV* key yields –79,231.28. Using the BAII PLUS calculator, the entries are: $PMT = 16274.54, I/Y = 10, N = 7$. Pressing CPT, then PV will yield $-79,231.28$.

Future Value of an Annuity

In some instances, particularly in personal finance, we are interested in finding the future value of equal payments received over time. In this type of problem, we could apply the future value formula described above to each payment individually using the proper exponent n and then add the results of each calculation, but this can be simplified by using the future value of an annuity formula.

Consider the following example: Suppose you invest $100 at the end of each year for the next five years in an interest-earning bank account paying 10 percent interest per year. How much money would you have in the account at the end of five years?

The first payment will be deposited one year from today and will earn interest for four years. The second deposit will earn interest over three years, and so on for the third and fourth deposits. Note that the fifth payment will not earn any interest because it will be deposited at the end of the fifth year. We can solve for the future value at the end of five years using the future value factor for each of the five deposits:

$$FV = \$100 \ (1.1)^4 + \$100 \ (1.1)^3 + \$100 \ (1.1)^2$$
$$+ \$100 \ (1.1)^1 + \$100 \ (1.1)^0 = \$610.51$$

To solve this problem quickly, however, we can use the **future value of an annuity** formula given in equation (4).

$$FVA = A \left[\frac{(1 + i)^n - 1}{i} \right] \qquad \textbf{(4)}$$

In this example

$$FVA = \$100 \left[\frac{(1.1)^5 - 1}{.10} \right] = \$610.51$$

$$FVA = \$100 \ (6.1051) = \$610.51$$

Our trusty financial calculators are useful in this type of problem as well. To solve for the future value of this annuity, enter 100 for PMT, 5 for number of years and 10 for the interest rate. Solving for the future value yields -610.51.

Sinking Fund Payments

The next time value of money principle, the **sinking fund payment** formula, is algebraically equivalent to the future value of an annuity formula. The important difference is that the unknown variable is not the future value of the stream of payments, but the amount of each payment required to accumulate the future amount.

Suppose, for example, that you wish to buy a home, but do not have the required down payment of $20,000. You decide that you will save that much over the next five years by making equal, annual deposits into a savings account paying 10 percent annually. How much must you deposit each year to accumulate $20,000? This type of problem is known as a *sinking fund*. That is, how much must you "sink" into the account each year to accumulate the desired amount in the future? Just as we solved the future value formula in equation (1) to get present value on the left side of the equality sign in equation (2), we can also solve equation (4) for the annuity A. To avoid possible confusion, we replace the variable A with the symbol *SFP* to represent the sinking fund payment. These manipulations of the *FVA* formula provide the formula for finding sinking fund payments:

$$ SFP = FVA \left[\frac{i}{(1 + i)^n - 1} \right] \qquad \textbf{(5)} $$

Applying the sinking fund formula to this problem shows you must deposit $3,275.94 into the account each year for five years to accumulate $20,000 at 10 percent interest:

$$ SFP = \$20,000 \left[\frac{.10}{(1.1)^5 - 1} \right] = \$3,275.94 $$

$$ SFP = \$20,000 \, (.163797) = \$3,275.94 $$

Using a financial calculator, the entries are as follows: $FV = 20000$, I/YR (or I/Y) $= 10$ and $N = 5$. Solving for the payment (PMT) yields $-3,275.94$.

Mortgage Payments

The sixth and final time value of money formula to be considered is the **mortgage payment** formula. This formula is used to calculate payments due on a fully amortizing loan. We will consider the concept of amortization in greater detail later in this chapter, so our discussion here is limited to using this formula to calculate mortgage payments.

Suppose you wish to borrow $100,000 to buy a parcel of real estate. The bank is willing to lend the money at 10 percent interest, provided that you amortize the debt with annual payments over the next ten years. How much will your payments be? Notice the similarity between this problem and the one we examined during our discussion of the present value of annuities. In both examples, we know the interest rate and the number of periods. In the present value of annuity problem, we know the amount of the annuity, but do not know the present value. In this problem, we know the present amount, but do not know the amount of the payment, or, in other words, the annuity. Because the problems are identical except for the unknown variable, we can solve equation (3) to move the annuity (variable A) to the left side of the equality sign. To avoid confusion, we then rename A to PMT to represent the mortgage payment. This results in the mortgage payment formula:

$$PMT = PVA \left[\dfrac{i}{1 - \dfrac{1}{(1 = i)^n}} \right] \qquad \textbf{(6)}$$

One item remains to be resolved. Why does the symbol PVA appear in the formula for mortgage payments? The answer to this question is simple, but very important. From the lender's point of view, a mortgage is an investment in the borrower's ability to repay the debt. In return for giving the borrower cash today, the lender will receive an annuity for n periods into the future. The lender is willing to give the borrower the present value of that annuity today in the form of a loan. To the borrower, the present value of the series of future payments represents the loan amount. Thus, the loan amount, or the remaining amount outstanding, can always be thought of as the present value of an annuity, where the annuity is the future mortgage payments. Applying equation (6) to the problem at hand shows the annual mortgage payment the lender will require for a ten-year loan of $100,000 at 10 percent interest:

$$PMT = \$100,000 \left[\dfrac{.10}{1 - \dfrac{1}{(1.1)^{10}}} \right] = \$16,274.54$$

Using a financial calculator, the entries are as follows: $PV = 100000, I/YR$ (or $I/Y) = 10$ and $N = 10$. Solving for the payment (PMT) yields $-16,274.54$.

Monthly Compounding

We now have developed the six time value of money formulas, but in each of the examples used thus far, we have dealt with annual time periods. In many instances, however, the compounding and discounting periods in real estate problems are semiannually, quarterly or even monthly. For example, almost all residential mortgage loans call for monthly payments. The preceding analysis remains valid for periods of any length, but with one word of caution. Time and interest must always be measured in the same unit. That is, if we wish to solve for a monthly mortgage payment, we must use a monthly interest rate.

Suppose, for example, we wish to calculate the monthly payment required to amortize a $100,000 loan at 12 percent annual interest for 30 years. The number of compounding periods becomes 360 (12 × 30), and the periodic interest rate becomes 1 percent (12 percent ÷ by 12). Substituting these numbers into the formula for finding the mortgage payment yields a monthly payment of $1,028.61.

We can generalize each of the six formulas to account for any compounding period by dividing i by m and multiplying n by m, where m is the number of compounding or discounting periods per year and i is the annual interest or discount rate. Applying this rule restates the six time value of money formulas as follows:

$$FV = PV \left[(1 + \dfrac{i}{m})^{nm} \right] \qquad \textbf{(7)}$$

$$PV = FV \left[\frac{1}{(1 + \frac{i}{m})^{nm}} \right] \tag{8}$$

$$PVA = A \left[\frac{1 - \frac{1}{(1 + \frac{i}{m})^{nm}}}{\frac{i}{m}} \right] \tag{9}$$

$$FVA = A \left[\frac{(1 + \frac{i}{m})^{nm} - 1}{\frac{i}{m}} \right] \tag{10}$$

$$SFP = FVA \left[\frac{\frac{i}{m}}{(1 + \frac{i}{m})^{nm} - 1} \right] \tag{11}$$

$$PMT = PVA \left[\frac{\frac{i}{m}}{1 - \frac{1}{(1 + \frac{i}{m})^{nm}}} \right] \tag{12}$$

Most financial calculators can be set to automatically convert the time value of money formulas for any compounding or discounting frequency. Of course, you can do this manually by dividing the interest rate and multiplying the number of years by the number of compounding or discounting periods per year before you press the appropriate keys. If you wish to take advantage of your calculator's built-in features, the following steps show how to use the HP-10B and BAII PLUS to calculate monthly mortgage payments on a $100,000 loan amount for 30 years at 12 percent interest.

HP-10B Keystrokes: Monthly Mortgage Payments

1. Set the number of discounting periods per year at 12	12, *goldkey, P/YR*
2. Enter the loan amount	100000, *PV*
3. Enter the number of months	30, *goldkey, N*
4. Enter the interest rate (calculator divides by *P/YR*)	12, *I/YR*
5. Solve for the monthly payment	*PMT* (calculator displays −1,028.61)

BAII PLUS Keystrokes: Monthly Mortgage Payments

1. Set the number of periods per year at 12	*2nd, P/Y, 12, ENTER, 2nd, QUIT*
2. Enter the loan amount	100000, *PV*
3. Enter the number of months	30, *2nd, xP/Y, N*
4. Enter the interest rate (calculator divides by *P/Y*)	12, *I/Y*
5. Solve for the monthly payment	*CPT, PMT* (calculator displays –1,028.61)

FINANCIAL DECISION RULES: NPV AND IRR

Now that we understand the concept of risk and the time value of money formulas, we will examine a framework for making decisions concerning investment choices. This framework compares the benefits of an investment to its costs, including risk and the time value of money. The key concept is **net present value** (NPV), which is the difference between how much an investment is worth to an investor and how much it costs. Suppose an investment promises to pay you a stream of cash flows that has a present value of $10,000. If the asking price of this investment is $9,000, the investor obviously would decide to buy it. In this case, the net present value is $1,000 ($10,000 – $9,000).

The question is, how do we determine the present value of the stream of cash flows? We discount the cash flows at the proper discount rate, which is the rate of return we require to compensate for the riskiness of the investment. If the stream occurs in uneven amounts, we use the present value of a lump sum formula to discount each cash flow. If the stream is an annuity, we can simplify the calculations by using the present value of an annuity formula. The appropriate discount rate to use is one that accounts for the risk of the investment opportunity, usually determined by comparing the rates of return on alternative investment choices of similar risk. Formally, we can define net present value as follows:

NPV = Present value of cash inflows – Present value of cash outflows

In decision-making situations, we use the NPV concept as part of the **NPV decision rule:** If the NPV of an investment is greater than or equal to zero, we choose to invest because the investment is worth at least as much as it costs, given our required rate of return. If NPV is less than zero, we choose not to invest because we would not earn our required rate of return. Remember that the required rate of return reflects both the time value of money and the riskiness of the investment opportunity. We can take this rule a step further and say that if faced with several alternative investment choices, we should accept the one with the highest positive NPV because it will increase our wealth more than the others.

| Table 14.2 | NPV and IRR Decision Rule Example |

Year	Cash Flow		Present Value	Discounted Cash Flow at 12%
0	-$10,000.00	outflow	-$10,000/1.12^0	-$10,000.00
1	100.00	inflow	100/1.12^1	89.29
2	1,600.00	inflow	1,600/1.12^2	1,275.51
3	1,800.00	inflow	1,800/1.12^3	1,281.20
4	450.00	inflow	450/1.12^4	285.98
5	12,500.00	inflow	12,500/1.12^5	7,092.84

NPV = PV of inflows – PV of outflows
NPV = $89.29 + $1,275.51 + $1,281.20 + $285.98 + $7,092.84 – $10,000
NPV = $24.82
IRR = 12.0646%

This leads us to another important concept in financial decision making: If the NPV of an investment is greater than or equal to zero, we must be earning at least our required rate of return. In fact, if the NPV equals zero, the rate of return on the investment is exactly equal to the required rate. If the NPV is not zero, what rate are we earning? We can define the **internal rate of return** (IRR) of an investment as the discount rate that makes the NPV exactly equal to zero. To determine an investment's IRR, we can search a variety of discount rates by trial and error until we find one that makes the NPV equal zero. This rate will be the internal rate of return on the investment. Fortunately, most financial calculators have a feature that allows automatic searches for the internal rate of return for a series of cash flows.

The definition of IRR provides another rule for financial decision making: If the IRR is greater than or equal to our required rate of return, we choose to invest; otherwise, we forgo the investment opportunity. While the IRR rule and the NPV rule are based on the same principles, the NPV rule is generally better to use because IRR calculations may yield multiple discount rates that set the NPV equal to zero. When our objective is to determine the rate of return provided by an investment, however, the IRR calculation is extremely useful. The following example demonstrates the NPV rule and the IRR rule using both the present value formula approach and financial calculators.

NPV and IRR Decision Rule Example

Suppose you are faced with making a decision about whether to invest $10,000 today in a risky real estate investment. In return for your investment, you expect to receive the following stream of cash flows: year one, $100; year two, $1,600; year three, $1,800; year four, $450; year five, $12,500. You believe other investment opportunities with similar risk offer 12 percent rates of return. What are the NPV and IRR of this investment? Should you invest?

We can find the NPV of this investment by applying the NPV definition: NPV equals the present value of cash inflows minus the present value of cash outflows. Table 14.2 shows the intermediate results from the calculation presented below:

$$NPV = \frac{\$100}{1.12^1} + \frac{\$1,600}{1.12^2} + \frac{\$1,800}{1.12^3} + \frac{\$450}{1.12^4} + \frac{\$12,500}{1.12^5} - \$10,000$$

$$NPV = \$24.82$$

Because the NPV is greater than zero, the investment is worth more than it costs and we should accept this opportunity. Likewise, we know that the IRR must be greater than our required rate of return, simply because the NPV is positive. To determine the IRR of this investment, we could apply different discount rates in the above calculation until the NPV becomes exactly zero, but this process is greatly simplified by a financial calculator. To find the NPV and IRR using a financial calculator, follow the steps outlined below. You should find that the IRR of this investment is 12.0646 percent.

HP-10B Keystrokes: NPV and IRR Calculations for Unequal Cash Flows

1. Set the number of periods per year at 1	1, *goldkey, P/YR*
2. Enter the initial cash outflow (a negative amount)	10000, +/-, *CF^j*
3. Enter the cash flow for year one	100, *CF^j*
4. Enter the cash flow for year two	1600, *CF^j*
5. Enter the cash flow for year three	1800, *CF^j*
6. Enter the cash flow for year four	
7. Enter the cash flow for year five	450, *CF^j*
8. Enter the required rate of return	12500, *CF^j*
9. Solve for the NPV	12, *I/YR*
	goldkey, NPV (calculator displays 24.82)
10. Solve for the IRR	*goldkey, IRR/YR* (calculator displays 12.0646)

BAII PLUS Keystrokes: NPV and IRR Calculations for Unequal Cash Flows

1. Set the number of periods per year at 1	*2nd, P/Y, 1, ENTER, 2nd, QUIT*
2. Enter the initial cash outflow (a negative amount)	*CF, 10000, +/−, ENTER*
3. Enter the cash flow for year one	*↓, 100, ENTER*
4. Enter the cash flow for year two	*↓, ↓, 1600, ENTER*
5. Enter the cash flow for year three	*↓, ↓, 1800, ENTER*
6. Enter the cash flow for year four	*↓, ↓, 450, ENTER*
7. Enter the cash flow for year five	*↓, ↓, 12500, ENTER*
8. Enter the required rate of return	*NPV, 12, ENTER, ↓*
9. Solve for the NPV	*CPT* (calculator displays 24.82)
10. Solve for the IRR	*IRR, CPT* (calculator displays 12.0646)

MORTGAGE MECHANICS

Because most real estate investments involve long-term commitments of relatively large amounts of money, most real estate transactions involve long-term mortgage financing from third parties. Understanding the mechanics of mortgage financing is important for students of real estate and real estate practitioners. In this section, we explore mortgage mechanics in detail. Our first tasks are to distinguish between amortizing loans and interest-only loans and to fully explore the concept of amortization.

Interest-Only versus Amortizing Loans

As we discussed in Chapter 13, most loans used to finance real estate purchases prior to the 1930s were short-term, interest-only loans. In these loans, the borrowers pay interest on the full loan amounts each period, and when the loan terms expire, the borrowers repay the loans in one lump sum. During the Depression era, many borrowers could barely afford to make the required interest payments on these loans, much less repay the loan balances when the loans matured. One of the most successful activities of the Federal Housing Administration was the promotion of long-term, amortizing loans for home financing rather than short-term, interest-only loans. Amortizing loans are much easier to budget for most borrowers and, when combined with mortgage insurance, are much less risky for most lenders. Amortizing loans are the dominant loan type in the housing finance industry. To fully understand the process of amortization, it is often useful to first understand how the payment streams differ between interest-only loans and amortizing loans.

Interest-only loans require a borrower to pay interest each period during the loan term and to repay the full loan amount in one lump sum at the end of the loan term. In contrast, **amortizing loans** require equal periodic payments composed of both interest and principal. As payments in this type of loan are made, the balance of the loan is gradually reduced to zero by the end of the loan term. Interest-only loan payments are calculated by multiplying the periodic interest rate by the loan amount. Amortizing loan payments are calculated using the mortgage payment formula, one of the six time value of money formulas discussed earlier.

The difference in payment streams between an amortizing loan and an interest-only loan is illustrated in Figure 14.2. Repayment of a five-year, $1,000 interest-only loan carrying a 10 percent interest rate requires a $100 interest payment for each of the first four years. At the end of the fifth year, the entire principal amount of $1,000 plus $100 interest is due. (This much larger final payment is often referred to as a **balloon payment.**) The same $1,000 loan can be amortized by five annual payments of $263.80. Notice that although the periodic payments are higher for the amortizing loan, the payment is the same in each period. No balloon payment at the end of the loan is required because the loan balance is gradually reduced by the periodic payments. Also, notice that the total amount of interest paid to the lender ($500) is higher in the interest-only loan because none of the principal is repaid until the final payment. In the amortizing loan, part of the principal is repaid with each payment, so the total interest paid is less ($319).

Understanding the Amortization Process

An **amortization schedule** can be developed for any amortizing loan. A loan amortization schedule describes the payments in each period, the interest and principal contained in each payment and the amount outstanding in each period. Table 14.3 shows an amortization schedule for a $100,000, ten-year annual payment loan at 10 percent interest. Figure 14.3 plots the periodic payments and the interest and principal components of each payment. Note that while the payment amount is constant over the life of the loan, the portion going to interest decreases with each payment as the balance owed falls. Conversely, the portion going to payment of principal increases over the life of the loan. Also, the loan balance decreases slowly in the earlier years of the loan and more rapidly as the loan approaches maturity.

Understanding the amortization process requires careful consideration of the principal and interest components of each payment, as well as the changing loan balance over time. Table 14.3 shows that $10,000 of the first year's payment on the above loan goes for interest, while only $6,274.54 reduces the principal owed. With the loan balance reduced to $93.725.46, interest for the second year drops to $9,372.55, while the principal component of the payment rises to $6,901.99. The process continues until the last year, when interest is only $1,479.51, and principal is $14,795.05. The total amount of principal repaid equals the original loan amount, $100,000, and the total interest paid is $62,745.40. If the loan had been an interest-only loan, the borrower would have paid a total of $200,000 to the lender: $100,000 interest and $100,000 principal.

Figure 14.2   Repayment of Five-Year, $1,000 Interest-Only Term and
Fully Amortizing Loans, Each Carrying 10 Percent Annual Interest

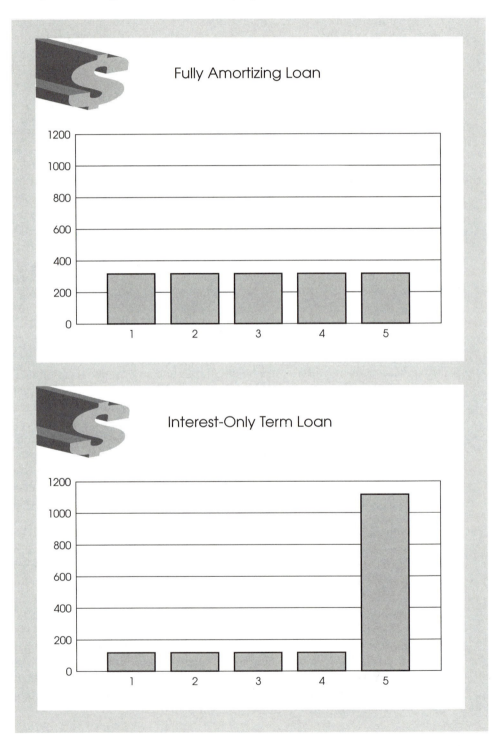

Amortization of a $100,000 Loan over Ten Years at 10 Percent   **Figure 14.3**

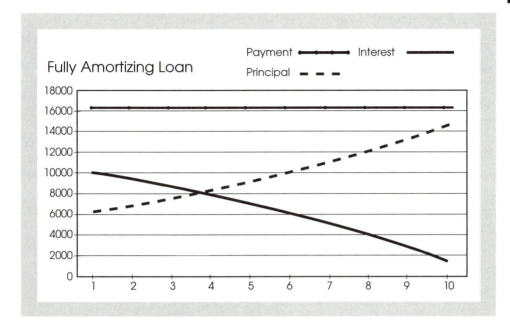

From this example, we can establish several principles regarding the amortization of real estate mortgage loans:

- With a level, constant payment, the portions of each payment going to interest and principal vary greatly over time.
- The interest portion of each payment decreases over time.
- The principal portion of each payment increases over time.
- The amount outstanding declines to zero at the end of the loan term.

An amortization table is a valuable tool in many real estate decisions. While most financial calculators have built-in amortization functions, we believe it is important for students to be able to construct a simple table manually. To construct an amortization table, begin by calculating the periodic payment required to amortize the loan using the mortgage payment formula. Rather than solving the equation directly, enter the necessary information into your financial calculator using the steps previously outlined. Because the payments on this type of loan are the same in each period, this calculation need be done only once. To complete the amortization schedule, proceed down the rows of the table, one row at a time, by calculating the interest due, subtracting the interest from the payment to get the principal for the period, then subtracting the principal paid in the period from the previous year's balance to get the new balance for the period.

These steps, for the first two years of the loan in Table 14.3, are summarized below. As you can see, each year's principal, interest and amount outstanding are found in the same manner. The following notations will prove useful as we consider more complicated aspects of mortgage mechanics: PMT = mortgage payment, I_t = interest due in period t, i = periodic interest rate, P_t = principal paid in period t, and AO_t = amount outstanding at the end of period t.

Table 14.3 Amortization Schedule for a $100,000 Loan at 10 Percent Annual Interest for Ten Years

Year	Payment PMT	Interest I_t	Principal P_t	Amount Outstanding AO_t
0	–	–	–	$100,000.00
1	$16,274.54	$10,000.00	$6,274.54	93,725.46
2	16,274.54	9,372.55	6,901.99	86,823.47
3	16,274.54	8,682.35	7,592.19	79,231.28
4	16,274.54	7,923.13	8,351.41	70,879.87
5	16,274.54	7,087.99	9,186.55	61,693.32
6	16,274.54	6,169.33	10,105.21	51,588.11
7	16,274.54	5,158.81	11,115.73	40,472.38
8	16,274.54	4,047.24	12,227.30	28,245.08
9	16,274.54	2,824.51	13,450.03	14,795.05
10	16,274.54	1,479.51	14,795.05	0.00
Total	$162,745.40	$62,745.40	$100,000.00	

Note: Component items may not add to totals due to rounding error.

Amortization: Period One

1. $I_t = AO_{t-1} \times i$ $10,000   = $100,000 \times .10$
2. $P_t = PMT - I_t$ $6,274.54   = $16,274.54 - $10,000$
3. $AO_t = AO_{t-1} - P_t$ $93,725.46   = $100,000 - $6,274.54$

Amortization: Period Two

1. $I_t = AO_{t-1} \times i$ $9,372.55   = $93,725.46 \times .10$
2. $P_t = PMT - I_t$ $6,901.99   = $16,274.54 - $9,372.55$
3. $AO_t = AO_{t-1} - P_t$ $86,823.47   = $93,725.46 - $6,901.99$

UNDERSTANDING THE FIXED-RATE MORTGAGE: PREPAYMENT

Now that we have explored the concept of amortization, we can take a closer look at other mechanics of mortgage loans. The most common mortgage loan is one in which the interest rate is fixed at the time of origination. We have already seen how this type of loan is amortized by the payment calculated using the mortgage payment formula, and we now examine the concepts of prepayment, refinancing, discount points, origination fees and effective interest rates.

For a variety of reasons, borrowers may decide to extinguish an outstanding mortgage loan by repaying the loan balance before the end of the loan term. Because all loans require repayment, we use the word **prepayment** to indicate that the loan is repaid before its full term expires. Based on historical evidence, many residential borrowers prepay their loans after five to seven years. Because the loan balance declines with each payment due to amortization, it is important that we be able to calculate the amount outstanding on a loan at any point in time. To simplify the calculations, we assume that all prepayments occur on payment dates, rather than between payment dates.

Consider a **fixed-rate mortgage** with the following characteristics: loan amount of $133,000, 30 years to maturity, monthly payments and an annual interest rate of 7.5 percent. Assume the borrower decides to sell the collateral and buy a new property. The loan contract contains a due-on-sale clause (see Chapter 13), so the borrower must prepay the loan if the property is sold. If the borrower prepays at the end of month 60, what is the amount outstanding on this loan at the time of prepayment?

To answer this question, we could construct an amortization schedule for the first 60 months of this loan. Fortunately, there is a less time-consuming method to answer this question that uses the annuity concept. Recall that an annuity is a series of equal payments over time. Obviously, the remaining payments on a mortgage meet our definition of an annuity. If we want to find the amount outstanding on a mortgage loan on any payment date, we calculate the present value of the remaining payments by discounting them at the interest rate on the loan. We can find the present value of an annuity (or amount outstanding at month 60, AO_{60}) using the appropriate formula or calculator keystrokes. First, find the monthly payment amount, then calculate the present value of the 300 payments remaining at the end of month 60. In this example, AO_{60} equals $125,841.19. The steps for solving this problem using financial calculators are given below.

HP-10B Keystrokes: Monthly Mortgage Payments and Amount Outstanding at Time t

1. Set the number of discounting periods per year at 12	12, *goldkey*, *P/YR*
2. Enter the loan amount	133000, *PV*
3. Enter the number of months	30, *goldkey*, *n*
4. Enter the interest rate (calculator divides by *P/YR*)	7.5, *I/YR*
5. Solve for the monthly payment	*PMT* (calculator displays –929.96)
6. Enter the number of remaining payments	300, *n*
7. Solve for the amount outstanding (AO_{60})	*PV* (calculator displays 125,841.19)

BAII PLUS Keystrokes: Monthly Mortgage Payments and Amount Outstanding at Time t

1. Set the number of discounting periods per year at 12	*2nd, P/Y, 12, ENTER, 2nd, QUIT*
2. Enter the loan amount	133000, *PV*
3. Enter the number of months	30, *2nd, xP/Y, N*
4. Enter the interest rate (calculator divides by *P/YR*)	7.5, *I/Y*
5. Solve for the monthly payment	*CPT, PMT* (calculator displays −929.96)
6. Enter the number of remaining payments	300, *N*
7. Solve for the amount outstanding (*AO60*)	*CPT, PV* (calculator displays 125,841.19)

Using the present value of an annuity formula to determine the amount outstanding on a loan is useful in many situations. For example, how can we determine the amount of principal repaid during the sixth year of a loan? First, find the amount outstanding at the end of month 60 (300 payments remaining). Second, find the amount outstanding at the end of month 72 (288 payments remaining). Then subtract AO_{72} from AO_{60} to get $1,781.80. Taking this idea a step further, we can also find the amount of interest paid in the sixth year by subtracting the principal paid in that year from total payments. In the example above, total payments in any year amount to $11,159.52. Subtracting the principal amount of $1,781.80 leaves $9,377.72 as interest paid in payments 63 through 72.

This technique of finding the amount outstanding is also useful when we are interested in determining the amount of interest or principal contained in any one monthly payment. How much interest is contained in payment 61? We know that interest is paid on the outstanding balance after the last payment was made, so we multiply AO_{60} by .075/12 (the monthly interest rate) to determine the interest contained in payment 61. Just as we saw in the amortization table, $I_t = AO_{t-1} \times i/m$. In this case, $I_{61} = \$125{,}841.19 \times .075/12 = \$786.51$. To find the principal contained in payment 61, we use the following relationship: $P_t = PMT - I_t$. In this case, $P_{61} = \$929.96 - \$786.51 = \$143.45$.

UNDERSTANDING THE FIXED-RATE MORTGAGE: REFINANCING

In many cases, borrowers find that the interest rate on an outstanding loan is substantially higher than rates available on new mortgages in the market. If the rate on the existing loan is higher than the market interest rate, the borrower can reduce total borrowing costs by refinancing the loan amount at the prevailing market rate. **Refinancing** involves retiring the existing loan with the proceeds of a new loan for the same property. The borrower may obtain the new loan from the same or a different lender. A reduction in borrowing cost can be obtained by either reducing the payment amount or by reducing the number of payments required to amortize the loan.

Consider the loan described in the previous example. At the end of 60 months, suppose that current interest rates are at 6 percent. If the borrower obtains a new loan for the same amount for 25 years, the monthly payments will be $810.80, which results in payment reduction of $119.16. Therefore, refinancing this loan will provide interest savings of $35,748 over the remaining 25 years of the loan.

On the other hand, if the borrower wishes to take advantage of the lower interest rates available in the market and is comfortable making the larger payments, refinancing can reduce the remaining term of the loan. In this case, if the borrower refinances the loan amount of $125,841.19 at 6 percent annual interest, but continues making payments of $929.96 each month, the number of monthly payments required to repay this debt falls from 300 to 227 (the last payment made will be for less than the full amount). Thus, refinancing the loan at a lower interest rate, but keeping the payments at the same level, reduces the time required to retire the debt by six years and one month. To reach these conclusions using the HP-10B or BAII PLUS financial calculator, follow the steps outlined below.

HP-10B Keystrokes: Mortgage Refinancing When Interest Rates Decline

1. Set the number of discounting periods per year at 12	12, *goldkey, P/YR*
2. Enter the loan amount	133000, *PV*
3. Enter the number of months	30, *goldkey, n*
4. Enter the interest rate (calculator divides by *P/YR*)	7.5, *I/YR*
5. Solve for the monthly payment	*PMT* (calculator displays –929.96)
6. Enter the number of remaining months	300, *n*
7. Solve for the present value of the annuity (*AOt*)	*PV* (calculator displays 125,841.19)
8. Enter the new interest rate	6, *I/YR*
9. Calculate the payment on the new loan	*PMT* (calculator displays –810.80)

To determine the number of months remaining if the payment is left at $929.96 per month:

10. Enter the original payment amount (negative)	–929.96, *PMT*
11. Solve for the new number of months remaining	*n* (calculator displays 227)

BAII PLUS Keystrokes: Mortgage Refinancing When Interest Rates Decline

1. Set the number of periods per year at 12	*2nd, P/Y,* 12, *ENTER, 2nd, QUIT*
2. Enter the loan amount	133000, *PV*
3. Enter the number of months	30, *2nd, xP/Y, N*
4. Enter the interest rate (calculator divides by *P/YR*)	7.5, *I/Y*
5. Solve for the monthly payment	*CPT, PMT* (calculator displays –929.96)
6. Enter the number of remaining months	300, *N*
7. Solve for the present value of the annuity (*AO_i*)	*CPT, PV* (calculator displays 125,841.19)
8. Enter the new interest rate	6, *I/Y*
9. Calculate the payment on the new loan	*CPT, PMT* (calculator displays –810.80)

To determine the number of months remaining if the payment is left at $929.96 per month:

10. Enter the original payment amount (negative)	–929.96, *PMT*
11. Solve for the new number of months remaining	*CPT, N* (calculator displays 226.33)

UNDERSTANDING THE FIXED-RATE MORTGAGE: DISCOUNT POINTS AND EFFECTIVE INTEREST RATES

Another important aspect of mortgage financing is the use of discount points and origination fees to increase a lender's yield on a loan. The charges represent additional income to the lender and therefore additional cost of borrowing to the borrower. When expressed as a percentage of the loan amount, the charges are called **discount points.** One discount point equals 1 percent of the loan amount. When expressed as a dollar amount, the charges are generally classified as **origination fees.** These charges cover the lender's cost of processing the loan application and obtaining credit reports, as well as other costs associated with loan origination. Of course, the lender could simply increase the interest rate on the loan, but many choose to charge these fees at the time of origination rather than throughout the term of the loan.

From the borrower's perspective, discount points and other fees result in an effective interest rate that may be substantially higher than the stated interest rate on the loan. The term **effective interest rate** refers to the actual cost of borrowing funds from a lender, expressed as an annual rate, after consideration of discount points and origination fees. Comparing one loan to another requires careful consideration of the effective interest rate. The calculations presented here are similar to those used by lenders to calculate the annual percentage rate (APR), which must be disclosed to all loan applicants under Regulation Z (see Chapter 13).

The table below shows a sample of interest rates and discount points offered by competing lenders. The quotes are based on a $100,000, 30-year loan for an owner-occupied, single-family home. Which loan provides the lowest effective interest rate? The answer to this question requires use of the IRR concept discussed previously in this chapter.

Lender	Interest Rate	Points
Loan Shack	7.875	0.50%
Marley Lenders	7.625	1.00
First Bank	8.000	0.00
Spider Savings	7.250	3.50

To determine which loan provides the lowest effective interest rate, we first must calculate the payments required under each loan. Notice that payments are based on the full loan amount of $100,000. In three of these loans, borrowers must pay points to the lenders at the time of origination. Therefore, the net amount disbursed by a lender at origination is determined by subtracting the fee from the loan amount. Using the definition of discount points and the mortgage payment calculations described early, the cash flows for each loan are as follows:

Lender	Cash Flow at Origination	Cash Flow in Periods 1–360 (payments)
Loan Shack	–$ 99,500	$725.07
Marley Lenders	– 99,000	707.79
First Bank	– 100,000	733.76
Spider Savings	– 96,500	682.18

The effective interest rate for each of these loans equals the IRR of the cash flow stream. We can find the IRR of the cash flows in each loan using our financial calculators. The keystrokes for finding the effective interest rate for the first loan using the HP-10B and BAII PLUS are described below.

HP-10B Keystrokes: IRR Calculations for Effective Interest Rates

Note that this problem requires the use of the *Nj* key. This key allows us to tell the calculator that a cash flow will occur for a specified number of periods. The largest value that can be entered with the *Nj* key is 99. Therefore, we must use it several times to enter all 360 monthly loan payments.

1. Set the number of compounding periods at 12 per year	12, *goldkey, P/YR*
2. Enter the initial cash outflow (a negative amount)	99,500, +/−, *CF^j*
3. Enter cash flow one	725.07, *CF^j*
4. Enter 99 for the number of times cash flow one will occur	99, *goldkey, N^j*
5. Enter cash flow two	725.07, *CF^j*
6. Enter 99 for the number of times cash flow two will occur	99, *goldkey, N^j*
7. Enter cash flow three	725.07, *CF^j*
8. Enter 99 for the number of times cash flow three will occur	99, *goldkey, N^j*
9. Enter cash flow four	725.07, *CF^j*
10. Enter 63 for the number of times cash flow four will occur	63, *goldkey, N^j*
11. Solve for the IRR	*goldkey, IRR/YR* (calculator displays 7.9275)

BAII PLUS Keystrokes: IRR Calculations for Effective Interest Rates

Note that this problem requires the use of the cash flow frequency function of the calculator. This function allows us to tell the calculator that a cash flow will occur for a specified number of periods.

1. Set the number of periods per year at 12	*2nd, P/Y, 12, ENTER, 2nd, QUIT*
2. Enter the initial cash outflow (a negative amount)	*CF, 99500, +/–, ENTER*
3. Enter the cash flow amount	*↓, 725.07, ENTER*
4. Enter the number of months (frequency)	*↓, 360, ENTER*
5. Solve for the monthly IRR	*IRR, CPT (calculator displays .66)*
6. Calculate the annual IRR	*X, 12, = (calculator displays 7.9275)*

Repeating this calculation for each of the loans provides the effective interest rates shown below. Notice that the effective interest rate on the loan from First Bank is the same as the stated interest rate because no points are involved. The answer from our calculators (7.9999 percent) is slightly less than the stated rate because we rounded the payment amount to the nearest penny. Of all four loans, the loan from Spider Savings provides the lowest effective interest rate, in spite of the large amount of points charged at origination.

Lender	Stated Interest Rate	Points	Effective Interest Rate
Loan Shack	7.875	0.50%	7.9275
Marley Lenders	7.625	1.00	7.7287
First Bank	8.000	0.00	7.9999
Spider Savings	7.250	3.50	7.6123

Discount points and origination fees can have a dramatic impact on effective interest rates if a borrower prepays the loan. As we mentioned earlier, most loans are prepaid within five to seven years. To determine the effective interest rate when a loan is prepaid, we must calculate the amount outstanding on the loan at the time of prepayment. To demonstrate the effect of discount points and prepayment on effective interest rates, assume that the loan from Spider Savings is prepaid at the end of month 60. What is the effective interest rate on the loan? To answer this question, first find AO_{60} as described above, then enter the cash flows into your financial calculator as shown below.

HP-10B Keystrokes: Effective Interest Rates with Discount Points and Prepayment

1. Set the number of periods at 12 per year	12, *goldkey, P/YR*
2. Enter the initial cash outflow (a negative amount)	96500, +/–, *CFⱼ*
3. Enter cash flow one	682.18, *CFⱼ*
4. Enter 59 for the number of times cash flow one will occur	59, *goldkey, Nⱼ*
5. Enter cash flow two (payment 60 + AO₆₀)	95060.96, *CFⱼ*
6. Solve for the IRR	
	goldkey, IRR/YR (calculator displays 8.1252)

BAII PLUS Keystrokes: Effective Interest Rates with Discount Points and Prepayment

1. Set the number of periods per year at 12	*2nd, P/Y,* 12, *ENTER, 2nd, QUIT*
2. Enter the initial cash outflow (a negative amount)	*CF,* 96500, +/–, *ENTER*
3. Enter cash flow one	↓, 682.18, *ENTER*
4. Enter the number of months (frequency)	↓, 59, *ENTER*
5. Enter cash flow two	↓, 95060.96, *ENTER*
6. Solve for the monthly IRR	*IRR , CPT* (calculator displays 0.6771)
7. Calculate the annual IRR	*X,* 12, = (calculator displays 8.1252)

As you can see, prepaying a loan with high origination costs can increase the effective interest rate considerably. Prepaying the Spider Savings loan at the end of five years raises the effective interest rate to 8.1252 percent, which is significantly greater than the stated interest rate of 7.250 percent. Notice that the loan from First Bank has an effective interest rate of 8 percent regardless of prepayment. Furthermore, realize that the earlier you prepay a loan with discount points, the greater the effective interest rate. When shopping for a new mortgage among competing lenders, consider how long you expect to keep the loan before making a final choice.

ALTERNATIVES TO THE FIXED-RATE MORTGAGE

In addition to shopping for the best deal on a mortgage by comparing effective interest rates resulting from discount points or origination fees, borrowers may wish to consider various alternatives to the fixed-rate mortgage. Several alternative mortgage types are available, including two-step mortgages and adjustable-rate mortgages. The distinguishing feature of each of these loans is that the payments are not necessarily the same in each period. In the **two-step mortgage,** the payment amount is reestablished once during the life of the loan, usually at the end of year five or year seven. Payments in an **adjustable-rate mortgage** (ARM) change more frequently, usually at the end of each year. Lenders are able to offer these loans at lower interest rates because the borrowers assume some of the risk of future interest rate increases. If the general interest rate in the economy increases, a lender's yield on an outstanding loan increases as well. Borrowers who are willing to accept this additional risk enjoy a lower initial interest rate. Borrowers who plan on prepaying a loan before it matures find this two-step loan, as well as the adjustable-rate loan, especially attractive. The tools we have developed in earlier sections help us understand the mechanics of these alternative loan types.

Understanding the Mechanics of Two-Step Mortgages

Two-step mortgages (also known as *reset mortgages*) are a relatively new type of loan in the residential lending market. Initial payments on this type of loan are calculated using the mortgage payment formula. At the end of five or seven years, depending on the contract terms, the payment is recalculated for the remaining balance and term of the loan based on the prevailing interest rate. The prevailing interest rate is usually defined as the yield on ten-year Treasury bonds plus two percentage points. In other words, the interest rate is indexed to the Treasury bond yield with a margin of 2 percent. Because the new interest rate may be higher or lower than the original interest rate, the payment amount changes accordingly.

This loan is advantageous to borrowers because the interest rate used to determine the initial payments is lower than the interest rate on a fixed-rate mortgage. Borrowers who do not expect to hold their loans for the full term find the two-step mortgage especially attractive. Even if a loan is held to maturity, the borrower is protected against large payment changes by an interest rate cap that limits the increase in the interest rate to a maximum of five percentage points. The following example demonstrates the payment stream required in a typical two-step mortgage.

Two-Step Mortgage Example

Consider a 30-year two-step mortgage for $110,000. The initial interest rate is 6 percent, but the loan contract requires that the interest rate be adjusted at the end of year seven to two percentage points more than the ten-year Treasury bond yield. The maximum increase in the interest rate is capped at five percentage points over the initial rate. At the end of year seven, the ten-year Treasury yield is 6.9 percent. Assuming the loan is held to maturity, monthly payments are determined as follows.

First, calculate the payment due in months 1 through 84 using the loan amount of $110,000, 6 percent interest and 30 years. The payment amount is $659.51. Second, find the amount outstanding at the end of month 84 ($98,603.32). Third, determine the new interest rate of 8.9 percent by adding the margin and the current Treasury yield. Notice that the new interest rate is 2.9 percentage points more than the initial rate, which is well within the limits of the interest rate cap. Finally, calculate the payment due in months 84 through 360 using the current loan balance, 23 years and the new interest rate of 8.9 percent. The new payment is $840.68. The financial calculator keystrokes necessary to find the payment amounts are outlined below.

HP-10B Keystrokes: Two-Step Mortgage Payments

1. Set the number of periods per year at 12	12, *goldkey, P/YR*
2. Enter the loan amount	110000, *PV*
3. Enter the number of months	30, *goldkey, N*
4. Enter the interest rate (calculator divides by *P/YR*)	6, *I/YR*
5. Solve for the monthly payment	*PMT* (calculator displays −659.51)
6. Enter the number of remaining months	276, *N*
7. Solve for the present value of the annuity (AO_{84})	*PV* (calculator displays 198,603.32)
8. Enter the new interest rate	8.9, *I/YR*
9. Calculate the new payment	*PMT* (calculator displays −840.68)

BAII PLUS Keystrokes: Two-Step Mortgage Payments

1. Set the number of periods per year at 12	*2nd, P/Y,* 12, *ENTER, 2nd, QUIT*
2. Enter the loan amount	110000, *PV*
3. Enter the number of months	30, *2nd, xP/Y, N*
4. Enter the interest rate (calculator divides by *P/Y*)	6, *I/Y*
5. Solve for the monthly payment	*CPT, PMT* (calculator displays –659.51)
6. Enter the number of remaining months	276, *N*
7. Solve for the present value of the annuity (AO*84*)	*CPT, PV* (calculator displays 198,603.32)
8. Enter the new interest rate	8.9, *I/Y*
9. Calculate the new payment	*CPT, PMT* (calculator displays –840.68)

Understanding the Mechanics of Adjustable-Rate Mortgages

Adjustable-rate mortgages are a common type of loan in both residential and commercial lending. As with two-step mortgages, the interest rate on an adjustable-rate mortgage is subject to change as the general interest rate level in the economy changes. The key difference is that the rate changes more than once during the term of the mortgage. In fact, most ARMs require annual rate adjustments, though some require adjustments every three or five years. In general, the initial interest rate on an ARM is lower than the rate on fixed-rate or two-step mortgages, which makes this an attractive loan type for many borrowers. Of course, ARM borrowers must be confident that they can afford the payment increases that are likely to occur over the life of the mortgage.

ARM interest rates are indexed to some general interest rate in the capital market. The most common index for residential ARMs is the one-year Treasury bill. The contract interest rate in any year of an ARM is defined as the index rate plus a margin of two or three percentage points. In the first year of an ARM, some lenders offer a teaser that reduces the margin by one or two percentage points. At each adjustment period, the contract interest rate is adjusted, and the payments are recalculated. To protect borrowers (and lenders) against large payment changes, most ARMs have two types of interest rate caps. Generally, the annual cap limits the change in the contract interest rate to two percentage points more than the prior year's contract rate, and the lifetime cap establishes maximum and minimum contract rates that are within five percentage points of the initial contract rate. The calculations required to determine the payment stream for a residential ARM with known T-bill rates are demonstrated in the following example.

HP-10B Keystrokes: ARM Payments

1. Set the number of discounting periods per year at 12	12, *goldkey, P/YR*
2. Enter the loan amount	110000, *PV*
3. Enter the number of months	30, *goldkey, N*
4. Enter the interest rate (calculator divides by *P/YR*)	5, *I/YR*
5. Solve for the monthly payment	*PMT* (calculator displays –590.50)
6. Enter the remaining number of months	348, *N*
7. Solve for the loan balance (*AO12*)	*PV* (calculator displays 108,377.10)
8. Enter the new interest rate	7, *I/YR*
9. Calculate the new payment	*PMT* (calculator displays –728.44)
10. Enter the number of remaining months	336, *N*
11. Solve for the loan balance (*AO24*)	*PV* (calculator displays 107,184.49)
12. Enter the new interest rate	5, *I/YR*
13. Calculate the new payment	*PMT* (calculator displays –593.35)
14. Enter the number of remaining months	324, *N*
15. Solve for the loan balance (*AO36*)	*PV* (calculator displays 105,382.65)
16. Enter the new interest rate	7, *I/YR*
17. Calculate the new payment	*PMT* (calculator displays –724.84)

ARM Example

Consider a 30-year ARM for $110,000. The interest rate is indexed to the one-year Treasury bill yield, with a margin of two percentage points. The lender offers a teaser of one percentage point for the first year. The loan requires annual rate adjustments, with an annual cap of two percentage points and a lifetime cap of five percentage points. We can use the following assumptions regarding the T-bill yield to determine the payment stream for the first four years of this loan.

Time	T-Bill Yield	Margin	Teaser	Contract Rate	Payment
At origination	4%	2%	–1%	5%	$590.50
At end of first year	5	2	0	7	728.44
At end of second year	3	2	0	5	593.35
At end of third year	6	2	0	7	724.84

For each year, calculate the monthly payment using the current loan amount, remaining years and contract interest rate. Finding the current loan amount is accomplished by finding the amount outstanding at the end of each year. Notice that the teaser rate reduces the contract rate in the first year to 5 percent and that the annual cap limits the contract rate at the end of the third year to 7 percent. The financial calculator keystrokes necessary to find the payment amounts for the first four years are outlined below.

BAII PLUS Keystrokes: ARM Payments

1. Set the number of periods per year at 12	*2nd, P/Y, 12, ENTER, 2nd, QUIT*
2. Enter the loan amount	110000, *PV*
3. Enter the number of months	30, *2nd, xP/Y, N*
4. Enter the interest rate (calculator divides by *P/Y*)	5, *I/Y*
5. Solve for the monthly payment	*CPT, PMT* (calculator displays –590.50)
6. Enter the remaining number of months	348, *N*
7. Solve for the loan balance (AO₁₂)	*CPT, PV* (calculator displays 108,377.10)
8. Enter the new interest rate	7, *I/Y*
9. Calculate the new payment	*CPT, PMT* (calculator displays –728.44)
10. Enter the number of remaining months	336, *N*
11. Solve for the loan balance (AO₂₄)	*CPT, PV* (calculator displays 107,184.49)
12. Enter the new interest rate	5, *I/Y*
13. Calculate the new payment	*CPT, PMT* (calculator displays –593.35)
14. Enter the number of remaining months	324, *N*
15. Solve for the loan balance (AO₃₆)	*CPT, PV* (calculator displays 105,382.65)
16. Enter the new interest rate	7, *I/Y*
17. Calculate the new payment	*CPT, PMT* (calculator displays –724.84)

Chapter Review

1. All financial decisions can be thought of as comparisons of the expected benefits from particular courses of action and the costs of pursuing them. In addition to the purchase price, however, prudent investors consider the costs of an investment resulting from uncertainty about those future benefits and the forgone use of the investment capital over time (risk and the time value of money).

2. Because most people are risk averse rather than risk seeking, a positive relationship between risk and return exists. The greater the risk of an investment, the greater the investor's required rate of return.

3. The six time value of money formulas are useful tools for evaluating financial choices whose risky cash flows are distributed over time. These formulas allow calculation of the present value of a lump sum, the future value of a lump sum, the present value of an annuity, the future value of an annuity, sinking fund payments and mortgage payments.

4. By definition, net present value is the present value of cash inflows minus the present value of cash outflows. If the net present value of an investment opportunity is negative, the investment is not worth its cost and should therefore be rejected by the investor.

5. The internal rate of return is defined as that discount rate that sets net present value equal to zero. This is the actual return provided by an investment opportunity. If the IRR is less than the investor's required rate of return, the investor should reject the investment.

6. In contrast to interest-only loans, amortizing loans require periodic payments of both principal and interest. The balance outstanding on a loan decreases gradually through amortization of the principal.

7. The amount outstanding on an amortizing loan at any regular payment date can be determined by finding the present value of the remaining payments. This rule is useful when an investor is faced with prepayment and refinancing decisions.

8. The effective interest rate on a loan can be much higher than the stated contract rate, especially if the lender charges discount points or origination fees. One discount point means that the borrower must pay 1 percent of the loan amount at the time of origination. The internal rate of return provides a measure of the effective interest rate for loans that charge discount points or origination fees.

9. Alternatives to the fixed-rate mortgage include the two-step mortgage and the adjustable-rate mortgage. In both of these types of loans, the

interest rate adjusts, which causes an adjustment in the payment amount. The borrower accepts some of the risk of future interest rate changes in exchange for a lower initial interest rate.

―――――――――――――――――――――   **Key Terms**   ―――――――――――――――――――――

adjustable-rate mortgage a loan whose interest rate is periodically adjusted based on the current interest rate environment.

amortization schedule a table showing the breakdown of principal and interest paid over the life of a mortgage.

amortizing loan a loan whose balance is gradually retired by periodic payments.

annuity a series of equal amounts, received one at the end of each period, for a specified number of periods.

balloon payment a lump sum payment due on a specified date in the future.

business risk uncertainty arising from changing economic conditions that affect an investment's ability to generate returns.

compounding the process of converting present amounts into future amounts.

compound interest interest earned on a principal amount plus any interest previously earned.

discounting the process of converting future amounts into present amounts.

discount point 1 percent of the loan amount.

effective interest rate the actual cost of borrowed funds expressed as an interest rate.

financial risk uncertainty associated with the possibility of defaulting on borrowed funds used to finance an investment.

fixed-rate mortgage a loan with a fixed interest rate over the loan term.

future value of a lump sum

$$FV = PV\,(1 + i)^{n}$$

future value of an annuity

$$FVA \;=\; A\left[\frac{(1 + i)^{n} - 1}{i}\right]$$

interest-only loan a nonamortizing loan that requires periodic payments of interest and a single balloon payment of the principal at the end of the loan term.

internal rate of return the discount rate that sets net present value exactly equal to zero.

IRR decision rule   if the internal rate of return is greater than or equal to the required rate of return, accept the investment.

liquidity risk   possibility of loss resulting from not being able to convert an asset into cash quickly should the need arise.

mortgage payment

$$PMT = PVA \left[\frac{i}{1 - \frac{1}{(1 = i)^n}} \right]$$

net present value   present value of inflows minus present value of outflows.

NPV decision rule   if the net present value is greater than or equal to zero, accept the investment.

origination fees   fees charged by lenders in the loan origination process.

prepayment   early repayment of principal.

present value of a lump sum

$$PV \; = \; FV \left[\frac{1}{(1 + i)^n} \right]$$

present value of an annuity

$$PVA \; = \; A \left[\frac{1 - \frac{1}{(1 + i)^n}}{i} \right]$$

purchasing power risk   uncertainty associated with the possibility that the amount of goods and services that can be acquired with a given amount of money will decline.

refinancing   the process of obtaining a new loan and using the proceeds to repay an existing loan.

risk   uncertainty about the actual rate of return an investment will provide over the holding period.

sinking fund payment

$$SFP \; = \; FVA \left[\frac{i}{(1 + i)^n - 1} \right]$$

time value of money   a dollar in hand is worth more than a dollar to be received in the future because it can either be consumed immediately or put to work to earn a return.

two-step mortgage   a loan whose interest rate is adjusted once during the term of the loan.

Study Exercises

1. Define the following concepts: risk, business risk, financial risk, purchasing power risk, liquidity risk.

2. Describe the risk/return relationship.

3. What is the time value of money principle?

4. Joe Saver deposits $1,000 in the Granite City Savings and Loan. To what value will his money accumulate in five years if the account pays 5 percent interest compounded annually? (future value of a lump sum)

5. How much should Joe Saver be willing to pay today for an investment that is expected to pay $1,000 ten years in the future if he requires a 10 percent rate of return? (present value of a lump sum)

6. Define the following: compound interest, compounding, discounting.

7. Joe Saver is offered the opportunity to receive $1,000 each year for ten years. How much would he be willing to pay for this future income stream if he desires a 10 percent return? (present value of an annuity)

8. Joe Saver expects to receive $1,000 each year for the next ten years beginning one year from today. If he deposits each payment into an account earning 8 percent interest annually, what will the balance of the account be when the last payment is deposited? (future value of an annuity)

9. Joe Saver hopes to accumulate $20,000 with ten annual deposits into a savings account earning 6 percent interest annually. What amount must Joe deposit each year to achieve his objective? (sinking fund payment)

10. Harold and Helen purchase a $150,000 house using a down payment of $15,000 and a fixed-rate mortgage for $135,000. The annual interest rate on the loan is 10 percent, and the term is 30 years. What monthly payment is necessary to amortize this loan?

11. Define the following: net present value, internal rate of return, NPV decision rule, IRR decision rule.

12. An investor considers purchasing a small retail property at a price of $82,000. The investor has established a required rate of return of 14 percent. Based on the following cash flow forecast, what is the NPV of this investment opportunity? Cash flows: year one, $10,000; year two, $12,000; year three, $11,000; year four, $14,000; year 5, $95,000. Should the investor purchase this property?

13. What is the internal rate of return for the investment in question 12?

14. Define the following: interest-only loan, amortizing loan, balloon payment.

15. Construct an amortization schedule for a loan with the following characteristics: loan amount, $10,000; term, five years; interest rate, 8 percent; payments, annual.

16. Bill and Ami borrowed $120,000 at 9 percent interest using a fixed-rate mortgage with a maturity of 25 years.
    (a) What is the monthly payment necessary to amortize this loan?
    (b) If the loan required annual payments instead of monthly, what would the annual payments be?
    (c) Multiply the answer in question (a) by 12. Why does this amount not equal the answer in question (b)?

17. Ron borrows $300,000 to purchase a warehouse. The annual interest rate on the loan is 10.25 percent, and the term of the loan is 15 years.
    (a) What is the monthly payment necessary to amortize this loan?
    (b) What is the balance on the loan at the end of month 36?
    (c) How much interest will Ron pay in month 37?
    (d) How much principal will Ron pay in month 37?
    (e) How much principal will Ron pay in the fourth year of this loan (payments 37 through 48)?

18. Suppose the loan in question 17 required two discount points at the time of origination.
    (a) If Ron keeps this loan for the full term, 180 months, what is his effective interest rate?
    (b) If Ron prepays the loan at the end of month 48, what is his effective interest rate?

19. Suppose Ron refinances the loan described above at the end of month 48 at the prevailing interest rate in the market (8 percent). Rather than reducing his monthly payment, however, Ron keeps making the same monthly payment.
    (a) How many months must Ron continue to make payments on this new loan?
    (b) By how many months has Ron shortened the term of the loan with this strategy?

20. Consider a 30-year two-step mortgage for $135,000. The initial interest rate is 5.5 percent, but the loan contract calls for a rate adjustment at the end of year five. The new rate will be two percentage points more than the ten-year Treasury bond yield. The interest rate is capped at five percentage points more than the initial interest rate. If the T-bond yield is 7.5 percent at the time of the adjustment, what will the payments be for the last 25 years of this loan?

21. Consider a 30-year ARM for $135,000. The loan is indexed to the one-year T-bill yield, which is currently at 5.25 percent. The margin is two percentage points, and the teaser is 1.5 percent. The contract rate adjusts once at the end of each year, but the loan has annual and lifetime interest rate caps of two and five percentage points, respectively. Answer the following questions assuming that the actual T-bill yields for the first four years of this loan are as shown below.

Time	T-Bill Yield	Margin	Teaser	Contract Rate
At origination	5.25%	2%	–1.5%	?
At end of first year	6.50	2	0.0	?
At end of second year	7.75	2	0.0	?
At end of third year	4.25	2	0.0	?

(a) What is the monthly payment during months 1 through 12?
(b) What is the amount outstanding at the end of month 12?
(c) What is the monthly payment during months 13 through 24?
(d) What is the amount outstanding at the end of month 24?
(e) What is the monthly payment during months 25 through 36?
(f) What is the amount outstanding at the end of month 36?
(g) What is the monthly payment during months 37 through 48?

22. A prospective homebuyer can afford to make monthly loan payments of no more than $475. If the best rate she can obtain on a mortgage is 10 percent (for a 25-year term), what is the maximum amount she can borrow?

23. Congratulations! You won the sweepstakes. The sweepstakes rules entitle you to a choice of one of the following prizes. Using the concept of present value, which choice is the most valuable to you if your opportunity rate is 8 percent?

Choice A: $40,000 per year for the next 20 years
Choice B: $25,000 today plus $35,000 per year for the next 25 years
Choice C: $200,000 today plus $12,000 per year for the next 40 years

24. Nikki's mortgage requires her to pay $1,230 per month for the next 180 months. The balance on her loan is $130,000. What is the annual interest rate on Nikki's loan?

For Further Reading

Dennis, M. W., and M. S. Robertson. *Residential Mortgage Lending*, 4th ed. (Englewood Cliffs, N.J.: Prentice Hall, 1995).

Clauretie, T. M., and G. S. Sirmans. *Real Estate Finance: Theory and Practice*, 2nd ed. (Upper Saddle River, N.J.: Prentice-Hall, 1996).

CHAPTER 15

Title Examination and the Closing Process

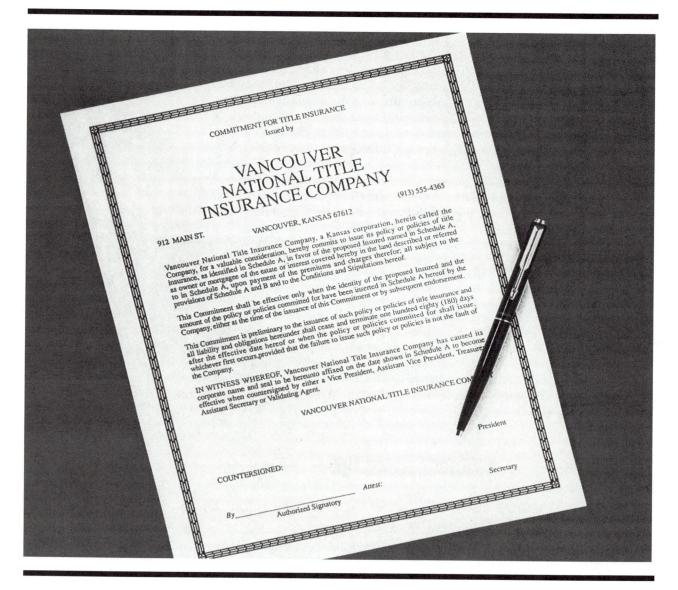

A title insurance policy protects the owner or lender against loss due to a defect in the title.

Chapter Preview

AS WE SAW in Chapter 11, the typical real estate transaction involves a sales contract between the buyer and seller that indicates the agreement to transfer the property and specifies the conditions by which that transfer will occur. The transfer of ownership will occur only when these conditions are satisfied. Before accepting ownership, the buyer must examine the title to the property to verify its validity. The objectives of this chapter are to consider the processes of (1) examining the title to the property and (2) closing, or settling, the transaction.

Under the topic of title examination, we will consider

- transfer of title;
- acquiring good title;
- title insurance; and
- the Torrens system.

Under the topic of closing, we will study

- the buyer's responsibilities;
- the seller's responsibilities;
- closing costs and the closing statement;
- events at closing; and
- escrow closing.

TITLE EXAMINATION

In the typical real estate transaction, the buyer's chief desire is to acquire **title,** or ownership, to the property involved. More specifically, the buyer wants good title from the seller. The phrase *good title* usually is used in conjunction with some combination of the words *marketable, insurable* or *perfect of record.*

Sales contracts usually require that the seller furnish good and marketable title to the buyer. A **marketable title** is one that is free and clear of all past, present or future claims that would cause a reasonable purchaser to reject such title. An **insurable title** is one that a reputable title insurance company is willing to insure. And **title perfect of record** means that the public records related to the particular title involved show no defects whatsoever. This last condition usually provides the buyer with the most protection. Suppose, for example, the seller's title reveals that years ago, a deed was signed improperly by a previous title holder. A reasonable buyer might not hesitate to accept the title, and a title insurance company might be willing to insure it, but the seller's title still is not perfect of record.

Any prospective buyer of real estate must find out all possible defects in the seller's title. This responsibility generally is satisfied by means of a lawyer's title opinion or by title insurance. A **title opinion** is a statement by a lawyer that summarizes the findings disclosed by a search through all public documents that may relate to the title. **Title insurance** is a policy that insures the title received by the grantee against any deficiencies that may have been in existence at the time title was transferred. Before a title insurance policy or title opinion can be given concerning a particular property, a search of the title must be completed.

Title Search

A **title search** reveals the ownership history, or **chain of title,** for a property. An examination of the chain of title might show that the seller has good title, or it could show that the seller is only one of several parties claiming to own the real estate being sold. The title search is made possible by the recording system provided by each state.

Recording System Each state's recording statute provides that any document affecting title to real estate must be recorded. Although recording schemes vary from state to state, the purpose of all such systems is to protect potential interest holders, including fee simple owners, tenants and mortgagees. The documents related to those interests are, of course, the deed, the lease and the mortgage. As a result of the recording requirement, anyone concerned with the validity of a real estate title can determine that validity by means of a title search.

Most states require that the recorded document be signed by the grantor. To be filed in the public record, the instrument must be witnessed and acknowledged by a notary public or another person authorized to acknowledge such documents. If this formality is not satisfied, the document cannot be recorded.

The location for the recording of real estate documents varies from state to state. State law generally creates a recorder's office in the local courthouse. The official in charge of that office may be called the clerk of the court, county clerk, recorder or registrar of deeds.

Because the public has constructive notice of all interests that are properly recorded, any buyer or lender can determine easily whether a seller or borrower has title to the real estate he or she claims. Failure to record an interest may cause the holder to lose the right to a subsequent good-faith purchaser because such a person would have no notice of unrecorded interests.

Assume, for example, that Otis had good and marketable title to a parcel of land. Assume further that Otis sold the parcel to Bill, but Bill failed to record the deed he received. Between the two, Bill has the superior title to the property. Assume, however, that Otis has wrongfully deeded the lot to George, who is unaware of Bill's interest. When George searches Otis's title, he finds no record that Otis previously sold the lot to Bill. Therefore, as far as George can ascertain, Bill has no right to the lot. Because George had no notice of Bill's interest and because George recorded his deed before Bill did, all states would say that George, as a good-faith purchaser, has title to the property.

The recording requirement is the key element that creates an efficient method of transferring title to real estate. Without public records, the confusion that existed in England centuries ago still would occur. Prospective buyers or mortgagees can gain near certainty as to their predecessors' titles because of public records. To reach any level of certainty about the validity of a real estate title, the method of conducting a title search must be understood.

Title Search   Although real estate title records are public and open to inspection by any interested person, real estate title searches normally should be conducted by attorneys or abstractors who are trained specifically in this field. A title examiner must trace a grantor's chain of title to be sure that no defects exist from previous transactions. For example, in a previous transaction of property, a spouse may not have signed the deed even though both the husband and wife jointly owned the property. This type of title defect raises the possibility that the spouse who did not sign still has a legal interest in the property. This defect should be corrected before the new buyer accepts the current grantor's deed.

The chain of title can be followed through grantor and grantee indexes. Each county in the United States maintains indexes of people (**grantors**) who have given any interests in real estate to others and people (**grantees**) who have received such interests. For a particular property, the current owner is listed in the grantee index. When ownership of the property is transferred, the previous owner's name is added to the grantor index, and the new owner's name is entered into the grantee index. The title examiner begins by tracing the property involved back through the grantee indexes to verify that the seller is in fact the current owner of record. Then the examiner searches the applicable grantor indexes to verify that the current owner has not granted any interest in the property to another person. Generally, a title search covers a period of 40 to 60 years. The Legal Highlight on page 335 demonstrates the use of the grantor and grantee indexes in title searches.

Merely examining the grantor and grantee indexes is not enough to ensure an accurate title search. The examiner also must check the tax records to discover whether any tax payments are delinquent. Furthermore, the examiner must search the local court records to determine whether any judgment has been awarded or any lien has been filed against the property. Only after these additional factors have been researched can a precise title opinion be given.

Of course, any recorded document that appears to relate to the property at issue must be checked for its legal description. Only if a tax lien or an attempted transfer by an owner concerns part or all of the property under contract does that record have to be examined.

For example, in the Legal Highlight, Charles Edwards owned the lot and house the Barrs are buying between June 17, 1965, and March 28, 1984. Edwards's name may appear several times in the grantor index for this time period. The lawyer searching the Stewarts' title must decide which, if any, grants involved the Stewarts' property. This is done by examining the legal description found in each document representing a grant by Charles Edwards. Edwards may have owned several pieces of property that are totally unrelated to the house and lot now being sold. Those grants of interest in property other than the Stewarts' land may be disregarded in the title search. The importance and types of precise legal description are discussed in Chapter 7.

In some states, a title examination is made much easier by the use of title abstracts. A **title abstract** is a written summary of the chain of title for a given piece of real estate. Generally, such abstracts are prepared by employees of abstract companies who are not licensed lawyers, but are trained specifically to search titles. When an abstract is readily available, the buyer's attorney does not have to go through the detailed search of the grantor and grantee indexes. The attorney obtains the proper abstract, studies it and issues an opinion to the buyer on the validity or defectiveness of the title. When abstracts are used widely, the attorney's fees in a real estate transaction may be much lower than they are when the attorney must perform the entire title examination.

Title Insurance

The lawyer's title-opinion letter is not the only type of protection a buyer can obtain to ensure that the seller can deliver marketable title. In many parts of the country, title insurance, which grew out of the expanded function of abstract companies or a group of lawyers, is purchased to provide protection in case the acquired title is defective. In addition to preparing abstracts or writing opinion letters, these companies or associations began to issue insurance that the title to a parcel of real estate was good and marketable.

Upon receiving a request for title insurance, the title insurance company conducts its own search of the grantor's title. The company then evaluates the validity of this title and determines the risk it must take to ensure the title's marketability. The title insurance policy includes a schedule of exceptions, which might list liens, easements or other encumbrances that appear in an examination of the public record. Often, the policy states that all restrictions of record are excluded from coverage. In addition, the policy can exclude those defects created by any party who possesses the property at the time the policy is delivered. Other risks excluded might include defects revealed by an accurate survey of the property or defects not recorded as required. The insured under a title insurance policy must be certain what defects are excepted from the policy and either have the seller-grantor clear the title of these defects or encumbrances or protect himself or herself by receiving credit from the seller for existing financial liens and paying them off thereafter. In a real estate transaction, title insurance may be purchased for the buyer-grantee or for the institution

Real Estate Today *Legal Highlight*

Grantor and Grantee Indexes

Through several of the previous chapters, we have followed a hypothetical residential real estate transaction between homesellers, the Stewarts, and homebuyers, the Barrs. The Stewarts listed their house in St. Joseph, Missouri, with Smith & Smyth Realty Company. Tom Smith, as broker, sold the house to the Barrs for $120,000. The sales contract in Figure 11.1 on page 231 was signed by all the parties, and this contract requires the transaction to be closed within 60 days after signing. The third section of that contract requires the Stewarts to furnish good and marketable title. The contract provides further that the Barrs must furnish the Stewarts with a written statement specifying any deficiencies in the title. To find out any possible title defects, the Barrs hire an attorney to examine the Stewarts' title.

By using the grantor and grantee indexes, the Barrs' attorney finds the following information. First, by looking through the grantee index, the lawyer discovers that the Stewarts bought the house now being sold on March 28, 1984, from Charles Edwards. Again via the grantee index, she finds that Edwards purchased the land on which the Stewarts' house sits on June 17, 1965, from J. William Martin. The Barrs' lawyer then discovers that Martin had owned the property since November 12, 1916, after inheriting it from his mother.

Having determined that the chain of title can be traced back more than 70 years, the Barrs' attorney must come forward with the title to make sure that each grantor had the right and power to transfer title. Beginning with the grantor index, the attorney examines it to see whether Mrs. Martin's executor deeded the land involved to anyone other than J. William Martin on November 12, 1916. The Barrs' lawyer must take similar measures to learn what Martin did with the property between November 12, 1916, and June 17, 1965. When she is satisfied that Charles Edwards received good title on June 17, 1965, she finds next that Edwards mortgaged the land to finance the construction of the house the Barrs now want to buy. A satisfaction of that mortgage—that is, a discharge of the obligation—was filed when Edwards sold the house and lot to the Stewarts in 1984. Therefore, it appears that as of the date of their purchase, the Stewarts had good, clear, marketable title. To complete the job, the Barrs' lawyer must check the grantor index under the name Stewart from March 28, 1984, to the present. Again, the land and house were mortgaged when the Stewarts bought the property. Because they have not paid off that mortgage, at the closing, the Barrs will insist that some document be recorded showing that the Stewarts have totally paid the mortgage. The satisfaction form generally is filed at the same time as the deed conveying the property from the Stewarts to the Barrs. ■

(mortgagee) financing the purchase price and taking a security interest in the real estate. In the typical transaction, the policy is paid for by the buyer, or mortgagor, as a condition of obtaining financing.

Title insurance differs from liability, life or property-hazard insurance in several important ways. First, the insured under title insurance is charged a premium only once, and it is payable when the policy is delivered. Second, a title insurance policy protects only the named insured; therefore, when the insured transfers the title that is covered, the insurance does not protect the new owner. Third, in contrast with most types of insurance (which protect against future events), title insurance protects against past events only. The schedule of exceptions normally exempts from coverage any liens, encumbrances or other defects that arise after the title is insured.

A title insurance policy may act as a substitute for the lawyer's title-opinion letter. Indeed, the practice in many states is to purchase a title policy rather than obtain a title opinion because many people feel the title policy provides more protection at a better price. Alternatively, a title policy may be purchased as supplemental protection to the lawyer's opinion, although most would consider this redundant and a waste of money.

In essence, a title insurance company provides protection to the insured to the extent that the title was free from unknown defects when the insured acquired title. Primarily, this protection covers the possibility that the recording system has failed to disclose a proper claim to the property. For example, if a previous owner received title through a forged deed, and later the true owner appears, the title insurance company would be obligated to defend the insured's title in court, reach a monetary settlement with the lawful owner or make good the insured's loss. In such a situation, title insurance can provide very valuable protection.

Mortgage companies usually require a title insurance policy before they will loan money to purchase property. Although the buyer normally must pay for this policy as part of the costs of obtaining the loan, the policy protects only the lender. If the property owner also wants title insurance to protect his or her interest, the owner must purchase a separate policy. In any case, the buyer can file suit against the seller for breach of warranty if the title turns out to be defective. The seller, however, may be insolvent and unable to pay any judgment the buyer might obtain. Legal action also involves attorney's and other expenses, as well as considerable time and inconvenience.

If a lawyer for a title abstract company has given an opinion on a title that later turns out to be defective, and the defect was overlooked because of the negligence of the abstractor or the attorney, the title holder has a cause of action against the negligent party. Here again, however, recovering from a title insurance company normally is much cheaper and less time consuming than having to pursue a lawsuit for negligence.

The Torrens System

The **Torrens system** of land registration provides the landowner with a title certificate similar to that used to show title to a car. To obtain the Torrens certificate of title, the purported owner must be willing to go through a legal registration proceeding. After reviewing all potential interests in the land, the judge issues a decree naming the true owner of the land and any valid claims, such as mortgages, easements or other restrictions, against the land. The judge's decree is entered on the court's records, an original certificate of title is recorded and a duplicate certificate is given to the landowner. To transfer title under the Torrens system, the old certificate of title must be returned to the original registrar, who then issues a new certificate to the new owner.

Although the Torrens system simplifies the real estate transfer process, it is permitted as an optional method of land transfer in only eleven states (Colorado, Georgia, Hawaii, Massachusetts, Minnesota, New York, North Carolina, Ohio, Oregon, Virginia and Washington), and even in those areas, it has been applied on a very limited basis.

Real Estate Today *Legal Highlight*

The Case of the Disappearing Island

The power of "Old Man River" can result in some confusing land titles. Consider the case of Stack Island, a six-mile-long finger of land separated by a levee and a narrow channel of the Mississippi River from downtown Lake Providence, Louisiana, about 50 miles north of Vicksburg, Mississippi. Who owns Stack Island? Does it still exist? If so, what state is it in? This is a bizarre tale of accretions, thalwegs and riparian rights. Much of Stack Island is submerged for part of the year, but the river channel between the island and the Louisiana shore is dry during other seasons. The island is uninhabitable and has value only for growing timber and for selling hunting leases. In 1881, the island was separated from the Mississippi shoreline by a 100-foot-wide to 200-foot-wide channel. Although narrow, this channel was the main navigable thread, or thalweg. (We bet that's a new word for you, and probably one you will never hear again.) Because the thalweg of the river fixes the boundary between the two states, this would seem to place the island in Louisiana. However, when dikes were constructed in 1882, a sudden shift of the main channel, or avulsive change, occurred to the west side of the island. About 1912, the thalweg shifted again to the east side. Where was the state line? Was Stack Island in Mississippi or Louisiana? All this was further complicated by the island's gradual erosion; it migrated downstream and across the river.

The Houston family gained title to Stack Island in 1938 "with all the accretions or additions thereto." By the 1950s, the island was located almost entirely in a new location, and a dispute arose over whether it was still the Houstons' property or whether the accretions belonged to the landowner on the Louisiana side, whose deed also included "all accretions adjoining or in any way connected with the above described land . . . and any islands located between the above described lands and the Louisiana–Mississippi state line." This issue of ownership was finally settled in 1981 when the courts ruled that the Houstons had gained title by virtue of adverse possession because for many years, they had sold grazing leases, planted tree seedlings and hunted on the property.

When the Houstons later attempted to clear up the title so they could sell the land, Louisiana officials jumped into the fray, contending that Stack Island was really located in their state, not in Mississippi. They argued that the original Stack Island had disappeared and that what is now called Stack Island is just sediment from upriver. This sediment, the state of Louisiana maintained, belonged to the riparian owners, or those who own the land on the Louisiana side of the river.

The central issue in this dispute was the historical location of the thalweg. The Federal Circuit Court of Appeals ruled that the 1881 location east of the island established the boundary, placing Stack Island in Louisiana. Even though the thalweg shifted to the west side between 1882 and 1912, the court held that the avulsive change did not alter the legal boundary. The U.S. Supreme Court eventually upheld the lower court's ruling.

Yes, the power of the mighty Mississippi River can certainly create some interesting legal property title questions. ∎

Source:

Houston v. United States Gypsum Company, 652 F.2d 467 (1981); *Houston v. Thomas,* 937 F.2d 247 (1991); *Lousiana v. Mississippi,* 116 S. Ct. 290 (1995).

There are three main reasons for this. First, the high initial cost of the proceeding discourages owners from having their land registered. Second, if a certificate is lost or stolen, the title must be registered by legal process again. Third, and perhaps most important, lawyers, abstractors and title insurance companies have fought against the use of the Torrens system because land transfers under this system would eliminate or greatly diminish the need for their services.

TITLE CLOSINGS

When all the conditions of the sales contract have been met, the last step in the transaction process is to close, or settle, the transaction. In fact, a real estate transaction may involve several types of closings. The borrower and the lending institution must close the loan; the escrow agent, if one is employed, must close the escrow arrangement; and the grantor and grantee must close or transfer the title to the property involved. Generally, but not always, the various closings occur at the same meeting. Therefore, the phrase *closing of the transaction* can include the conclusions to several different relationships. Remember that the ultimate purpose of the real estate sales process is to transfer title from the seller to the buyer. To look at closing properly, we must first examine each party's prior responsibilities.

Buyer's Responsibilities

Once the right house is located and a sales contract is signed, the real estate transaction begins. Indeed, during the time period (usually 60 days) between the signing of a contract and the closing of the transaction, the buyer takes on many new responsibilities, including

- obtaining financing;
- obtaining an opinion on the title's validity;
- having the property surveyed;
- purchasing property insurance; and
- inspecting the property's utilities and appliances.

Financing the Purchase   A house is the largest financial investment the average American family makes. Very few families are able to pay cash for a home; indeed, even those who have such large amounts of cash are encouraged to borrow money because the interest paid on a loan is deductible from income taxes, and the money otherwise spent on a house is available for other forms of investment. Typically, buyers of residential real estate finance 70, 80, 90 or even 95 percent of the total purchase price. Buyers' reliance on borrowed money requires that they insist on a contractual clause similar to that in section II(e) of Figure 11.1. Then, if a buyer is unable to secure the specified financing, he or she may cancel the sales contract and have all earnest money refunded.

Under a clause conditioning a sale on the buyer's ability to obtain adequate financing, the buyer must use good faith and honesty in all attempts to borrow the required amount. The buyer must apply for the loan within a short time after the contract is signed. He or she cannot delay such an attempt until there is not enough time for the lending institution to approve the loan before the closing date. If the buyer's failure to secure adequate financing is a result of the buyer's lack of good faith, the seller can sue for damages as a consequence of the buyer's inability to close the transaction. If the money market is exceedingly tight, however, or if the bank is unwilling to risk the loan because it doubts the buyer's ability to pay, or if the loan is not approved for some reason over which the borrower has no direct control, the buyer is relieved of the contractual obligation.

Failure to include in the sales contract the clause conditioning the sale on the buyer's ability to obtain financing can cause great hardship to the buyer. In that case, failure to secure adequate financing does not relieve the buyer of his or her contractual duties; therefore, the buyer who cannot pay the purchase price at closing has breached the contract and is liable for the seller's damages.

Obtaining a Title Opinion   Another principal responsibility of the buyer before closing is to get a title opinion. Even though a seller may agree to pass title by general warranty deed, the buyer must check on the state of the seller's title for at least two important reasons. First, the seller's deed usually promises that there are no encumbrances other than restrictions of record. It then becomes the buyer's responsibility to learn of any restrictions of record. Second, the sales contract normally requires the buyer to inform the seller of any defects found in the seller's title and give the seller the opportunity to correct them. (See Figure 11.1, section III.) As discussed above, title defects are discovered through a title examination.

Having the Property Surveyed   An actual survey of the property's boundaries is not always required before title can be transferred, particularly in subdivisions that have been platted. The plat in the public records normally suffices in lieu of a survey. If some confusion exists as to the actual property lines, however, or if the lending institution requires that a survey be made, the buyer usually must pay for it. Of course, the sales contract can provide that the seller must bear the cost of any survey.

Obtaining Property Insurance   Again, because of the magnitude of real estate costs, most people cannot bear the risk of losing a property's value as a result of fire, vandalism or other potential hazards. When a buyer borrows money to purchase real estate, the lender requires the buyer to purchase property insurance. Indeed, the lending institution will refuse to close the loan unless the borrower has given proof that the property is insured for at least the amount of the loan.

Such proof typically is provided by a letter from the insurance company to the bank or savings and loan association, a document often referred to as an **insurance binder.** Property insurance is indirectly vital to the title closing because the property insurance must be obtained before the loan can be completed, and the loan is crucial to the overall performance of the sales contract. Property insurance is the subject of Chapter 12 .

Inspecting the Property   Except in the most unusual circumstances, a buyer will have visited the real estate once or twice, or many times, before the sales contract is signed. Despite numerous visits to view the property, the prospective buyer seldom investigates thoroughly the home's plumbing, wiring or heating system. At times, buyers feel great pressure to sign a sales contract so that they will not lose the opportunity to buy a particular home they have set their hearts on. The major utilities and appliances, if included, often remain uninspected as well.

The high cost associated with the plumbing, wiring, heating and air-conditioning unit, stove, oven, dishwasher and other appliances makes it extremely important that these items be in good working order. If they are not working properly, the buyer should know so that the offer to purchase can be adjusted accordingly.

Assume that Frank and Elizabeth Barr believed that all of the major appliances and utilities were in good shape when they agreed to buy the Stewarts' house. How are the Barrs protected in regard to these items? One source of protection is section VII of their sales contract. (See Figure 11.1.) There, the seller guarantees that all utilities and appliances will be working normally on the closing date. Although this clause provides some assurances to the Barrs, it is inadequate by itself. If the heating system works when the Barrs move in but quits two weeks later, must the Stewarts fix it? No. The Stewarts promised only that the system would be working at the time of closing, and it was. In the absence of any fraud, the Stewarts are relieved of any further obligation in regard to the heating unit or other utilities and appliances.

The Barrs, like all other buyers, should inspect the premises during the time period before the closing. The seller must cooperate in allowing access to the buyer for this purpose. Although it does cost money to have someone knowledgeable inspect the major items of concern, the expense is far smaller than that of replacing the heating unit two weeks after the transaction is closed. If something is found to be wrong with any of the utilities or appliances, the seller is responsible for repairing the problem before the closing. Depending on the importance of the problem, failure of the seller to make the required repairs either relieves the buyer of his or her contractual obligations or constitutes a breach of the seller's promise concerning the utilities and appliances.

Other Responsibilities   A buyer who purchases land for commercial purposes should investigate the zoning restrictions on the parcel involved. A sales contract for commercial land should contain a provision permitting the buyer to cancel the contract if the zoning regulations do not permit the intended use or cannot be changed to permit it by the stipulated closing date. A buyer of rental property should study the current lease's terms and conditions, as well as the schedule of rental payments. Of course, because the parties are the masters of their contracts, a sales agreement may include other duties owed by the buyer before the closing of the transaction.

Seller's Responsibilities

A seller's work, like a buyer's, really begins when a sales contract is signed. Before actually going to the closing, a seller must

- prepare the required deed;
- remove all encumbrances;

- prepare papers with respect to the seller's loan; and
- obtain a termite and pest-inspection bond.

Preparing the Deed   Earlier in this book (see Chapter 7), we discussed the various types of deeds that can be used to transfer title. The sales contract always should specify the kind of deed to be delivered by the seller.

As we have noted, the normal sales transaction involves a warranty deed of a general nature. For example, section III of Figure 11.1 provides that the Stewarts are required to furnish a general warranty deed to the Barrs at closing. Such a deed, which would be similar to the one shown in Figure 7.1, must be drafted by a lawyer in most states.

Removing Encumbrances   Assuming that a seller is required to present a general warranty deed, he or she will covenant that the real estate is free of encumbrances other than those specified in the deed. Encumbrances that the seller may have to remove include unrecorded claims of ownership, easements, covenants and liens. One of the most frequently filed liens is the tax lien, resulting from the owner's failure to pay state, county and city property taxes. Therefore, before the closing, a seller must have paid all taxes due on the property.

Paying the Seller's Loan   Loans for the purchase of residential property usually are to be paid back over a period of 20 to 30 years. Because of the longevity of such loans, most owners do not complete their house payments before they sell the properties. Therefore, a major encumbrance on the real estate being purchased is the seller's mortgage. From the title search described earlier, we saw that the Stewarts bought the house they now sell on March 28, 1984. If their loan was for the usual 25 or 30 years, the Stewarts probably have not yet paid it off.

One of two things can happen with respect to the seller's loan at closing: it will be satisfied out of the sale's proceeds or it will be assumed by the buyer. Whichever event occurs, the seller must have the proper papers ready at the closing. With the aid of the seller's lender and lawyer, either a certificate of satisfaction or the loan-assumption papers must be prepared. For the purposes of our example, the Barrs are not assuming the Stewarts' loan; thus, a certificate stating that the Stewarts' loan and mortgage are satisfied is needed at the closing.

Obtaining a Termite Bond   In the areas of the United States where termite or other pest infestation can cause substantial damage to a house, the buyer will want assurance that the property being purchased is without such infestation. Generally, the sales contract should require the seller to furnish a certificate from a bonded pest control company stating that the property is free from any wood-destroying organisms. (See Figure 11.1, section VI.) Before the closing, the seller must obtain such a certificate. In addition, the seller sometimes assigns to the buyer his or her rights and duties under a service-maintenance contract with a pest control company.

Other Responsibilities   If the property being sold is commercial, the seller may have contractual duties to assist the buyer in changing the zoning restrictions. On closing a transaction involving rental property, the seller must turn over all valid leases to the buyer. In addition, the rent schedules and copies of letters to all tenants informing them of the change of ownership must be provided.

Once again, a sales contract can place special duties on both the buyer and seller, and generally, these contractual obligations must be performed before the transaction is closed. Failure to do so may void the contract, as the buyer in the Legal Highlight on page 343 discovered.

Costs at Closing

A prospective purchaser of real estate may save up money for the down payment only to learn that he or she needs more cash to cover the **closing costs.** The elements of closing costs vary from time to time and from location to location, but generally, the buyer must pay for the following items in cash:

- Loan origination fee
- Loan discounts, or points
- Appraisal fee
- Credit report fee
- Lender's inspection fee
- Mortgage insurance premium
- Fee of the buyer's attorney and of the attorney representing the mortgagee
- Hazard-insurance premium
- Recording fees for the deed the buyer receives and the mortgage he or she gives

The loan origination fee, the points and the mortgage-guarantee insurance premium usually are based on percentages of the loan. For example, the loan origination fee—the fee charged by the bank to process the loan—may be 1 to 3 percent of the amount of the loan. Points are an extra charge made by the bank; each point is 1 percent of the amount of the loan. (Points are discussed in Chapter 14.) The typical mortgage insurance premium is 2 percent of the amount of the loan, of which .5 percent is due at the closing. The other 1.5 percent is paid over a ten-year period. These types of closing costs generally total 2 to 6 percent of the money borrowed.

For example, we have assumed the Barrs are borrowing $108,000. In addition to the $12,000 down payment, their closing costs may amount to $5,000. Therefore, rather than needing only $12,000, the Barrs may need $17,000 or more in cash.

The seller also has to pay closing costs, which may include the

- real estate brokerage commission;
- attorney's fees for preparing the deed or other documents;
- tax transfer stamps (a tax charged on the equity the seller receives), where required; and
- recording fees for the certificate of satisfaction of the seller's mortgage.

A seller, however, generally does not have to worry about coming up with the cash to pay for these items. Such costs simply are subtracted from the proceeds of the sale. We will examine the breakdown of the buyer's and seller's closing costs in detail in Figure 15.1.

Proration of Homeowner's Costs   Certain homeowner's costs must be prorated or shared by the buyer and seller. Such costs normally include state and

Real Estate Today
Legal Highlight

Necessity to Meet Concurrent Conditions by Date of Closing

As illustrated in our example of the sale of the Stewarts' house to the Barrs, a real estate sales contract usually creates conditions that both parties must fulfill by the closing date. These are called **concurrent conditions.** Failure to do so can void the contract, as one purchaser found to his sorrow.

On November 24, 85-year-old Lily Canham agreed to sell a 56-acre parcel of land in San Luis Obispo County, California, to real estate broker Jeffrey Pittman for $250,000. The contract called for an initial deposit of $1,000 and a further deposit of $24,000 before closing. The balance of the purchase price was to be paid by a note secured by a deed of trust on the property. The closing of escrow was to be within 30 days, and the contract provided that "time is of the essence."

About the second week of December, Canham sent a signed copy of the deed to the escrow agent, which—he pointed out—had not been notarized. When broker Pittman contacted Canham, she told him she would have the deed notarized at an escrow agent near her home. By the closing date of December 24, Canham still had not sent the signed deed to the escrow agent, nor had Pittman tendered the $24,000, promissory note or deed of trust. There the matter rested

until the following May, when Canham told Pittman she had entered into a contract with other purchasers to buy her property for $600,000. Pittman wrote her a letter demanding she sell the property to him as agreed in the earlier contract, but she refused and sold it to the other buyers. Pittman sued for breach of contract. He lost.

Under the contract, Canham was supposed to tender a signed and notarized deed by the closing date of December 24; Pittman was supposed to tender a $24,000 deposit, note and deed of trust. The court ruled that neither party had fulfilled the concurrent conditions called for in the contract by the closing date, resulting in a discharge of both parties' duties to perform.

We appreciate the reluctance of a buyer to act first by placing money into escrow. But in a contract with concurrent conditions, the buyer and seller cannot keep saying to one another, "NO, you first." Ultimately, in such a case the buyer seeking enforcement comes in second; he loses. ■

Source:
Pittman v. Canham, 3 Cal. Rptr. 2d 340 (1992).

---

local taxes, the hazard-insurance premium if that insurance policy is to be assigned to the buyer, and the monthly mortgage payment, should the buyer assume the seller's loan.

The costs of any other contracts that exist during the seller's and buyer's ownerships should be prorated. For example, the cost of a pest extermination contract purchased by the seller and not canceled by the buyer must be shared. Whether this proration appears as a credit to the seller or to the buyer depends on which party pays the amount owed. Also, if the home is heated by oil, the buyer must pay the seller for the oil remaining in the storage tank, usually at the current price per gallon. In commercial sales, the collection or payment of rents also must be prorated equitably.

Figure 15.1	Uniform Settlement Statement

A. **Settlement Statement**

U.S. Department of Housing
and Urban Development

OMB No. 2502-0265

B. Type of Loan						
1. ☐ FHA　2. ☐ FmHA　3. ☒ Conv. Unins.　4. ☐ VA　5. ☐ Conv. Ins.		6. File Number	7. Loan Number	8. Mortgage Insurance Case Number		

C. **Note:** This form is furnished to give you a statement of actual settlement costs. Amounts paid to and by the settlement agent are shown. Items marked "(p.o.c.)" were paid outside the closing; they are shown here for information purposes and are not included in the totals.

D. Name and Address of Borrower	E. Name and Address of Seller	F. Name and Address of Lender
Frank L. and Elizabeth M. Barr 1097 Timbers Crossing St. Joseph, MD	Harold J. and Gladys A. Stewart 7451 6 Court St. Joseph, MD	Barber Savings Association 5050 Avenue M St. Joseph, MD

G. Property Location	H. Settlement Agent	
1097 Timbers Crossing St. Joseph, MD	Ana Farrell	
	Place of Settlement	I. Settlement Date
	Barber Savings Association	2/5/96

J. SUMMARY OF BORROWER'S TRANSACTION:		K. SUMMARY OF SELLER'S TRANSACTION:	
100. **GROSS AMOUNT DUE FROM BORROWER**		400. **GROSS AMOUNT DUE TO SELLER:**	
101. Contract sales price	120,000.00	401. Contract sales price	120,000.00
102. Personal property		402. Personal property	
103. Settlement charges to borrower (line 1400)	4,924.30	403.	
104.		404.	
105.		405.	
Adjustments for items paid by seller in advance		**Adjustments for items paid by seller in advance**	
106. City/town taxes to		406. City/town taxes to	
107. County taxes to		407. County taxes to	
108. Assessments to		408. Assessments to	
109. Pest Control Contract		409. Pest Control Contract	
110. 2/5/96 to 12/31/96	238.33	410. 2/5/96 to 12/31/96	238.33
111.		411.	
112.		412.	
120. **GROSS AMOUNT DUE FROM BORROWER**	125,162.63	420. **GROSS AMOUNT DUE TO SELLER**	120,238.33
200. **AMOUNTS PAID BY OR IN BEHALF OF BORROWER**		500. **REDUCTIONS IN AMOUNT DUE TO SELLER**	
201. Deposit or earnest money	4,000.00	501. Excess Deposit (see instructions)	
202. Principal amount of new loan(s)		502. Settlement charges to seller (line 1400)	9,194.50
203. Existing loan(s) taken subject to	108,000.00	503. Existing loan(s) taken subject to	
204.		504. Payoff of first mortgage loan	71,245.00
		Spider Savings	
205.		505. Payoff of second mortgage loan	
206.		506.	
207.		507.	
208.		508.	
209.		509.	
Adjustments for items unpaid by seller		**Adjustments for items unpaid by seller**	
210. City/town taxes 1/1/96 to 2/5/96	25.20	510. City/town taxes 1/1/96 to 2/5/96	25.20
211. County taxes 1/1/96 to 2/5/96	47.40	511. County taxes 1/1/96 to 2/5/96	47.40
212. Assessments to		512. Assessments to	
213.		513.	
214.		514.	
215.		515.	
216.		516.	
217.		517.	
218.		518.	
219.		519.	
220. **TOTAL PAID BY/FOR BORROWER**	112,072.60	520. **TOTAL REDUCTION AMOUNT DUE SELLER**	80,512.10
300. **CASH AT SETTLEMENT FOR OR TO BORROWER**		600. **CASH AT SETTLEMENT TO OR FROM SELLER**	
301. Gross amount due from borrower (line 120)	125,162.63	601. Gross amount due to seller (line 420)	120,238.33
302. Less amounts paid by/for borrower (line 220)	112,072.60	602. Less reduction amount due seller (line 520)	80,512.10
303. CASH to BORROWER	13,090.03	603. CASH to SELLER	39,726.23

Uniform Settlement Statement *(Continued)*

Figure 15.1

U.S DEPARTMENT OF HOUSING AND URBAN DEVELOPMENT
SETTLEMENT STATEMENT
PAGE 2

L. SETTLEMENT CHARGES:	PAID FROM BORROWER'S FUNDS AT SETTLEMENT	PAID FROM SELLER'S FUNDS AT SETTLEMENT
700. TOTAL SALES/BROKER'S COMMISSION based on price $ 120,000 @ 7% = $8,400.00		
Division of commission (line 700) as follows:		
701. $8,400 to Smith and Smyth Realty Company		
702. $ to		
703. Commission paid at Settlement		8,400.00
704.		
800. ITEMS PAYABLE IN CONNECTION WITH LOAN		
801. Loan Origination Fee 1 % Barber Savings Association	1,080.00	
802. Loan Discount %		
803. Appraisal Fee to Michele Tipton	250.00	
804. Credit Report to Barber Savings Association	50.00	
805. Lender's Inspection Fee to		
806. Mortgage Insurance Application Fee to		
807. Assumption Fee to		
808.		
809.		
810.		
811.		
900. ITEMS REQUIRED BY LENDER TO BE PAID IN ADVANCE		
901. Interest from to @$ /day		
902. Mortgage Insurance Premium for 1 Year to MGIC	1,188.00	
903. Hazard Insurance Premium for 1 yrs. to P&C Insurance (408.00 paid by		
904. buyer)		
905.		
1000. RESERVES DEPOSITED WITH LENDER FOR		
1001. Hazard Insurance 2 mo. @ $ 34.00 /mo.	68.00	
1002. Mortgage insurance 2 mo. @ $ 42.25 /mo.	84.50	
1003. City property taxes 10 mo. @ $ 25.20 /mo.	252.00	
1004. County property taxes 6 mo. @ $ 47.40 /mo.	284.40	
1005. Annual assessments mo. @ $ /mo.		
1006. mo. @ $ /mo.		
1007. mo. @ $ /mo.		
1008. mo. @ $ /mo.		
1100. TITLE CHARGES		
1101. Settlement or closing fee to		
1102. Abstract or title search to Land Title, Inc.	75.00	
1103. Title examination to		225.00
1104. Title insurance binder to		
1105. Document preparation to Land Title, Inc.	175.00	110.00
1106. Notary fees to		
1107. Attorney's fees to		
(includes above items No:)		
1108. Title insurance to Land Title, Inc.	900.00	
(includes above items No:)		
1109. Lender's coverage $ 350.00		
1110. Owner's coverage $ 550.00		
1111.		
1112.		
1113.		
1200. GOVERNMENT RECORDING AND TRANSFER CHARGES		
1201. Recording fees: Deed $ 15 ; Mortgage $ 15 ; Releases $ 12.00	30.00	12.00
1202. City/county tax/stamps: Deed $; Mortgage $		
1203. State tax/stamps: Deed $ 447.50 ; Mortgage $ 212.40	212.40	447.50
1204.		
1205.		
1300. ADDITIONAL SETTLEMENT CHARGES		
1301. Survey to Stiner and Associates	275.00	
1302. Pest inspection to		
1303.		
1304.		
1305.		
1400. TOTAL SETTLEMENT CHARGES (enter on lines 103 and 502, Sections J and K)	4,924.30	9,194.50

CERTIFICATION: I have carefully reviewed the HUD-1 Settlement Statement and to the best of my knowledge and belief, it is a true and accurate statement of all receipts and disbursements made on my account or by me in this transaction. I further certify that I have received a copy of HUD-1 Settlement Statement.

_____   _____

Buyers   Sellers

To the best of my knowledge, the HUD-1 Settlement Statement which I have prepared is a true and accurate account of the funds which were received and have been or will be disbursed by the undersigned as part of the settlement of this transaction.

_____   _____

Settlement Agent   Date

WARNING: It is a crime to knowingly make false statements to the United States on this or any similar form. Penalties upon convictions can include a fine or imprisonment. For details see: Title 18: U.S. Code Section 1001 and Section 1010.

REV HUD-1 (3/86) LSS 0190-2

Understanding the Settlement Statement

In residential transactions involving mortgage loans, the Real Estate Settlement Procedures Act (RESPA) of 1974 requires that lenders fully disclose the financial details of a transaction to the buyer and seller in writing using the Uniform Settlement Statement approved by the U.S. Department of Housing and Urban Development. At the closing, the buyer and seller sign this **closing statement,** and each receives a copy. The Uniform Settlement Statement shown in Figure 15.1 is completed in accordance with the Stewart-Barr transaction.

Although the Uniform Settlement Statement appears rather complex at first glance, it simplifies and summarizes financial transactions. Page 2 is a worksheet to help determine the seller's and buyer's closing costs. A quick study of the worksheet will show that most items are self-explanatory. After page 2 is completed, the totals are transferred to the appropriate lines on page 1.

The first calculation on page 1 appears at lines 106 through 112. Here, any item the seller has paid for that the buyer also will enjoy must be prorated. The example is a pest control contract for which the Stewarts paid $260 in January 1996. Because this contract covers the entire year during which the house was sold, it is only fair that the Barrs reimburse the Stewarts for the period from February 5, 1996 (closing date), to December 31, 1996. Line 120 represents the total amount to be paid by the buyer. Similar calculations must be made on the seller's side at lines 406 through 412, resulting in the total amount due to the seller (line 420).

Next, lines 200 to 209 describe how the Barrs are paying the total owed. Lines 500 to 509 include items that are payable by the Stewarts. Certain payments that were made by the seller now must be assumed by the buyer. These items, such as property taxes, must be prorated, as they are on lines 210 through 219 and 510 through 519. For example, the Barrs will have to pay the 1996 city taxes later in the year. It is projected that these taxes will amount to $302.40. The Stewarts are liable for the portion of the taxes covering the period from January 1, 1996, to the closing date, February 5, 1996. The same procedure follows for the county taxes, which are projected to be $568.80.

At line 1003 of Figure 15.1, the Barrs are required to pay ten months of city taxes in advance. The next line, 1004, indicates that they are to pay only six months of county taxes at closing. The reason for this difference is that city taxes in St. Joseph, Missouri, are due for the calendar year on June 1 of each year. Buchanan County taxes are payable for the calendar year on October 1. In other words, the Stewarts paid the 1995 city taxes on June 1, 1995, and the county taxes on October 1, 1995. The Barrs (through their lender) must pay 1996 city and county taxes on June 1, 1996, and October 1, 1996, respectively. Because the closing date is February 5, 1996, the time between June 1 and February 5 is approximately eight months. In this case, the lender collects eight months of city taxes plus a cushion of two extra months (one-sixth of the annual amount), which equals ten months. In addition to the principal and interest payments due each month on their loan, the lender will require the Barrs to pay a portion of the anticipated property taxes into escrow each month. After the Barrs have made their monthly mortgage payments for February through May 1996, there should be enough in the escrow account to pay the 1996 city taxes with a cushion left over.

The same analysis is used to determine that only six months of county taxes can be collected as reserve deposits at the closing, while line 1001 of Figure 15.1 indicates only two months of advance payments for the hazard-insurance premiums. This is because the Barrs had to purchase the first year's policy outside of the closing costs. (See line 903.) The lender will require the Barrs to pay an additional amount into the escrow account to cover the insurance premium when it comes due.

Line 220 is the total amount paid by the buyer in lines 201 through 219. Line 520 is the total amount owed by the seller as reflected in lines 501 through 519. Finally, the amount paid by the buyer is subtracted from the amounts owed, and line 303 indicates the cash the buyer needs to close the transaction. Likewise, the amount payable by the seller is deducted from the amounts due the seller, and line 603 shows the total cash the seller will take home. In other words, Frank and Elizabeth Barr must pay $13,090.03 in cash at closing, while Harold and Gladys Stewart receive $39,726.23 free and clear from the sale.

Parties Present at the Closing

Although a closing can be handled through the mail without ever having a group meeting of interested parties, the closing of a real estate sale normally is held at the lending institution, the office of the seller's lawyer or the office of the buyer's attorney.

Present at the closing are the buyer, the seller, a representative of the lender, the lawyer who represents the buyer and the listing real estate broker. The broker often helps arrange the meeting and attends to collect a commission and to turn over any of the buyer's earnest money the broker may have held pursuant to the sales contract. Other parties who may attend include the lender's lawyer, the seller's lawyer and a title insurance company representative. These individuals are present only if they have been involved in the transaction.

For example, the seller may not have employed an attorney except to draft the deed, or the buyer may not be purchasing title insurance. Under these circumstances, neither the seller's attorney nor a title insurance company representative would be present.

In addition to the people already mentioned, the escrow agent must be present if an escrow arrangement was used. The Stewart-Barr sales contract provided that the Barrs would pay $4,000 as earnest money in escrow. The Stewarts were obligated to deliver the signed warranty deed to the escrow agent within five days of signing the contract.

To close the entire transaction, the escrow also must be terminated, and the escrow agent is needed to turn over the earnest money and the deed. Often, the escrow agent will be the same bank that lends the buyer money; therefore, the lender's representative also may represent the escrow agent.

Events at the Closing

After the parties have completed all contractual obligations, it is time for the closing. Before the title is transferred from the seller to the buyer, the buyer's loan and the escrow arrangement must be closed. This process can be somewhat confusing and bewildering to the uninitiated, with buyers and sellers caught up

Real Estate Today   *Legal Highlight*

The Closing

The person in charge of the closing normally is the lawyer for one of the parties. This lawyer makes sure everyone has met and notes those in attendance. After the introductions, the lawyer presents the loan-related papers to Frank and Elizabeth Barr for their consideration and signatures. These papers include the promissory note, which is the legal document stating that the Barrs, as borrowers, will pay back the money lent to them. In addition to the promissory note, the Barrs are presented with a loan settlement statement, the required truth-in-lending papers (if they have not already been given to the Barrs) and the mortgage instrument. The mortgage, in essence, gives the lender a security interest in, or lien on, the real estate subject to the loan's repayment. Some states use a deed of trust in lieu of a mortgage. Such a specialized deed actually transfers the buyer's newly acquired title to a third party or the lender for as long as the loan is being repaid. A final, vital document is the closing statement, copies of which are given to the sellers and the buyers.

While the Barrs read the loan papers, the lawyer in charge obtains the signed deed from the escrow agent or presents the unsigned deed to the sellers for their signatures. In this case, Harold and Gladys Stewart had previously signed the warranty deed and delivered it to the escrow agent in accordance with the sales contract. The legal documents to be signed may be lengthy; nevertheless, the parties should study and read them before signing. No one should be afraid to take extra time or to ask questions to clarify ambiguous points.

A real estate closing is an important event, and problem areas can be handled much more easily before the documents are signed than afterward. Indeed, if any of the papers is not prepared properly, the closing should not be concluded, but postponed until a later date.

Let us assume the Barrs are satisfied with the various loan papers, and they sign them. These papers are delivered to the lender's representative, and the loan is thereby closed. The Barrs then must write a check for the amount not covered by the loan. This amount includes the down payment plus closing costs. Figure 15.1 shows that the Barrs owe $13,090.03 in cash. The $4,000 earnest money is received from the escrow agent and applied to the purchase price. After the purchase price and closing costs have been paid, the signed deed is delivered to the Barrs. Actually, the deed is taken by the Barrs' attorney to the courthouse to be filed with the public records. Thereafter, the Barrs will receive the deed in the mail.

Although the delivery of the deed represents passage of title, the closing is not yet completed. The money must be distributed. The Stewarts' lender is paid the amount still due on the Stewarts' loan and mortgage. That lender then executes and delivers a certificate of satisfaction, which also is filed with public records. Next, the real estate broker receives the commission.

Whatever remains after these items are paid goes to the Stewarts. This amount is commonly called the *seller's equity and profit.* Figure 15.1 indicates that the Stewarts receive $39,726.23.

These events may take only 10 to 15 minutes in a simple residential closing, or the closing may last an hour or more in a more complex transaction. No matter how long it takes, a successful closing accomplishes its goal of completing the real estate transaction by transferring title from the seller to the buyer. ■

in what appears to be a vast paper shuffle. To help demystify this process, the events at the Stewart-Barr closing are examined in the Legal Highlight on page 348. The actual procedures and amounts of closing costs vary, however, depending on local custom and practice.

Escrow Closing

Instead of the conventional closing described above, the escrow closing is practiced in some communities in the eastern United States and in the majority of western states. Instead of the buyer and seller coming face to face, a third party called an *escrow agent* acts as an intermediary to facilitate the closing. The escrow agent is usually an attorney, a title company, a trust company, an escrow company or the escrow department of a lending institution.

The seller deposits a fully executed deed with the escrow agent, who then delivers the deed to the purchaser after receiving the purchase price. The agent then delivers the deed to the purchaser and the purchase price to the seller.

Some of the advantages of the escrow closing are (1) the seller is ensured of receiving the buyer's money before title passes because the check must clear before this occurs, (2) the buyer's money is not paid until the seller's title is acceptable and free from liens and (3) the parties need not be present. The last is particularly advantageous if one or both of the parties reside in other areas.

──────────────⟨ **Chapter Review** ⟩──────────────

1. Title to land signifies the legal right to ownership. A buyer of real estate is concerned fundamentally with acquiring good title. Good title is title that is specified as marketable, insurable, perfect of record or any combination thereof. To protect against inadvertent acceptance of a defective title, every buyer should obtain a title opinion, title insurance or both. Title opinions are written by lawyers after they have searched the applicable titles or examined the title abstracts. Title insurance provides protection in that any defect or claim to a property that is not recorded is handled by the insurance company.

2. A title search is conducted by trained personnel who examine the grantor and grantee indexes, the tax records and the judgment records to determine whether the grantor has the right and power to grant the stated interest. An abstractor searches a title and compiles all records applicable to a piece of real estate; the resulting compilation is called an *abstract*.

3. Title insurance can be beneficial in conjunction with or in lieu of a title opinion. In essence, a title policy insures the title against any defects or claims that exist as of the date title is acquired. Title insurance does not cover potential defects or claims that come into existence after the policy is issued. Although title insurance is important in some situations, it

should not be purchased automatically when a title opinion is obtained because that opinion may provide sufficient protection.

4. The Torrens system of land registration provides an alternative to the more traditional method of exchanging title to real estate by delivery of a deed. Through a legal action to register the land, the judge determines the true owner of the land and the valid claims that exist. A certificate of title is issued then, and transfer of title occurs only when the old certificate is turned in to the proper official and a new certificate is issued. This registration system has not gained wide acceptance in the United States because of the high cost of the required legal proceeding and the opposition of lawyers and abstractors.

5. The real estate transaction is closed when title to real property passes from the seller to the buyer. In essence, a closing—or *settlement,* as it is sometimes called—includes the closing of the loan, of the escrow arrangement and of the title.

6. Between the signing of the sales contract and the closing of the deal, both seller and buyer have certain responsibilities that must be completed. The buyer must obtain an opinion about the status of the title and attempt in good faith to secure the needed financing. Among other obligations, the seller must make sure that all encumbrances are removed and obtain the type of written deed the contract requires.

7. Closing costs are the charges incurred by the buyer and seller at the close of the transaction. Such costs to the buyer include the loan origination fee, loan discount points and attorney's fees. Costs to the seller may consist of the real estate brokerage commission and various recording fees. The buyer's closing costs and the down payment must be paid in cash. The seller's closing costs are deducted from the amount due to the seller.

8. At the closing, many papers are examined, signed and exchanged by the parties. A successful closing of the transaction results in the transfer of the seller's title to the buyer. Thereafter, all necessary papers should be taken to the courthouse and filed in the public record.

Key Terms

chain of title　ownership history of a specific property.

closing costs　costs associated with closing a real estate transaction.

closing statement　a worksheet showing the sources and uses of funds in a real estate transaction.

grantee　the party who receives a freehold estate in real property from a grantor.

grantor   the party who transfers a freehold estate in real property to a grantee.

insurable title   a title in real estate that a reputable title insurance company is willing to insure. An insurable title most frequently is one without major defect.

insurance binder   temporary evidence of insurance.

marketable title   a title free and clear of all past, present or future claims that would cause a reasonable purchaser to reject such title.

title   the legal right to ownership.

title abstract   a written history of a property's chain of title.

title insurance   a policy that insures the title received by the grantee against any deficiences that may have been in existence at the time title was transferred.

title opinion   an attorney's opinion of the quality of title for a specific property.

title perfect of record   a property for which there are no defects.

title search   the process of verifying the quality of title.

Torrens system   a system of land registration used by a few states as an alternative to grantor/grantee indexes.

Study Exercises

---

1. Define the following: grantor, grantee, title search, chain of title, title abstract, title opinion, title insurance.

2. Attorney James Hudson has been retained to search the title of a house owned by Bobby Newton at 1024 College Station Road. Bobby, who purchased the property in 1988, is selling the house to John and Karen Gillespie. Describe the process that Bobby would go through in searching this title.

3. Define the following: marketable title, insurable title, title perfect of record.

4. Karen's offer to purchase Scott's house was accepted on August 17, and a contract was signed by both parties on that day, with closing scheduled for October 4. It was Karen's responsibility to check the marketability of Scott's title. Karen hired an attorney, who said the title was free from all defects on September 23. Before the scheduled closing of the transaction on October 4, Karen's attorney updated his title search and found that a tax lien had been filed against the property because Scott had failed to pay last year's property taxes. Does this lien's existence make

Scott's title defective? Does Karen have the right to complain about this lien, as it did not appear in the first title search?

5. Suppose that Karen (see question 4) had employed a title insurance company to check Scott's title. If the company had delivered on September 23 a policy exempting from coverage all future liens, would Karen be protected from the tax lien filed on October 2?

6. How does the Torrens system work? Why is it not used more widely?

7. The Hoods and the Wakeleys entered into a formal contract whereby the Hoods agreed to buy the Wakeleys' partially restored 80-year-old house. During the time between the signing of the contract and the closing of the transaction, what things should the Hoods accomplish? What responsibilities do the Wakeleys have?

8. In a typical residential transaction, what closing costs must the buyer normally pay? Which are usually paid by the seller?

9. Trace the events that occur at a typical closing of a real estate sales transaction.

10. At the closing of the sale of William's house to Barlow, it was discovered that the deed had a typographical error. Broker Maynard agreed that he would deliver the corrected deed to Barlow the next day. When Maynard arrived at Barlow's house with the deed, Barlow was called to the phone. The message was that his wife had been in an accident. Maynard placed the deed on a table, and the two left. A few days later, Barlow called Maynard to report that his wife would be bedridden for several months, and they did not want the house. What arguments can Barlow use to resolve this situation? What arguments are accessible to William?

11. Assume that Maynard (see question 11) delivered the deed to Barlow at 11:55 AM. on March 12. Later in the day, it was learned that William had died at 11:10 AM. Was the sale of the house consummated?

12. Barnes's and Bradley's adjacent properties, which they bought ten years ago, were originally part of a small estate. Barnes decides to sell to Soames, but a survey shows that running the length of the lot, a three-foot strip Barnes had thought was his actually belongs to Bradley. What advice would you give to Barnes on how to clear up the title?

13. It is common for real estate agents to assume that each month has 30 days and a year has 360 days for purposes of prorating items at the time of closing. Using this 30-day convention, find the buyer and seller shares of a three-year hazard-insurance policy taken out by the sellers on February 1, 1995, for $690 when the closing date was July 1, 1996.

14. Property taxes for the 1996 year are due on October 1 and will be $1,875 for a property being sold on July 1, 1996. Using the 30-days-per-month assumption, how much should the sellers be responsible for?

15. Property taxes for a property sold on June 15, 1996, are due on October 15. If the taxes will be $987, what is the seller's responsibility for this item at closing?

16. As part of a purchase transaction, the buyers have taken out a loan for $75,000 at 10.5 percent annual interest with monthly payments of $702. The closing date is to be March 16, but the first loan payment will not be made until May 1. At the closing, how much interest must the buyers pay for the remainder of March?

PART FIVE

Real Estate Investment Analysis

CHAPTER 16

Home Purchase Decisions

The American dream of home ownership requires thoughtful planning and careful decsion making. The information presented in this book should well prepare you for your future real estate decisions.

Chapter Preview

BUYING A HOME is the most important investment decision that the average U.S. family ever makes. Too often, however, it is made with the buyer at a distinct disadvantage and without the complete information needed to make the best choice at the most favorable terms. By now, you should be far better informed about real estate transactions than the usual homebuyer because you already know the basic principles of real estate.

This chapter will cover four topics specifically related to buying a home:

- the rent or buy decision,
- how much home you can afford,
- choosing the right property and
- the negotiation, purchase and closing process.

THE RENT OR BUY DECISION

Everyone needs a place to live, and housing expense is a dominant portion of most families' budgets. A major question facing these families is the rent or buy decision.

Should you rent, or should you buy? That depends on a great number of factors, many of which are not economic. For example, many families derive great satisfaction from owning their own homes; to others, the responsibility of home ownership is a psychological burden.

To make the correct economic decision, you really need an all-seeing crystal ball that accurately reveals the future. What will happen to home prices in the future? Will they rise, making your investment in a home more valuable? How much will they rise? Or will home prices fall, making your investment an unwise decision? What will happen to income tax laws that affect the deductions you can take for mortgage interest and property taxes? If these deductions are reduced or eliminated, home ownership will be relatively less desirable than renting. How long will you live in the home? Will your work require that you move within a relatively short time, or will you remain in the home for many years? Will you and your spouse continue to live in marital bliss, or will you split, making your home just one more thing to fight over?

We could go on and on conjuring up more and more imponderables, but let's try to analyze the rent or buy decision based on some reasonable assumptions regarding the future. Suppose that Carlos and Mary Mallory, a financially successful young couple, are pondering the purchase of a home. They currently live in an apartment, which costs them $1,000 per month plus utilities, but they have found a $180,000 house they like. They can finance the home with a down payment of $36,000 and a 30-year, 7.5 percent, $144,000 mortgage. In addition to the down payment, closing costs on the loan will add $3,800 to the required investment.

Monthly payments for principal and interest on the mortgage will be $1,006.87, plus another $230 per month for property taxes and $80 for property insurance—a total of $1,316.87. The first year's interest charges will be approximately $10,755, and property taxes will total $2,760. These two items are deductible from taxable income, and for their analysis, Carlos and Mary assume a marginal federal and state tax rate of 30 percent. This means they can save $4,055 in income taxes during the coming year, or $337.88 per month, if they purchase the house. This reduces their after-tax monthly payment on the new home to $978.99, approximately the amount they currently pay in rent.

Of course, home ownership also entails additional maintenance expenses, but because the house is new, Carlos and Mary believe these will be relatively minor during the analysis period.

(The amount of income tax savings depends on many factors. With their assumed income of $79,200, the Mallorys are entitled to a standard deduction of $6,000. Until their itemized deductions exceed this amount, they gain no tax advantage. Let us assume that the Mallorys pay $4,000 in state income taxes, but they have no additional deductions other than the $2,760 in property taxes and $10,755 in mortgage interest. Under these assumptions, the tax savings would be only $3,245 annually, not $4,055, as assumed above. If they live in a state with no state income tax, the tax savings would be even less; however, if

The Mallory's Home Ownership Analysis

Table 16.1

Assumptions

1. House will cost $180,000. It will appreciate 3 percent annually over five years. House will sell for $208,669 in five years.

2. Real estate sales commission will be 6 percent of sales price.

3. House will be financed by a down payment of $36,000 and a 30-year, 7.5 percent, $144,000 mortgage. Financing costs will be $3,800.

4. Income taxes on any profit will be 30 percent.

Sales price after five years	$208,669
Sales commission	12,520
Net sales receipts	$196,149
Loan repayment	136,249
Cash to Mallorys	$ 59,900
Income taxes on profit ($16,149 × 30%)	4,845
Cash after taxes	$ 55,055

After-tax return on investment of $39,800 = 6.7% annually
After-tax return on alternative investment = 4.3% annually

they have other allowable deductions, such as charitable contributions or unreimbursed employee expenses, their income tax savings from buying the house could equal or exceed the assumed $4,055. Life is not simple!)

Their jobs may require that the Mallorys move sometime in the next several years, but they do not know when that might occur or whether it will be necessary or desirable at all. This is one of the uncertainties that make the rent or buy decision difficult. For this analysis, however, the Mallorys assume they will move after five years.

The next question is what will happen to home prices. This, of course, is a critical assumption. Carlos and Mary initially assume a 3 percent annual growth rate, but recognize that they must also analyze other possibilities.

Given these assumptions, the Mallorys arrive at the analysis summarized in Table 16.1. At a 3 percent annual rate of appreciation, the home can be sold for $208,669 in five years, or $196,149 after deducting a 6 percent real estate sales commission. From the mortgage loan repayment schedule in Table 16.2, we find that the principal of the mortgage has been reduced by only 5.4 percent, leaving a balance of $136,249.

Because they are relatively young and probably would move to a larger house, the Mallorys likely would postpone any taxes due, but for our analysis, let us assume that for some reason, they do not buy another house. In this case, they must pay income taxes on the profit, $16,149, which leaves an after-tax balance of $55,055. This represents a 6.7 percent annual return on their $39,800 investment.

| Table 16.2 | | Mortgage Loan Repayment Schedule |

Year	6%	7.5%	9%
1	1.2	.9	.7
2	2.5	1.9	1.4
3	3.9	3.0	2.2
4	5.4	4.1	3.1
5	6.9	5.4	4.1
6	8.6	6.7	5.2
7	10.4	8.2	6.4
8	12.2	9.7	7.6
9	14.2	11.4	9.0
10	16.3	13.2	10.6
15	28.9	24.6	20.7
20	46.0	41.1	36.5
25	69.0	65.1	61.2
30	100.0	100.0	100.0

After the real estate sales commission has been paid, the Mallorys receive $59,900. Here, Carlos and Mary encounter another great tax break for home-owners, the tax-free exchange. If they purchase another home of at least equal value, any tax due on the gain is postponed. Furthermore, they can buy and sell houses many times, continuing to postpone any income taxes due on the cumulative sales. When they are 55 years old, they can sell their house and elect to take the one-time exemption of $125,000 on cumulative profit on sales of their principal residences.

Alternative Investment

We must not forget that if Carlos and Mary do not buy the home, they can invest the $39,800 elsewhere. They might buy Amalgamated Whitzadiddle stock, which could be worth 100 times their initial investment. But Amalgamated Whitzadiddle might also go bankrupt, leaving their investment worthless. For simplicity, let's suppose the Mallorys invest the money very conservatively in U.S. government savings bonds, an investment that pays 6 percent annually, with income taxes on the interest not due until the bonds are cashed. This investment yields a 4.3 percent after-tax annual rate of return on the Mallorys' $39,800 investment—slightly less than the yield on the investment in the home.

Impact of Inflation or Deflation on Home Prices

Suppose, however, that Carlos and Mary purchase the home just before a period of rapid inflation, during which home prices rise 10 percent annually. Under this assumption, the Mallorys' house could be sold for $289,892 at the end of five years, yielding a profit of $92,498 after the sales commission and giving the Mallorys $108,500 in cash after they repay the loan and pay income taxes on the profit. This would yield a 22.2 percent annual return on their investment of $39,800.

In this type of inflationary situation, it would be extremely likely that the cost of renting an apartment would also rise rapidly. If the cost of renting their apartment should rise at this assumed 10 percent annual rate, the Mallorys' $1,000-per-month apartment would cost $1,600 per month in five years. On the other hand, if they buy the house and finance the purchase with a fixed-rate mortgage, the mortgage payment would not rise. This is another factor that makes home ownership more advantageous in inflationary times.

Now, let's make the pessimistic but often realistic assumption that home prices decline by 3 percent annually during the five-year analysis period. Under this grim scenario, the Mallorys could sell their house for only $154,572 in five years, leaving them with $9,049 after paying a real estate brokerage commission and repaying the mortgage. This means they would lose $30,751 of their $39,800 investment—a decidedly negative return.

Are Carlos and Mary likely to experience a 10 percent annual increase in the value of their home during the analysis period? Probably not. Are they likely to experience a 3 percent annual decline? Probably not. But these extremes set realistic parameters for their analysis.

Impact of Mortgage Interest Rates

In this evaluation of the rent or buy decision, the Mallorys have benefited from a relatively low mortgage interest rate of 7.5 percent. Suppose, however, that the best rate they can obtain is 9 percent. This would affect the analysis in two principal ways. First, of course, the Mallorys would face much higher monthly payments for principal and interest—$1,158.66 compared to $1,006.87. This would make the total monthly payment $1,468.66, or $1,062 after taxes the first year assuming they benefit from the entire mortgage interest and property tax deduction.

In addition, as indicated in Table 16.2, the mortgage payback is much slower with the higher interest rate. If we assume our initial 3 percent annual rate of appreciation in home prices, the Mallorys will receive a lower cash return because they have a larger mortgage repayment—$138,067 compared to $136,249 with the 7.5 percent mortgage. This reduces their rate of return to only 5.9 percent annually.

Period of Ownership

Generally, because of the inflation in home prices, the longer the period of ownership, the greater the relative advantage of home ownership over renting. For example, let's return to our original assumptions for the Mallorys' rent versus buy analysis, with one exception.

Let's now assume that Carlos and Mary will own the home for ten years rather than five. The results of this analysis are shown in Table 16.3. The sales price of the house would increase to $241,905, leaving the Mallorys with $88,189 in cash after paying the brokerage commission and income taxes and repaying the mortgage.

| Table 16.3 | The Mallorys' Rent versus Buy Analysis—Ten-Year Ownership Period |

Assumptions

1. House will cost $180,000. It will appreciate 3 percent annually over ten years. House will sell for $241,905 in ten years.

2. Real estate commission will be 6 percent of sales price.

3. House will be financed by a down payment of $36,000 and a 30-year, 7.5 percent, $144,000 mortgage. Financing costs will be $3,800.

4. Income taxes on any profit will be 30 percent.

Sales price after ten years	$241,905
Sales commission	14,514
Net sales receipts	$227,391
Loan repayment	124,985
Cash to Mallorys	$102,406
Income taxes on profit ($47,391 × 30%)	14,217
Cash after taxes	$ 88,189
After-tax return on investment of $39,800 in home = 8.3% annually	
After-tax return on alternative investment = 4.3% annually	

This represents an 8.3 percent after-tax annual rate of return on their original $39,800 investment. We might also note that if apartment rents increase at the same 3 percent annual rate, in ten years, the Mallorys will pay more than $1,345 a month if they stay in their apartment.

Some Conclusions

After all this, should Carlos and Mary rent, or should they buy? That depends on what assumptions they make regarding these future imponderables. However, at least we now know the parameters for the decision. Given the history of the past several decades, homeowners have done well compared to renters because their homes have served as hedges against inflation. Although it appears that rates of inflation will be lower in future years, don't count on it.

And what will happen to present income tax breaks enjoyed by homeowners? Will proponents of a flat tax remove the deductions for mortgage interest and property taxes? Will homeowners be forced to pay taxes immediately on any profits from selling their homes, rather than being allowed to make tax-free exchanges? Will the tax forgiveness on up to $125,000 in accumulated profit on the sales of principal residences for those older than 55 years of age be done away with? We don't know, although these tax breaks have broad support.

Of course, the Mallorys' decision may well rest on noneconomic factors. Perhaps the intangibles of owning a home are very important to the Mallorys.

Table 16.4	The Mallorys' Estimated Monthly Income

Salary (gross)	$6,200
Self-employment income	500
Dividends	300
Interest on $20,000	100
Total	$7,100

Perhaps they love to garden and will enjoy working on their home. If so, they may want to buy even if they feel the investment probably will not be economically profitable. Or perhaps they hate yard work and all forms of home maintenance. They might want to be able to simply call the landlord when the heating system conks out, rather than having to deal with it themselves. If so, they may even be willing to pay a premium to live in a rental unit.

HOW MUCH HOME CAN YOU AFFORD?

After working through the rent or buy analysis, Carlos and Mary decide that they want to explore the option of buying a house further. The next question is how much house can they afford? In other words, how big a mortgage can they expect a lender to extend, given their income and financial obligations? First, the Mallorys need to estimate their income, including gross salary, self-employment income, wages from a second job, dividends, interest, pensions, Social Security, rental income and child support or alimony received, but excluding one-time events, such as inheritances, insurance settlements and capital gains.

Carlos and Mary have combined gross monthly salaries of $6,200. In addition, Carlos earns an average of $500 monthly in tax work for outside clients and has done so for several years. Mary receives an average of $300 in dividends on some Amalgamated Whitzadiddle stock that she inherited from her uncle. They also receive $300 in monthly interest on $60,000 of savings and Mary's additional inheritance they have in a bank, but they would need to use almost $40,000 of this money for the down payment and closing costs if they buy the home they are considering. See Table 16.4 for a breakdown of the Mallorys' monthly income.

Next, the Mallorys calculate their monthly payments. These include items such as payments on loans for automobiles, furniture, appliances, boats or recreational vehicles, revolving credit and student loans. Carlos and Mary's monthly payments, shown in Table 16.5, are $1,100: $450 for a car, $200 for furniture, $300 for revolving credit and $150 for a student loan.

As noted earlier, lenders use qualifying ratios as rules of thumb to estimate maximum mortgage payments. Generally, these ratios range between 25/33 and 28/36. The first figure of both ratios is the percentage of gross income a lender will allow as a maximum monthly mortgage payment. For the Mallorys' $7,100 monthly gross income, this amount would range from the conservative 25 percent ($1,775) to the more generous 28 percent ($1,988).

Table 16.5	The Mallorys' Monthly Payments

Car	$ 450
Furniture	200
Appliances	0
Boat or recreational vehicle	0
Revolving credit	300
Student loan	150
Other	0
Total	$1,100

The second calculation reduces this amount to account for payments on other indebtedness. Using the 33 percent conservative figure, a lender would calculate the Mallorys' maximum monthly payment as follows:

Monthly gross income	$7,100
Times 33% (one-third)	2,367
Less other monthly payments	1,100
Amount available for payment	$1,267

Using the more liberal 36 percent ratio, the maximum monthly payment could be $1,456. In other words, the Mallorys' maximum monthly payment would be reduced significantly to reflect the impact of their existing debts.

In addition to principal and interest, the typical house payment includes one-twelfth of yearly property taxes and property insurance. Thus, the $1,267 to $1,456 that Carlos and Mary have available for a monthly house payment must be reduced to reflect these items before the Mallorys can estimate the maximum mortgage they can afford. The amount of property taxes depends on several factors, including the value of the home and the community in which it is located. Property taxes for the house the Mallorys are considering would be $280 each month, with another $80 for property insurance. This means they are left with $957 to $1,146 for the actual mortgage payment.

Because the monthly payment for principal and interest on the 7.5 percent, 30-year, $144,000 loan they need to buy the house is $1,007, the Mallorys have adequate income to qualify for this loan. The fact that Mary owns the Amalgamated Whitzadiddle stock and they would still have $20,000 in the bank after expending $39,800 for the down payment and closing costs also makes them a more favorable credit risk.

CHOOSING A PROPERTY

Now that Carlos and Mary know the price range of the home they can afford, they need to decide whether their chosen house is really their best buy. The search for a home has two aspects. First, they must decide on a general area in which to look, and second, they must decide on a particular property. While the decision is very important, it is not one they will have to live with forever—the average first-time homebuyer moves after five years—and the decision must be based partly on the Mallorys' desires and preferences and what will appeal to prospective future buyers.

Choosing an Area

If the Mallorys buy in a small or medium-sized town, choosing an area may be quite uncomplicated. But if they live in a large metropolitan area, the choice can be quite complex. Let's suppose the latter is the case. Not only do Carlos and Mary have to decide what type of home they would like and what development they might like to live in, they must also choose a community.

The Mallorys begin their search by deciding how far they want to commute to work. Some people do not like commuting and choose residences that are close to their employment. Others will endure longer commutes to enjoy the suburban lifestyle they prefer. Carlos and Mary decide they will limit their hunt to a maximum commuting distance of 60 minutes during rush hour. Within this area, they concentrate on six basic criteria for choosing one community over another:

1. Property tax base
2. Quality of general public services
3. Available recreational facilities
4. Quality of public school system
5. Crime statistics
6. Overall quality of community

Property Tax Base and Quality of Public Services   In a metropolitan area, property tax rates and the quality of public services can vary considerably from one community to another. Other things equal, a low tax rate is desirable if it is not achieved by cutting necessary services. Both factors are important.

Available Recreational Facilities   Good public recreational facilities and established sports programs may be very important factors in locational decisions for some families. For others, they may not be important at all. Carlos and Mary, who have no children, are much more interested in access to cultural events and good shopping.

Quality of Public School System   Having no children, the Mallorys are not concerned significantly about the local school system, although they know it may be quite important in the future. In addition, they realize that quality of schools probably will be a vital consideration for potential future buyers of their home.

Crime Statistics   Carlos and Mary, like most homebuyers today, are very concerned about their security. Thus, crime statistics and the quality of the local police force are extremely important considerations in their locational decision.

Overall Quality of Community   In the final analysis, the locational decision may come down to what the Mallorys perceive as the overall quality of the community. Is it attractive? Does it control signage, or are its thoroughfares visual litterboxes? Are homes in the community well maintained? And, finally, does the community control its growth and require quality real estate development, or does mediocrity abound? The answers to these questions may be based partly on fact and partly on perception, but the quality of a community is vital to property values.

Many sources of information are available on these community factors, including real estate agents, building and real estate publications, and bankers or lenders. Another extremely good source of information is people in a neighborhood. If they respond favorably to inquiries about their area, this almost certainly indicates a desirable community.

Evaluating the Individual Home

Even more than the selection of a community or housing area, selection of an individual property is governed by personal preferences. Carlos and Mary prefer a home with traditional architecture, for example, and want large, open rooms that are good for entertaining.

If a house has a swimming pool, they will not even consider buying it because neither likes to swim, and they don't want the maintenance burden that goes with a pool. To others, a pool would be a very desirable feature.

Despite these individual preference items, all homebuyers should consider certain basic factors. The first rule is to buy a home that is less expensive than the average for the neighborhood. The more expensive homes will tend to raise its value. Conversely, never buy the most expensive home in a neighborhood. The others will drag down its value.

Also, look carefully at other factors that affect a home's investment potential. Does it have a good exterior design? Is the floor plan well arranged? Does it have convenient traffic flow? Is the home well placed on the lot? Is the lot well drained, with good landscaping?

Finally, the structural integrity of the home is extremely important, as the Case Study on page 367 shows. In fact, even if the home is new, but particularly if it is not, it may be very prudent to have the home inspected by a professional. But there are many items that anyone armed with a flashlight and a bit of common sense can examine. Carlos and Mary did this with several houses they considered, covering the following items:

Attic   Does inspection of the attic reveal water leaks or signs of rodent infestation? Are insulation and ventilation adequate?

Walls and Ceilings   Are there cracks in plaster walls or ceilings? Are seams in wallboard smooth and invisible?

Floors   What is the condition of the floors? Do they show signs of buckling or sagging? What is the condition of any carpets?

Roof   Does the roof show signs of wear? An asphalt roof usually lasts only 15 to 20 years, for example, and bare spots can mean it will have to be replaced soon.

Basement or Crawlspace   Are there signs of water damage under the house? If so, a professional should evaluate the problem. Is there evidence of rot or termites? Almost all lenders require an inspection by a professional from a pest control firm.

Electrical System   A professional should inspect the electrical system, but the potential buyer can check some important things on his or her own. For example,

Real Estate Today

Case Study

The House That Came off the Mountain

Why should you obtain a professional home inspection before you purchase a home? Let's look at a dramatic example.

Philip and Phyllis McDonald bought a mountainside house with a spectacular view in an exclusive resort area of western North Carolina. Even though the house was placed over a 40-foot-high concrete block foundation wall, the McDonalds did not have the house inspected before they purchased it for $375,000. They should have!

Less than six years later, the McDonalds came up from Florida to open their summer mountain home. That night, Philip awoke to hear loud cracking noises. The next day, he had the house inspected by a local contractor and later by an engineer. Both informed him that the structure was very unsafe and could collapse at any time. They noted separated and bulging foundation walls, twisted and leaning deck supports, separation of roof sections and walls and separation of concrete blocks throughout the basement area. The house was in such dangerous and deteriorated condition that the only practical course of action was to move out immediately and have the house demolished. The demolition cost $25,000.

The McDonalds, sadder but wiser, suffered a loss of more than $400,000. They could not recover anything from their homeowner's insurance policy because no "occurrence" caused the loss. For the same reason, they could not claim a casualty loss on their income tax return. The contractor who built the home had gone out of business, so the McDonalds were advised that legal action against him was not practical. The loss fell on them alone.

This financial tragedy could have been avoided if the McDonalds had only spent perhaps $200 to have the house inspected before they bought it, as any qualified inspector could have spotted the inadequate construction methods and the potential for disaster. This sad tale also points out the need for adequate building codes to protect consumers. ∎

does the home have adequate electrical capacity? A modern home should have at least a 150-ampere entrance. Are there enough outlets throughout the home?

Heating and Cooling System   How old is the heating and air-conditioning system? Older units are less efficient and may need to be replaced soon. Again, the services of a professional may be necessary.

Water Supply and Waste Disposal   If the home is connected to a municipal water and sewerage system, the potential buyer need worry about only the adequacy of the household plumbing. If the home depends on a well, the water should be tested before purchase. Is the supply adequate throughout the year? How old is the pump? If the home uses a septic tank disposal system, this also needs to be checked by a professional. In many states, inspection by the state health department is required before the property can be sold.

Two Final Thoughts

Following these guidelines can help you make an informed decision regarding where and what home to buy. And remember—you can always find a buyer for a good home in a good location. Take the time and effort to do the job right.

Finally, remember that this home is probably not your last. Consider your future needs, but unless you are an extremely unusual buyer, you will move in a few years.

MAKING AND CLOSING THE DEAL

Carlos and Mary have now completed the preliminary steps to buying a home. They have determined how much home they can afford. They have researched communities and specific neighborhoods and developments to determine where they might like to locate. They also have learned some of the factors they should look for in a home and have thought carefully about what features are important to them.

Now they are ready to choose a property, negotiate its purchase, obtain financing and close the deal.

In this process, always remember one thing: in the normal sales transaction, no one works for you. The real estate broker works for the seller (unless you have hired a buyer's broker); the lender works for the mortgage company; even the closing attorney, whose fee you pay, does not really look out for your interests. This does not mean that these people are dishonest or out to cheat you, but *they do not work for you*. It is not their job to look out for your interests.

The Real Estate Agent

A real estate broker or salesperson can be a valuable source of information on neighborhoods and homes for sale. He or she can also save you considerable time by narrowing your search to properties that might really fit your needs and desires. But remember, unless you hire an agent specifically to represent you, the real estate broker does not work for you. He or she works for the seller and is legally bound to represent the seller's interests, not yours. Even though the salesperson spends long hours showing you around town, taking you to lunch and, in general, being a wonderful person, don't forget that simple fact. For example, you certainly shouldn't tell the agent that you probably would be willing to make a higher offer on a particular house. The agent is duty bound to take that information to the seller, thereby weakening your position.

As discussed earlier in this book, buyers are increasingly being represented by buyer's brokers. This may be a very good idea, particularly when you move to a community that you do not know thoroughly.

The Negotiating Process

Suppose you have found a home that fits your needs. Now comes the tricky part—negotiating a price and terms. In this process, there are two rules:

1. Set a top limit above which you will not go.
2. Be prepared to walk away from the deal.

If you fall in love with a home and just have to have it, you are in a very poor bargaining position. Be prepared to walk away. On the other hand, if you really have found the home of your dreams, it may be worth spending a little more to get it, rather than going through the time-consuming process of extending the search. But be certain it really is the home you want. Don't fall in love with the first thing you see.

Not everyone, and particularly not a first-time homebuyer, is an experienced and shrewd negotiator. This may be one more reason to engage an agent to represent your interests. For one thing, the buyer's broker probably knows conditions in the market better than you do. Your agent may know that the house you are considering has been on the market for some time, and the owners are eager to sell. This information may place you in position to obtain a much better deal, which may more than pay for your representative's fee.

Finally, don't forget a fundamental rule of contracts: Verbal agreements are not worth the paper they are written on. Unless something is written down as part of a contract, it is *not* part of the contract. If promises or agreements are made, be certain they are contained in the written contract. If not, they are worthless.

Dealing with the Lender

Lenders sell money, and naturally, they want to get the highest price (the interest rate) they can. You should shop as carefully for a mortgage loan as you do for a home. Don't take the first offer, and check with several lenders to find the best deal.

Also, remember that any appraisal and inspections required by the lender are to protect the lender, not necessarily you. For example, the purpose of the appraisal, which you normally pay for, is to ensure that the home has value high enough to enable the lender to be able to recover its money in case of foreclosure. The appraisal does not tell you whether the home is a good investment for you, although it certainly should help in this determination. (It is amazing how many appraisals for lending purposes arrive at values that are almost exactly the selling prices.)

The Closing Attorney or Escrow Agent

The closing attorney's or escrow agent's job is to prepare the necessary documents relating to the sale and loan and to make sure the title is in order, the requirements of the lender and the title insurance company have been met, all funds have been collected and properly disbursed and the necessary documents have been recorded. All of this is important to the buyer, but again, the closing agent is not paid to look after the buyer's interests. The agent does not negotiate for you, draft a purchase contract favorable to you, make certain the contract has no clauses that are unfavorable to your interests, help arrange favorable financing or make sure that the seller fully honors his or her agreement with you. To

Real Estate Today

Close-Up

What Will Happen to Home Prices?

Perhaps the most critical element in the rent or buy decision is the question of future home prices. Thus, let us examine the question of what is likely to happen to home prices in the United States over the next two decades.

The change in home prices depends on many factors, particularly changes in population, the level of general inflation, general economic growth, and growth or decline in the local economy. During the 1960s, for example, there was great upward pressure on home prices because of the large expansion in the number of households—the Baby Boom effect. General inflation in the 1970s was the primary factor causing home prices to rise more than 10 percent annually in some years of that decade, but increases in other demand factors caused home prices to rise 50 percent faster than the general level of inflation.

The increase in home prices moderated during most of the 1980s, but some areas such as Southern California and Boston experienced large increases, partially fueled by speculative fever. Conversely, local economic factors caused declines in other markets. For example, the drop in oil prices caused a bust in the Houston market.

Finally, the general economic recession of the early 1990s triggered a decline in home prices in many areas, particularly those that had experienced speculative run-ups in earlier years. Some homeowners in Southern California and the Northeast were faced with ugly financial leverage, and saddled with mortgages greater than the values of their homes.

But all that is in the past. What of the future? Let us examine some of the factors that will influence the general level of home prices in the future, always recognizing that real estate markets are local in nature and heavily influenced by local economic conditions.

In contrast to earlier periods, the number of Americans in the age 25 to 34 first-time homebuyers group is declining and will be through about 2005. Only about 27 million of the possible 40 million Baby Boomers will want to sell their homes over the next few years. This has led some economists to predict an absolute decline in home prices over this analysis period.

Recent population estimates by the Census Bureau contradict this gloomy prediction, however. The current forecast predicts a population increase of 27 million for the 1990s, resulting in a total household formation about the same as that of the 1980s. A major factor in this estimate of increase is the large number of immigrants. Studies show that immigrants, particularly those coming from Asian countries, highly value home ownership.

The large group of aging Baby Boomers with accumulated home equity and relatively large disposable income bodes well for both the trade-up market for more expensive homes and the second home market for vacation homes. Preferred retirement areas should also benefit from the existence of this group.

Rapid inflation is the friend of debtors, particularly heavily leveraged homeowners. Thus, the greatly reduced rates of inflation in recent years have made home ownership somewhat less attractive, while also making it more affordable. Slow growth in home prices and relatively low interest rates combined to make housing more affordable in 1996 than at any time in the past 20 years. These factors have also increased the home ownership rate to its highest level in many years.

A big unknown is the future of the mortgage interest deduction from taxable income. This deduction now costs the Treasury about $50 billion annually, and many, particularly those advocating a flat tax, are calling for its repeal. If this were to occur, many feel that the negative impact on home prices would be severe, a factor that makes the deduction's repeal unlikely.

So, what's likely to happen to home prices during the time when most readers of this book will be faced with the rent or buy decision? The most likely scenario appears to be that prices will keep up with, or possibly slightly exceed, the rate of general inflation. But that is also the general outlook; home prices where you might buy a home also depend heavily on what happens in the local economy. ∎

the contrary, the closing agent's job is to see that the transaction meets legal requirements and is closed.

Perhaps we have been too forceful in warning you of the pitfalls in the sales, lending and closing transactions when buying a home. Certainly, the intention is not to convey that real estate brokers, lenders and attorneys are dishonest or unethical. But do remember whom they work for. If you feel you need someone to represent your interests, don't depend on these individuals; hire your own representative.

Chapter Review

1. Important factors in the rent or buy decision are (1) the future of home prices, (2) the probable period of ownership, (3) the mortgage interest rate and (4) noneconomic factors.

2. Lenders will normally make a mortgage loan with a monthly payment equal to between 25 and 28 percent of monthly gross income or, if the payment is less, an amount equal to 33 to 36 percent of monthly gross income reduced by the amount of existing monthly debt payments.

3. Important factors in choosing a community in which to buy a home are (1) commuting distance to work, (2) property tax base, (3) quality of general public services, (4) available recreational facilities, (5) quality of the public school system, (6) crime statistics and (7) overall quality of the community.

4. In choosing a home, it is a good rule to buy one priced lower than the average for the neighborhood. Also, the buyer should consider a home that has a good design and should carefully check the home's structural integrity.

5. In the negotiating, lending and closing process, always remember that in the normal sales transaction, no one works for the buyer, and therefore, no one really looks out for the buyer's interests.

Study Exercises

1. What are some of the important factors to consider in the rent or buy decision?

2. Jack and Jill Jolly are thinking about buying a home. Their combined monthly income is $5,000, and they have $30,000 savings in a bank. They also have existing debt that requires monthly payments of $350 for a car, $200 for furniture and $250 for revolving credit. How large a

mortgage loan could they expect to get if the current interest rate is 8.5 percent? How expensive a home could they buy?

3. In choosing a location and home, what factors should Jack and Jill consider?

4. Is the assertion really true that in the negotiating, lending and closing process, no one works for the buyer? Why or why not?

CHAPTER 17
Investing in Income-Producing Properties

Investment in income-producing property, such as an office building, requires a very different set of considerations than an investment in owner-occupied real estate.

Real Estate Today

- *Close-Up*
  Renaissance
  Center—The Story
  of an Investment
  Failure

Chapter Preview

ONE OF THE most exciting aspects of the real estate industry is investment in income-producing properties. History is filled with the names of people who have made, and sometimes lost, fortunes through real estate investments. The primary question to be considered in this chapter is "How do investors decided whether to invest in a particular project?" Successful investment decision making requires careful analysis of the risks and returns offered by an investment opportunity.

The objective of this chapter is to describe the analysis methods successful investors use to make real estate investment decisions. In general, this process involves (1) evaluating a project's competitive environment, (2) forecasting the cash flows expected to accrue to the investor and (3) making a final decision about whether to proceed with the project. Our focus throughout this chapter is on decision-making situations facing equity investors who are considering investing in existing income properties. In this chapter, we will

- discuss the advantages and disadvantages of real estate investment;
- review the concepts of investment and wealth maximization; and
- discuss how investors compare the costs and benefits of investment opportunities using NPV, IRR and the discounted cash flow model.

ADVANTAGES AND DISADVANTAGES OF REAL ESTATE INVESTMENT

What makes real estate an attractive investment category? While numerous motivations exist for pursuing real estate investments, investors often cite cash flow from operations, the possibility of value appreciation, portfolio diversification and financial leverage as the major incentives for pursuing real estate projects.

Cash Flow from Operations

For many investors, the primary attraction to real estate investment is the operating cash flow generated by income-producing property. The source of this cash flow is the rent paid by tenants for the use of space in the property. Because real estate is a durable asset, most properties are capable of generating rental revenue for many years into the future. From this revenue, the investor must pay a property's operating expenses, debt service and income taxes. Operating expenses typically include utilities, maintenance, property management, insurance and property taxes. Debt service includes principal and interest payments on any outstanding mortgage debt. Income taxes are due on any taxable income generated by the property. Investors refer to the annual operating cash flow that remains after these items are paid as **after-tax cash flow** from operations. Often referred to by its acronym, ATCF, this cash flow represents the money the investor puts in his or her pocket at the end of each year of the investment holding period.

Appreciation

Another motivation for investing in income-producing real estate is the possibility of appreciation in property value over the investment holding period. While investment properties do not always increase in value, investors generally choose properties whose values are expected to grow at the rate of inflation or greater. Furthermore, changing market conditions can improve a property's competitive position in a market, allowing it to command higher rents and thereby increase its value to investors. When an investor sells an income-producing property, the proceeds from the sale, less selling expenses, are used to retire any outstanding mortgage debt and to pay any income taxes due as a result of the sale. To the investor, the sum of money that is generated by the sale of an investment is known as **after-tax equity reversion** (ATER). The term *equity reversion* refers to the return of funds originally invested in the property plus any change in the value of the investor's investment in the property.

Portfolio Diversification

Another important motivation for investing in real estate is the diversification real estate adds to a portfolio. Combining real estate investments with investments in stocks and bonds allows investors to develop diversified portfolios. Diversification allows investors to maximize their investment returns while spreading their risk exposure across different types of investments. Such a strategy provides protection against an economic downturn in any one sector of the economy. In addition, many people are attracted to the security offered by investments in tangible assets that are under their personal control.

Financial Leverage

Real estate investors are also attracted to real estate because it allows the use of **financial leverage,** or other people's money. The real estate finance industry makes debt capital readily available to most investors, with many lenders willing to provide 70 percent or more of the funds necessary to purchase investment properties. By borrowing additional investment funds from lenders, investors can control more real estate with less of their own funds. The use of borrowed funds has the effect of leveraging, or magnifying, the returns on funds invested. The benefits of leverage come at a price, however, because investors face increased risk. If a project fails to generate sufficient revenue to satisfy the debt service payments, the project may be forced into foreclosure.

Example of Financial Leverage   To understand the impact of leverage on an equity investor's rate of return, consider the following example. Lou Lever has $100,000 to invest. He can (1) purchase a $100,000 property without using any borrowed funds or (2) use the $100,000 to make a 10 percent down payment on a $1 million property and borrow $900,000 at 11 percent annual interest on an interest-only loan. If each of the two properties provides a 15 percent return before debt service and income taxes are considered, the second is clearly more advantageous due to the effects of financial leverage. To see why, calculate Lou's rate of return on his equity investment for both properties.

If Lou follows the first strategy, he would earn $15,000, or 15 percent, on his equity investment of $100,000. If he follows the second strategy, Lou would earn $51,000. This amount is calculated by first determining the total return on the investment (.15 × $1 million = $150,000), then subtracting the interest due on the borrowed funds (.11 × $900,000 = $99,000). As a percentage of his equity investment of $100,000, the $51,000 ($150,000 − $99,000) reflects a 51 percent rate of return.

As you can see, financial leverage can greatly magnify the rate of return on equity. If the property in the second strategy provides an overall return of 18 percent instead of 15 percent, Lou's rate of return on equity would jump to 81 percent; an overall return of 20 percent would balloon Lou's return to 101 percent.

Of course, the magnification of the return on equity also works in the opposite direction. If, for example, the second property provides a return of only 5 percent overall, Lou would suffer a negative rate of return on equity of 49 percent (.05 × $1 million − .11 × $900,000 = −$49,000). The ability of leverage to magnify returns on equity implies that leverage increases risk. The additional risk comes from the fact that Lou has a fixed liability (interest on the debt) that he must satisfy each year. If the property's earnings are insufficient to cover the debt service, Lou stands to lose cash out of his pocket to keep the investment alive.

As a rule, financial leverage increases the investor's return on equity as long as the cost (interest rate) of the borrowed funds is less than the overall return on the investment. If the interest rate exceeds the overall return, financial leverage reduces the return on the investor's return on equity, possibly causing it to be negative.

Disadvantages of Real Estate Investment

Though there are numerous advantages to investing in real estate, the disadvantages must not be ignored. For example, even with borrowed funds, real estate investments often require relatively large capital expenditures. Large-scale properties such as office buildings and shopping centers are often beyond the resources of individual investors. In addition, investing in real estate is risky, and the risk exposure may not be suitable for every investor.

In the preceding discussion, we saw how financial leverage could increase the risk of an investment. Another aspect of real estate risk comes from the lack of liquidity that real estate investments have in comparison with other types of investments. Liquidity refers to the ability to convert an asset into cash quickly without having to accept a low price. For example, stocks are considered liquid assets because an investor who wishes to sell a portfolio of common stocks can do so simply by calling a stock broker. The broker can immediately sell the shares at the current market price. Real estate investors should anticipate that selling a property quickly may mean that the property will sell at a lower price than could otherwise be obtained.

Real estate investors also face the risk of changing economic conditions that may adversely affect the rents they are able to charge tenants and the value of investment properties. Successful investors spend considerable time and effort evaluating the markets in which their properties compete to understand how changing market conditions affect the risk exposure of their portfolios.

Weighing the benefits and costs of a real estate investment opportunity requires a high degree of knowledge about the characteristics of real estate markets and transactions, as well as careful consideration of the risks involved in real estate investment. The next section takes a closer look at the process real estate investors use when making the investment decision.

FINANCIAL DECISION MAKING

As we discussed in Chapter 14, all financial decisions involve a comparison of the expected benefits from a proposed course of action with the expected costs arising from that course of action. In this context, **investment** is defined as present sacrifice in anticipation of expected future benefit. Based on this definition, the decision to continue your education is an investment, as is the decision to place money in a savings account for future use. If you do not expect the benefits of these activities to be greater than the sacrifices you must make, you would choose not to engage in them. Similarly, real estate investment decisions require a comparison of the benefits a project is expected to generate with the sacrifices one must make in order to engage in the project.

The Wealth Maximization Objective

To make investment decisions, investors must define their criteria for determining the acceptability of alternative projects. Some investors pursue projects that will generate income, while others are more interested in the appreciation potential real estate offers. Other investors are in search of projects that provide tax-sheltering benefits or those that have minimum management concerns. Although each investor has different interests, tastes and preferences, the ultimate goal of all investors is to accept those projects that will maximize their wealth. Wealth-maximizing investors choose only those projects that offer expected benefits in excess of the costs of pursuing them, and if faced with a choice between two or more projects that increase wealth, wealth-maximizing investors choose the project in which benefits exceed costs by the largest amount.

The NPV Rule

To evaluate the impact a project will have on wealth, investors use the net present value decision rule and the internal rate of return decision rule discussed in Chapter 14. We will review each of these rules in turn.

Recall that **net present value** (NPV) is defined as the present value of cash inflows less the present value of cash outflows. The conversion of future cash flows into present values is accomplished by discounting the future cash flows at the investor's **required rate of return.** The required rate of return reflects both the time value of money and the riskiness of the investment opportunity.

Investors use the NPV of a particular project as a decision rule by evaluating its sign (positive or negative). If the NPV of an investment is greater than or equal to zero, the investor should choose to invest because the investment is worth at least as much as it costs, given the investor's required rate of return. If the NPV is less than zero, the investor should not invest.

Taking this rule one step further, if we are faced with several alternative investment choices, we should accept the one with the highest positive NPV because it will increase our wealth more than the others. To use this rule in investment analysis, we must estimate the cash flows associated with an investment opportunity, then convert the cash flows into present values using the appropriate discount rate. The following example demonstrates the NPV decision rule.

Using the NPV Rule

Consider an investor who faces a choice between two alternative investments. The investor has performed a detailed analysis of the projects' competitive environment and has developed the cash flow forecasts shown below. He believes that both projects are equally risky and that the level of risk of the projects suggests an annual required rate of return of 15 percent for both projects. Which project should the investor choose?

	Project A	Project B
Initial investment	$ 90,000	$ 80,000
Cash flow in year one	10,000	9,100
Cash flow in year two	11,100	10,000
Cash flow in year three	12,000	11,000
Cash flow in year four	12,000	11,000
Cash flow in year five	120,000	104,000

Given that the investor's objective is to choose the project that increases his wealth by the greatest amount, he should calculate the NPV of each project and choose the one with the highest NPV. These calculations are shown below.

Project A

$$NPV = \frac{\$10,000}{(1.15)^1} + \frac{\$11,100}{(1.15)^2} + \frac{\$12,000}{(1.15)^3} + \frac{\$12,000}{(1.15)^4} +$$

$$\frac{\$120,000}{(1.15)^5} - \$90,000 = \$1,501$$

Project B

$$NPV = \frac{\$9,100}{(1.15)^1} + \frac{\$10,000}{(1.15)^2} + \frac{\$11,000}{(1.15)^3} + \frac{\$11,000}{(1.15)^4} +$$

$$\frac{\$104,000}{(1.15)^5} - \$80,000 = \$703$$

Both projects result in a positive NPV, which suggests that both are good projects that will result in a wealth increase to the investor above and beyond the cost of pursuing them. Because the NPV of project A is greater than the NPV of project B, the investor should choose A. By doing so, the investor expects to receive a return of 15 percent plus a wealth increase of $1,501.

Using the IRR Rule

The internal rate of return decision rule also provides us with a yes or no decision about whether to proceed with an investment opportunity. Notice that in project A above, the investor's required rate of return is 15 percent. Because the NPV is greater than zero, and because its NPV is larger than project B's NPV, the investor should accept this project. But what rate of return does the investor expect to earn? Obviously, the investor expects to earn some rate greater than 15 percent. To find the exact return the investor expects to earn, we can define the **internal rate of return** (IRR) of an investment as the discount rate that makes the NPV exactly equal to zero. To determine an investment's IRR, we can search a variety of discount rates by trial and error until we find one that makes the NPV equal zero. This rate is the internal rate of return on the investment. Fortunately, most financial calculators have a feature that allows automatic searches for the internal rate of return for a series of cash flows.

The steps outlined below show how to use a financial calculator to determine the NPV and IRR for the series of cash flows forecast for project A.

HP-10B Keystrokes: NPV and IRR Calculations for Project A

1. Enter the initial cash outflow (a negative amount)	90000, +/−, *CFj*
2. Enter the cash flow for year one	10,000, *CFj*
3. Enter the cash flow for year two	11,100, *CFj*
4. Enter the cash flow for year three	12,000, *CFj*
5. Enter the cash flow for year four	12,000, *CFj*
6. Enter the cash flow for year five	120,000, *CFj*
7. Enter the required rate of return	15, I/YR
8. Solve for the NPV	goldkey, NPV (calculator displays 1,501.29)
9. Solve for the IRR	goldkey, IRR/YR (calculator displays 15.47)

BAII PLUS Keystrokes: NPV and IRR Calculations for Project A

1. Set the number of periods per year at 1	2nd, P/Y, 1, ENTER, 2nd, QUIT
2. Enter initial cash outflow (a negative amount)	CF, 90000, +/−, ENTER
3. Enter cash flow for year one	↓, 10000, *ENTER*
4. Enter cash flow for year two	↓, ↓, 11100, *ENTER*
5. Enter cash flow for year three	↓, ↓, 12000, *ENTER*
6. Enter cash flow for year four	↓, ↓, 12000, ENTER
7. Enter cash flow for year five	↓, ↓, 120000, *ENTER*
8. Enter the required rate of return	*NPV,* 15, *ENTER,* ↓,
9. Solve for the NPV	CPT (calculator displays 1,501.29)
10. Solve for the IRR	IRR, CPT (calculator displays 15.47)

To use the IRR as a financial decision-making rule, we simply compare the IRR of an investment opportunity with the required rate of return. If the IRR is greater than or equal to our required rate of return, the investor invests; otherwise, he or she forgoes the investment opportunity. While the IRR rule and the

NPV rule are based on the same principles, the NPV rule is generally better to use because IRR calculations may yield multiple discount rates that set the NPV equal to zero. Furthermore, the NPV rule should be used when an investor is forced to choose between mutually exclusive projects such as those described above. When the objective is to determine the rate of return provided by an investment, however, the IRR calculation is extremely useful.

Real estate investors can use these decision rules to evaluate individual projects and to decide whether to pursue them. Applying the rules, however, requires a forecast of the cash flows that the investor expects to receive during the investment holding period. The discounted cash flow model described below provides a systematic framework for calculating the expected net present value and internal rate of return of real estate investment opportunities on an after-tax basis.

THE DISCOUNTED CASH FLOW MODEL

The NPV and IRR decision rules provide a sound basis for defining the suitability of an investment opportunity by identifying its impact on the investor's wealth. Using these rules, we know that a good investment is one that is worth more than it costs, assuming all benefits and sacrifices are identified correctly. To put the decision rules into practice, real estate investors often rely on the following discounted cash flow model.

$$NPV = \sum_{t=1}^{T} \frac{\text{ATCF}_t}{(1 + i)^t} + \frac{\text{ATER}_T}{(1 + i)^T} - \text{initial equity}$$

In this model, $ATCF$ is the annual after-tax cash flow from operations, $ATER$ is the after-tax equity reversion realized on the sale of the property at the end of the holding period, i is the investor's required rate of return, T is the expected number of years the property will be held and *initial equity* is the difference between the purchase price and any debt used to finance the purchase. Understanding the model requires careful consideration of the components ATCF and ATER. The following example describes each of these concepts in detail.

Applying the Discounted Cash Flow Model

To illustrate some of the issues involved in real estate investment analysis, consider the decision facing Susan Adrep, an advertising account executive who is considering adding real estate to her investment portfolio. Susan became interested in buying an income-producing property several months ago. She has discussed her interests with her accountant, local lenders, other real estate investors and several real estate brokers. Because this is her first real estate investment, she has decided to focus on smaller residential properties located in her neighborhood. After looking at several properties that are currently available in the market, Susan feels that one property, a four-unit apartment building, deserves further consideration.

The property is located on a quiet street between a commercial district and an area containing single-family homes. Property values in this area have been increasing at approximately 5 percent per year over the past ten years. The eight-year-old building was well-constructed, and the owner has maintained the property in excellent condition. The owner is moving to another city and has decided to sell the property, rather than manage it as an absentee owner.

John Block, a local real estate broker, has agreed to market the property for the owner at a firm asking price of $255,000. John provides Susan with a summary of the rental income and operating expenses for the past two years. In addition, Susan talks with several lenders and learns that a 25-year, monthly payment mortgage loan can be obtained at 9 percent interest for 70 percent of the property value. Based on this information, as well as her own analysis of local market conditions, Susan develops the following forecast for income and expenses for the property.

	Year 1
Rent ($725 per unit per month)	$34,800
Annual rent increases	5 percent
Operating expenses	
Lawn service	$ 800
Maintenance and repairs	4,000
Property taxes	2,100
Insurance	900
Property management services	2,100
Total	$9,900
Annual operating expense increase	3 percent

The question Susan faces is whether this property is a suitable investment for her portfolio. To reach a decision about buying the property, Susan must identify the sacrifices she must make to acquire the property, and she must compare those sacrifices with the benefits she expects to receive from this investment.

The sacrifices facing Susan in this project include the initial equity contribution she must make at the time of purchase and the risk she will be exposed to as a result of her decision to invest. Initial equity is the purchase price of a project less any debt used to complete the purchase. Risk is defined as the possibility that the actual benefits provided by the investment will deviate from the investor's initial expectations. The benefits Susan expects to receive from pursuing this opportunity include the net cash flows that will occur during the investment holding period.

Expected benefits from real estate investments are typically divided into two categories: after-tax cash flows from operations and after-tax equity reversion. The first category refers to income received each year of the investment holding period, and the second category refers to income realized when the property is sold. Because income taxes are an important consideration in any investment strategy, Susan must consider their impact on the income she expects to receive from this investment.

Forecasting ATCF

To forecast the after-tax cash flows from operations for the investment opportunity under consideration, Susan uses the relationships shown in Table 17.1.

Table 17.1		After-Tax Cash Flows from Operations for Year 1

Potential gross income	PGI	$34,800
− Vacancy and credit losses	−VCL	−1,392
Effective gross income	EGI	$33,408
− Operating expenses	− OE	−9,900
Net operating income	NOI	$23,508
− Annual debt service	−ADS	−17,976
Before-tax cash flow	BTCF	$ 5,532
− Taxes (determined below)	−Taxes	−302
After-tax cash flow	ATCF	$ 5,230
Determining Taxes from Operations		
Net operating income	NOI	$23,508
− Interest expense	−Int.	−15,984
− Depreciation deduction	−Dep.	− 6,447
Taxable income	TI	$ 1,077
× Marginal tax rate	× MTR	× .28
Taxes from operations	Taxes	$ 302

We will consider the second category of cash flows in real estate investments, after-tax equity reversion, in the next section.

The starting point for estimating annual cash flows from operations in a real estate investment is **potential gross income** (PGI). PGI is the total income potential of the investment, assuming all leasable space is rented and all rents are collected. Investors must have knowledge of the expected rent for the space in the property to estimate PGI. The source of this knowledge is usually a survey of rental rates for similar space in other properties in the marketplace. For the property Susan is considering, the PGI in the first year of her holding period is expected to be $34,800 ($725 rent per unit × 12 months × 4 units). Susan also believes that rents will increase at 5 percent per year for the next five years, which is her anticipated holding period.

Calculating Net Operating Income Because some of the PGI may not be received as a result of vacancies or uncollected rents, an allowance for these items should be deducted from PGI in the form of **vacancy and credit losses** (VCL). The forecasted allowance of VCL (often expressed as a percentage of PGI) depends on observations of historic data, comparable properties and general market conditions. For new properties, the vacancy rate may be quite high during the initial leasing period, and older properties in declining areas may experience high credit losses from faltering tenants. Susan believes that 4 percent of PGI is a reasonable allowance for the property she is considering, so she expects the VCL in year one to be $1,392 ($34,800 × .04). Subtracting VCL from PGI results in **effective gross income** (EGI), or the actual amount of rental revenue expected to be received each year.

With revenues accounted for, the next step is to subtract operating expenses (OE) from EGI to determine **net operating income** (NOI). Operating expenses include any expenditures made in the operation of the investment property, such as maintenance costs, management fees, property taxes, insurance premiums and utility fees. Net operating income is the amount of revenue left after paying the expenses of operation, but before paying the mortgage payments and income taxes on the investment. In this case, Susan feels that operating expenses for year one will be $9,900, resulting in NOI of $23,508. She also believes that these expenses will increase by 3 percent each year.

Annual Debt Service   Susan now must consider the impact of financing on this investment opportunity. Using the mortgage payment formula described in Chapter 14, Susan calculates the monthly payment required to amortize a 25-year loan for $178,500 ($255,000 × .70) at 9 percent annual interest. Multiplying this amount, $1,497.97 times 12 gives annual debt service (ADS) of $17,976. Subtracting ADS from NOI results in the **before-tax cash flow** (BTCF) of $5,532. Because taxes are a real expense, however, the analysis must be based on after-tax cash flow (ATCF). To calculate the annual income tax consequence of Susan's investment, she must first determine the taxable income (TI) generated by this project.

Taxable Income   Two items that require careful consideration when determining taxable income in most real estate investments are (1) interest expense and (2) depreciation deduction. Considering interest expense (int.) first, notice that Susan subtracts the annual debt service from NOI to get BTCF. ADS, however, also includes principal repayments which are not tax deductible. Therefore, BTCF is not the same as taxable income. To determine TI, Susan subtracts only the interest component of ADS from NOI. Recall from the discussion of amortizing loans in Chapter 14 that the amount of interest in each payment is reduced as the loan balance declines. Developing an amortization schedule for the loan used to finance the property investment allows Susan to determine the amount of interest paid each year. To construct an amortization schedule, the mortgage payment is calculated by the mortgage constant formula, then each payment is separated into interest and principal components. If payments are made more frequently than once each year, annual totals are necessary. An amortization schedule for Susan's loan is shown in Table 17.2. Interest in year one totals $15,984.

The second item to consider when calculating taxable income is the amount of the **depreciation deduction** (dep). Income tax laws allow depreciation deductions (also known as *cost recovery allowances*), which provide an investor with a means of recovering his or her original capital investment without paying taxes on this amount until the property is sold. Nonresidential and residential property improvements have depreciable lives of 39 and 27.5 years, respectively. Land is not depreciable under current tax laws, so the purchase price attributable to improvements must be identified separately.

To determine the annual depreciation deduction, Susan divides the value of the improvements by the appropriate depreciable life. Assuming that the value of the building alone is $185,000, the annual depreciation deduction is $6,727 ($185,000 ÷ 27.5). Under current tax laws, however, an investor must make some additional calculations to determine the depreciation deduction during the first and last years of ownership. As a rule, the investor is presumed to have purchased or sold the property in the middle of the month in which the property was

Table 17.2		Amortization Schedule (Annual Summary)		

Year	Payment	Interest	Principal	Amount Outstanding
0	0	0	0	$178,500
1	$17,976	$15,984	$1,991	176,509
2	17,976	$15,797	2,178	174,330
3	17,976	$15,593	2,383	171,948
4	17,976	$15,370	2,606	169,342
5	17,976	$15,125	2,851	166,491

purchased or sold, regardless of the actual day of the month the transaction occurs. For example, if an investor buys a property in January, the depreciation deduction for the first year of ownership is 11.5/12 of the annual amount. Similarly, if the investor sells the property in July of a later year, the depreciation deduction is 6.5/12 of the annual amount for the last year of ownership.

Assume that Susan buys the property in January of year one and sells the property in December of year five. The depreciation deductions in those two years will be $6,447 ($6,727 × 11.5/12). For years two, three and four, the full deduction of $6,727 is used. In this example, subtracting interest and depreciation from NOI yields taxable income of $1,077.

Income Taxes　Annual income taxes are calculated by multiplying taxable income by the investor's marginal tax rate. Susan faces a marginal tax rate of 28 percent, which means that any additional income she earns will be subject to a tax of 28 percent. Therefore, the taxes from operations in year one are $302 ($1,077 × .28). (In the event that taxable income is a negative number, which is sometimes the case in real estate investments, the tax loss may be used to offset taxable income from other investments in the investor's portfolio. A full discussion of the tax implications of real estate investment is beyond the scope of this text.) Subtracting taxes from BTCF yields ATCF in year one of $5,230.

These calculations are repeated for each year of the investment holding period as shown in Table 17.3 Thus far in her analysis of this property, Susan knows that she must invest $76,500 ($255,000 − $178,500) in return for annual cash flows from operations shown in the table for years one through five. Susan must now forecast the cash flow she will receive at the end of year five from the sale of the property.

Forecasting ATER

The second source of cash flows in a real estate investment is the proceeds from the sale of the property at the end of the holding period. *After-tax equity reversion* (ATER) is the term used to represent the after-tax cash flow to the investor when the property is sold. The relationships involved in the calculation of ATER for Susan's investment opportunity are presented in Table 17.4.

The starting point in determining the ATER is forecasting a future sales price. The sales price is the estimated transaction price that will be negotiated between

After-Tax Cash Flow Estimates, Years 1–5   **Table 17.3**

Forecasting After-Tax Cash Flows

	Year 1	Year 2	Year 3	Year 4	Year 5
PGI	$34,800	$36,540	$38,367	$40,285	$42,300
–VCL	1,392	1,462	1,535	1,611	1,692
EGI	33,408	35,078	36,832	38,674	40,608
–OE	9,900	10,197	10,503	10,818	11,143
NOI	23,508	24,881	26,329	27,856	29,465
–ADS	17,976	17,976	17,976	17,976	17,976
BTCF	5,532	6,906	8,354	9,880	11,490
–Taxes	302	660	1,123	1,613	2,210
ATCF	5,230	6,246	7,231	8,268	9,279

Forecasting Taxes from Operations

	Year 1	Year 2	Year 3	Year 4	Year 5
EGI	$33,408	$35,078	$36,832	$38,674	$40,608
–OE	9,900	10,197	10,503	10,818	11,143
NOI	23,508	24,881	26,329	27,856	29,465
–Int.	15,984	15,797	15,593	15,370	15,125
–Dep.	6,447	6,727	6,727	6,727	6,447
TI	1,077	2,357	4,009	5,759	7,893
× MTR	.28	.28	.28	.28	.28
Taxes	302	660	1,123	1,613	2,210

Note: Numbers may not add to totals due to rounding.

the buyer and the seller at the time of the transaction. To estimate sales price, Susan assumes that the value of her property will increase by about 5 percent each year. Therefore, if it is worth $255,000 at the time of purchase, it will sell for approximately $325,450 at the end of five years.

From this amount, Susan subtracts $16,500 for expenses she expects to incur during the sale, including such items as brokerage commissions and attorney's fees. The difference between the sales price and selling expenses gives the **net sales proceeds** of $308,950. Subtracting the amount outstanding ($166,491) on the mortgage from the net sales proceeds, where the amount outstanding on the loan is determined by the amortization schedule, gives the **before-tax equity reversion** of $142,459.

The next step is to calculate the taxable gain on the sale for tax purposes. The taxable gain on an investment is defined as net sales proceeds less original purchase price plus all depreciation deductions taken in previous years. (Notice that the depreciation deduction used in determining cash flows from operations only defers income tax payments until the sale of the asset.) In this example, the accumulated depreciation is $33,075. Therefore, the taxable gain is $87,025 ($308,950 – $255,000 + $33,075). Taxes due on sale are calculated by multiplying the taxable gain by the investor's marginal income tax rate. In this case, they

Table 17.4	After-Tax Equity Reversion

Sales price	$325,450
−Selling expenses	− 16,500
Net sales price	$308,950
−Amount outstanding	−166,491
Before-tax equity reversion	$142,459
−Taxes (determined below)	− 24,367
After-tax equity reversion	$118,092
Determining Taxes Due on Sale	
Net sales price	$308,950
− Purchase price	−255,000
+ Accumulated depreciation	+ 33,075
Taxable Gain	$ 87,025
× MTR	× .28
Taxes	$ 24,367

total $24,367 ($87,025 × .28). After-tax equity reversion is determined by subtracting taxes due on sale and from the BTER. Based on these calculations, Susan expects to receive an ATER of $118,092.

Now that Susan has carefully estimated ATCF and ATER for her investment opportunity, she can apply the discounted cash flow model and decide whether she should proceed with this project. Given a loan amount of $178,500 and a purchase price of $255,000, the equity required to buy this property is $76,500. Assume that Susan believes a required rate of return of 16 percent reflects the riskiness of the investment as well as the time value of money over the holding period. Using the estimated ATCF for each year of the holding period and the estimated ATER, Susan calculates NPV as follows:

$$NPV = \frac{\$5,230}{(1.16)^1} + \frac{\$6,246}{(1.16)^2} + \frac{\$7,231}{(1.16)^3} + \frac{\$8,268}{(1.16)^4} +$$

$$\frac{\$9,279}{(1.16)^5} + \frac{\$118,092}{(1.16)^5} - \$76,500 = \$2,493$$

$$IRR = 16.85\%$$

Based on the NPV and IRR decision rules, Susan should choose to purchase this property. While she has no guarantee that this property will be a profitable investment, the discounted cash flow model provides a systematic process for analyzing investment choices and evaluating them with the objective of maximizing investor wealth. The accuracy of the technique depends on the quality of the information used to develop the cash flow forecasts and on the appropriate evaluation of the risk of the investment when formulating a required rate of return.

Real Estate Today   *Close-Up*

Renaissance Center—The Story of an Investment Failure

Although most real estate has appreciated in value over the years, there are numerous and notable exceptions. One of the prominent failures is Renaissance Center, a $350 million multiuse complex on downtown Detroit's waterfront. The center, which opened in 1977, includes a 73-story hotel with 1,400 rooms, four 39-story office towers containing 2.2 million square feet of office space and a 340,000-square-foot retail mall area.

Renaissance Center was designed to serve as a catalyst for the redevelopment of Detroit's seriously declining central city. It became a reality only because of the personal efforts of the late Henry Ford II, who used his considerable personal and company resources and persuasive ability to secure both financing and tenants. Unfortunately, this was not enough to make the project a success in the face of the weak market for downtown Detroit office space. In fact, most analysts feel that rather than sparking a renewal, Renaissance Center merely drew tenants from other downtown buildings.

By 1983, the five institutions holding the $200 million first mortgage took over 53 percent ownership, with the 49 original investors retaining 47 percent. In 1995, the complex was put up for sale, with an asking price of $125 million, but even that price was not low enough to attract a buyer. Renaissance Center finally sold more than a year later for only $80 million, less than a fourth of its cost two decades earlier.

The message is clear. Real estate projects that defy economic logic will not be successful, regardless of the prestige and financial strength of their promoters. ■

Chapter Review

1. Investing in real estate is one of the most exciting aspects of the real estate industry. To be a successful real estate investor requires considerable knowledge about all of the topics addressed in this text. In addition, investors must have a clear understanding of the criteria they should use when evaluating an investment opportunity.

2. Advantages of investing in income-producing properties include cash flows from operations, appreciation in property value, portfolio diversification and financial leverage. Disadvantages include relatively large capital requirements, risk and the lack of liquidity of real estate investments.

3. The net present value decision rule provides a basis for sound financial decision making that is consistent with the objective of wealth maximization. To apply this rule to real estate investment opportunities, we must develop forecasts of the expected cash flows the projects are likely to generate.

4. The discounted cash flow model is the recommended framework for making real estate investment decisions. By forecasting the cash flows that are likely to result from operating a property during each year of the holding period and the cash flow that will result when the property is sold, we can calculate the expected net present value of the investment opportunity. Using the net present value rule, we can then make a decision about whether the project is expected to increase our wealth.

5. Estimating ATCF requires estimates of potential gross income, vacancy and credit losses, operating expenses and mortgage amortization, as well as a thorough understanding of income tax rules regarding real estate investment. An estimate of ATER is obtained by subtracting from the sales price of a property's selling expenses, taxes due on sale and the amount outstanding on any loans. Converting these cash flows into present value is accomplished by discounting them at the rate of return that reflects the time value of money and the riskiness of the investment opportunity.

6. If the present value of ATCF and ATER exceed the equity required, NPV is positive, and the investor should choose to accept the project.

Key Terms

after-tax cash flow   annual operating cash flow that remains after expenses, debt service and taxes have been paid.

after-tax equity reversion   the amount of money generated by the sale of an investment after taxes have been paid and any debts extinguished.

before-tax cash flow   annual operating cash flow that remains after expenses and debt service have been paid.

before-tax equity reversion   the amount of money generated by the sale of an investment before taxes have been paid.

debt service   total amount paid to lenders to service outstanding debt.

depreciation deduction   a noncash deduction permitted by the Internal Revenue Service (IRS) for capital recovery.

effective gross income   potential gross income less vacancy and credit losses.

financial leverage   the use of borrowed funds with the intention of magnifying investment returns.

internal rate of return   the discount rate that sets net present value exactly equal to zero.

investment   present sacrifice in anticipation of expected future benefit.

net operating income   annual operating cash flow that remains after expenses have been paid.

net present value   present value of inflows minus present value of outflows.

net sales proceeds   proceeds from sale after selling expenses have been paid.

potential gross income   the total income potential of an investment, assuming all space is leased and all rents are collected.

required rate of return   a minimum acceptable rate of return.

vacancy and credit losses   revenues not received due to vacancy in the property or uncollectible rents.

Study Exercises

1. What are the attractions of real estate as an investment?

2. What are the disadvantages of real estate as an investment?

3. Explain the logic behind the net present value decision rule and the internal rate of return decision rule.

4. Why do you suppose the depreciable life for a residential investment property is shorter than that of a nonresidential property? How does this fact influence an investor's decisions?

5. A real estate broker offers an apartment building for sale that has the following characteristics:

   (a) Asking price: $3.5 million, with the land valued at $500,000

   (b) The building contains 160 apartment units that rent for $450 per month, with rent expected to increase by 4 percent per year starting in year two.

   (c) Vacancy and bad debt allowance is 6 percent of the potential gross income.

   (d) Property taxes and insurance are expected to be constant over the investment horizon at $60,000 per year. Utilities, maintenance, management and other operating expenses are expected to be 25 percent of the annual effective gross income.

   (e) The real estate agent estimates that the value of the property will be $4.4 million at the end of the five-year investment horizon with 5 percent expected selling expenses.

   (f) A 12 percent, 20-year mortgage for $2.4 million with annual payments is available.

(g) The investment horizon is five years, beginning January 1997 and ending December 2001. The investor's marginal tax rate is 28 percent. The investor has several profitable real estate investments and can utilize any tax losses. The appropriate discount rate for this investment (the required rate of return) is 18 percent.

Calculate the relevant cash flows for this investment, and apply the NPV and IRR rules to decide whether the investor should pursue this project.

For Further Reading

Greer, G. E. *Investment Analysis for Real Estate Decisions,* 4th ed. (Chicago: Dearborn Financial Publishing, Inc., 1997).

Hoven, V. *The Real Estate Investor's Tax Guide,* 2nd ed. (Chicago: Real Estate Education Company, 1996).

PART SIX

Real Estate
Development

CHAPTER 18
Residential Land Uses

With land and other development costs escalating, single-family attached houses, such as these duplexes, are quickly becoming a popular residential alternative to the more traditional detached home.

Real Estate Today

- *Close-Up*
  Seaside, Florida

- *Close-Up*
  Fisher Island

- *Close-Up*
  Highlands Falls
  Country Club

- *Case Study*
  Market and
  Feasibility for the
  Milford Hills
  Subdivision

- *Close-Up*
  Biltmore House

Chapter Preview

THE PROCESS OF real estate development is one that requires extensive knowledge and practice of all aspects of real estate: legal, financial and markets. Because of the special character-istics of real estate improvements—large size, long life and long gestation period—success in real estate development is in large part determined by the accuracy of forecasts of long-term market potential for the project.

The final two chapters of this book examine the real estate development process. In this chapter, we will focus on residential land development, while the next chapter will deal with various types of commercial development.

Residential development takes various forms: single-family and multifamily dwellings, primary and secondary homes, cus-tom-built and factory-built houses. Whatever form a develop-ment takes, successful developers study carefully the market for the type of housing they contemplate and analyze carefully the financial feasibility of the proposed project.

The topics to be covered in this chapter are

- types of residential development, including (1) single-fam-ily detached houses, (2) single-family attached houses, (3) multifamily residences, (4) mobile homes and (5) second homes;
- time-sharing;
- market and feasibility analysis; and
- financial feasibility analysis.

TYPES OF RESIDENTIAL DEVELOPMENT

Although the single-family home on its own lot remains the ideal of most American families, other forms of single-family dwellings are becoming increasingly popular. Multifamily residences, too, take various forms. The five principal types of residential development are

1. single-family detached houses;
2. single-family attached houses;
3. multifamily residences;
4. mobile homes; and
5. second homes.

Single-Family Detached Houses

The single-family house separated from any adjoining house with at least some open land on all four sides remains the dwelling type most sought after by American families. Many accept a very basic house on a very small lot simply to attain this goal. The reason often given for the preference is that the detached house provides more privacy than an attached dwelling, though this is not always the case, especially if lots are small. Nevertheless, because of this perception, detached houses often have the best resale values.

In the years following World War II, the single-family detached dwelling overwhelmingly dominated housing markets in the United States. Land was cheap on the urban fringe, and large investments in public facilities such as roads, schools and sewer and water extensions made this type of horizontal sprawl feasible.

In more recent years, however, land and other developmental costs have escalated, making detached housing too expensive for many potential buyers. Design modifications, such as the clustering of such houses, will help conserve open space and reduce costs.

Single-Family Attached Houses

The attached row house is a form of housing that goes back to colonial times. This type of dwelling, on its own fee simple lot, but sharing common walls with its neighbors, was quite common in cities of the East and in San Francisco.

The first association of homeowners who owned streets and parkland in common was founded in Boston in 1826. Louisburg Square, which contains 18 row houses and a common park on 2.3 acres on Beacon Hill, remains a very desirable residential area even today.

The rise of the suburbs shortly after the turn of this century led to the domination of the detached house. The suburban form of the row house, the town house (see below), was a rarity until the 1960s; the overwhelming majority of such dwellings have been built since 1970. For projects that are owner-occupied, almost all have used the condominium form of ownership, with a community association managing common areas.

The single-family attached dwelling has several advantages over the detached project. Clustering requires less road frontage and shorter utility lines,

Real Estate Today

Close-Up

Seaside, Florida

The automobile-oriented, low-density suburban development that has dominated urban growth in the United States since the 1940s has met with growing criticism as urban sprawl, with its attendant congestion and negative environmental impacts, has gobbled up the rural landscape. Increasingly, urban planners are promoting higher-density, pedestrian-oriented residential developments that are more economical of land and less dependent on the automobile. Seaside, Florida is one of the most outstanding examples of this trend.

Developer Robert Davis owned an eighty-acre tract of land on Florida's northwest coast near Panama City that had been willed to him by his grandfather. Instead of building the typical high-rise condominiums that were dominating Florida beachfront development, Davis decided to build a community that would be in keeping with the small cottage, rocker-on-the-porch, pedestrian-oriented vacation villages he remembered from his youth. The result was Seaside.

The Seaside plan provides for approximately 300 houses. Its compact layout follows the principle of the "five-minute" walk, with most daily needs being inside that distance. The beach has been reserved as common open space with a series of varied pavilions providing access at the end of streets leading to the Gulf. A series of public pedestrian paths lead through the community, and every house is required to have a picket fence along the walkway. But not just any picket fence—the community development code requires that there cannot be two identical fences on the same street. All fences must be painted white, not just any white, but one of thirteen specific brands and shades of white. All utility wires must be run underground. Shutters must be real—not artificial—and operable.

While being very specific on certain items, the development code allows for great individuality in architectural styles, and it has accommodated Victorian, Neoclassical, Cracker, Modern and Postmodern styles. Many houses include towers and are painted in distinctive hyper-pastel colors such as hot pinks and purples, bright greens and yellows.

While the development code shaped the architectural and aesthetic character of Seaside, it also mandated height construction standards. When Hurricane Opal ravaged the Florida Panhandle coast in 1995, nearby communities suffered extensive damage. Seaside experienced almost none.

Both as a real estate development and as a planning statement, Seaside has been a definite success. Lot prices are now ten times higher than when the development began in 1981, and house prices have kept pace, with some homes selling for over $750,000. One was even recently offered at $995,000! But Seaside is far from a typical community. Fewer than one-third of the homes are occupied by permanent residents, and the question remains as to whether Seaside can really be a model for more typical, nonresort, bedroom suburbs. ∎

---

resulting in lower development costs per unit. The higher density of houses also permits lower land costs, further reducing cost per unit. This type of development also can result in less adverse ecological impact, with more of the site being left in its natural state and with more useful open space. A frequent complaint in conventional subdivisions is "I have to spend my weekends cutting all that grass, but there's no place for the kids to play." In a well-designed single-family attached project, yard maintenance by the homeowner is reduced greatly or eliminated, and children have a place to play.

Real Estate Today

Close-Up

Fisher Island

If you would like to go upscale, you might want to buy a home on Fisher Island. Located just five miles from downtown Miami in Biscayne Bay, the island was once owned by William Vanderbilt, who swapped his luxury yacht for the 216-acre isle in the 1920s. Vanderbilt, grandson of the famous and very wealthy tycoon Commodore Vanderbilt, built a Mediterranean-style, terra-cotta-roofed mansion with seven marble fireplaces and hand-carved mahogany paneling from Napoleon's palaces. The mansion also had several guest bungalows, a studio, swimming pools, tennis courts, a nine-hole golf course and an electrical generating plant. After Vanderbilt's death in 1944, the island passed through several hands before being purchased by Island Developers, Ltd., in 1979. The company decided to develop Fisher Island as an extremely exclusive resort and residential community. Current prices for the condominium ownership villa and apartments range from around $500,000 to more than $4 million, with an average price of $1.6 million for a 3,500-square-foot unit. In 1993, an 8,500-square-foot unit was on sale for $6.39 million. It contained five bedrooms, a gymnasium, a Jacuzzi on a 5,000-square-foot terrace and huge closet and dressing areas off the his-and-hers bathrooms.

Fisher Island has no causeway to the mainland. It is reached by private ferries, which run every 15 minutes, 24 hours a day. If you prefer, you can use the island's private seaplane ramp or helipad. Or if you would rather bring your yacht, two deep-water marinas can accommodate vessels of up to 200 feet. But don't come to the island unless you are a resident or guest. It is said to be easier to break into the White House than to get onto Fisher Island uninvited; privacy and tranquility are ensured by a 40-person security staff. Travel around the island is primarily by golf cart, one of which comes with each home and hotel room.

As for activities, in addition to the redesigned golf course, there are 18 lighted tennis courts and nearly a mile of beach "renourished" with 35,500 cubic yards of soft white sand barged in from the Bahamas. The restored Vanderbilt mansion is now the Fisher Island Club, with elegant dining and an international spa.

Fisher Island is obviously a development aimed at a narrow niche market, primarily very wealthy people in their early 40s who desire a full-time or winter haven that is relatively secluded and secure from most of the problems of the outside world. Security has been a major factor in attracting foreign buyers, particularly South American residents who worry about kidnappings. About 40 percent of Fisher Island residents are foreign, with 39 countries represented. ■

Single-family attached housing can be of several types, including the town house, the plex and the patio house.

Town Houses   The **town house** is similar to the old row house. Each unit has its own front door that opens to the outdoors, but shares one or both side walls with adjacent houses. Although the town house has no side yards, it may have front and rear yards. Town houses may front on a street or may be built in a series of five to ten units fronting on a common area.

Plexes   The **plex** shares the characteristics of the town house and the single-family detached house. Each building in a plex contains two or more units, each with its own outside entrance. A duplex is for two families; a triplex, for three families; a quadruplex, for four families; and so on.

The plex has fallen into disrepute in many communities because it is so often associated with dreary and styleless rental housing on small, conventional lots. If well designed, however, the plex can be a very attractive alternative to the detached house.

Patio or Zero-Lot-Line Houses   The **patio house,** or zero-lot-line house, is very similar to the detached house except that construction is from lot line to lot line, with an outdoor living area in an interior garden court.

The garden court is normally enclosed by the house or by the house and walls. Although small compared to the yard of the usual single-family detached house, the secluded area provides a great deal of privacy. The houses are usually one story, are often L-shaped and may have one small side yard to provide passage to the rear court area.

Multifamily Residences

Although the single-family home is still preferred by most families, it is too expensive for an increasing portion of the population. Multifamily housing may be the best alternative for such families, as well as for young couples who lack the down payments necessary to purchase their own homes, "empty nesters" who no longer need or desire as large a home as they did when their children lived with them and single-person households. Where land prices are extremely high, rental or owner-occupied apartments may be the only feasible type of new housing available. Multifamily housing can take the form of garden apartments and midrise or highrise apartments.

A **garden apartment** generally is a two-story or three-story building with a density of 10 to 20 units per acre, with open space between the buildings and convenient parking. They generally are built in suburban locations.

Many garden apartment projects contain precious little garden, consisting only of buildings separated by slivers of grass surrounded by a sea of asphalt paving. Good design and careful use of open space, however, can produce a very pleasant housing environment.

A **midrise apartment** building consists of four to eight stories with one or more apartments per floor. Elevators almost always are found in this type of development, and the eight-story maximum height is set by the capacity of a single residential elevator.

Most **highrise apartment** buildings contain more than eight stories and sometimes rise to nearly 100 stories, as does the John Hancock Building in Chicago. The highrise apartment project is more expensive to construct than the garden apartment project and typically contains only luxury apartments. Until recently, almost all highrise apartments were rental units, but condominium ownership has grown rapidly in the past few years.

Ownership Alternatives: Condominiums and Cooperatives As noted in Chapter 4, many potential homeowners look to condominiums and cooperatives as ownership alternatives. To review these concepts very briefly, the owner of a condominium (condo) holds title in fee simple to the particular unit occupied and shares ownership in common areas, such as recreational facilities, lobbies and parking lots. The owner of a cooperative (co-op) owns stock in a corporation that actually holds title to the property, but the individual has the right to live in a particular apartment. The condominium, which in the United States is a relatively recent development, is far more common than the older cooperative form; most cooperatives are located in New York City. Almost all condos and co-ops are attached or multifamily units.

Condominiums and cooperatives offer several economic advantages to the buyer when contrasted with renting. Like other homeowners, the owner of a condo or co-op can deduct property taxes and mortgage interest from taxable income for income tax purposes. Second, and perhaps of even greater importance, condominium or cooperative ownership serves as a hedge against potential inflation, enabling the owner to accumulate an equity position. Conversely, of course, it also exposes the owner to potential declines in housing prices.

The demand for condos and co-ops has increased during the past several decades, primarily in response to demographic trends and rapidly rising home prices. Many first-time buyers were forced out of the single-family detached market, but they still could afford a condominium or cooperative. The market was also helped by the growth in the number of households, by the smaller size of families and single-member households, by growing preference for in-town living and by increasing commuting costs.

Besides these demographic trends, economic factors affecting the rental market have also helped increase the popularity of condos and co-ops. Owners of rental property have been caught in a serious cost squeeze. Operating costs in many cities have increased far more rapidly than rents, and in cities with rent controls, the squeeze has been much worse. This has led to a large number of conversions from rental units to condominiums and cooperatives. The large-scale trend began in Chicago, then spread rapidly across the country.

Manufactured Homes

A **manufactured home,** or mobile home, is a dwelling manufactured in a factory and then moved to a particular site. The traditional image of mobile homes has been that of cheap, tacky and high-density housing in sleazy "shantytown" trailer parks. Unfortunately, in the past, much of this reputation was richly deserved. In contrast to the resale value of a conventional site-built house, which has generally appreciated, that of a mobile home generally fell each year. This caused many lenders to treat mobile homes as personal property, much like automobiles, and to provide only relatively short-term, high-interest installment loans. In many areas, it was impossible to obtain one mortgage that would cover the purchase of a mobile home and its site. Opposition to mobile-home developments led many communities either to zone them out completely or to limit them to generally undesirable or rural areas.

The image is changing, however, because the design and construction of manufactured homes have been greatly improved. With the introduction of new designs and materials, the "oversized aluminum shoebox" has been replaced by a structure much closer to a conventional house in appearance. Part of this process has been the trend toward wider units and the double-wide and triple-wide units that are assembled on site into 24-foot-wide to 36-foot-wide homes. Construction quality also has improved tremendously with the introduction of required national construction standards.

These factors, plus the trend toward owner-occupied manufactured-home subdivisions instead of rental parks, have led lenders to liberalize financing and make it more comparable to that for conventional homes. In the past, mobile homes were considered personal property and were financed with 10-year to 15-year consumer installment loans that generally carried interest rates approximately two percentage points more than conventional mortgage rates. Today, however, owners of manufactured homes located permanently on their lots can obtain 30-year, FHA-insured mortgages.

The rising absolute and relative cost of conventional "stick-built" housing and increasing rents in apartments have boosted manufactured housing's share of the market. It now accounts for about 25 percent of new single-family home sales and for more than 35 percent of home sales of less than $50,000.

Second Homes

By their very nature, second homes are very different from primary homes, and second-home markets are quite different from primary-home markets. The

Real Estate Today

Highlands Falls Country Club

It was not an outstanding golf club community or real estate development. In fact, the Highlands Falls Country Club was a failure. Located near the western North Carolina mountain resort town of Highlands, the club was first opened as the nine-hole Skylake golf course in the 1960s. It was a shoestring operation, with golfers depositing their greens fees in an honor box, where the money was picked up at the end of the day. Several developers worked on the project, the last adding nine more holes and a clubhouse. By 1980, there were about 85 homes, but sales were slow, and the project's mortgage was foreclosed.

The mortgage on the Highlands Falls Country Club was held by two real estate investment trusts. They had to decide whether the development could be made economically viable. Not only was Highlands Falls Country Club a failed project with a poor reputation, it also came with about 85 very disgruntled and suspicious existing homeowners. Thus, the new development firm, Golf Properties, Inc., was faced with the daunting task of not only developing a high-quality golf club that could yield a development profit, but also handling a near revolt of existing club members. It was no small task.

Noted golf architect Joe Lee completely redesigned the golf course, building several new holes and combining others to create longer ones, and the entire course was refurbished. While this made Highlands Falls a much better and more challenging golf course, it also made some of the old club members unhappy because they preferred the shorter course. A tennis and swim center was added, and extensive additions and renovations were made to the clubhouse.

Golf Properties worked very hard to upgrade the image of Highlands Falls, but this was a slow and uphill process. Both the members and the community had seen too much mediocre development and failure in the past. Rumors persisted that the club would soon be foreclosed again. Gradually, however, the sweeping physical facility improvements, increasing lot and home sales and small but important touches such as extensive landscaping and masses of flowers turned the country club's image around.

Today, Highlands Falls Country Club has a deserved reputation as one of the premier clubs in an area of very exclusive golf courses. Lot prices, which in 1980 ranged from $10,000 to $15,000, have reached up to $150,000 for view lots. There are more than 300 homes in the development, with only 25 lots remaining. Club memberships, which in 1984 sold for $1,100, now sell for $31,000. House prices range from about $190,000 for some of the older homes to $800,000 for a few of the newer ones.

The story of the Highlands Falls Country Club shows that even a failed development can be turned into an outstanding and profitable one if the basic elements for success are present and the project is managed by a knowledgeable developer with sufficient resources and a sincere desire to create a quality development. ■

---

principal reason for owning a second home is the desire to use it for leisure-time enjoyment, and certain amenities are ordinarily the main factors in its location: beaches, mountains, golf courses, tennis courts, ski lifts and so on.

Most second-home owners occupy their dwellings for only small portions of the year, often because of the seasonal nature of many resorts, but also because the owners are unable to get away from their jobs or other responsibilities for extended periods. Hence, many units are bought at least partially for their investment potential and rented for much of the year. As landlords, owners enjoy various tax benefits, including depreciation allowances and deduction of maintenance costs, but changes in tax laws and regulations have greatly reduced potential tax advantages in recent years. For example, there are limits on the time an owner can occupy a dwelling and still claim it as rental property.

Because ownership of a second home is so expensive, many buyers in recent years have turned to resort **time-sharing,** a concept discussed in Chapter 4. Under time-sharing, a single dwelling is sold to a number of buyers, each of whom receives exclusive ownership of the dwelling for a specified time period each year. Like other forms of fee simple ownership, this ownership interest can be willed, leased or sold.

The time-sharing concept of vacation property first appeared in the 1960s, grew rapidly with the collapse of the resort condominium market in the 1970s and peaked during the early years of the 1980s. Since that time, many buyers have turned away from the concept as the disadvantages of time-sharing have become apparent, particularly the questionable values offered by many projects and the slow appreciation or actual decline in price of existing time-share units.

MARKET AND FEASIBILITY ANALYSIS

We have covered in previous chapters some of the factors that determine the demand for housing at the national, regional and neighborhood levels. All such factors must be considered when analyzing the market for a particular project.

Both developers and lenders need to know what the market will be for a project in order to determine its feasibility. Essentially, they must determine what market conditions have been in the recent past and which factors that would affect the market for the project are likely to change in the near future. The four steps in such a market analysis are

1. delineation of the market area;
2. analysis of recent economic trends in the local market area;
3. determination of possible changes in demand factors, such as employment, disposable income, population, household characteristics and the **absorption rate** (the number of units being absorbed by the market); and
4. analysis of the potential supply, including other possible competing projects.

Delineation of the Market Area

To begin with, the project's market area—that is, the extent of the housing submarket in which it will compete—must be described. The market area is determined largely by employment opportunities and commuting ranges. In smaller communities, of course, all of the local employers will be within the market area, but local workers also may commute to jobs in nearby communities.

In larger urban areas, the analyst must determine the extent of employment available within relevant commuting ranges. Public transportation facilities can extend the commuting range and expand the market area.

Analysis of Recent Trends

What has been the demand for housing within the market area during the past few years, and what economic factors lie behind recent trends? What are the vacancy rates for local rental housing and the absorption rates for new owner-occupied units? Such data usually are available and are essential for an analysis of the market potential of a new project.

Determination of Future Demand

After past and present housing market conditions have been determined, the most important part of the analysis remains—the estimation of future demand. How much unfulfilled demand remains in the market? What changes in the economic base or in national or regional economic conditions will affect demand in the local area? Are new transportation facilities or other public facilities being completed that will influence demand? The developer must analyze such factors carefully to make a reasonably accurate estimation of potential demand for the project.

Of course, not even the most keen and careful analyst can always accurately prophesy the future. Indeed, one would need almost supernatural powers to totally forecast the impact on real estate of the interactions of international political and economic intrigues, the tax changes coming from Congress or state and local governments, the expansion or contraction plans of large corporations and the complexity of business locational decisions.

Analysis of Future Supply

Many developers correctly analyze demand factors, but court disaster by ignoring competitive projects. One of the primary characteristics of real estate improvements is their long gestation periods, and developers must estimate both demand and supply conditions during this time.

Suppose, for example, a potential demand exists for 500 new apartment units in a community within the next two years. If three developers respond to this potential demand by constructing three 500-unit complexes, it is impossible that each will be successful in the short run unless the market expands more than anticipated. At best, vacancy rates in the local market probably will rise to a high level, and the general profitability of all complexes will be reduced, or perhaps will be nonexistent, resulting in foreclosure and failure.

The second step in the analysis—determining what lies behind recent trends—sometimes is not given enough emphasis, much to the subsequent regret of the developer. Suppose that housing markets in a particular community have been very tight during the past five years; that is, there has been excess demand. Without proper analysis, this might indicate a continuing strong demand for housing in the next few years.

On more thorough investigation, however, the developer might determine that the tight market conditions resulted from an influx of workers to a major new manufacturing plant, which now operates at its designed level. Unless growth occurs in either the plant or some other part of the community's economic base, the absorption rate—and therefore absolute demand for new housing—will decline.

The analyst also must carefully evaluate potential demand in the particular submarket at which the project is aimed. For example, it may be that the new plant described above caused a significant expansion in demand for rental housing. The future demand for this segment of the market may decline, even though demand in other segments may expand, if the new workers move out of the rental units to owner-occupied homes.

FINANCIAL FEASIBILITY ANALYSIS

In addition to a market analysis, the developer should conduct a financial feasibility analysis of the proposed project. Such an analysis may be quite sophisticated for a large and complicated development or relatively simple for a small one. In either case, the purpose is to determine—on paper, at least—the probable success of the project.

Finally, bank financing, which is usually essential, also helps reduce the developer's risk because a large amount of the developer's own or company funds are not involved. On the other hand, any delays can be quite expensive when the interest rate meter is running. For example, if the site improvements cannot be constructed as rapidly as the developer anticipates, or if the homes do not sell as rapidly as expected, the result could be a greatly reduced profit or even default on the loan.

THE IMPORTANCE OF MARKET ANALYSIS

If the three most important factors in real estate are location, location and location, it should be clear to the readers of this book that the three most important factors in real estate development are the market, the market and the market. Real estate developers who forget this lesson usually fail; those who carefully and correctly analyze the market usually succeed .

Real Estate Today   *Case Study*

Market and Feasibility for the Milford Hills Subdivision

Developer Angus Talberson was considering developing a 19.5-acre tract into a subdivision of 30 single-family attached houses that would sell for approximately $95,000 each. Even though Talberson was well acquainted with the local market, he performed a careful analysis of the potential demand for the proposed project.

The subdivision site for Milford Mills was located in northern Rowan County, a desirable residential section of a metropolitan area containing a population of approximately 800,000. Talberson compared Milford Hills with ten existing subdivisions located in the same general area. As the map in Figure 18.1 shows, all of the subdivisions were located north of the beltway surrounding the city and had reasonable access to the freeway system. Milford Hills was farther from the beltway and the office park employment located there than most of the other subdivisions, but the site was near a freeway interchange and still within relatively easy commuting range.

Location Map of Milford Hills Subdivision   **Figure 18.1**

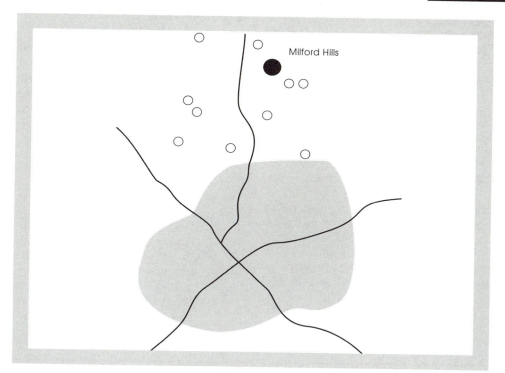

Table 18.1		Sales in Selected Rowan County Subdivisions				
Subdivision	Up to $70,000	$71,000–$85,000	$86,000–$100,000	$101,000–$115,000	$116,000–$130,000	More than $130,000
Brookwood		10	15	5		
Chimney Springs			4	13	10	
Hollyberry		2	23	11	1	
Huntcliffe				10	15	15
Lost Forest			5	7	11	
River Chase		22	48	24	1	
Rivermont			10	19	16	1
Saddle Creek			26	9	2	
Terramont	36	5				
Woodland Hills			16	10	2	
Total	36	39	147	108	58	16

Talberson obtained the sales figures for the existing subdivisions during the previous year, data that are presented in Table 18.1. Nearly 150 homes were sold in the price range that Talberson had proposed for Milford Hills, meaning that if the size of the market remained the same, to sell 30 homes in 15 months, he would have to capture approximately 16 percent of total sales in this category, certainly not an unreasonable expectation. Because the subdivision could not be developed and placed on the market for more than two years, Talberson also tried to determine any changes that might influence the size of the market two or three years into the future. The economy of the metropolitan area was widely diversified, with no dominant industry or employer. Hence, it seemed logical to assume that no dramatic shifts in employment would greatly affect the local housing market. On the contrary, the absorption of new housing units had been increasing at approximately 10 percent annually in this price bracket, and it seemed probable that this trend would continue, further reducing the market penetration needed to make Milford Hills a success.

Talberson also analyzed the supply of homes currently on the market in the price range of his proposed project and tried to find out whether other new projects were in the planning stage. From these studies, he determined that no large supply of competing homes was either currently on the market or planned that would create an excess supply in his market segment.

In summary, Talberson's analysis led to the conclusion that the market for the proposed project was adequate to support it and that he could proceed to determine its financial feasibility.

In analyzing the financial feasibility of Milford Hills, Talberson made several assumptions.

- The land would be purchased in quarter 1 of the development process for $136,500 with 10 percent in cash, the balance to be due in quarter 6. (The project was divided into 14 quarters over a three-and-one-half-year period.) The land acquisition would be financed by the seller, with a 9 percent rate of interest on the mortgage.
- Planning, engineering and subdivision approval would require 15 months.
- A development loan could be secured from a commercial bank at the following terms:
  - Line of credit up to $1.3 million
  - Loan to be repaid within 36 months
  - 9 percent annual interest, payable quarterly on the average funds outstanding the previous quarter
  - Three points ($39,000) payable to the bank at closing as an additional inducement to make the loan

- The houses could be started six months after site improvements had been begun. Six houses could be finished and sold in each quarter 10 to 14. All would be sold and the project completed by the end of quarter 14.
- Any increases in costs resulting from inflation would be reflected in the prices of the houses sold.

From these assumptions, Talberson constructed the cash flow statement shown in Table 18.2 on pages 410 and 411.

Several characteristics of subdivision development are apparent here. First, development requires a large negative cash flow for a long period before any positive cash flow occurs. For the Milford Hills project, no cash inflow would be received until quarter 10. By that time,

the project would have recorded a total negative cash outflow of $1.28 million because funds would have to be used for land acquisition, planning and engineering, site improvements, house construction, financing and administration. Milford Hills would not develop a positive cash flow until quarter 13.

Second, development loans are usually needed to absorb large negative cash flows during the early months of such projects. After Talberson secured a development loan from a commercial loan bank at the terms enumerated above, he constructed a revised cash flow statement to show the impact of the financing costs. The profit and loss statement shown in Table 18.3 on page 411, developed from these data, shows an expected profit of $541,000.

Table 18.2		Cash Flow Statement, Milford Hills Subdivision				

	Quarter					
	1	**2**	**3**	**4**	**5**	**6**
Sources of Funds						
Sales						
Less cost of sales	$ 0	$ 0	$ 0	$ 0	$ 0	$0
Net receipts						
Uses of Funds						122,850
Land acquisition	13,650					9,375
Planning and engineering site	9,375	9,375	9,375	9,375	9,375	110,000
Improvements						
Home construction						
Administration and other	15,000	15,000	15,000	15,000	15,000	15,000
Total	38,025	24,375	24,375	24,375	24,375	257,225
Net cash flow	(38,025)	(24,375)	(24,375)	(24,375)	(24,375)	(257,225)
Cumulative cash flow	(38,025)	(62,400)	(86,775)	(111,150)	(135,525)	(392,750)
Borrowings	122,850	122,850	85,000	25,000	24,000	351,000
	(land)					
Repayments						
Cumulative borrowings	122,850		207,850	232,850	256,850	485,000

Cash Flow Statement, Milford Hills Subdivision *(Continued)*   **Table 18.2**

			Quarter				
7	**8**	**9**	**10**	**11**	**12**	**13**	**14**
			$570,000	$570,000	$570,000	$570,000	$570,000
			19,950	19,950	19,950	19,950	19,950
$0	$0	$0	550,050	550,050	550,050	550,050	550,050
9,375	9,375						
140,000	100,000						
125,000	125,000	250,000	250,000	250,000	125,000	125,000	
15,000	15,000	15,000	15,000	15,000	15,000	15,000	15,000
289,375	249,375	265,000	265,000	265,000	140,000	140,000	15,000
(289,375)	(249,375)	(265,000)	285,000	285,050	410,050	410,050	535,050
(682,125)	(931,500)	(1,196,500)	(911,500)	(626,450)	(216,400)	193,650	728,700
290,000	250,000	265,000	285,000	285,000	410,000	300,000	
775,000	1,025,000	1,290,000	1,005,000	720,000	310,000	0	

Pro Forma Profit and Loss Statement, Milford Hills Subdivision   **Table 18.3**

Revenue	
Sale of houses: 30 × $95,000	$2,850,00
Less selling cost (3.5%)	99,750
	$2,750,250
Costs	
Land acquisition: 19.5 acres × $7,000 per acre	$136,500
Planning and engineering	75,000
Site improvements	350,000
House construction	1,250,000
Estimated financing costs	187,650
Administration and other costs	210,000
	$2,209,150
Expected profit	$541,100

Real Estate Today

Close-Up

Biltmore House

Biltmore House is the largest house ever built in the United States—three times the size of the White House, with 255 rooms, four and one-half acres of floor space and an 8,000-acre yard (nine times the size of New York City's Central Park). The house, built for George Vanderbilt in the 1890s at a cost of $7 million, is in the style of a French chateau and was considered very technologically advanced in its day, with full central heat, electricity, a fire alarm system, two elevators and telephones. In addition to 34 guest bedrooms (Vanderbilt liked to entertain), the house contains an indoor swimming pool, a bowling alley and a gymnasium.

But what would you do if you owned Biltmore House and had its huge maintenance costs staring you in the face? That was the dilemma facing Vanderbilt's grandson, William Cecil. He decided to leave a banking career in 1960 to return to North Carolina and the problems of the family home.

Biltmore House had been open to the public for about 30 years, but revenue from the 50,000 annual visitors fell $250,000 short of yearly maintenance costs. Cecil set out to market the property more effectively as a tourist attraction, and by 1968, 200,000 people visited annually, and the house turned its first profit—$16.34.

Today, more than 700,000 visitors each year, along with several restaurants, gift shops and a winery, generate $29 million in annual revenues.

In addition to the wonders of the house itself, Biltmore contains Vanderbilt's extensive collection of priceless paintings, porcelains, bronzes, carpets, other furnishings and antiques. The grounds include a four-acre English walled garden with more than 50,000 tulips and irises each spring and extensive landscaping with azaleas and other plants adorning the remainder of the estate. At Christmas, the house is decorated with some 30 trees, including a 40-foot Fraser fir in the huge banquet hall, with its 72-foot-high ceiling. In fact, Christmas has become the estate's busiest season, with more than 10,000 visitors crowding the grounds the day after Thanksgiving. To accommodate more guests during the holiday season, the house is now decorated for Christmas by early November (necessitating the erection of a second great tree in December), and special candlelight evening tours expand the visiting hours.

While turning Biltmore House from a financial burden into a financial success, William Cecil has also preserved an important part of our country's historical heritage. ■

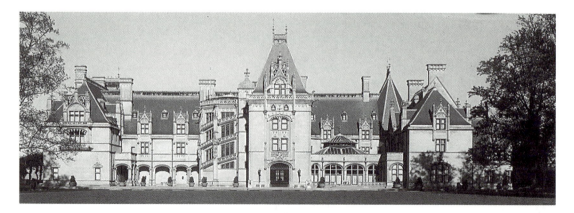

Chapter Review

1. The five principal types of residential development are (1) single-family detached houses, (2) single-family attached houses, (3) multifamily residences, (4) mobile homes and (5) second homes.

2. The single-family detached home has dominated housing markets for the past 50 years and remains the most sought after type of dwelling. Escalating land costs and growing environmental and energy concerns have made this type of housing less attractive than it once was, however.

3. Types of attached housing include (1) the town house, (2) the plex and (3) the patio house.

4. Multifamily residential projects are of three types: (1) garden apartments, which are generally two-story or three-story buildings; (2) mid-rises, consisting of four to eight stories, usually with an elevator; and (3) highrises, which contain more than eight stories and multiple elevators.

5. Condominium and cooperative ownership of multifamily and attached housing are increasing because of the economic benefits of such ownership, favorable demographic trends and the declining profitability of rental housing.

6. Manufactured or mobile homes gradually move toward greater acceptance by consumers, financial institutions and communities. As a result of improvements in design and quality, the availability of financing and the rising cost of conventional housing, manufactured homes probably will continue to capture increasing shares of the single-family market.

7. Amenities are the primary factors leading to the purchase of a second home. Because most buyers cannot occupy their units for much of the year, many dwellings are purchased for their investment potential.

8. Time-sharing enables a buyer to purchase the use of a second home for a specific time period each year. The buyer thus protects a large portion of his or her future vacation costs from inflation and benefits from any appreciation in the value of the interest.

9. The steps in analyzing the market for a residential project are (1) delineation of the market area, (2) analysis of recent trends in the local market area, (3) determination of possible changes in the demand factor of the project and (4) analysis of the potential supply, including other possible competing projects.

10. Market area is determined largely by employment opportunities within the relevant commuting range.

11. The market analyst essentially determines what market conditions have been in the recent past and which factors that would affect the market for a project are likely to change in the near future.

12. A developer should conduct a financial feasibility analysis that projects the probable cash flow and profit or loss of a proposed project.

Key Terms

absorption rate   the number of units capable of being absorbed by the market over a given time period.

garden apartment   a two-story or three-story building with a density of 10 to 20 units per acre.

highrise apartment   apartment buildings containing more than eight stories.

manufactured home   a dwelling unit that is manufactured in a factory and then moved to a particular site.

midrise apartment   apartment building consisting of four to eight stories.

patio house   a detached house with at least one wall that touches the property line.

plex   a form of attached housing containing two or more units, each with its own outside entrance.

time-sharing   a form of concurrent estate that splits ownership of a property across owners and across time.

town house   a form of attached housing in which each unit has its own front door but shares one or two walls with adjacent units.

Study Exercises

1. What are the five principal types of residential development?

2. What are the differences between condominium and cooperative ownership? What are some of the advantages of these types of ownership over renting?

3. What are the three types of single-family attached housing? What are the differences among the three?

4. What are the three types of multifamily residential housing? What are the differences among the three?

5. Discuss some of the factors that are leading to greater acceptance of manufactured or mobile homes.

6. What are the principal reasons for owning a vacation home, and how do they differ from the reasons for owning a principal residence?

7. Discuss the use of time-sharing in the marketing of vacation homes.

8. Describe the steps in analyzing the market for a residential project.

9. What factors determine the market for a residential project?

10. Describe the process of financial feasibility analysis for a proposed residential project.

CHAPTER 19
Commercial and Industrial Development

The Nichols Memorial Fountain serves as a focal point for the Country Club Plaza, which has the distinction of being known as the first suburban shopping center. For a complete description of the evolution of the shopping center, turn to the Close-Up on page 421.

Real Estate Today

- *Close-Up*
  The First Suburban
  Shopping Center:
  Country Club Plaza

- *Case Study*
  The Development
  of Willow Springs
  Center

Chapter Preview

SHOPPING CENTERS AND other buildings for retail trade, office buildings, hotels and motels, and restaurants are examples of income-producing commercial properties. Industrial properties include factory buildings and warehouses. The development of these types of properties is the focus of this chapter.

Specific topics to be discussed are

- shopping center development;
- evolution of the shopping center;
- development process of commercial properties, including (1) market and feasibility analysis, (2) site location, (3) tenant selection and (4) financial feasibility analysis;
- office buildings;
- industrial parks and distribution facilities; and
- hotels and motels.

417

SHOPPING CENTER DEVELOPMENT

The suburban shopping center is a creature of the automobile and is both a result and a cause of the suburban explosion that has taken place since World War II. As shopping centers have proliferated in suburban areas, the older central business districts of many cities have become economic backwaters. Others have been redeveloped, some as specialized shopping areas.

The traditional American shopping area was the **central business district,** an unplanned series of buildings constructed along major streets in the center of town. The modern shopping center is distinguished from the traditional commercial district by the following characteristics:

- One or more structures of unified architecture housing firms that are selected and managed as a unit for the benefit of all tenants
- A site that serves a particular trade area
- On-site parking
- Facilities for deliveries separated from the shopping area
- Single ownership and management

Although all shopping centers share these characteristics, not all shopping centers are alike. In fact, there are four major types, classified on the basis of type of tenants, size and function: the neighborhood center, the community center, the regional center and the superregional center. The types of shopping centers and their characteristics are shown in Figure 19.1 and listed in Table 19.1.

The **neighborhood shopping center,** sometimes called a *convenience center,* is designed to serve an area within a radius of approximately 1.5 miles and a population of 2,500 to 40,000. Its principal tenant usually is a supermarket, while the other stores largely provide convenience and shopping goods, such as pharmaceuticals, housewares and personal services. Its **gross leasable area**—that is, the total floor area designed for the tenants' use—ranges from 30,000 to 100,000 square feet, with 50,000 square feet typical. It usually is located on about three acres of land. Generally, the neighborhood center is a **strip shopping center**—that is, basically built in a straight line, with stores tied together by a canopy over a pedestrian walk. Parking space is provided adjacent to the stores and off the public street.

The **community shopping center** provides a wider range of merchandise and usually is built around a junior department store, variety store or discount store. It is designed to serve an area with a radius of approximately three to five miles and has a gross leasable area of 100,000 to 300,000 square feet located on from 10 to 30 acres.

When a discount store is the main tenant, the community shopping center sometimes is known as a **discount shopping center.**

The **regional shopping center** offers a full range of goods and services, usually has between 300,000 and 750,000 square feet of gross leasable area and occupies between 30 and 50 acres. It is anchored by at least one full-line department store, but usually has two or more. These shopping centers almost always are built as open or enclosed pedestrian malls, with the closed mall the overwhelming choice in recent years.

A **superregional shopping center** exceeds 750,000 square feet in gross leasable area, occupies 100 acres or more and includes at least three department

Types of Shopping Centers   **Figure 19.1**

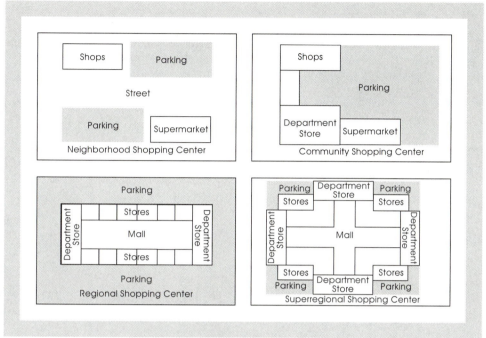

stores. Most centers exceed 1 million square feet and may draw customers from more than 50 miles. Most superregional centers are built with multiple levels to reduce walking distances for shoppers.

Variations on the major types of shopping centers include the superstore, the power center, the specialty shopping center and the factory outlet center. The **superstore** is a very large discount store with between 60,000 and 150,000 square feet under one roof. Such stores, which are found more often in Europe than in the United States, typically offer foodstuffs, general merchandise and hard lines, such as appliances, in a warehouse atmosphere. The **power center** is a large strip-type shopping center that is anchored by one or more "big box" retailers, along with smaller shops. The **specialty shopping center** focuses on unusual market segments, usually offering high-quality and high-priced merchandise in boutique-type stores, although a number of new specialty centers focus only on discount stores.

Another type of specialty center is the **factory outlet center,** which consists of retail outlet facilities, where goods are sold directly to the public in stores owned and operated by manufacturers. These centers began a decade or so ago when manufacturers opened factory-owned stores near their plants to sell off seconds, outdated or overproduced goods or goods sent back unsold by retailers. Then, in the 1980s, developers began constructing shopping malls catering specifically to outlet stores. Now more than 300 outlet malls exist. These malls bear little resemblance to the often dingy original stores and carry top-quality merchandise in extensive sizes and selections.

Table 19.1   Characteristics of Shopping Center, by Type

Type	Leasing Tenant	Typical Leasable Area (Square Feet)	Range of Gross Feasible Area (Square Feet)	Typical Site Area (Acres)	Minimum Support Required (Number of People)
Neighborhood or convenience center	Supermarket or drugstore	50,000	30,000–100,000	3	2,500–40,000
Community center	Variety, discount or junior department store	150,000	100,000–300,000	10–30	40,000–100,000
Regional center	One or more full-line department stores	400,000	300,000–750,000	30–50	150,000
Superregional center	Three or more full-line department stores	1,000,000	750,000–1,500,000	100 or more	200,000

The locational requirements of outlet malls are similar to those of full-price centers, with the exception that factory outlet malls generally must be located on the outskirts of large market areas or major tourist resorts. This requirement appeases major retailers, which are not happy to have factory stores in their markets selling the same merchandise at cheaper prices.

EVOLUTION OF THE SHOPPING CENTER

The tremendous rise in automobile ownership during the 1920s put a strain on downtown shopping areas, designed for pedestrians and public transportation. Congested streets, parking meters and the limited curbside areas available for parking in most cities encouraged a shift to new concentrations of shopping facilities with adequate provisions for parking.

The automobile also encouraged population movement to the suburbs, and these areas on the outskirts of cities became the logical sites for the new shopping facilities. A few developers built the first true suburban shopping centers with unified architecture, a planned mix of tenants and the essential ingredient—off-street parking. The surge in the number of centers came after World War II, with the explosion of residential suburbs.

The first suburban shopping center was Country Club Plaza in Kansas City, profiled on page 421. The first regional shopping center to contain a major full-line department store as the leading tenant was the Northgate Shopping Center

Real Estate Today

Close-Up

The First Suburban Shopping Center: Country Club Plaza

The first suburban shopping center generally is considered to be Country Club Plaza in Kansas City, although strictly speaking, it is a shopping district rather than a shopping center. At any rate, it was the first suburban area to incorporate unified architecture, common management, tenant selection and off-street parking.

J. C. Nichols Company began to develop the Country Club district shortly after the turn of the century, when it was the extreme southern suburb of Kansas City. To the north of this area and between it and the developed portion of the city was Brush Creek Valley, a largely overgrown area that was occupied by a brick kiln, several trash dumps and an old goat farm. In these unpromising surroundings, Nichols developed a new shopping center that featured off-street parking in what he termed "parking stations" and architecture reminiscent of that of Seville, Spain.

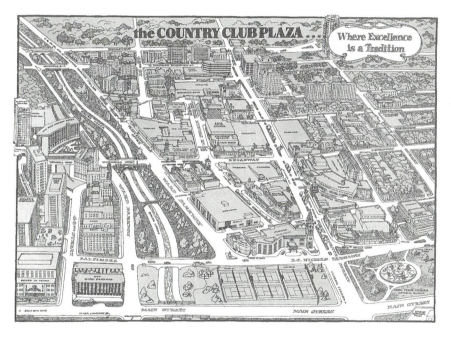

The first building was completed in 1923, and the center has been under almost continuous development and redevelopment since that time. It expanded greatly after World War II into a prestige shopping area containing more than 180 retail and service shops. A more recent major redevelopment was the conversion of the old Sears building into Seville Square, housing 42 boutiques and restaurants around an atrium.

Country Club Plaza pioneered many of the concepts that are commonplace in suburban shopping centers today. Because of the high quality of its design and architecture and continuing good management that has successfully adapted the center's facilities to keep abreast of evolving marketing trends, Country Club Plaza has retained its rank as a prestige shopping center for more than half a century. ■

in Seattle, constructed in 1950. The center contains several features that soon became familiar, including a central pedestrian mall, a truck tunnel to separate deliveries from the shopping areas and vast seas of parking spaces surrounding the central building.

THE SHOPPING CENTER DEVELOPMENT PROCESS

A developer who contemplates the construction of a shopping center must undertake several exhaustive studies if the proposed project is to have any hope of succeeding. The first task is to analyze the market to determine whether the proposed project is economically feasible. If it is, the developer must determine the precise site that will be most likely to ensure the project's success. Having settled on a site, the developer must secure the commitments of the key anchor tenants and the proper supplementary tenants to ensure a complementary mix of shopping facilities.

Market and Feasibility Analysis

Before a developer can build a shopping center, before a lender will make a mortgage loan and before potential anchor tenants will sign leases, several questions need to be answered regarding the proposed center's market and economic feasibility. Can the proposed center generate enough sales volume—and therefore rental income—to justify its development? Can the community absorb the proposed new retailing space? Are the population and purchasing power of the potential trade area expanding? If the market is not expanding, can the proposed center and its particular merchandising mix succeed in taking business away from existing stores or shopping centers?

A new center can do little to create business; basically, it must take business away from other retailers or capture expanded trade in a growing area. It is essential therefore that the developer also carefully analyze the status of the competition and the future prospects of the trade area.

Defining the Trade Area   The first step in a market and feasibility analysis is to define the **trade area**—that is, the geographic area from which the major portion of the patronage necessary to support the shopping center is to be drawn. This area varies with the types and quality of merchandise offered. For example, families generally purchase food and sundries close to their homes, but for more expensive items, such as clothing, furniture and major appliances, they often drive long distances to secure a better selection or lower prices. Similarly, those seeking specialty items, such as sports equipment or high-quality cameras, also will travel longer distances to shop.

These factors are reflected in the trade areas for the various types of centers. The **primary trade area**—that is, the area that accounts for 60 to 70 percent of a center's sales—has a radius of approximately 1.5 miles for a neighborhood shopping center, three to five miles for a community shopping center and eight to ten miles for a regional shopping center. Additional shoppers may come from the **secondary trade area**—the area for a regional center that is 15 to 20

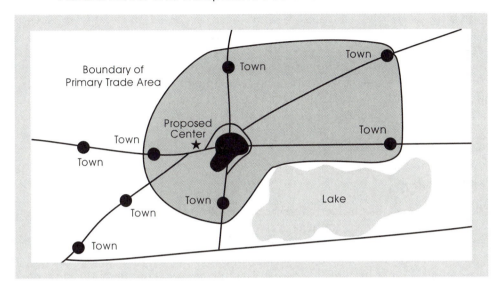

Primary Trade Area of a Proposed Shopping Center, Skewed by a Natural Barrier and Competitive Facilities

Figure 19.2

minutes' driving time from the primary trade area and that normally accounts for 15 to 20 percent of sales.

Besides the type of goods desired, the main factors that determine the size and shape of the trade area are the nature and location of competitive centers, the location of major transportation facilities, and natural barriers. For example, the defined trade area for the proposed center shown in Figure 19.2 is skewed toward the east and north because there is little or no competition exists in those directions. A lake forms a natural barrier in the southeast, and competitive facilities in the south and particularly the west greatly reduce the radius of the trade area in those directions.

Determining the Size of the Market After the extent of the trade area has been determined, the next step is to calculate the size of the potential market within the trade area. Basic data can be obtained from the Census of Population and Housing and the Census of Retail Trade. They can be supplemented by other public and private data sources, such as the annual estimates of personal income by county, supplied by the Bureau of Economic Analysis, and the *Survey of Buying Power*, published annually by *Sales and Marketing Management* magazine.

Analyzing the Competition After the current size and characteristics of the trade area's population have been determined, these data must be projected into the future. Projections are critical to the center's potential success because it is in the future that the center must compete in the marketplace.

It often is tempting simply to extrapolate recent trends into the future, but this method provides a very poor basis for decision making unless the best evidence indicates that a recent trend *will* continue. The experienced analyst or investor goes behind recent trends to find their causes and then attempts to project those trends on the basis of his or her findings.

Competitive Survey After the probable future purchasing power and retail purchases of the defined trade area have been estimated, the analyst must estimate the percentage of the total that can be captured by the proposed development.

One obvious step in this analysis is to make a competitive survey to determine the extent and strength of existing centers in the market. It also is essential to find out what other potential competitors are planned. A market study that indicates a potential demand sufficient to support a new shopping center probably will lead to a very unsuccessful project if the developer fails to take into account another proposed new center.

Site Location

The market and feasibility analysis can substantiate the practicability of a center within the defined trade area, but it does not pinpoint the exact site, and site selection is a crucial factor in the success of a shopping center.

Several factors are important in selecting the shopping center site, including size, shape, topography, drainage, utilities and zoning. The most important considerations by far, however, are location and access. The neighborhood or convenience shopping center requires easy access from the supporting residential area. It usually is located on a collector street, and in a planned community, it also may be located to encourage pedestrian access. The community center normally is located along a major thoroughfare, while the principal location requirement for regional and superregional centers is easy access to major freeways and, increasingly, mass-transit facilities.

It is not necessary for shopping centers to be located far from other centers; in fact, centers located across the street from or adjacent to each other may be complementary. For example, a specialty fashion center may draw customers to an adjacent regional shopping center from competing centers in the area because the specialty center enhances the general location for shoppers. Alternatively, one center may not compete with another nearby because it handles different types of goods. For example, a convenience or neighborhood shopping center may be located near a regional center and actually benefit from this location.

Developers say that there are only three important considerations in real estate development: location, location and location. The maxim is especially applicable in choosing a shopping center site. Selection of any but the best site not only means a less successful center initially; it usually means that a competing center eventually will be built on the best site and will use this advantage to secure the lion's share of the business.

Tenant Selection

The success of most shopping centers depends upon the securing of key anchor tenants. For regional and superregional centers, the anchors are major department stores; for community centers, they are junior department stores or discount stores; and for neighborhood centers, they are supermarkets or drugstores. Consequently, the negotiating strength of such firms is great, and they usually secure very favorable lease terms. Often, the major tenants in a regional center purchase land from the developer and construct their own buildings.

The major tenants are expected to attract shoppers to the supplementary tenants. These tenants must be chosen carefully to be complementary to each other and to the anchor stores. For example, men's stores—shoes, clothing and sporting goods—tend to reinforce each other. The same principle holds for women's clothing and related shops, including food products and personal services. To yield the highest return, continuing careful attention is also crucial to ensure that the tenant mix changes when necessary to reflect new trends.

OFFICE BUILDINGS

The demand for office space in a community depends on the level of certain types of business activity and government employment. Nationally, the increasing percentage of the work force in white-collar occupations and the growth in service industries in the past several decades have added to the demand for additional office space. Increased business activity in expanding areas, particularly in the Sunbelt region, has also fueled the demand for additional office space. Within cities, the growth of suburban office parks has greatly expanded the supply of office buildings in these locations.

Location of Office Activity

Office buildings traditionally have been located in downtown business districts, and in recent years, they have become the dominant form of land use in many city centers. Downtown office buildings most likely are used as the main offices of financial institutions, corporate headquarters, attorneys' offices and government facilities.

Most cities also have at least one secondary "uptown" office node, usually located along a major thoroughfare leading to the suburbs. Other specialized nodes may develop near governmental installations, shopping centers, hospitals and universities.

Another more recent type of development is the **office park,** a community of office structures under central management and administration, usually located in the suburbs and adjacent to a major freeway. Such parks generally consist of lowrise buildings in a campuslike setting. They attract tenants in sales, manufacturing and similar activities that do not need downtown locations. The office park's advantages are its location near suburban residential areas, with resultant reduction in commuting time, ease of parking and pleasant environment.

Types of Office Projects

Office buildings can be classified in several ways. Building location, discussed above, is one way. Another is by number of tenants. Single-tenant buildings are very common. They range in size from a 1,000-square-foot suburban structure

Real Estate Today   *Case Study*

The Development of Willow Springs Center

Cindy Owensby and Carlos Slawson had taken an option on a three-acre site and were considering developing a small shopping center called the Willow Springs Center. Before they could proceed, they had to answer the following questions:

- Was there sufficient market demand to support a new center at the proposed location?
- What type of center should they build?

The site was located just off a heavily traveled arterial street in a rapidly growing high-income suburb of a major city. A recent study conducted by a consulting firm indicated that the general area had great potential for retail stores. The population of the primary trade area (approximately a two-mile radius) was 45,000 and was forecast to increase to 65,000 in 15 years. The secondary trade area (the fan-shaped area shown in Figure 19.3, lying principally to the north of the proposed center and away from the central city) had a population of 70,000 and a projected population in 15 years of 95,000. The area's population was relatively young and affluent; only 6 percent were older than age 65, and the average household income was 75 percent higher than the average for the entire metropolitan area. Even though these data indicated a strong market potential, it was still not clear whether that site would be viable for a new shopping center.

| **Figure 19.3** | Trade Area for Willow Springs Center |

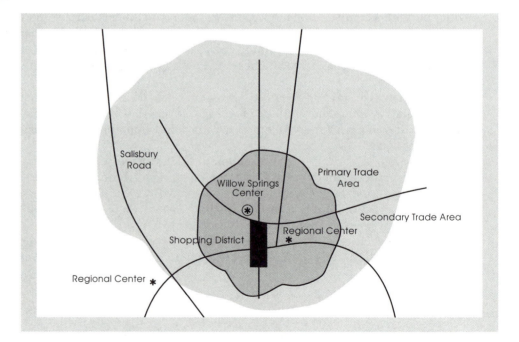

Specifically, the site for the Willow Springs Center lay on the northern edge of a shopping district that had developed along Salisbury Road. (See Figure 19.4.) There were several neighborhood specialty store centers in the district, but none contained a major department store. The only large discount department store in the area was located in a new center across from the subject property.

Willow Springs Center Site   **Figure 19.4**

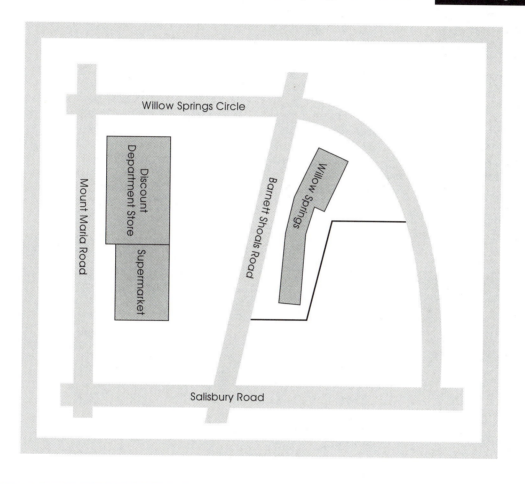

Slawson and Owensby realized that the discount department store and large supermarket in this center provided a major attraction for shoppers that could benefit their proposed center as well. Accordingly, they reasoned that a strip center containing specialty and local service shops would have the greatest probability of success.

Working with an architect and a site planner, Slawson and Owensby developed a plan for a 32,550-square-foot center with 12 shops ranging in size from 1,200 to 6,500 square feet. From their knowledge of the local market, the two developers felt that these shops could be leased for an average annual rental of approximately $16.80 per square foot, with escalation clauses raising the rates in future years.

An insurance company agreed to finance 75 percent of the estimated value of the center ($3.84 million) at 9 percent interest provided the developers secured an adequate number of tenants approved by the lender. Expenses the first year, excluding debt service on the line, were estimated at $72,783. (See Table 19.2.)

From the data in this table, an income and expense statement was prepared, which is shown in Table 19.3. It indicated a $173,092 cash flow the first year, a return

that would make the project financially feasible—if the market assumptions were correct.

The next step was to secure tenants. Jolly Charlie's, a branch of a prominent local liquor and wine store, signed a 20-year lease at $15.40 per square foot that provided for escalation based on the consumer price index. A textile mill outlet was a second major tenant, signing a ten-year lease for 35,800 square feet at an annual rental of $16 per square foot. Other tenants included a furniture and decorating shop, a drugstore, a children's clothing shop, a ladies' high-fashion clothing store, a sporting goods shop, an arts and craft shop, a florist, a dry cleaner, a beauty shop and an ice cream parlor.

Rents for these businesses ranged from $16.40 to $19.70 a square foot, with lease terms ranging from three to ten years. Most of the leases provided for percentage rents in addition to the base rates; the others contained escalation clauses.

Despite inflationary pressures, Willow Springs was completed within its budget. Sales during the first 18 months were quite good, and actual rents the first year averaged $17 per square foot.

| **Table 19.2** | Estimated First-Year Expenses, Willow Springs Center |

Expense	Amount
Property taxes	
32,550 sq. ft. × 61 cents per sq. ft.	$19,856
Insurance	
32,550 sq. ft. × 13.3 cents per sq. ft.	4,329
Utilities	
32,550 sq. ft. × 19.5 cents per sq. ft.	6,347
Maintenance	
32,550 sq. ft. × 21 cents per sq. ft.	6,836
Reserves	
32,550 sq. ft. × 8 cents per sq. ft.	2,604
Management	
4% of gross income ($546,840)	21,874
Leasing commissions	
2% of gross income	10,937
Total	$72,783

Income and Expense Statement, Willow Springs Center   **Figure 19.3**

First-year income	$546,840
Less vacancy, 2%	10,937
Effective income	$535,903
Less expenses	72,783
Net operating income	$463,120
Less debt service	290,028
Cash flow	$173,902

Mortgage

Amount	$2,880,000
Rate	9%
Monthly debt service	$ 24,169

for a small firm or physician to a 1-million-square-foot skyscraper for a large corporation. They may be owner occupied or leased from an investor.

Many office buildings, particularly the larger ones, are built by investors on a speculative basis for lease to multiple tenants. Sometimes a large company leases a major portion of a building, which then is named for the firm. In other cases, ownership is organized on a condominium basis, with the individual firms owning their office space and sharing ownership of the common areas.

INDUSTRIAL PARKS AND DISTRIBUTION FACILITIES

Early industrial facilities were located wherever transportation facilities, water power and other such features were adequate. Around the turn of the century, however, **industrial parks**—controlled, parklike developments designed to accommodate specific types of industry and providing all necessary utilities—came into existence. These parks provided location advantages and also avoided conflicts with other land uses.

Several planned industrial districts were pioneered in Chicago, beginning with the Original East District in 1902. These districts were served by railroads, and their success led to the establishment of other railroad-sponsored industrial districts in other parts of the country. Following World War II, the industrial park concept spread widely. Most recent parks depend primarily on road access, but most also are served by rail facilities.

Some industrial parks contain manufacturing plants, but many allow only light manufacturing activities. Others are devoted exclusively to warehousing and distribution activities.

Analysis of Industrial Sites

The task of determining the feasibility of developing a site for industrial use is much like that of analyzing other types of property. The basic technique is to

- determine the amount of existing or potential supply;
- forecast the demand for additional developed industrial acreage or building space in the general area;
- estimate the absorption rate during the analysis period; and
- compare the competitiveness of the subject site with that of other properties.

HOTEL, MOTEL AND RESORT DEVELOPMENTS

The demand for lodging services comes from several sources, including pleasure travelers, business travelers and conventioneers. The various types of lodging customers necessitate different types of facilities, although considerable overlap often exists. For example, many pleasure travelers seek easy access to and from major highways, and so do many business travelers. Pleasure travelers seek resort locations, and so do many convention groups.

The distinction between motels and hotels was quite marked in the early days of the motel. Motels usually were small structures of one or two stories offering parking space adjacent to rooms and a minimum of services. Today, many motels are almost indistinguishable from hotels, the primary distinction being that hotels generally offer a wider range of services.

Lodging facilities usually are classified as commercial hotels, highway or airport hotels and resort hotels.

Commercial hotels cater primarily to businesspeople and conventioneers. Their occupancy is usually relatively stable throughout the year, but often drops to low levels on weekends. Many depend heavily on convention trade and have extensive facilities to attract this type of business.

A **highway hotel,** or an **airport hotel,** caters primarily to businesspeople or vacationers who are in transit. Such facilities range from the small highway motel that offers little more than a sparsely furnished room to elaborate facilities with extensive amenities.

Resort hotels, also known as *destination* or *seasonal hotels,* cater to individuals or families on vacation. By definition, the hotels must be located near scenic, historic or other attractions that appeal to pleasure travelers. To enhance their appeal further, most offer extensive facilities—golf courses, tennis courts, swimming pools and the like. Many are seasonal, often closing completely in the off-season or catering to convention groups.

Lodging facilities differ in several ways from other types of real estate. Their revenues are very susceptible to changes in business activity or pleasure travel, as rentals usually are from night to night rather than on the basis of the long-term leases used for other types of rental property. Conversely, rates can be adjusted quickly in periods of rapid inflation, a desirable characteristic for investors. Management is of critical importance to the success of such facilities, usually making the difference between a successful and an unsuccessful project.

Even a well-designed and well-located lodging facility will have difficulty overcoming inadequate management.

Chapter Review

1. The shopping center is distinguished from the traditional commercial district by the following characteristics: (1) one or more structures of unified architecture housing firms that are selected and managed as a unit, (2) a site that serves a particular trade area, (3) on-site parking, (4) facilities for deliveries separated from the shopping area and (5) single ownership and management.

2. Four major types of shopping centers are classified on the bases of tenant type and functions: (1) the neighborhood or convenience center, with a typical gross leasable area of 50,000 square feet and a supermarket or drugstore as leading tenant; (2) the community center, with a typical gross leasable area of 150,000 square feet and a variety, discount or junior department store as leading tenant; (3) the regional center, with one or more full-line department stores and 400,000 square feet of gross leasable area; and (4) the superregional center, with three or more full-line department stores and 1 million square feet of gross leasable area.

3. The factory outlet center was a development of the 1980s. These centers contain stores where goods are sold directly to the public by manufacturers.

4. The steps involved in a market and feasibility analysis for a shopping center are (1) define the trade area—that is, the geographic area from which the major portion of the center's patronage will be drawn; the primary trade area (the area from which 60 to 70 percent of sales are expected to come) will have a radius of approximately 1.5 miles for a neighborhood shopping center, three to five miles for a community shopping center and eight to ten miles for a regional shopping center; (2) determine the size of the market in terms of population, purchasing power and expected sales; (3) analyze existing and potential competition; and (4) estimate the percentage of sales of the total trade area that can be captured by the proposed center.

5. Several factors are important in selecting the shopping center site, including size, shape, topography, drainage, utilities and zoning. Most important is location.

6. The demand for office space in a community depends on business activity and government employment.

7. Office buildings generally are located in downtown business districts, in office nodes along major thoroughfares leading to the suburbs and in office parks.

8. A firm's selection of an industrial site is influenced by many factors, including (1) the availability of land, (2) the availability of utilities and (3) access to major transportation facilities.

9. The steps in determining the feasibility of developing a site for industrial use are (1) determine the amount of existing or potential supply, (2) forecast the demand for additional developed industrial acreage or building space in the general area, (3) estimate the absorption rate during the analysis period and (4) compare the competitiveness of the subject site with that of other properties.

10. Demand for lodging services comes from several sources, including pleasure travelers, business travelers and conventioneers.

11. Transient hotels and motels usually are classified as (1) commercial hotels, which cater primarily to businesspeople and conventioneers; (2) highway or airport hotels, which cater primarily to businesspeople and vacationers who are in transit; and (3) resort hotels, which cater to individuals or families on vacation.

Key Terms

airport hotel   a hotel near an airport that caters to business travelers.

central business district   an unplanned series of buildings constructed along major streets in the center of town.

commercial hotel   a hotel that caters primarily to businesspeople and conventioneers.

community shopping center   a shopping center containing between 100,000 and 300,000 square feet of gross leasable area that is designed to serve an area within a radius of three to five miles.

discount shopping center   a community shopping center that contains a discount store as the main tenant.

factory outlet center   a shopping center consisting of retail outlet facilities where goods are sold directly to the public in stores owned and operated by the manufacturers.

gross leasable area   the total floor area of a building designed for the tenants' use.

highway hotel   a hotel that caters primarily to businesspeople and vacationers who are in transit.

industrial park   controlled, park-like developments designed to accommodate specific types of industry.

neighborhood shopping center   a shopping center designed to serve an area within a radius of 1.5 miles and a population of 2,500 to 40,000.

office park   a community of lowrise office structures under central management and administration, usually located in the suburbs and adjacent to a major freeway.

power center   a large strip-style shopping center that is anchored by one or more "big box" retailers, along with smaller shops.

primary trade area   the geographic area immediately surrounding a shopping center that typically accounts for 60 percent to 70 percent of the center's sales.

regional shopping center   a shopping center that contains between 300,000 and 750,000 square feet in gross leasable area and contains at least one full-line department store.

resort hotel   a hotel that caters to individuals or families on vacation.

secondary trade area   the area outside the primary trade area that typically accounts for 15 percent to 20 percent of sales at a shopping center.

specialty shopping center   a shopping center that focuses on unusual market segments and usually offers high-quality, high-priced merchandise in boutique-type stores.

strip shopping center   a neighborhood shopping center built in a straight line, with stores tied together by a canopy over a pedestrian walk.

superregional shopping center   a shopping center that exceeds 750,000 square feet of gross leasable area and includes at least three department stores.

superstore   a very large discount store with between 60,000 and 150,000 square feet under one roof.

trade area   the geographic area from which the major portion of the patronage necessary to support the shopping center is to be drawn.

Study Exercises

1. What characteristics distinguish a shopping center from the traditional commercial district?

2. What are the four major types of shopping centers?

3. Describe the characteristics of (1) the neighborhood shopping center, (2) the community center, (3) the regional center and (4) the superregional center.

4. Discuss the steps involved in a market and feasibility analysis for a proposed shopping center.

5. Define the primary trade area. What is its typical size for each of the major types of centers?

6. What factors are most important in selecting a successful shopping center site?

7. What is a specialty shopping center? What is a discount shopping center?

8. What factors determine the demand for office space in a community?

9. What types of firms tend to lease space in downtown office locations? Why do financial institutions and attorneys often choose downtown locations?

10. Where are office nodes likely to develop?

11. What factors have led to the growing popularity of the suburban office park?

12. What factors determine a firm's selection of a specific industrial site?

Glossary

absorption rate the number of units capable of being absorbed by the market over a given time period.

acceleration clause clause in a promissory note that permits the lender to demand payment in full of any unpaid principal and any interest due in the event of default.

acceptance an expression of satisfaction with an offer.

accrued depreciation loss in value from any cause.

actual cash value the cost of replacing an insured item minus the amount by which the item has depreciated in value since it was new.

adaptive use use of a building in a manner different from the use for which it was originally designed.

adjustable-rate mortgage a loan whose interest rate is periodically adjusted based on the current interest rate environment.

ad valorem tax a tax levied as a percentage of the value of the taxed item.

adverse possession the acquisition of property as a result of "actual and exclusive, open and notorious, hostile and continuous" possession under a claim of right for a statutory period of time.

after-tax cash flow annual operating cash flow that remains after expenses, debt service and taxes have been paid.

after-tax equity reversion the amount of money generated by the sale of an investment after taxes have been paid and any debts extinguished.

agency a legal relationship between a principal and an agent.

agent the party authorized to conduct business on the principal's behalf.

airport hotel a hotel near an airport that caters to business travelers.

air rights property rights associated with the space above the surface of the earth.

alienable a property owner's right to transfer interests owned in a property during his or her lifetime.

amortization the process of gradually retiring a loan or other asset; also, the requirement that a nonconforming use be discontinued after a stated period of time.

amortization schedule a table showing the breakdown of principal and interest paid over the life of a mortgage.

amortizing loan a loan whose balance is gradually retired by periodic payments.

annuity a series of equal amounts, received one at the end of each period, for a specified number of periods.

anticipation the idea that the current value of a property depends on the anticipated utility or income that will accrue to the property owner in the future.

appraisal an estimate of value.

appraisal process a systematic procedure employed to arrive at an estimate of value and convey that estimate to the appraisal user.

assessed value the estimated value of a property for tax purposes.

asset manager a company executive charged with management of the firm's real estate facilities and activities.

assignment the act of passing all of one's rights and responsibilities under a legal agreement to a third party.

axial model a model of urban growth patterns based on transportation routes.

balloon payment a lump sum payment due on a specified date in the future.

bargain and sale deed a deed which simply states that the grantor has title to the property and the right to convey it, but which does not contain any express covenants or warranties to the title's validity.

base lines east-west lines used as reference points in the rectangular survey system.

before-tax cash flow annual operating cash flow that remains after expenses and debt service have been paid.

before-tax equity reversion the amount of money generated by the sale of an investment before taxes have been paid.

blockbusting the illegal practice of encouraging property owners to sell their homes when minorities begin moving into an area.

broker an intermediary who brings together buyers and sellers, assists in negotiating agreements between them, executes their orders and receives compensation for services rendered.

building codes regulations that establish standards for the construction of new buildings and the alteration of existing ones.

bulk regulations regulations that control the percentage of the lot area that may be occupied by buildings on a site.

businessowner's policy an insurance policy for small and medium-sized businesses.

business risk uncertainty arising from changing economic conditions that affect an investment's ability to generate returns.

buyer representation agreement the legal agreement between a buyer and a broker hired to represent the buyer's interests.

buyer's agent a broker who is legally obligated to represent a buyer's interests.

capacity legal ability to understand and accept the terms of a contract.

capitalization rate the relationship between income and value, where the capitalization rate equals net operating income divided by property value.

central business district an unplanned series of buildings constructed along major streets in the center of town.

certified general appraiser an appraiser who is certified by the state to perform appraisals on all property types.

certified residential appraiser an appraiser who is certified by the state to perform residential appraisals regardless of complexity.

chain of title ownership history of a specific property.

change the idea that economic, social, political and environmental forces are constantly causing changes that affect the value of real estate.

closing costs costs associated with closing a real estate transaction.

closing statement a worksheet showing the sources and uses of funds in a real estate transaction.

coinsurance the joint assumption of risk by two or more parties.

commercial hotel a hotel that caters primarily to businesspeople and conventioneers.

commission the compensation received by a broker for services rendered.

community property theory under which all property acquired during a marriage is considered to be equally owned by the husband and wife, regardless of the financial contribution each spouse actually made to the property's acquisition.

community shopping center a shopping center containing between 100,000 and 300,000 square feet of gross leasable area that is designed to serve an area within a radius of three to five miles.

compounding the process of converting present amounts into future amounts.

compound interest interest earned on a principal amount plus any interest previously earned.

comprehensive general plan a statement of land-use policies that shape the future development of a community.

comprehensive zoning division of a community's land into specific land-use districts to regulate the use of land and buildings and the intensity of various uses.

concentric-circle model a model of urban growth patterns based on concentric zones surrounding a central business district.

concurrent estate ownership interests held jointly by two or more owners.

condominium a form of joint ownership whereby the property owners own their individual units separately but share ownership of common areas; a building owned in this manner.

condominium declaration legal document that describes the individual units and common areas of a property owned as a condominium, creates an association to govern the property and sets forth restrictions on use.

consideration anything that incurs legal detriment or the forgoing of a legal benefit.

contract a legal device used by two or more persons to indicate they have reached an agreement.

contribution the idea that the value of a component part of a property depends on the amount it contributes to the value of the whole.

conventional loan mortgage loans not insured or guaranteed by a government agency but may carry private mortgage insurance.

cooperative a form of joint ownership whereby the property owners own shares of stock in a corporation that owns the property and are entitled to occupy space within the building.

cost approach a method used to estimate value by implementing the following steps: (1) estimate the value of the site as though it were vacant, (2) estimate the cost to produce the improvements, (3) subtract accrued depreciation and (4) add site value to the estimated depreciated cost of the improvements.

counteroffer a response to an offer that represents a new offer.

covenant a promise or guarantee made by a grantor in a deed.

covenant against encumbrances an assurance made by the grantor that no liens or encumbrances other than those of public record exist against the property.

covenant of further assurances an assurance made by the grantor that the grantor will execute any future documents needed to perfect the grantee's title.

covenant of quiet enjoyment an assurance made by the grantor that no other party will disturb the grantee claiming to own the property or to have a lien on it; a promise from the lessor that the tenant has the right of exclusive possession of the property during the term of the lease.

covenant of seisin an assurance made by the grantor that he or she is in full possession of the interest being conveyed by a deed and thus has the right to convey it.

debt service total amount paid to lenders to service outstanding debt.

deed a written document that evidences ownership.

deed in lieu of foreclosure a process by which a borrower transfers ownership of a mortgaged property to the lender rather than face foreclosure.

deed of trust a security instrument that conveys title to the property pledged as collateral to a trustee until the loan is repaid.

defeasible estate an estate that can be lost should some event or stated condition come to pass.

deficiency judgment a judgment against a borrower following a foreclosure that permits the lender to recover any shortfall between the sale price and the balance of the loan.

depreciation deduction a noncash deduction permitted by the Internal Revenue Service (IRS) for capital recovery.

descendible a property owner's right to transfer interests owned in a property to legal heirs should the owner die without a valid will.

devisable a property owner's right to transfer interests owned in a property via a will.

direct losses costs of replacing or repairing property destroyed or damaged.

discounting the process of converting future amounts into present amounts.

discount point 1 percent of the loan amount.

discount shopping center a community shopping center that contains a discount store as the main tenant.

dominant estate the property benefitted by the existence of an easement appurtenant.

dual agency a legal relationship that exists when an agent is legally obligated to represent the best interests of two competing principals.

due-on-sale clause a clause in a promissory note that requires the borrower to repay all amounts due immediately upon transferring the property to a new owner.

easement a right given to another party by a landowner to use a property in a specified manner.

easement appurtenant an easement with clearly identifiable dominant and servient estates.

easement by prescription a method of creating an easement as a result of "actual and exclusive, open and notorious, hostile and continuous" use for a statutory period of time.

easement in gross an easement with only a servient estate.

economic base employment in industries that bring income into a region from beyond its borders.

economic obsolescence loss in value resulting from factors outside the property that affect its income-producing ability or degree of use.

effective gross income potential gross income less vacancy and credit losses.

effective interest rate the actual cost of borrowed funds expressed as an interest rate.

eminent domain the government's power to take private property for public use upon payment of just compensation.

encroachment an unauthorized invasion or intrusion of a fixture, building or another improvement onto another person's property.

encumbrance restriction or limitation on ownership rights.

escheat the government's right to own real estate following the owner's death in the absence of a valid will or legal heirs.

estate in land ownership interests in real property.

estate in severalty term used to describe ownership interests without regard to the number of owners.

exclusive-agency listing a listing agreement that guarantees the broker's right to a commission if the property is sold by any licensed real estate broker or salesperson.

exclusive-right-to-sell listing a listing agreement that guarantees the broker's right to a commission if the property is sold by the seller or any licensed real estate broker or salesperson.

executor's deed a special use deed used by the executor of an estate to transfer ownership without any assurances regarding the quality of title being transferred.

export activities activities that produce goods and services for sale or consumption outside an area's borders.

express grant method of expressly creating an easement on a grantor's property.

express reservation method of expressly creating an easement on a grantee's property.

factory outlet center a shopping center consisting of retail outlet facilities where goods are sold directly to the public in stores owned and operated by the manufacturers.

fair housing laws laws that protect the rights of certain citizens in housing transactions.

Fannie Mae Federal National Mortgage Association.

fee interest time-share a type of concurrent estate that splits ownership of a property over time across joint owners.

fee simple absolute estate the fullest and most complete set of ownership rights one can possess in real property.

FHA-insured loan a loan insured against default by the Federal Housing Administration.

fiduciary a person who is obligated to act in the best interest of another.

filtering the passage of housing to less affluent families as the housing ages.

financial leverage the use of borrowed funds with the intention of magnifying investment returns.

financial risk uncertainty associated with the possibility of defaulting on borrowed funds used to finance an investment.

fixed-rate mortgage a loan with a fixed interest rate over the loan term.

fixed-rent lease a lease contract that stipulates a fixed rent amount for the period of the lease.

fixture an item that was once personal property but has become part of the real estate.

floor-area ratio relationship between the total floor area of a building and the total area of a site.

foreclosure the process of seizing control of the collateral for a loan and using the proceeds from its sale to satisfy a defaulted debt.

fraud a false statement made with the intention to mislead, that is material to a transaction, that is justifiably relied upon by a client and that results in injury to the client.

Freddie Mac Federal Home Loan Mortgage Corporation.

freehold estate ownership interests in real property.

functional obsolescence loss in value that occurs because a property has less utility or ability to generate income than a new property designed for the same use.

future value of a lump sum $FV = PV (1 + i)^n$

future value of an annuity

$$FVA = A\left[\frac{1 + i^n - 1}{i}\right]$$

garden apartment a two-story or three-story building with a density of 10 to 20 units per acre.

general lien a security interest on all property owned by an individual.

general warranty deed the deed that offers the most protection to the grantee, complete with all relevant covenants and warranties.

gestation period the time between conception of the idea for a development project and its completion and entry into the available supply.

Ginnie Mae Government National Mortgage Association.

graduated-rent lease a lease contract that stipulates scheduled rent increases over the period of the lease.

grantee the party who receives a freehold estate in real property from a grantor.

grantor the party who transfers a freehold estate in real property to a grantee.

gross income multiplier the relationship between income and value, where the gross income multiplier equals value divided by gross income.

gross leasable area the total floor area of a building designed for the tenants' use.

gross lease a lease contract stipulating that the landlord will pay all operating expenses, taxes and insurance for the property during the period of the lease.

gross rent multiplier the relationship between rent and value, where the gross rent multiplier equals value divided by gross rent.

ground lease a long-term lease for vacant land.

highest and best use that use, found to be legally permissible, physically possible and financially feasible, that results in the highest land value; that use of land most likely to result in the greatest long-term economic return to the owner.

highrise apartment apartment buildings containing more than eight stories.

highway hotel a hotel that caters primarily to businesspeople and vacationers who are in transit.

homeowner's policy an insurance policy that provides coverage of losses from fire and other perils, personal liability, medical payments and theft.

housing finance system the arrangements and institutions that facilitate the financing of residential buildings.

hypothecation the practice of leaving borrowers in possession of their property while repaying a loan with interest.

impact fees fees charged to developers to raise funds for expansion of public facilities needed as a result of the new development.

implied grant a method of implicitly creating an easement on a grantor's property.

implied reservation a method of implicitly creating an easement on a grantee's property.

incentive zoning a practice used by communities to encourage developers to provide certain publicly desired features in their developments in exchange for relaxed enforcement of the zoning code.

income approach a method used to estimate value by discounting or capitalizing the expected future income that is expected to accrue to the property owner.

index lease a lease in which rent payments are adjusted based on changes in the cost of living.

indirect losses additional living expenses or loss of business income suffered before a damaged property is restored.

industrial park controlled, park-like developments designed to accommodate specific types of industry.

infrastructure investment in public facilities such as roads, schools, etc.

inheritable freehold estate an ownership interest that passes to heirs upon the death of the owner.

insurable title a title in real estate that a reputable title insurance company is willing to insure. An insurable title most frequently is one without major defect.

insurable value an estimate of value for insurance purposes.

insurance binder temporary evidence of insurance.

interest-only loan a nonamortizing loan that requires periodic payments of interest and a single balloon payment of the principal at the end of the loan term.

interim use temporary use of a property until such time that conditions are favorable to convert it to another use intended to be permanent.

internal rate of return the discount rate that sets net present value exactly equal to zero.

inverse condemnation a lawsuit initiated by a property owner to force the government to purchase a property whose value has been diminished by a governmental action.

investment present sacrifice in anticipation of expected future benefit.

investment value the worth of a property to a particular investor, based on that investor's personal standards of investment acceptability.

IRR decision rule if the internal rate of return is greater than or equal to the required rate of return, accept the investment.

joint tenancy joint ownership in which all owners have an equal, but undivided, interest in a property.

judicial foreclosure a court ordered sale of the property following default by the mortgagor.

land contract a contract that establishes an obligation to transfer title from a seller to a buyer at some future date based on an agreed-upon payment schedule.

land rent the return that a parcel of land will bring in the open market.

lease a legal agreement between lessor and lessee.

leasehold estate a tenant's rights to use and possess (but not own) a property as defined in a lease agreement.

lessee the person who receives a leasehold interest in a property from the lessor.

lessor the person who gives a leasehold interest in a property to a lessee.

liability insurance insurance that protects the insured against lawsuits brought in response to supposed acts of negligence that result in injury or loss of property to the public.

license a revocable personal privilege to use land for a particular purpose.

licensed appraiser a person licensed by the state to perform noncomplex residential appraisals.

lien a claim on a property as security for a debt or fulfillment of some monetary charge or obligation.

lien theory a concept adopted by some states that recognizes that the mortgagee must foreclose on the property through a court action to acquire possession in the event of default.

life estate an ownership interest in real property that normally ends upon the death of a named person.

liquidity risk possibility of loss resulting from not being able to convert an asset into cash quickly should the need arise.

listing agreement the legal agreement between a broker and a property owner that authorizes the broker to attempt to sell the property.

listing broker the broker who negotiates the listing agreement with the seller.

littoral proprietor owner of land that adjoins navigable bodies of water.

loan origination the process of creating a new loan agreement between a borrower and a lender.

loan-to-value ratio the ratio obtained by dividing the loan amount by an estimate of property value.

management agreement a legal agreement authorizing a property manager to conduct business on behalf of the landlord.

mandatory dedication a requirement that developers donate property to the community for public use as a condition for obtaining development approval.

manufactured home a dwelling unit that is manufactured in a factory and then moved to a particular site.

marketable title a title free and clear of all past, present and future claims that would cause a reasonable purchaser to reject such title.

market value the most probable price that a property should bring in a competitive and open market under all conditions requisite to a fair sale, the buyer and seller each acting prudently and knowledgeably, and assuming the price is not affected by undue stimulus. Implicit in this definition is the consummation of a sale as of a specified date and the passing of title from seller to buyer under conditions whereby:
1. buyer and seller are typically motivated;
2. both parties are well informed or well advised and acting in what they consider their best interests;
3. a reasonable time is allowed for exposure in the open market;
4. payment is made in terms of cash in U.S. dollars or in terms of financial arrangements comparable thereto; and
5. the price represents the normal consideration for the property sold unaffected by special or creative financing or sales concessions by anyone associated with the sale.

mechanic's lien a claim on a property held by a supplier of materials or labor for nonpayment of a debt.

metes and bounds a legal method for describing the exact boundaries of a property; metes refer to the distances and bounds refer to the directions of the property's boundaries.

midrise apartment apartment building consisting of four to eight stories.

mill one one-thousandth, or 0.001.

millage rate the tax rate imposed on property owners, expressed as the dollars of tax for each $1,000 of property value.

mineral rights ownership rights associated with minerals that may be located below the surface of the earth.

misrepresentation a false statement that is material to a transaction, that is justifiably relied upon by a client and that results in injury to the client.

mortgage a contract by which real property is pledged as security for a loan.

mortgage-backed securities securities issued by mortgage holders to investors who wish to invest indirectly in the mortgage market.

mortgage debt ratio the percentage of a borrower's gross monthly income that is required to meet housing expenses.

mortgagee the lender in a mortgage loan transaction.

mortgage life insurance a diminishing term life insurance policy whose amount is keyed to the outstanding mortgage balance.

mortgage payment

$$Pmt = PVA \left[\frac{i}{1 - \frac{1}{(1 + i)^n}} \right]$$

mortgagor the borrower in a mortgage loan transaction.

multiple-listing service an arrangement in which brokers share their listings with other brokers in exchange for a share of the commission generated by a transaction.

multiple-nuclei model a model of urban growth patterns that emphasizes more than one center of commercial activity.

negative renewal clause a clause in a lease contract that automatically renews the lease in the event neither party desires to terminate the agreement.

neighborhood an area containing properties of similar type. It also can be defined by reference to geographical area; to social, religious or ethnic ties; or to income group.

neighborhood shopping center a shopping center designed to serve an area within a radius of 1.5 miles and a population of 2,500 to 40,000.

net lease a lease that stipulates that the lessee will pay operating expenses for a property during the lease period.

net listing a listing agreement in which the broker is entitled to receive as commission any amount above a base price.

net net lease a lease that stipulates that the lessee will pay operating expenses and insurance for the property during the lease period.

net net net lease a lease that stipulates that the lessee will pay operating expenses, insurance and property taxes for the property during the lease period.

net operating income annual operating cash flow that remains after expenses have been paid.

net present value present value of inflows minus present value of outflows.

net sales proceeds proceeds from sale after selling expenses have been paid.

nonconforming use a use of land that does not conform to the current land-use controls imposed by the government.

nonjudicial foreclosure a situation in which the security instrument grants the lender power of sale should the borrower default.

NPV decision rule if the net present value is greater than or equal to zero, accept the investment.

nuisance the use of property in such a way as to harm the property of others.

offer a statement that specifies the position of its maker (offeror) and indicates that the offeror is willing to be bound by the conditions stated.

office park a community of lowrise office structures under central management and administration, usually located in the suburbs and adjacent to a major freeway.

open listing a listing agreement in which a broker is entitled to receive a commission only in the event the broker procures a buyer for the property.

option-to-buy contract a contract that gives one party the right, but not an obligation, to purchase a property within a specified time horizon at a specified price.

origination fees fees charged by lenders in the origination process.

partial performance fulfillment of the terms of an agreement to such an extent that the existence of the agreement may be reasonably inferred.

patio house a detached house with at least one wall that touches the property line.

percentage lease a lease for a property used for commercial purposes under which the rental payments are based on some percentage of sales made on the premises.

performance zoning regulations that restrict land-use based on the environmental carrying capacity of the site.

personal articles floater policy an insurance policy that insures specific personal property items for specific amounts.

personal excess liability policy an insurance policy that insures against disastrous liability claims involving a home, automobile or boat.

personal property movable items such as cars, clothing, books, etc.

personal property replacement cost endorsement an insurance policy that allows the holder to recoup the full replacement cost of stolen or damaged goods rather than the actual cash value of the goods.

physical deterioration loss in value that occurs from ordinary wear and tear, vandalism or neglect.

plat a detailed land survey drawing, usually prepared by a professional surveyor, that shows the features of a property and its legal description.

plex a form of attached housing containing two or more units, each with its own outside entrance.

police power the government's power to regulate the way private property is used to protect the health, safety, morals and general welfare of the public.

policy a contract providing insurance coverage.

population-serving activities activities that produce goods and services for sale or consumption within an area's borders.

positive renewal clause a clause on a lease that states that if no notice of renewal is given properly, normally one to two months prior to the expiration of the lease, the lease terminates at the end of the lease period.

possibility of reversion the future interest that follows a qualified fee determinable estate.

potential gross income the total income potential of an investment, assuming all space is leased and all rents are collected.

power center a large strip-style shopping center that is anchored by one or more "big box" retailers, along with smaller shops.

power of termination the future interest that follows a qualified fee conditional estate.

premium the consideration paid for an insurance policy.

prepayment early repayment of principal.

prepayment clause a clause in a promissory note that determines the borrower's right to prepay any or all of the principal before it is due.

prescriptive easement an easement created when someone other than the owner uses the land "openly, hostilely and continuously" for a statutory time period.

present value of a lump sum

$$PA = FV\left[\frac{1}{(1+i)^n}\right]$$

present value of an annuity

$$PVA = A\left[1 - \frac{1}{\frac{(1+i)^n}{i}}\right]$$

price actual amount paid for a property in a particular transaction.

primary mortgage market transactions that occur between a borrower and a lender.

primary trade area the geographic area immediately surrounding a shopping center that typically accounts for 60 percent to 70 percent of the center's sales.

principal the person who authorizes an agent to conduct business on his or her behalf.

principal meridians north-south lines used as reference points in the rectangular survey system.

prior appropriation doctrine theory which states that the first person to use a body of water for some beneficial economic purpose has the right to use all the water needed, even though landowners who later find a use for the water may be precluded from using it.

private mortgage insurance nongovernment insurance that provides protection for the lender against the borrower's default.

profit a prendre a nonpossessory interest in real property that permits the holder to remove specified natural resources from a property.

promissory note a written promise to pay money owed.

property manager a person authorized by a property owner to manage the property on his or her behalf.

purchasing power risk uncertainty associated with the possibility that the amount of goods and services that can be acquired with a given amount of money will decline.

qualified estate an estate that can be lost should an event or stated condition come to pass.

qualified fee conditional estate an estate that a court may rule has been terminated should some condition be violated.

qualified fee determinable estate an estate that terminates automatically should some condition be violated.

quitclaim deed a deed used to transfer any interest a grantor may or may not have in a property, without implying that the grantor has a valid interest to convey.

range lines north-south lines that run parallel to principal meridians in the rectangular survey system.

real estate land and structures that are attached to it.

real estate broker an individual licensed by a state to represent others in real estate transactions in exchange for compensation.

real estate salesperson an individual licensed by a state to assist real estate brokers in arranging real estate transactions in exchange for compensation.

real property the legal interests associated with the ownership of real estate.

reappraisal lease a lease that stipulates that the rent will be adjusted periodically as the value of the building changes, as determined by an appraisal.

rectangular survey system a grid-based system used to legally describe the location of a property.

refinancing the process of obtaining a new loan and using the proceeds to repay an existing loan.

regional shopping center a shopping center that contains between 300,000 and 750,000 square feet in gross leasable area and contains at least one full-line department store.

remainder the future interest associated with a life estate held by someone other than the grantor.

renewal option a clause in a lease agreement that defines the parties agreement regarding renewal of the lease upon termination.

replacement cost the estimated cost of replacing the property being appraised with a property built at today's prices, by current construction methods and with the same usefulness as the one being appraised.

reproduction cost the cost of constructing an exact replacement of the property being appraised with the same or similar materials, at today's prices.

required rate of return a minimum acceptable rate of return.

residential mortgage credit report a standardized credit report used in the underwriting process for residential loans.

resort hotel a hotel that caters to individuals or families on vacation.

restrictive covenant limitations placed on a property by a landowner or previous landowner that prevents the property from being used in certain ways.

reversion the future interest associated with a life estate held by the grantor.

right of survivorship the right of surviving joint owners to automatically divide the share owned by a deceased owner.

right-to-use time-share a form of leasehold estate that permits the holder to use a property for a certain period each year.

riparian rights doctrine theory that permits landowners whose land underlies or borders nonnavigable bodies of water to use all the water needed as long as the use does not deprive other landowners who are also entitled to use some of the water.

risk the chance of loss; also, the uncertainty about the actual rate of return an investment will provide over the holding period.

sale-leaseback an arrangement whereby a property owner sells the property to an investor and immediately leases the property back from the investor.

sales comparison approach a method used to estimate value by comparing the property to other properties that have recently sold for known prices.

secondary mortgage market transactions involving mortgages that occur between investors.

secondary trade area the area outside the primary trade area that typically accounts for 15 percent to 20 percent of sales at a shopping center.

section 1-square-mile rectangles that divide townshps into 36 equal areas of 640 acres each.

secured loan a loan for which a specific item has been pledged as collateral.

security deposit an amount required by a lessor in advance of occupancy as security against potential damages caused by the lessee.

seller's agent a real estate broker who is obligated to represent the best interest of the seller.

selling broker the broker who actually locates a buyer for a property.

servient estate the property burdened by the existence of an easement appurtenant or easement in gross.

setback a common land-use regulation that requires a certain amount of space between improvements on a property and the property lines.

sinking fund payment

$$SFP = FVA\left[\frac{i}{(1+i)^n - 1}\right]$$

special lien a security interest that relates only to real estate.

special warranty deed similar to a general warranty deed, except the covenants and warranties apply only to events that occurred during the grantor's period of ownership.

specialty shopping center a shopping center that focuses on unusual market segments and usually offers high-quality, high-priced merchandise in boutique-type stores.

specific performance a requirement that the terms of a contract be exactly complied with.

statute of frauds a law designed to prevent fraudulent practices involving contracts.

steering the illegal practice of steering potential home buyers into certain areas to influence the racial or ethnic composition of the areas.

strip shopping center a neighborhood shopping center built in a straight line, with stores tied together by a canopy over a pedestrian walk.

strict foreclosure a situation in which the lender is entitled to immediate ownership of the property should the borrower default.

subagent an agent of an agent of a principal.

subdivision regulations the standards and procedures that regulate the subdivision of land for development and sale.

subleasing the act of transferring a portion of the leasehold estate to a third party.

substitution the idea that a prudent buyer will pay no more for a property than the cost of acquiring an equally desirable substitute in the open market.

superregional shopping center a shopping center that exceeds 750,000 square feet of gross leasable area and includes at least three department stores.

superstore a very large discount store with between 60,000 and 150,000 square feet under one roof.

tenancy at sufferance a leasehold estate that defines a tenant's rights to occupy the property against the wishes of the lessor.

tenancy at will an informal leasehold estate of indeterminable length that may last as long as the parties agree.

tenancy by the entirety a form of concurrent estate in which a husband and wife can own property jointly.

tenancy for a stated period a leasehold estate that has definite starting and ending dates.

tenancy from period to period a leasehold estate that continues to automatically renew each period unless terminated by either party.

tenancy in common a form of concurrent estate in which each owner has an undivided interest in the property.

time-sharing a form of concurrent estate that splits ownership of a property across owners and across time.

time value of money principle a dollar in hand is worth more than a dollar to be received in the future because it can either be consumed immediately or put to work to earn a return.

title the legal right to ownership.

title abstract a written history of a property's chain of title.

title insurance an insurance policy that protects property owners and lenders against undiscovered defects in a property's chain of title.

title opinion an attorney's opinion of the quality of title for a specific property.

title perfect of record a property for which there are no defects.

title search the process of verifying the quality of title.

title theory a concept adopted by some states that recognizes that the mortgagee has the right to immediate possession of mortgaged property in the event of default.

Torrens system a system of land registration used by a few states as an alternative to grantor/grantee indexes.

total debt ratio the percentage of a borrower's gross monthly income required to meet monthly contractual expenses.

town house a form of attached housing in which each unit has its own front door but shares one or two walls with adjacent units.

township a 36-square mile area formed by township and range lines in the rectangular survey system.

township lines east-west lines that run parallel to base lines in the rectangular survey system.

trade area the geographic area from which the major portion of the patronage necessary to support the shopping center is to be drawn.

trade fixture personal property used in a trade or business.

transfer of development rights a system whereby landowners can sell their development rights to other property owners so the other property owners can use their property more intensely.

two-step mortgage a loan whose interest rate is adjusted once during the term of the loan.

underwriting process of evaluating the risk of a loan applicant and the property being pledged in order to make a decision regarding the loan application.

unsecured loan a loan for which no specific item has been pledged as collateral.

vacancy and credit losses revenues not received due to vacancy in the property or uncollectible rents.

VA-guaranteed loans a loan in which the lender is protected from the borrower's default by a guarantee of repayment from the Department of Veterans Affairs.

variance permission granted by a government for a landowner to use the property in a manner not ordinarily permitted.

voidable capable of being rescinded, as a contract entered into by a minor or by a person who has been declared insane.

warranty a promise or guarantee made by a grantor in a deed.

warranty forever an assurance made by the grantor to always defend the title conveyed to the grantee.

warranty of habitability an assurance made by a lessor that the property is fit for its intended use.

APPENDIX

Time Value of Money Tables

This appendix presents time value of money tables (often called *capitalization tables*) for interest rates of 6, 8, 10, 12, 14, 20 and 25 percent. They are adapted from *Financial Compound Interest and Annuity Tables,* Sixth Edition (Boston: Financial Publishing Co., 1980). Other rates and other periods can be found in this publication or with the aid of a financial calculator.

Time Value of Money at 6%

Periods	Future Value Factors	Future Value of Annuity Factors	Sinking Fund Factors	Present Value Factors	Present Value of Annuity Factor	Mortgage Constant
1	1.060 000	1.000 000	1.000 000	.943 396	.943 396	1.060 000
2	1.123 600	2.060 000	.485 437	.889 996	1.833 393	.545 437
3	1.191 016	3.183 600	.314 110	.839 619	2.673 012	.374 110
4	1.262 477	4.374 616	.228 591	.792 094	3.465 106	.288 591
5	1.338 226	5.637 093	.177 396	.747 258	4.212 364	.237 396
6	1.418 519	6.975 319	.143 363	.704 961	4.917 324	.203 363
7	1.503 630	8.393 838	.119 135	.665 057	5.582 381	.179 135
8	1.593 848	9.897 468	.101 036	.627 412	6.209 794	.161 036
9	1.689 479	11.491 316	.087 022	.591 898	6.801 692	.147 022
10	1.790 848	13.180 795	.075 868	.558 395	7.360 087	.135 868
11	1.898 299	14.971 643	.066 793	.526 788	7.886 875	.126 793
12	2.012 196	16.869 941	.059 277	.496 969	8.383 844	.119 277
13	2.132 928	18.882 138	.052 960	.468 839	8.852 683	.112 960
14	2.260 904	21.015 066	.047 585	.442 301	9.294 984	.107 585
15	2.396 558	23.275 970	.042 963	.417 265	9.712 249	.102 963
16	2.540 352	25.672 528	.038 952	.393 646	10.105 895	.098 952
17	2.692 773	28.212 880	.035 445	.371 364	10.477 260	.095 445
18	2.854 339	30.905 653	.032 357	.350 344	10.827 603	.092 357
19	3.025 600	33.759 992	.029 621	.330 513	11.158 116	.089 621
20	3.207 135	36.785 591	.027 185	.311 805	11.469 921	.087 185
21	3.399 564	39.992 727	.025 005	.294 155	11.764 077	.085 005
22	3.603 537	43.392 290	.023 046	.277 505	12.041 582	.083 046
23	3.819 750	46.995 828	.021 278	.261 797	12.303 379	.081 278
24	4.048 935	50.815 577	.019 679	.246 979	12.550 358	.079 679
25	4.291 871	54.864 512	.018 227	.232 999	12.783 356	.078 227
26	4.549 383	59.156 383	.016 904	.219 810	13.003 166	.076 904
27	4.822 346	63.705 766	.015 697	.207 368	13.210 534	.075 697
28	5.111 687	68.528 112	.014 593	.195 630	13.406 164	.074 593
29	5.418 388	73.639 798	.013 580	.184 557	13.590 721	.073 580
30	5.743 491	79.058 186	.012 649	.174 110	13.764 831	.072 649
31	6.088 101	84.801 677	.011 792	.164 255	13.929 086	.071 792
32	6.453 387	90.889 778	.011 002	.154 957	14.084 043	.071 002
33	6.840 590	97.343 165	.010 273	.146 186	14.230 230	.070 273
34	7.251 025	104.183 755	.009 598	.137 912	14.368 141	.069 598
35	7.686 087	111.434 780	.008 974	.130 105	14.498 246	.068 974
36	8.147 252	119.120 867	.008 395	.122 741	14.620 987	.068 395
37	8.636 087	127.268 119	.007 857	.115 793	14.736 780	.067 857
38	9.154 252	135.904 206	.007 358	.109 239	14.846 019	.067 358
39	9.703 507	145.058 458	.006 894	.103 056	14.949 075	.066 894
40	10.285 718	154.761 966	.006 462	.097 222	15.046 297	.066 462
41	10.902 861	165.047 684	.006 059	.091 719	15.138 016	.066 059
42	11.557 033	175.950 545	.005 683	.086 527	15.224 543	.065 683
43	12.250 455	187.507 577	.005 333	.081 630	15.306 173	.065 333
44	12.985 482	199.758 032	.005 006	.077 009	15.383 182	.065 006
45	13.764 611	212.743 514	.004 700	.072 650	15.455 832	.064 700
46	14.590 487	226.508 125	.004 415	.068 538	15.524 370	.064 415
47	15.465 917	241.098 612	.004 148	.064 658	15.589 028	.064 148
48	16.393 872	256.564 529	.003 898	.060 998	15.650 027	.063 898
49	17.377 504	272.958 401	.003 664	.057 546	15.707 572	.063 664
50	18.420 154	290.335 905	.003 444	.054 288	15.761 861	.063 444

[1] How $1 left at compound interest will grow
[2] How $1 deposited periodically will grow
[3] Periodic deposit that will grow to $1 at future date

[4] What $1 due in the future is worth today
[5] What $1 payable periodically is worth today
[6] Annuity worth $1 today. Periodic payment necessary to pay off a loan of $1

Time Value of Money at 8%

Periods	Future Value Factors	Future Value of Annuity Factors	Sinking Fund Factors	Present Value Factors	Present Value of Annuity Factor	Mortgage Constant
1	1.080 000	1.000 000	1.000 000	.925 926	.925 926	1.080 000
2	1.166 400	2.080 000	.480 769	.857 339	1.783 265	.560 769
3	1.259 712	3.246 400	.308 034	.793 832	2.577 097	.388 034
4	1.360 489	4.506 112	.221 921	.735 030	3.312 127	.301 921
5	1.469 328	5.866 601	.170 456	.680 583	3.992 710	.250 456
6	1.586 874	7.335 929	.136 315	.630 170	4.622 880	.216 315
7	1.713 824	8.922 803	.112 072	.583 490	5.206 370	.192 072
8	1.850 930	10.636 628	.094 015	.540 269	5.746 639	.174 015
9	1.999 005	12.487 558	.080 080	.500 249	6.246 888	.160 080
10	2.158 925	14.486 562	.069 029	.463 193	6.710 081	.149 029
11	2.331 639	16.645 487	.060 076	.428 883	7.138 964	.140 076
12	2.518 170	18.977 126	.052 695	.397 114	7.536 078	.132 695
13	2.719 624	21.495 297	.046 522	.367 698	7.903 776	.126 522
14	2.937 194	24.214 920	.041 297	.340 461	8.244 237	.121 297
15	3.172 169	27.152 114	.036 830	.315 242	8.559 479	.116 830
16	3.425 943	30.324 283	.032 977	.291 890	8.851 369	.112 977
17	3.700 018	33.750 226	.029 629	.270 269	9.121 638	.109 629
18	3.996 019	37.450 244	.026 702	.250 249	9.371 887	.106 702
19	4.315 701	41.446 263	.024 128	.231 712	9.603 599	.104 128
20	4.660 957	45.761 964	.021 852	.214 548	9.818 147	.101 852
21	5.033 834	50.422 921	.019 832	.198 656	10.016 803	.099 832
22	5.436 540	55.456 755	.018 032	.183 941	10.200 744	.098 032
23	5.871 464	60.893 296	.016 422	.170 315	10.371 059	.096 422
24	6.341 181	66.764 759	.014 978	.157 699	10.528 758	.094 978
25	6.848 475	73.105 940	.013 679	.146 018	10.674 776	.093 679
26	7.396 353	79.954 415	.012 507	.135 202	10.809 978	.092 507
27	7.988 061	87.350 768	.011 448	.125 187	10.935 165	.091 448
28	8.627 106	95.338 830	.010 489	.115 914	11.051 078	.090 489
29	9.317 275	103.965 936	.009 619	.107 328	11.158 406	.089 619
30	10.062 657	113.283 211	.008 827	.099 377	11.257 783	.088 827
31	10.867 669	123.345 868	.008 107	.092 016	11.349 799	.088 107
32	11.737 083	134.213 537	.007 451	.085 200	11.434 999	.087 451
33	12.676 050	145.950 620	.006 852	.078 889	11.513 888	.086 852
34	13.690 134	158.626 670	.006 304	.073 045	11.586 934	.086 304
35	14.785 344	172.316 804	.005 803	.067 635	11.654 568	.085 803
36	15.968 172	187.102 148	.005 345	.062 625	11.717 193	.085 345
37	17.245 626	203.070 320	.004 924	.057 986	11.775 179	.084 924
38	18.625 276	220.315 945	.004 539	.053 690	11.828 869	.084 539
39	20.115 298	238.941 221	.004 185	.049 713	11.878 582	.084 185
40	21.724 521	259.056 519	.003 860	.046 031	11.924 613	.083 860
41	23.462 483	280.781 040	.003 561	.042 621	11.967 235	.083 561
42	25.339 482	304.243 523	.003 287	.039 464	12.006 699	.083 287
43	27.366 640	329.583 005	.003 034	.036 541	12.043 240	.083 034
44	29.555 972	356.949 646	.002 802	.033 834	12.077 074	.082 802
45	31.920 449	386.505 617	.002 587	.031 328	12.108 402	.082 587
46	34.474 085	418.426 067	.002 390	.029 007	12.137 409	.082 390
47	37.232 012	452.900 152	.002 208	.026 859	12.164 267	.082 208
48	40.210 573	490.132 164	.002 040	.024 869	12.189 136	.082 040
49	43.427 419	530.342 737	.001 886	.023 027	12.212 163	.081 886
50	46.901 613	573.770 156	.001 743	.021 321	12.233 485	.081 743

Time Value of Money at 10%

Periods	Future Value Factors	Future Value of Annuity Factors	Sinking Fund Factors	Present Value Factors	Present Value of Annuity Factor	Mortgage Constant
1	1.100 000	1.000 000	1.000 000	.909 091	.909 091	1.100 000
2	1.210 000	2.100 000	.476 190	.826 446	1.735 537	.576 190
3	1.331 000	3.310 000	.302 115	.751 315	2.486 852	.402 115
4	1.464 100	4.641 000	.215 471	.683 013	3.169 865	.315 471
5	1.610 510	6.105 100	.163 797	.620 921	3.790 787	.263 797
6	1.771 561	7.715 610	.129 607	.564 474	4.355 261	.229 607
7	1.948 717	9.487 171	.105 405	.513 158	4.868 419	.205 405
8	2.143 589	11.435 888	.087 444	.466 507	5.334 926	.187 444
9	2.357 948	13.579 477	.073 641	.424 098	5.759 024	.173 641
10	2.593 742	15.937 425	.062 745	.385 543	6.144 567	.162 745
11	2.853 117	18.531 167	.053 963	.350 494	6.495 061	.153 963
12	3.138 428	21.384 284	.046 763	.318 631	6.813 692	.146 763
13	3.452 271	24.522 712	.040 779	.289 664	7.103 356	.140 779
14	3.797 498	27.974 983	.035 746	.263 331	7.366 687	.135 746
15	4.177 248	31.772 482	.031 474	.239 392	7.606 080	.131 474
16	4.594 973	35.949 730	.027 817	.217 629	7.823 709	.127 817
17	5.054 470	40.544 703	.024 664	.197 845	8.021 553	.124 664
18	5.559 917	45.599 173	.021 930	.179 859	8.201 412	.121 930
19	6.115 909	51.159 090	.019 547	.163 508	8.364 920	.119 547
20	6.727 500	57.274 999	.017 460	.148 644	8.513 564	.117 460
21	7.400 250	64.002 499	.015 624	.135 131	8.648 694	.115 624
22	8.140 275	71.402 749	.014 005	.122 846	8.771 540	.114 005
23	8.954 302	79.543 024	.012 572	.111 678	8.883 218	.112 572
24	9.849 733	88.497 327	.011 300	.101 526	8.984 744	.111 300
25	10.834 706	98.347 059	.010 168	.092 296	9.077 040	.110 168
26	11.918 177	109.181 765	.009 159	.083 905	9.160 945	.109 159
27	13.109 994	121.099 942	.008 258	.076 278	9.237 223	.108 258
28	14.420 994	134.209 936	.007 451	.069 343	9.306 567	.107 451
29	15.863 093	148.630 930	.006 728	.063 039	9.369 606	.106 728
30	17.449 402	164.494 023	.006 079	.057 309	9.426 914	.106 079
31	19.194 342	181.943 425	.005 496	.052 099	9.479 013	.105 496
32	21.113 777	201.137 767	.004 972	.047 362	9.526 376	.104 972
33	23.225 154	222.251 544	.004 499	.043 057	9.569 432	.104 499
34	25.547 670	245.476 699	.004 074	.039 143	9.608 575	.104 074
35	28.102 437	271.024 368	.003 690	.035 584	9.644 159	.103 690
36	30.912 681	299.126 805	.003 343	.032 349	9.676 508	.103 343
37	34.003 949	330.039 486	.003 030	.029 408	9.705 917	.103 030
38	37.404 343	364.043 434	.002 747	.026 735	9.732 651	.102 747
39	41.144 778	401.447 778	.002 491	.024 304	9.756 956	.102 491
40	45.259 256	442.592 556	.002 259	.022 095	9.779 051	.102 259
41	49.785 181	487.851 811	.002 050	.020 086	9.799 137	.102 050
42	54.763 699	537.636 992	.001 860	.018 260	9.817 397	.101 860
43	60.240 069	592.400 692	.001 688	.016 600	9.833 998	.101 688
44	66.264 076	652.640 761	.001 532	.015 091	9.849 089	.101 532
45	72.890 484	718.904 837	.001 391	.013 719	9.862 808	.101 391
46	80.179 532	791.795 321	.001 263	.012 472	9.875 280	.101 263
47	88.197 485	871.974 853	.001 147	.011 338	9.886 618	.101 147
48	97.017 234	960.172 338	.001 041	.010 307	9.896 926	.101 041
49	106.718 957	1057.189 572	.000 946	.009 370	9.906 296	.100 946
50	117.390 853	1163.908 529	.000 859	.008 519	9.914 814	.100 859

Time Value of Money at 12%

Periods	Future Value Factors	Future Value of Annuity Factors	Sinking Fund Factors	Present Value Factors	Present Value of Annuity Factor	Mortgage Constant
1	1.120 000	1.000 000	1.000 000	.892 857	.892 857	1.120 000
2	1.254 400	2.120 000	.471 698	.797 194	1.690 051	.591 698
3	1.404 928	3.374 400	.296 349	.711 780	2.401 831	.416 349
4	1.573 519	4.779 328	.209 234	.635 518	3.037 349	.329 234
5	1.762 342	6.352 847	.157 410	.567 427	3.604 776	.277 410
6	1.973 823	8.115 189	.123 226	.506 631	4.111 407	.243 226
7	2.210 681	10.089 012	.099 118	.452 349	4.563 757	.219 118
8	2.475 963	12.299 693	.081 303	.403 883	4.967 640	.201 303
9	2.773 079	14.775 656	.067 679	.360 610	5.328 250	.187 679
10	3.105 848	17.548 735	.056 984	.321 973	5.650 223	.176 984
11	3.478 550	20.654 583	.048 415	.287 476	5.937 699	.168 415
12	3.895 976	24.133 133	.041 437	.256 675	6.194 374	.161 437
13	4.363 493	28.029 109	.035 677	.229 174	6.423 548	.155 677
14	4.887 112	32.392 602	.030 871	.204 620	6.628 168	.150 871
15	5.473 566	37.279 715	.026 824	.182 696	6.810 864	.146 824
16	6.130 394	42.753 280	.023 390	.163 122	6.973 986	.143 390
17	6.866 041	48.883 674	.020 457	.145 644	7.119 630	.140 457
18	7.689 966	55.749 715	.017 937	.130 040	7.249 670	.137 937
19	8.612 762	63.439 681	.015 763	.116 107	7.365 777	.135 763
20	9.646 293	72.052 442	.013 879	.103 667	7.469 444	.133 879
21	10.803 848	81.698 736	.012 240	.092 560	7.562 003	.132 240
22	12.100 310	92.502 584	.010 811	.082 643	7.644 646	.130 811
23	13.552 347	104.602 894	.009 560	.073 788	7.718 434	.129 560
24	15.178 629	118.155 241	.008 463	.065 882	7.784 316	.128 463
25	17.000 064	133.333 870	.007 500	.058 823	7.843 139	.127 500
26	19.040 072	150.333 934	.006 652	.052 521	7.895 660	.126 652
27	21.324 881	169.374 007	.005 904	.046 894	7.942 554	.125 904
28	23.883 866	190.698 887	.005 244	.041 869	7.984 423	.125 244
29	26.749 930	214.582 754	.004 660	.037 383	8.021 806	.124 660
30	29.959 922	241.332 684	.004 144	.033 378	8.055 184	.124 144
31	33.555 113	271.292 606	.003 686	.029 802	8.084 986	.123 686
32	37.581 726	304.847 719	.003 280	.026 609	8.111 594	.123 280
33	42.091 533	342.429 446	.002 920	.023 758	8.135 352	.122 920
34	47.142 517	384.520 979	.002 601	.021 212	8.156 564	.122 601
35	52.799 620	431.663 496	.002 317	.018 940	8.175 504	.122 317
36	59.135 574	484.463 116	.002 064	.016 910	8.192 414	.122 064
37	66.231 843	543.598 690	.001 840	.015 098	8.207 513	.121 840
38	74.179 664	609.830 533	.001 640	.013 481	8.220 993	.121 640
39	83.081 224	684.010 197	.001 462	.012 036	8.233 030	.121 462
40	93.050 970	767.091 420	.001 304	.010 747	8.243 777	.121 304
41	104.217 087	860.142 391	.001 163	.009 595	8.253 372	.121 163
42	116.723 137	964.359 478	.001 037	.008 567	8.261 939	.121 037
43	130.729 914	1081.082 615	.000 925	.007 649	8.269 589	.120 925
44	146.417 503	1211.812 529	.000 825	.006 830	8.276 418	.120 825
45	163.987 604	1358.230 032	.000 736	.006 098	8.282 516	.120 736
46	183.666 116	1522.217 636	.000 657	.005 445	8.287 961	.120 657
47	205.706 050	1705.883 752	.000 586	.004 861	8.292 822	.120 586
48	230.390 776	1911.589 803	.000 523	.004 340	8.297 163	.120 523
49	258.037 669	2141.980 579	.000 467	.003 875	8.301 038	.120 467
50	289.002 190	2400.018 249	.000 417	.003 460	8.304 498	.120 417

Time Value of Money at 14%

Periods	Future Value Factors	Future Value of Annuity Factors	Sinking Fund Factors	Present Value Factors	Present Value of Annuity Factor	Mortgage Constant
1	1.140 000	1.000 000	1.000 000	.877 193	.877 193	1.140 000
2	1.299 600	2.140 000	.467 290	.769 468	1.646 661	.607 290
3	1.481 544	3.439 600	.290 731	.674 972	2.321 632	.430 731
4	1.688 960	4.921 144	.203 205	.592 080	2.913 712	.343 205
5	1.925 415	6.610 104	.151 284	.519 369	3.433 081	.291 284
6	2.194 973	8.535 519	.117 157	.455 587	3.888 668	.257 157
7	2.502 269	10.730 491	.093 192	.399 637	4.288 305	.233 192
8	2.852 586	13.232 760	.075 570	.350 559	4.638 864	.215 570
9	3.251 949	16.085 347	.062 168	.307 508	4.946 372	.202 168
10	3.707 221	19.337 295	.051 714	.269 744	5.216 116	.191 714
11	4.226 232	23.044 516	.043 394	.236 617	5.452 733	.183 394
12	4.817 905	27.270 749	.036 669	.207 559	5.660 292	.176 669
13	5.492 411	32.088 654	.031 164	.182 069	5.842 362	.171 164
14	6.261 349	37.581 065	.026 609	.159 710	6.002 072	.166 609
15	7.137 938	43.842 414	.022 809	.140 096	6.142 168	.162 809
16	8.137 249	50.980 352	.019 615	.122 892	6.265 060	.159 615
17	9.276 464	59.117 601	.016 915	.107 800	6.372 859	.156 915
18	10.575 169	68.394 066	.014 621	.094 561	6.467 420	.154 621
19	12.055 693	78.969 235	.012 663	.082 948	6.550 369	.152 663
20	13.743 490	91.024 928	.010 986	.072 762	6.623 131	.150 986
21	15.667 578	104.768 418	.009 545	.063 826	6.686 957	.149 545
22	17.861 039	120.435 996	.008 303	.055 988	6.742 944	.148 303
23	20.361 585	138.297 035	.007 231	.049 112	6.792 056	.147 231
24	23.212 207	158.658 620	.006 303	.043 081	6.835 137	.146 303
25	26.461 916	181.870 827	.005 498	.037 790	6.872 927	.145 498
26	30.166 584	208.332 743	.004 800	.033 149	6.906 077	.144 800
27	34.389 906	238.499 327	.004 193	.029 078	6.935 155	.144 193
28	39.204 493	272.889 233	.003 664	.025 507	6.960 662	.143 664
29	44.693 122	312.093 725	.003 204	.022 375	6.983 037	.143 204
30	50.950 159	356.786 847	.002 803	.019 627	7.002 664	.142 803
31	58.083 181	407.737 006	.002 453	.017 217	7.019 881	.142 453
32	66.214 826	465.820 186	.002 147	.015 102	7.034 983	.142 147
33	75.484 902	532.035 012	.001 880	.013 248	7.048 231	.141 880
34	86.052 788	607.519 914	.001 646	.011 621	7.059 852	.141 646
35	98.100 178	693.572 702	.001 442	.010 194	7.070 045	.141 442
36	111.834 203	791.672 881	.001 263	.008 942	7.078 987	.141 263
37	127.490 992	903.507 084	.001 107	.007 844	7.086 831	.141 107
38	145.339 731	1030.998 076	.000 970	.006 880	7.093 711	.140 970
39	165.687 293	1176.337 806	.000 850	.006 035	7.099 747	.140 850
40	188.883 514	1342.025 099	.000 745	.005 294	7.105 041	.140 745
41	215.327 206	1530.908 613	.000 653	.004 644	7.109 685	.140 653
42	245.473 015	1746.235 819	.000 573	.004 074	7.113 759	.140 573
43	279.839 237	1991.708 833	.000 502	.003 573	7.117 332	.140 502
44	319.016 730	2271.548 070	.000 440	.003 135	7.120 467	.140 440
45	363.679 072	2590.564 800	.000 386	.002 750	7.123 217	.140 386
46	414.594 142	2954.243 872	.000 338	.002 412	7.125 629	.140 338
47	472.637 322	3368.838 014	.000 297	.002 116	7.127 744	.140 297
48	538.806 547	3841.475 336	.000 260	.001 856	7.129 600	.140 260
49	614.239 464	4380.281 883	.000 228	.001 628	7.131 228	.140 228
50	700.232 988	4994.521 346	.000 200	.001 428	7.132 656	.140 200

Time Value of Money at 20%

Periods	Future Value Factors	Future Value of Annuity Factors	Sinking Fund Factors	Present Value Factors	Present Value of Annuity Factor	Mortgage Constant
1	1.200 000	1.000 000	1.000 000	.833 333	.833 333	1.200 000
2	1.440 000	2.200 000	.454 545	.694 444	1.527 778	.654 545
3	1.728 000	3.640 000	.274 725	.578 704	2.106 481	.474 725
4	2.073 600	5.368 000	.186 289	.482 253	2.588 735	.386 289
5	2.488 320	7.441 600	.134 380	.401 878	2.990 612	.334 380
6	2.985 984	9.929 920	.100 706	.334 898	3.325 510	.300 706
7	3.583 181	12.915 904	.077 424	.279 082	3.604 592	.277 424
8	4.299 817	16.499 085	.060 609	.232 568	3.837 160	.260 609
9	5.159 780	20.798 902	.048 079	.193 807	4.030 967	.248 079
10	6.191 736	25.958 682	.038 523	.161 506	4.192 472	.238 523
11	7.430 084	32.150 419	.031 104	.134 588	4.327 060	.231 104
12	8.916 100	39.580 502	.025 265	.112 157	4.439 217	.225 265
13	10.699 321	48.496 603	.020 620	.093 464	4.532 681	.220 620
14	12.839 185	59.195 923	.016 893	.077 887	4.610 567	.216 893
15	15.407 022	72.035 108	.013 882	.064 905	4.675 473	.213 882
16	18.488 426	87.442 129	.011 436	.054 088	4.729 561	.211 436
17	22.186 111	105.930 555	.009 440	.045 073	4.774 634	.209 440
18	26.623 333	128.116 666	.007 805	.037 561	4.812 195	.207 805
19	31.948 000	154.740 000	.006 462	.031 301	4.843 496	.206 462
20	38.337 600	186.688 000	.005 357	.026 084	4.869 580	.205 357
21	46.005 120	225.025 600	.004 444	.021 737	4.891 316	.204 444
22	55.206 144	271.030 719	.003 690	.018 114	4.909 430	.203 690
23	66.247 373	326.236 863	.003 065	.015 095	4.924 525	.203 065
24	79.496 847	392.484 236	.002 548	.012 579	4.937 104	.202 548
25	95.396 217	471.981 083	.002 119	.010 483	4.947 587	.202 119
26	114.475 460	567.377 300	.001 762	.008 735	4.956 323	.201 762
27	137.370 552	681.852 760	.001 467	.007 280	4.963 602	.201 467
28	164.844 662	819.223 312	.001 221	.006 066	4.969 668	.201 221
29	197.813 595	984.067 974	.001 016	.005 055	4.974 724	.201 016
30	237.376 314	1181.881 569	.000 846	.004 213	4.978 936	.200 846
31	284.851 577	1419.257 883	.000 705	.003 511	4.982 447	.200 705
32	341.821 892	1704.109 459	.000 587	.002 926	4.985 372	.200 587
33	410.186 270	2045.931 351	.000 489	.002 438	4.987 810	.200 489
34	492.223 524	2456.117 621	.000 407	.002 032	4.989 842	.200 407
35	590.668 229	2948.341 146	.000 339	.001 693	4.991 535	.200 339
36	708.801 875	3539.009 375	.000 283	.001 411	4.992 946	.200 283
37	850.562 250	4247.811 250	.000 235	.001 176	4.994 122	.200 235
38	1020.674 700	5098.373 500	.000 196	.000 980	4.995 101	.200 196
39	1224.809 640	6119.048 200	.000 163	.000 816	4.995 918	.200 163
40	1469.771 568	7343.857 840	.000 136	.000 680	4.996 598	.200 136
41	1763.725 882	8813.629 408	.000 113	.000 567	4.997 165	.200 113
42	2116.471 058	10577.355 289	.000 095	.000 472	4.997 638	.200 095
43	2539.765 269	12693.826 347	.000 079	.000 394	4.998 031	.200 079
44	3047.718 323	15233.591 617	.000 066	.000 328	4.998 359	.200 066
45	3657.261 988	18281.309 940	.000 055	.000 273	4.998 633	.200 055
46	4388.714 386	21938.571 928	.000 046	.000 228	4.998 861	.200 046
47	5266.457 263	26327.286 314	.000 038	.000 190	4.999 051	.200 038
48	6319.748 715	31593.743 576	.000 032	.000 158	4.999 209	.200 032
49	7583.698 458	37913.492 292	.000 026	.000 132	4.999 341	.200 026
50	9100.438 150	45497.190 750	.000 022	.000 110	4.999 451	.200 022

Index

Index

Credits and Acknowledgements

Chapter 1 Introduction to Real Estate Decision Making
1—Courtesy of the U.S. Department of Agriculture.

Chapter 2 Understanding Real Estate Markets
16—Courtesy of the U.S. Department of Agriculture.

Chapter 3 The Economics of Regional and Community Growth
34—Supplied by Century 21® Real Estate Corporation; 48—Courtesy of the I.N. Phelps Stokes Collection, Miriam and Ira D. Wallach Division of Art, Prints and Photographs, The New York Public Library, Astor, Lenox and Tilden Foundations.

Chapter 4 Property Rights and Ownership Interests
60—Permission granted by the Missouri Division of Tourism; 65—Courtesy of Charles Floyd.

Chapter 5 Private Restrictions on Ownership
80—Courtesy of the Louisiana Office of Tourism.

Chapter 6 Public Restrictions on Ownership
96—Courtesy of the Louisiana Office of Tourism.

Chapter 7 Deeds and Legal Descriptions
124—Courtesy of the Louisiana Office of Tourism; 136—Courtesy of Charles Floyd; 137—Courtesy of Charles Floyd; 139—Courtesy of Charles Floyd.

Chapter 8 Real Estate Brokerage
146—Photo provided by ERA® Real Estate.

Chapter 9 Property Management and Leasing
170—Photo provided by ERA® Real Estate.

Chapter 10 Real Estate Appraisal
190—Courtesy of the U.S. Department of Agriculture.

Chapter 11 Contracts in Real Estate Transactions
224—Photo provided by ERA® Real Estate.

Chapter 12 Property Insurance
240—Courtesy of the U.S. Department of Agriculture; 248-249—Courtesy of American Appraisal Associates, Inc.

Chapter 13 Financing Residential Property
258—Courtesy of the U.S. Department of Agriculture.

Chapter 14 Basic Financial Concepts and Mortgage Mechanics
288—Photo provided by ERA® Real Estate.

Chapter 15 Title Examination and the Closing Process
330—Photo provided by ERA® Real Estate.

Chapter 16 Home Purchase Decisions
356—Photo provided by ERA® Real Estate.

Chapter 17 Investing in Income-Producing Properties
374—Courtesy of the Texas Department of Transportation.

Chapter 18 Residential Land Uses
394—Courtesy of the U.S. Department of Agriculture; 398—Printed with permission by Fisher Island; 402—Courtesy of Charles Floyd; 412—Courtesy of The Biltmore Company.

Chapter 19 Commercial and Industrial Development
416—Courtesy of J.C. Nichols Company; 421—Courtesy of J.C. Nichols Company.